CAMBRIDGE GREEK AND LATIN CLASSICS

GENERAL EDITORS

E. J. KENNEY
Emeritus Kennedy Professor of Latin, University of Cambridge

AND

P. E. EASTERLING
Regius Professor of Greek, University of Cambridge

PLATO ON POETRY

Ion; Republic 376e–398b9;
Republic 595–608b10

EDITED BY

PENELOPE MURRAY

Lecturer in Classics, University of Warwick

CAMBRIDGE UNIVERSITY PRESS
Cambridge, New York, Melbourne, Madrid, Cape Town,
Singapore, São Paulo, Delhi, Tokyo, Mexico City

Cambridge University Press
The Edinburgh Building, Cambridge CB2 8RU, UK

Published in the United States of America by
Cambridge University Press, New York

www.cambridge.org
Information on this title: www.cambridge.org/9780521349819

First published 1996
Eighth printing 2008

A catalogue record for this publication is available from the British Library

Library of Congress Cataloguing in Publication data
Plato. [Selections. 1995]
Plato on poetry/edited by Penelope Murray.
p. cm. – (Cambridge Greek and Latin Classics)
Preface, introduction, and commentary in English with text in Greek
Includes bibliographical references and index.
Contents: Iōn – Platōnus politeia 376c–398bg – Platōnos politeia 595–608b 10.
ISBN 0 521 34182 5 (hardback) – ISBN O 521 34981 8 (paperback)
1. Poetics.   I. Murray, Penelope.   II. Plato. Iōn.   III. Plato.
Republic. Book 9. Selections.   IV Platō. Republic. Book 10.
Selections.   V Title.   VI. Title: Iōn.   VII. Title: Republic
3766–39809.   VIII. Title: Republic 595–608b10.   IX. Series.
PA4279.A3   1995
808.1–dc20   95 13249 CIP

ISBN 978-0-521-34182-0 Hardback
ISBN 978-0-521-34981-9 Paperback

CONTENTS

PREFACE

Plato's views on poetry, and particularly those expressed in the *Ion* and *Republic*, have had a profound effect on the history of Western poetics. Plato writes on poetry not as a disinterested observer, but as a passionate participant in a struggle between poetry and philosophy whose repercussions are still being felt today. Much has been written in recent years on Plato as a critic of literature; but no commentaries have appeared in English on the *Ion*, or on the opening books of the *Republic* in which Plato launches his attack on poetry, since the early years of this century. This volume brings together these texts and the relevant section of *Republic* 10. It aims to provide the reader with a commentary which takes account of modern scholarship on the subject, and which explores the ambivalence of Plato's pronouncements on poetry through the analysis of his own skill as a writer. A general introduction sets Plato's views in the wider context of attitudes to poetry in Greek society before his time, and indicates the main ways in which his writings on poetry have influenced the history of aesthetic thought in European culture.

I wish to thank the University of Warwick for granting me a period of study leave in which I was able to complete this commentary. Thanks are also due to Mark Vermes, who provided valuable assistance in preparing the text for publication. My colleagues Andrew Barker and Angela Hobbs willingly discussed the interpretation of various problematic passages, and I am particularly grateful to Angela Hobbs for her generosity in lending me a copy of her unpublished Ph.D. thesis. A series of seminars at the University of Warwick's Centre for Research in Philosophy and Literature provided a stimulating context in which to discuss Plato's ideas on poetry. Oswyn Murray read and commented on the Introduction, and sustained me in other ways during the writing of this book. I am particularly indebted to Professor S. R. Slings of the Free University of Amsterdam for putting at my disposal his expert knowledge of the text of the *Republic*, and for the time and trouble he has taken in answering my queries on points of difficulty. I must thank Professors Pat Easterling and Ted Kenney for their encouragement, and for the astuteness of their comments. My greatest debt, and one which it is a pleasure to record, is to Pat Easterling, who introduced me to the delights of Plato's *Ion* in my first term as an undergraduate at Newnham.

University of Warwick
January 1995   P. A. M.

ABBREVIATIONS AND REFERENCES

1. Abbreviations for ancient authors and works usually follow those of the *Oxford Classical Dictionary*. S. throughout refers to the Socrates of the Platonic dialogues.

2. Modern works are abbreviated as follows:

   D–K   H. Diels (ed.), revised by W. Kranz, *Die Fragmente der Vorsokratiker*, 6th edn. (Berlin 1961)

   EGF   M. Davies (ed.), *Epicorum Graecorum Fragmenta* (Göttingen 1991)

   FGH   F. Jacoby (ed.), *Die Fragmente der griechischen Historiker* (Berlin 1923)

   LSJ   H. G. Liddell and R. Scott (edd.), revised by H. Stuart Jones and R. Mackenzie, *A Greek–English Lexicon*, 9th edn (Oxford 1968)

   N–H   R. G. M. Nisbet and M. Hubbard (edd.), *A commentary on Horace: Odes book I* (Oxford 1970); *A commentary on Horace: Odes book II* (Oxford 1978)

   PMG   M. Davies (ed.), *Poetarum melicorum Graecorum fragmenta, post D. L. Page* (Oxford 1991)

3. Works cited by author and date only are listed in the Bibliography.

INTRODUCTION

A. N. Whitehead once remarked that the European philosophical tradition could be characterised as 'a series of footnotes to Plato'.[1] The same might be said of the history of Western thinking about poetry and art. When P. banished poetry from the ideal state in *Republic* 10 (607d6–e2) he suggested, however equivocally, that if lovers of poetry could show that poetry is not only pleasurable, but also useful to civic society and to human life, he would be prepared to listen. Aristotle was not the only one to take up that challenge. From antiquity to the Italian Renaissance, from Sir Philip Sidney's *Defence of poetry* (1595) to Shelley's essay of the same name (1821), in twentieth-century writers as diverse as Jacques Derrida and Iris Murdoch, the potency of P.'s influence can be felt.[2]

The Greeks had no word to denote those activities that we now subsume under the term 'art'. *Techne* covered anything from poetry, painting and sculpture to shoemaking, carpentry and shipbuilding, there being no linguistic or conceptual distinction in the Greek world, or in antiquity generally, between crafts and the 'fine arts'. Moreover, art was not thought of as something that could be separated from morality. As Tolstoy put it, 'the ancients had not that conception of beauty separated from goodness which forms the basis and aim of aesthetics in our time'.[3] Indeed aesthetics as a distinct field of study goes back no further than the eighteenth century, when the German philosopher, Alexander Baumgarten, first coined the term

[1] *Process and reality* (New York 1930) 63.

[2] For P.'s influence on Aristotle's *Poetics* see Halliwell (1986) 1–6, 19–27, 331–6; for the Neoplatonist defence of poetry against P.'s attack see Russell (1981) 65–6, 104–10; A. Sheppard, 'Plato and the Neoplatonists', in Baldwin and Hutton (1994) 12–18; for bibliography on Platonism in Renaissance poetics see nn. 59 and 60 below; on Sidney see pp. 26 and 31 n. 75; for Shelley see J. A. Notopoulos, *The Platonism of Shelley: a study of Platonism and the poetic mind* (Durham 1949) and below pp. 31–2. For the twentieth century see e.g. J. Derrida, *Dissemination*, trans. B. Johnson (Chicago 1981); Murdoch (1977) and (1993); P. Conradi, 'Platonism in Iris Murdoch', in Baldwin and Hutton (1994) 330–42.

[3] *What is art?*, trans. A. Maude (Oxford 1930) 91; cf. Murdoch (1977) 6–7, 12 where she notes that for P. 'the aesthetic is the moral'.

with the publication of his *Aesthetica* in 1750. But in a very real sense the history of Western aesthetics begins with P.[4] Many of the questions which we still debate today were first raised in P.'s work. What is poetry, and indeed art in general, and how does it operate? What is and should be the function of imaginative literature in society? Is it dangerous in that it encourages emotions and feelings which ought to be kept in check, or is it therapeutic in that it allows us to give vent to our emotions in a harmless way? Should there be censorship? Is literature (which now, of course, includes television and film) a form of escapism or does it deepen our insight into the nature of people and the world around us?

The extent of P.'s influence is all the more remarkable in that, unlike Aristotle, he never wrote a treatise on the subject of poetry. His views have to be extracted from a number of different dialogues, and his discussions of poetry are always embedded in some wider context; poetry is never treated as a subject in itself. Indeed to talk of P.'s 'view of poetry' is already to imply a systematisation of his thought which diminishes its richness. We cannot speak of a Platonic theory of poetry, but rather of a collection of texts in which various attitudes, images and myths about poetry are expressed.[5] In the *Ion* and the *Phaedrus* poets are described in what appear to be terms of extravagant praise, yet in the *Republic* poets are categorised as at best worthless, at worst dangerous, and expelled from the ideal society. The very diversity of P.'s treatment of poetry has generated a range of responses quite unlike that provoked by any other author. Thus he has been seen as a puritan, a philistine and the enemy of poetry, indeed Nietzsche described him as 'the greatest enemy of art Europe has yet produced'.[6] But he has also been hailed as the originator of the Renaissance conception of the divinity of poetry, and of the

---

[4] See Schaper (1968), a thoughtful and perceptive study. The topic is also discussed by e.g. S. Halliwell, 'The importance of Plato and Aristotle for aesthetics', in *Proceedings of the Boston area colloquium in ancient philosophy* v (1989), edd. J. J. Cleary and D. C. Shartin, 321–57.

[5] For a comprehensive survey see Vicaire (1960). The following general discussions are also useful: Else (1986) 3–64; Halliwell (1988) 3–16; Ferrari (1989) 92–148; Asmis (1992).

[6] *Genealogy of morals*, trans. W. Kaufmann and R. J. Hollingdale (New York 1969) 3.25.

Romantic myth of the artist. It would be impossible to cover every aspect of P.'s thinking about poetry within the confines of the present study. Instead I shall focus my discussion on the two great themes which dominate P.'s treatment of poetry: the idea of poetry as *mimesis*, and the concept of poetic inspiration.

1. *MIMESIS*

Mimesis is a protean term, whose precise connotations vary according to context, but broadly speaking *mimesis* and its cognates indicate a relation between something which is and something made to resemble it.[7] Already before P. the *mimeisthai* word group covered a wide range which included vocal mimicry, dramatic enactment or impersonation, the imitation of behaviour in a more general sense (e.g. modelling oneself on someone else) and visual representation.[8] P.'s own use of the terms is highly flexible: mimetic language is used not only of the arts of poetry, painting, music and dance, but also, for example, of the relationship between language and reality, and of that between the material world and its eternal paradigm; even the life of the philosopher is said to 'imitate' the forms.[9] McKeon (1952)

[7] For this definition see McKeon (1952) 152.

[8] See e.g. Hom. *h. Ap.* 163, the earliest occurrence of the word group; Aesch. *Cho.* 564; Ar. *Thesm.* 156, 850, *Frogs* 109; Eur. *Ba.* 980; Thuc. 2.37; Eur. *Hipp.* 114, *El.* 1037; Aesch. fr. 78a7 Radt; Hdt. 2.78, 3.37; Eur. *Hel.* 74. These various meanings are not, of course, mutually exclusive. Pre-Platonic usages of the μιμεῖσθαι word group are discussed by Else (1958) cf. (1986) 26, who discerns three main strands of meaning: (1) miming, that is the mimicking or impersonation of another as in a dramatic performance; (2) imitating or copying another's behaviour in a more general way; (3) making a visual replica of something as e.g. in a wooden image. See also Havelock (1963) 57–60. Nehamas (1982) 55–8 has some pertinent points to make, noting in particular that the μιμεῖσθαι word group 'as it was traditionally applied to poetry, speaking, and dancing, meant primarily *acting like* someone else' (58). See also Halliwell (1986) 109–16 for a thorough and judicious discussion of the pre-Platonic evidence.

[9] For μίμησις and poetry see e.g. *Rep.* 595b4–5, 597e6, 600e4–5; for painting *Rep.* 596c–e, *Crat.* 430b, *Soph.* 234b–c; for music and dance *Rep.* 399a–c, 400a, *Laws* 655d, 798d–799b, 816a. On language see *Crat.* 423b–424b; on the material world as an 'imitation' of the eternal see *Tim.* 39e, 48e, 50c; for the philosopher imitating the Forms see *Rep.* 500c. For further discussion of the subject of *mimesis* in general in P.'s work see McKeon (1952) and Halliwell (1986) 116–21.

150 draws attention to the scope of *mimesis* terminology in P.'s work, pointing out that though these words are defined in the course of the various dialogues, they do not have fixed or univocal meanings.

The notion of *mimesis* is first introduced in the *Republic* in connexion with literature at 392d5 in terms which suggest that what follows will not be entirely familiar to P.'s readers (see on 392d7–8). Socrates is considering the whole question of what kind of literature his putative guardians should study, and having considered the content of such literature, he then moves on to its form. Any story or poem, he says, narrates things past, present or future, and for the purposes it employs either *diegesis*, or *mimesis*, or a mixture of both. For example, when a poet speaks in his own person as Homer does at the beginning of the *Iliad*, Μῆνιν ἄειδε θεά κτλ., that is *diegesis*, which we might translate as 'pure narrative'. But when he speaks as if he were one of his characters, as, for example, when Homer speaks in the voice of the aged priest Chryses, addressing the Achaeans in the opening scene of the poem at lines 17–21, that is *mimesis*. On the basis of this distinction S. divides literature into three kinds: one kind uses *mimesis* alone, the obvious examples being tragedy and comedy; another, such as the dithyramb, consists entirely of narrative; a third kind, exemplified by Homer's poetry, uses a mixture of *diegesis* and *mimesis*, with the poet speaking sometimes in his own person, sometimes in that of his characters. The notion of *mimesis* is introduced here in the context of a discussion of *lexis*, but it rapidly becomes clear that more is at stake than verbal expression. For when someone speaks in the voice of another (whether poet or reciter) he makes himself like that person not just in voice, but also in character: he adopts his looks, his gestures and even his thoughts, so that in a sense he almost becomes that person (see on 393c5–6, 395c7–d3). *Mimesis* thus has profound effects on character.

S. expands on this theme a little later at 400c–403c when he summarises the aims of the first stage of the guardians' education in *mousike* in a passage which highlights the significance of imitation in general.[10] Emphasising the paramount importance of environment for the training of character, S. says that if the young are surrounded by images of goodness and beauty they will absorb good-

[10] Else (1986) 37–8. See also Gill (1985).

ness into their souls like people living in healthy climes, where 'the breeze brings health from salubrious regions' (401c6–d1). It is therefore necessary to give orders, not only to poets, but also to all artists and craftsmen, that they should portray the image of goodness in their works and avoid everything that is ugly and bad (401b1–8). The implication of this passage is that poetry and art have a vital role to play in the education of the young, and indeed this is why S. takes such pains to discuss the content of primary education in the preceding section, laying down guidelines (τύποι) for poets to follow (376e–400b). It is clear, of course, that poets and artists will be subject to the dictates of the rulers, who will give them orders about what can and cannot be portrayed (401b cf. 398b1–3). Nevertheless the models of goodness which they produce will make a deep impression on the souls of the young, and train them to appreciate goodness wherever they find it.

In the light of all that is said here we would expect S. to advocate the virtues of poetic *mimesis* in his discussion of *lexis* at 392d5–398b4. But in fact he concludes (*a*) that potential guardians should imitate only good men (396c5–d3), and (*b*) that they should imitate as little as possible, using the mixed style exemplified by Homer, but with a small amount of *mimesis* (396e4–7, cf. 395c3–7). These views are not incompatible, but there is a certain ambivalence in P.'s attitude: if imitating a good man fosters goodness of character why restrict the amount of *mimesis* a young person can use? Why shouldn't young guardians spend all their time impersonating good characters? P. seems to be caught between the view that *mimesis* is beneficial provided that its object is suitable, and the feeling that there is something potentially harmful about *mimesis* in itself.[11]

The ambivalence deepens when S. returns to the subject of poetry in book 10 and says that they were right to have excluded mimetic poetry from their city (595a5). But in book 3 it was expressly stated that the austere poet who imitates the speech of a good man would be acceptable in a well governed state (398a8–b1).[12] Furthermore in

---

[11] See Annas (1981) 99. Havelock (1963) 11 (see also 22–35) draws attention to the 'strong undercurrent of suspicion and dislike for the dramatic empathy as such' which is evident in P.'s discussion of *mimesis* in book 3.

[12] For attempts to resolve this discrepancy see on 595a5.

the course of book 10 a more complex view of *mimesis* is developed with reference to the Platonic theory of Forms, according to which a metaphysical hierarchy is established, consisting of Forms, the sensible world, and imitations of the sensible world (595c7–597e10). Taking painting as the paradigm of *mimesis*, S. argues that the painter is like someone holding up a mirror (596d8–e6), who produces reflections of objects in the sensible world, which are themselves less real than the Forms which alone have true existence. Since poets are also imitators, they, like painters, are condemned to operate at the third level of reality, their products being nothing but worthless imitations of an imitation of reality (597e6–8, 600e4–5). The notion of *mimesis* developed here, which depends on the example of painting, seems quite different from that expounded in book 3 in the context of what kind of poetry the guardians ought to perform. There *mimesis* involved a deep identification on the part of the imitator with the object of his imitation, whereas now *mimesis* involves the notion of a counterfeit copy (see on 597e3–4). P. seems to oscillate between regarding the poet's *mimesis* as potentially beneficial (398a8–b1, cf. 401b1–3) and condemning it as trivial play (602b8). This ambivalence arises partly from the fact that the products of *mimesis* can be evaluated in two distinct ways, either in terms of the objects imitated (whether they are good or bad), or in terms of the quality of the imitation (how good the likeness is). As far as P. is concerned, existing poetry fails on both counts: poets imitate the wrong kind of behaviour and therefore corrupt the souls of their listeners (605c10–608b2); but they are also incapable of producing a true likeness of goodness and the other moral qualities because they do not know what goodness is (598d7–600e6). Hence Homer and his fellow poets are to be banished entirely from the ideal state. There might be room for poetry of a very restricted sort, provided that poets are prepared to follow the guidelines laid down for them by the rulers (398b2–3, 401b1–3 and see on 607a3–5) and imitate only what is good. But this is the death of poetry as we know it.

2. POETRY AND INSPIRATION

P.'s view that poetry is a worthless imitation of an imitation of reality would seem at first sight to be incompatible with the picture of the poet as a god-like being who pours forth beautiful poetry when inspired by the Muses' power. And it is noticeable that, with one exception to which I shall return, P. keeps the ideas of *mimesis* and inspiration apart. P.'s descriptions of poetic inspiration occur over a long period of time, ranging from his earliest works to his latest,[13] and there is considerable uniformity in what he says. Throughout P.'s work the mental state of the inspired poet is described in similar terms: the poet, when composing, is in a frenzy and out of his mind; he creates by divine dispensation, but not with knowledge. So much is certain. But critics are, and always have been, deeply divided over the question of how seriously we should take P.'s mythical account of the poet's divine inspiration.[14]

Greek poetry before P. abounds with allusions to the idea of poetic inspiration. From Homer onwards poets invoke the Muses' aid, calling on them, as daughters of Memory, to provide them with knowledge, to instil sweetness into their song, or to assist them generally in the composition and performance of their poems.[15] Poetry is regularly portrayed as a divine gift, which the Muses bestow or teach,[16] and a whole range of imagery is developed to express the relationship between the goddesses and their chosen protégés. For example, the poet is the messenger, servant or herald of the Muses, he rides in their chariot or culls his songs from their gardens and glades.[17] But despite the poet's dependence on the Muse, it is never suggested that he is merely the unconscious instrument of the divine: poetry is presented both as a gift of the Muses and as a product of the poet's own invention.[18] His gift may be inexplicable, but it is not irrational.

---

[13] The most important texts are *Ion, passim; Ap.* 22a–c; *Men.* 99c–e; *Phdr.* 245; *Laws* 719c–d. See Appendix, pp. 235–8. For discussion of the topic see the authoritative article by Tigerstedt (1969).

[14] See Tigerstedt (1969) 18–29 for a survey of interpretations of the dialogue.

[15] See e.g. Hom. *Il.* 2.484–92; Hes. *Th.* 104; Alcm. fr. 27; Ibyc. fr. 1. 23–6; Sol. fr. 17; Pi. *Nem.* 7.23–4, *Pae.* 6.50–8; Ar. *Ach.* 665–75, *Thesm.* 107–10. For further references, bibliography and discussion of pre-Platonic concepts of inspiration see Murray (1981); Verdenius (1983) 37–46; Nagy (1989) 24–9.

[16] See e.g. Hom. *Od.* 8.44–5, 62–4, *h. Ap.* 440–2; Hes. *Th.* 22–34, *Op.* 661–2; Sol. fr. 440–2 and in general Sperduti (1950).

[17] See e.g. Pi. *Ol.* 9.80–1, *Pae.* 6.6, fr. 150; Bacch. 5.14, 9.3, 13.230; Ar. *Frogs* 1300 and see on *Ion* 534c5–7.

[18] See e.g. Hom. *Od.* 22.347–8; Pi. *Ol.* 3.4–6, 7.7–8 and Murray (1981) 96–7.

And hand in hand with the notion of inspiration goes the idea of poetry as a craft.[19] Already in the *Odyssey* (17.382-5) the bard is described as a *demioergos*, a worker who is prized for his technical skill, and there are frequent references to the poet's expertise in early Greek poetry, expressed by terms such as *oida, epistamai, sophos* and *sophia*.[20] The increasing use of craft metaphors to describe the poet's activity from Pindar onwards is also indicative of the importance attached to the craft elements in poetic composition, and by the end of the fifth century we find the poet himself referred to as a *poietes* (maker), and his art as a *techne*.[21] Thus in pre-Platonic literature poets are portrayed both as *sophoi*, 'wise men', who have access to knowledge through the inspiration of the Muses, and as skilled craftsmen.

Poetic inspiration is one of the major themes of P.'s *Ion*. The ostensible subject of the dialogue is the nature of the rhapsode's skill: why is it that Ion excels in speaking about Homer, but is at a loss as far as any other poets are concerned? The reason, S. claims, is that Ion's ability as a rhapsode depends not on *techne*, but on a divine force which emanates from the Muses (533d1-2). Just as a magnet attracts iron rings and induces in those rings the power to attract others, so the Muse inspires a chain of people possessed by divine enthusiasm, and the rhapsode is the middle link in that chain: first comes the poet, then the rhapsode, then the audience. This image of the magnet underlines the interconnexion between the various elements in the chain of poetic communication, but in what follows S. puts the emphasis increasingly on poets, and his own language becomes increasingly poetic. In the dazzling central speech of the dialogue (533e-534e) S. builds up a picture of the poet as a 'light, winged, holy creature', who cannot compose until he is out of his mind and possessed by the Muses' power. Beautiful poetry can only be produced when the poet is devoid of reason and filled with

---

[19] See Harriott (1969) 92-104; Murray (1981) 98-9; Verdenius (1983) 20-4; Nagy (1989) 18-24.

[20] See e.g. Hom. *Od.* 11.368; Archil. fr. 1.2; Sol. 13.52; Theogn. 770, 772 and for further references Verdenius (1983) 21-2.

[21] *Poietes* is first used of the poet at Hdt. 2.53; for *techne* of the poet's work see e.g. Ar. *Peace* 749, *Frogs* 762, 770, 780, 850, and see further Verdenius (1983) 23-4.

divine enthusiasm, like a Corybantic dancer or a participant in the ecstatic rites of Dionysus. The god takes away the poet's senses and uses him, like a seer or a prophet, as a mouthpiece for the god's message so that the poems he utters are 'not human and of men, but divine and of the gods' (534e2–4).

Here P. takes over the traditional view that poets are inspired by the Muses, and revitalises it, partly by breathing new life into a cluster of metaphors about poets and poetry which, though not entirely dead, had nevertheless become conventional, partly by inventing some extraordinarily powerful images of his own, notably the poet as Corybant or Bacchant.[22] The total effect of his highly skilful 'collage' (Velardi (1989) 57) is to provide an overwhelming image of irrationality, at least so far as the poetic process is concerned. The value of the end product is not overtly questioned in the *Ion*, and in so far as S. touches on the subject, he is apparently complimentary: poems are consistently described as *kala* ('fine') throughout the dialogue. But P. transforms the traditional notion of poetic inspiration by emphasising the passivity of the poet and the irrational nature of the poetic process. He differs most significantly from his predecessors in maintaining that inspiration is incompatible with *techne*.[23] As we have seen, the craft elements in poetry had always been important, and by the time P. was writing, the word *poietes* had come to designate the poet *par excellence*. The poet might claim to be divinely inspired, but he was also a professional, a master of his *techne*, just like any other craftsman. P., however, is not interested in the mechanics of composition or in the technical aspects of the poet's work. He denies poets *techne* not because he regards them as shoddy craftsmen, but because they have no knowledge of what they say. The more irrational the poetic process, the less can the poet claim knowledge either of how he makes his poetry or of what his poetry says. Although in other dialogues P. occasionally implies that poets know about such things as diction, metre, rhythm and melody (see on *Rep.* 393d8) he always insists that they do not understand the subject-matter of their poetry, whether it concerns chariot-driving, medicine or virtue.

---

[22] For details see on 534a1–d1.

[23] On the radical nature of P.'s views see Tigerstedt (1969) and (1970); Murray (1981) and (1992); Woodruff (1982).

P. constructs his account of poetic inspiration in the *Ion* ambiguously. By using the language of divine possession he maintains a link with the traditional concept of poetic inspiration, but turns that concept upside down. In the early Greek poets, the divine origin of poetry is used to guarantee its truth and quality,[24] and there is still an implication of that sort in S.'s words here, especially at 534d. Despite its eulogistic tone, however, the central speech of the *Ion* undermines the authority traditionally accorded to poets by depriving them of *techne*. And we cannot ignore its context: the image of the magnet at the beginning (533d3 cf. 535e7–9) emphasises the interconnexion between the various elements in the chain of poetic communication – Muse, poet, rhapsode and audience – so that it is difficult to separate our judgement on the activity of the rhapsode (which must surely be negative) from our judgement on the activity of the poet. Like Ion himself we are left in a state of *aporia*, unable to decide how to read S.'s apparent eulogy of poets.

The negative implications of P.'s idea of inspiration are also apparent in other dialogues. For example, in the *Apology* (22b–c, quoted on p. 235) S. professes to be dismayed to find that the poets whom he questioned were quite incapable of explaining the meaning of their poetry, and concludes that they compose not through wisdom (*sophia*) but by a kind of instinct and inspiration (φύσει τινὶ καὶ ἐνθουσιάζοντες) like seers. Again, as with the *Ion*, the value of the poetry itself is not necessarily diminished by the fact that poets cannot understand their own productions; but the status of poets is inevitably called into question.[25] The implication of this passage is that poets are neither *sophoi* in the traditional sense, nor craftsmen, a point which S. underlines by comparing them unfavourably with *cheirotechnai*, skilled craftsmen, who at least have technical expertise in relation to the crafts which they practise. P.'s reluctance to grant poets the status even of skilled craftsmen, both here and elsewhere in his work (see on *Rep.* 601d1–2), must surely be seen against the background of the increasing professionalism of the poet's vocation in contemporary society.

The same opposition of inspiration and *techne* occurs in the fa-

---

[24] See Murray (1981) 90–2; Verdenius (1983) 27–8.
[25] Cf. *Men.* 99c–e quoted on pp. 235–6.

mous passage on poetic *mania* at *Phaedrus* 245a (quoted on p. 237), where the poet who relies on skill pales into insignificance beside the one whose tender, virgin soul is possessed by the frenzy of the Muses. This is a compelling image, beloved of all who seek validation in P.'s work for the view of the poet as an inspired being in touch with some higher level of reality through intuitive powers which have nothing to do with the intellect.[26] But even here there is an ambivalence about the presentation of poetry: despite the eulogy at 245a, later on in the dialogue (248d–e) the life of the poet is rated sixth in order of merit after the philosopher, the king, the man of affairs, the trainer or the doctor, and the seer. The language used here is significant: the highest form of life is that of 'the lover of wisdom or beauty, a follower of the Muses or of love' (φιλοσόφου ἢ φιλοκάλου ἢ μουσικοῦ τινος καὶ ἐρωτικοῦ), whereas the sixth is that of 'a poet or a practitioner of some other imitative art' (ποιητικὸς ἢ τῶν περὶ μίμησίν τις ἄλλος). The contradiction between P.'s low rating of the poet's life and his earlier exaltation of the recipient of the Muses' *mania* suggests that his attitude to poets and poetry in this dialogue is just as equivocal as in the *Ion*. Poetry remains a mimetic art, and the *Phaedrus* does not, after all, rehabilitate poets; for the true devotee of the Muses proves to be the philosopher, who devotes himself to the highest form of *mousike*, which proves to be philosophy.[27] The difference between the *Phaedrus* and other dialogues lies not in its conception of poetry, but in its conception of philosophy as a 'Muse-loving' activity in which inspiration and irrationality have a part to play.[28] The ending of the dialogue (278c–d), where P. asserts the superiority of the spoken over the written word, also suggests very little change in his attitude to existing poets: if Homer and the poets along with speech writers and law-givers had knowledge of the truth when they wrote, and could defend their words in conversation, they would deserve to be called lovers of wisdom. But a man who has

---

[26] For the importance of this passage for the Renaissance theory of *furor poeticus* see Weinberg (1961) I 250–1; Tigerstedt (1969) 50; M. J. B. Allen, *The Platonism of Marsilio Ficino* (Berkeley and Los Angeles 1984) 41–67; Hankins (1990) I 71–2.

[27] See 248d3 with Rowe (1986) *ad loc.*, 259a–e, and cf. *Phaed.* 61a3–4.

[28] For further discussion see Nussbaum (1986) 223–7; Else (1986) 47–59; Ferrari (1989) 142–8.

nothing more valuable than what he has composed or written, who has spent his time twisting words, sticking them together and pulling them apart is rightly called a poet or speech writer or a maker of laws. The one thing poets are consistently unable to do throughout P.'s work is to give an account of what they have composed. So the conclusion of the *Phaedrus* suggests that the poet is merely a manipulator of words, with no more grasp on the truth than anyone else.

In one passage, and one passage alone, P. combines the themes of inspiration and imitation. At *Laws* 719c, quoted and discussed on pp. 237–8, P. claims that there is an 'old story ... that when the poet sits on the tripod of the Muses, he is not in his right mind, but like a spring lets whatever is at hand flow forth. Since his skill is that of imitation he is often forced to contradict himself, when he represents contrasting characters, and he does not know whose words are true.' Here we see that the poet's art of imitation is just as irrational as the inspiration which comes from the Muses: in both cases the poet does not know what he is doing and is therefore incapable of judging his productions. It is the poet's lack of knowledge which P. consistently attacks, whether that attack is veiled in the ambiguous language of praise, as in the *Ion* and *Phaedrus*, or is more explicitly hostile as in the *Republic*.

3. PLATO AS POET

P.'s praise of poets in the *Ion* and *Phaedrus* is equivocal, his condemnation of them in the *Republic* uncompromising. Yet he was clearly drawn towards poetry like no other philosopher before or since. There are references to, and discussions of, poetry in dialogues from all periods of his life, and his work itself displays distinctly poetic qualities. As Sir Philip Sidney remarked:

Plato whosoever well considereth shall find that in the body of his work, though the inside and strength were philosophy, the skin, as it were, and beauty depended most of poetry: for all standeth upon dialogues, wherein he feigneth many honest burgesses of Athens to speak of such matters, that, if they had been set on the rack, they would never have confessed them, besides his poetical describing the circumstances of their meetings, as the well ordering of a banquet, the delicacy of a walk, with interlacing mere tales, as Gyges' ring and others, which who knoweth not be flowers of poetry did never walk into Apollo's garden.

These words from *A defence of poetry* (1595) highlight some of the peculiarities of P.'s work, in which we find philosophical arguments expressed in a form of literary fiction which often borders on poetry. The poetic nature of P.'s style has, of course, been recognised since antiquity: Aristotle, according to Diogenes Laertius (3.37), remarked that 'the style of the dialogues is half-way between poetry and prose', and Longinus (13.3–4) comments on the poetical language of P.'s prose. According to the ancient Lives there was a tradition that P. had written poetry himself in his youth, but abandoned his early passion when he met Socrates and turned to philosophy. We even possess some epigrams attributed to P., but these are now generally thought to be spurious.[29] Attractive as these stories are, like so much ancient biography, they were almost certainly invented out of P.'s own work.[30] If the tradition has a certain plausibility it is because P.'s work is indeed poetic.

The paradox that the most poetic of philosophers banished poets from his ideal state and condemned *mimesis*, yet used the mimetic techniques of poetry in his own work, has often been noted.[31] As we have seen, P. himself distinguishes between two different types of *lexis* or forms of speech, *diegesis* (narrative) when the author speaks in

[29] Perhaps the most famous of the poems attributed to P. is the epitaph to Aster, translated by Shelley:

> Thou wert the morning star among the living,
> Ere thy fair light had fled; –
> Now, having died, thou art as Hesperus, giving
> New splendour to the dead.

The epigrams are collected together in E. Diehl (ed.), *Anthologia lyrica graeca: poetae elegiaci*, 3rd edn (Leipzig 1949) 102–9. On the question of their authenticity see W. Ludwig, 'Plato's love epigrams', *G.R.B.S.* 4 (1963) 59–82; Riginos (1976) 48.

[30] See Riginos (1976) 43–51.

[31] On the dramatic elements in P.'s work and on his use of the dialogue form see e.g. R. Schaerer, *La question platonicienne*, 2nd edn (Paris 1969) 218–34; D. Tarrant, 'Plato as dramatist', *J.H.S.* 75 (1955) 82–9; Gadamer (1980) 39–72; Nussbaum (1986) 122–9 with further bibliography.

his own person, and *mimesis* when he speaks in the voice of another, as in the case of drama and direct speech in general. According to this definition all P.'s dialogues would fall under the category of *mimesis*, since the author (i.e. P. himself) never speaks *in propria persona*. The *Republic* itself is presented in the form of mimetic discourse: S. and his interlocutors are, as it were, characters conversing in a drama, with no authorial voice controlling the response of the audience. But how does this square with the conclusion S. reaches at 396e, that the good man will use the mimetic mode sparingly? The problem becomes more acute in book 10 when the concept of *mimesis* is broadened (see on 595a5, 597e3–4, 607a3–5), and it is suggested that all mimetic literature should be banished from the perfect society they have constructed. How can we reconcile this hostility to mimetic literature with the fact that P. appears to be a *mimetes* himself?[32] Should his own dialogues be banned from the ideal state? Various kinds of explanation have been offered for this embarrassing impasse, some people arguing that P. does not banish all *mimesis*, but only that which imitates the wrong kind of objects (see on 595a5, 607a3–5), others that the Platonic dialogues are precisely the kind of mimetic literature which P. would allow into his ideal state when he leaves open the possibility of welcoming back 'poetry for pleasure and imitation' (ἡ πρὸς ἡδονὴν ποιητικὴ καὶ ἡ μίμησις, 607c4–5).[33] But although the dialogues are poetic they are not poetry, and it is poetry which is his real target.

4. THE BATTLE BETWEEN POETRY AND PHILOSOPHY

The question of what kind of poetry might be permitted in the ideal state is not one on which P. spends a great deal of time: he is far

[32] See e.g. M. Haslam, 'Plato, Sophron and the dramatic dialogue', *B.I.C.S.* 19 (1972) 23; L. A. Kosman, 'Silence and imitation in the Platonic dialogues', in Klagge and Smith (1992) 73–92; D. M. Halperin, 'Plato and the erotics of narrativity', *ibid.* 93–129.

[33] See e.g. Friedländer (1958) 121–5. It has also been pointed out that several of the dialogues are not dialogues in the formal sense, since they are recounted by a narrator. See Plut. *Mor.* 711b–c; Halperin, in Klagge and Smith (1992) 93–6.

more concerned with banishing all existing poetry than with envisaging suitable alternatives. Despite his insistence at 400d11–402a6 that poetry and the arts in general have a vital role to play in developing the right kind of habits and fostering goodness of character in the young (provided, that is, that poets and artists follow their orders and portray only what is good), we hear very little more on the subject of 'good' poetry beyond the comment on the difficulty of imitating the good man in book 10 (604e2–4). Hymns to the gods and encomia to good men will be permitted in the ideal state, but there will be no place for poetry as we know it. The epics of Homer, the tragedies of Aeschylus, Sophocles and Euripides, and all the great masterpieces of Greek literature, long since canonised as high art, will be banished. Such uncompromising hostility to poetry strikes the modern reader as very odd. Why is P. so afraid of poetry that he has to abolish it altogether?

In order to answer this question it is important to remember first of all that poetry in P.'s day was not simply a minority interest indulged in by the leisured few, but a central feature in the life of the community. Greek education was based on *mousike*, that is all the arts over which the Muses presided: poetry, music, song and dance. English has no equivalent for the Greek *mousike*, but 'poetry' will not be too misleading a translation, provided we remember that for the Greeks poetry was inseparable from its musical elements: we should not think primarily of a written text, but rather, of a performance combining words and music. It was through poetry in this broad sense that one was trained to become a good citizen.[34] When children go to school, says Protagoras in P.'s dialogue (325e–326b), the masters make them learn by heart the works of good poets 'in which there is much admonition (πολλαὶ ... νουθετήσεις), many stories and eulogies and encomia of the good men of old, so that the child may eagerly imitate these and want to be like them'. Similarly when the children have learned to play the lyre they are taught the works of the good lyric poets in order that they may become balanced and harmonious people. In the *Laws* (810e–811a) the Athenian refers to the standard practice of making children learn large amounts of poetry off by heart, in order that they may grow up to be good and

[34] See Marrou (1965) 80–3 and Comm. on *Rep.* 376e2–3.

wise. Poetry is studied not for its aesthetic qualities, but for its ethical content, a point which is made abundantly clear in S.'s detailed critique of literature in books 2 and 3 of the *Republic*. The discussion of *mimesis* which begins at 392d5 centres on poetry's power to influence behaviour, since a major part of the poet's function was to provide role models for the young by glorifying the great heroes of the past.

But it was not only in the early stages of education that poetry had this formative role. In Ar. *Frogs* (727–9) the chorus sing the praises of the *kaloi kagathoi*, the good men of old, who were brought up 'on the wrestling floors and in choruses and on poetry' (ἐν παλαίστραις καὶ χοροῖς καὶ μουσικῆι). Choral singing and dancing played a major part in Greek life, and training young people to participate in choral performances such as the dithyrambic choruses at Athens was part of the educational process in its broadest sense. In the chorus the young were taught how to sing and dance, but they also learned how to become members of the community, since it was here, through the medium of poetry, that the values of society were transmitted. Hence in the *Laws* (654a) P. can define the uneducated person as one who cannot take part in a chorus, *apaideutos achoreutos*.[35] In the city he envisages there, the entire community, men, women and children, will be involved in choral performances, which will reinforce the values of the *polis* and promote social cohesion amongst its members: *choreia is paideia*.[36] The *Laws* is not, of course, a historical work, but the prominence which P. gives to choral singing and dancing in his Cretan city is based on the reality of Greek life, in which choral performances were indeed an important means of reinforcing social and cultural values. When, in the political turmoil of 404 B.C., a democratic army faced an oligarchic army in the port of Piraeus, the herald of the Eleusinian mysteries stood between the lines and reminded his fellow citizens of the bonds they shared:

[35] On the importance of the chorus as an educational institution see especially C. Calame, *Les choeurs de jeunes filles en Grèce archaïque* (Rome 1977) 1 386–411.

[36] See in particular *Laws* 664b–667b, but the entire discussion of education in books 2 and 7 is relevant. See further S. H. Lonsdale, *Dance and ritual play in Greek religion* (Baltimore 1993) 21–43.

Fellow citizens, why are you driving us out of the city? Why
do you want to kill us? We have never done you any harm. We
have shared with you in the most holy rites, in sacrifices and
in splendid festivals; we have danced in choruses with you
and gone to school with you and fought in the army with you,
braving together with you the dangers of land and sea in defence of our common safety and freedom. (Xen. *Hell.* 2.4.20)

Poetry continued to play a major part in the lives of adult citizens
through their participation (both as performers and as audience) in
the various public festivals at which drama, lyric and epic were performed. At Athens ordinary citizens took part as members of the
chorus in the tragedies and comedies which were staged annually at
the City Dionysia, and the dithyrambic contests involved ten choirs
of fifty boys and the same number of men.[37] P.'s *Ion* gives us a
vivid description of a rhapsode in performance. Decked in fine
robes, wearing a golden crown, and standing on a platform, he en-
acts scenes from Homeric epic, before an audience of 20,000 people
(530b6–8, 535d2–5). Like an actor he throws himself into the part
of the characters whom he portrays, stirring up the emotions of his
audience, who weep and visibly express their fear as they participate
in the rhapsode's performance (535b–e; cf. 532d6–7). Being a mem-
ber of a Greek audience was evidently not a passive experience.
Apart from the public world of festivals, poetry, music and song
were also a central feature of the more private environment of the
symposium, which continued to be a focus of social life long after
the aristocratic culture in which it had arisen had disappeared.[38]
Here poetry circulated amongst the guests like the wine which they
drank, and each symposiast was expected to take his turn, improvis-
ing a song of his own, or performing one from the standard repertoire of drinking songs. Greece was indeed a 'song culture' until well
into the fifth century (Herington (1985) 3–4).

The educative function of poetry was taken for granted, not simply in the education of the young, but in Greek life generally. So in
Ar. *Frogs* 1009–10 both Aeschylus and Euripides agree that a poet

[37] See Pickard-Cambridge (1988) 66, 75; Herington (1985) 96.
[38] See Marrou (1965) 81–2; O. Murray (ed.), *Sympotica. A symposium on the symposion* (Oxford 1990).

should be admired for 'his skill and admonition and because he makes men better citizens' (δεξιότητος καὶ νουθεσίας, ὅτι βελτίους τε ποιοῦμεν | τοὺς ἀνθρώπους ἐν ταῖς πόλεσιν) and Aeschylus claims at 1054–6 that 'children have a master to teach them, grown-ups have the poets'.[39] Poetry always had been a medium for communicating ethical teaching, indeed in the oral culture of early Greece it was the chief means by which ideas of any importance could be transmitted.[40] The distinction which we now make between poets and moral philosophers is not one which would have occurred to pre-Platonic thinkers: some of the most influential of those whom we now categorise as early Greek philosophers – Xenophanes, Parmenides and Empedocles – wrote in verse. Equally it was quite natural to regard poets as purveyors of moral truths, as we can see from P.'s own dialogues, where poets are often cited as authorities on ethical matters.[41] The 'ancient quarrel' between poetry and philosophy to which P. refers (*Rep.* 607b5–6) is not as old as P. himself would like to think.

Such was the hold of poetry on the Greek imagination that it continued to play an important part in the curriculum even when the old system of education, lamented by Right in Ar. *Clouds* 964–86, began to be replaced by newer teaching methods associated primarily with the sophists. The interpretation of poetry remained a feature of sophistic education, as we can see from Protagoras' claim at *Prot.* 338e7–339a3, that the most important part of a man's education is 'cleverness about words (περὶ ἐπῶν δεινόν). This means being able to understand what poets say, both the good things and the bad, to know how to distinguish them, and to give one's reasons when asked'. The famous discussion of Simonides' poem which then follows (339b) seems to reflect sophistic methods of literary criticism with reasonable accuracy, despite P.'s obvious parody of those methods.[42] We find

---

[39] For discussion of these lines see Dover (1993) 12–16, and on the poet as teacher Harriott (1969) 105–9.

[40] See Havelock (1963) 36–60; Thomas (1992) 113–17. On the priority of poetry over prose see Nagy (1989) 8–10.

[41] See e.g *Rep.* 331a, 331d, 334a–b; *Prot.* 339a–341e, 343d–347a; *Men.* 95c–96a; *Phaed.* 94d6–95a2, 112a2–3. For a good discussion of these issues see Nussbaum (1986) 123–5.

[42] See Pfeiffer (1968) 32–9; R. Rutherford, 'Unifying the *Protagoras*' in Barker and Warner (1992) 150–2.

another example of this kind of sophistic interpretation of poetry in the *Hippias Minor*, which debates the relative merits of the characters of Achilles and Odysseus as role models.

5. PLATO AND HOMER

One poet above all dominated Greek education and Greek cultural life: Homer. P. himself refers to Homer as 'the best and most divine of poets' (*Ion* 530b9–10 cf. *Rep.* 607a2–3), 'the educator of Greece' (*Rep.* 606e2–3), and it is clear that the Homeric poems did have a canonical status akin to that of the Bible in later ages.[43] At school Homer was the primary text: in a fragment from Aristophanes' comedy *Daitales*, for example, a boy is questioned about archaic Homeric vocabulary, and the recital of Homeric poetry seems to have been a standard feature in the curriculum.[44] It is not by chance that P. chooses a passage from the beginning of the *Iliad* to illustrate what he means by *mimesis* at *Rep.* 392e, since this is a text that every schoolboy would know. 'Homer was not a man, but a god' was one of the first sentences children learned to copy in the Hellenistic period, and papyri and ostraca containing numerous fragments of the Homeric poems, particularly the *Iliad*, confirm their central place in the education of Greek Egypt.[45]

Homer's poems were not only studied in school, they were also performed by rhapsodes in public contests which go back to at least the sixth century: Herodotus (5.67.1) records that Cleisthenes, tyrant of Sicyon, stopped rhapsodic competitions of Homeric epic when at war with Argos on the grounds that the Argives were too much praised in Homer's poetry. And it was during this period that rhap-

---

[43] See Marrou (1965) 31–41, 246–7, 332–3; Buffière (1956) 10–13; Goldhill (1986) 139–42.

[44] Ar. fr. 233 in *Poetae comici Graeci*, ed. R. Kassel and C. Austin (Berlin 1984). When Alcibiades was unable to obtain a volume of Homer from a school master, he punched the unfortunate man, according to a story in Plutarch's *Life of Alcibiades* (7.1). On the other hand he was very impressed by another teacher who said that he had a copy of Homer which he had 'corrected' himself. 'Are you teaching boys to read when you know how to edit Homer? Why aren't you teaching young men?' (*ibid*). Cf. Plut. *Mor.* 186e and Ael. *V.H.* 13.38.

[45] See Marrou (1965) 246–7.

sodic recitations of Homer were instituted at the Panathenaea, where the poems were recited in their entirety, each rhapsode taking his cue from where the previous one had left off (see further on *Ion* 530b2). In the fifth and fourth centuries professional rhapsodes such as Ion earned their living travelling round Greece, reciting poetry at public festivals and games, where they competed for prizes (*Ion* 535e4–6). In the *Laws* (764d–e) P. takes it as a matter of course that a state should have rhapsodic competitions just as it should have contests for musicians and choral performers. Elsewhere in the same work (658d) he says that old men, who are competent by virtue of their age and wisdom to make sound judgements, will enjoy rhapsodic recitals of Homer and Hesiod above all other types of performance. The popularity of rhapsodes is also attested by Diodorus (14.109), who tells us that when Dionysius, tyrant of Syracuse, sent a group of the best available rhapsodes along with several four-horse teams to the Olympic games in 388 B.C., people flocked to hear their performance and were amazed at the beautiful sound of their voices. Inscriptions attest that rhapsodes continued to compete in performances of Homeric epic at festivals and games until at least the third century A.D.[46]

Rhapsodes also seem to have given performances of a more intimate sort, as is suggested by the remarks of Niceratus in Xenophon's *Symposium* (3.6), who says that he listens to the recitations of rhapsodes practically every day. The same character describes how his father, being concerned to make him a good man (ἀγαθὸς ἀνήρ), had made him learn the works of Homer so that he could now repeat by heart the entire *Iliad* and *Odyssey* (Xen. *Symp.* 3.5–6, cf. *Mem.* 4.2.10). Later on, when he is asked what benefits such knowledge of Homer confers he replies: 'Doubtless you know that Homer, the wisest of men, (σοφώτατος) has dealt with practically all human affairs in his poetry. So let anyone cultivate me who wishes to become an expert in domestic economy, public speaking or strategy (οἰκονομικὸς ἢ δημηγορικὸς ἢ στρατηγικός), or to be like Achilles, Ajax, Nestor or Odysseus. For I understand all these things' (*Symp.* 4.6, cf. *Ion* 536e1–3). Knowledge of Homer's poetry could impart technical expertise, but it was also essential for the cultivated man since it

---

[46] See M. L. West (1981) 114.

provided him with the moral and ethical examples on which he should model his own behaviour.[47]

In the *Ion* S. takes the rhapsode to task for not having technical knowledge of the skills which Homer depicts in his poems – divination, medicine, warfare and so on. How can he interpret Homer's poetry if he does not know what Homer is talking about? At this stage S. refrains from saying that Homer himself knows nothing, and confines his criticism to the poet's interpreter. But in the *Republic* he focuses his attention on Homer directly. In the critique which begins at 377c5 S. objects to most existing poetry because it is morally harmful in content: the ideas expressed by Homer and the other poets about the gods and their attitude to human life are quite simply wrong in terms of the information that they impart (377d4–9, 379c2–d8). Equally objectionable is the portrayal of gods and heroes as morally weak. Heroes who are afraid of death, who lament excessively or who indulge in violent laughter encourage similar behaviour in others and therefore provide unsuitable role models for the young (386a6–392a2). The prominence of Homer's Achilles in this discussion is no accident, for he is the hero *par excellence*, the embodiment of the heroic ideal. Alexander the Great, the historical counterpart of this legendary hero, took his copy of the *Iliad* with him on his campaigns, and dreamt of being a second Achilles.[48] But for P., Achilles' obsession with personal glory, his highly emotional nature, and his pessimistic view of the gods and of human life make him the antithesis of the good man.[49]

In *Rep.* books 2 and 3 S. advocates strict censorship of the literature

---

[47] See e.g. *Prot.* 325 quoted above, and 312b3–4 where S. suggests that one studies poetry ἐπὶ παιδείᾳ, ὡς τὸν ἰδιώτην καὶ τὸν ἐλεύθερον πρέπει ('for the purposes of a liberal education, as a layman and a gentleman should'); cf. *Hipp. Min.* 365b. Homer's didactic role in Greek education and culture is strongly emphasised by Havelock (1963) 61–86, who summarises the function of poetry in Greek society before P. thus: 'it provided a massive repository of useful knowledge, a sort of encyclopaedia of ethics, politics, history and technology which the effective citizen was required to learn as the core of his educational equipment' (27).

[48] See e.g. Plut. *Alex.* 8.2, 15.8–9, 26.2; *Mor.* 327f–328a, 331c–d; Marrou (1965) 40, 44; J. Mossman, 'Tragedy and epic in Plutarch's *Alexander*', *J.H.S.* 108 (1988) 83–93.

[49] See on 386a6–7, c5–7, 388b1–2, 389d7 and, in general, Hobbs (1990).

on which Greek education is based, and concludes that the only poetry acceptable in the ideal state will be that which imitates the good man in accordance with guidelines laid down by S. himself (398a–b). S. does not mention specific poets to be banished at this stage, but Homer dominates the discussion (see on 398a8–b4) in a way that prepares us for the final assault on poetry in book 10, which begins and ends with Homer. At 595b9–c3 S. professes that the love and respect (φιλία ... καὶ αἰδώς) he has had for Homer since childhood make him hesitate before launching his devastating attack on poetry. These words are ironically echoed in the closing lines of that attack, which expose this love and respect for what it is: an ἔρως, a passion, engendered and nurtured by the society in which he has been brought up (607e6–608a1). S.'s emphasis on the triviality of poetry and his insistence on Homer's ignorance about all matters human and divine strike at the heart of Greek *paideia*. Homer, the educator of Greece, must be banished in order to make way for a new system of *paideia* in which poetry will be replaced by philosophy. In the *Laws* when the question arises as to whether serious poets (σπουδαῖοι) who compose tragedies will be allowed to put on their plays, the Athenian replies, 'We ourselves are composers of the finest and noblest tragedy we can make; for the whole of our state has been constructed as an imitation (*mimesis*) of the finest and noblest life, which, we say, really is the truest tragedy' (817b).[50] The *Republic* too presents us with a vision of an ideal society in which philosophers will take the place of poets: instead of poetry we will have Platonic dialogues, instead of Achilles, the philosopher king. P. deliberately sets himself up as a rival to Homer, as Nietzsche saw: 'Plato versus Homer; that is the complete, the genuine antagonism'.[51]

The crucial importance of banishing poetry from the ideal state is underlined in S.'s words at 608b4, which bring his attack on poetry to a close: 'Great is the struggle, my dear Glaucon, greater than it seems: for the choice is between becoming a good man or a bad, so it's not right to be tempted by honour, or money or power, or even

---

[50] Cf. *Laws* 811c, where the Athenian suggests that children need no longer learn poetry at school, they can learn passages from the *Laws* instead.

[51] *On the genealogy of morals*, trans. W. Kaufmann and R. J. Hollingdale (New York 1969) 3.25.

by poetry, to neglect justice and the rest of virtue.' Poetry must go because it is dangerous: it has the power to corrupt even the best of men, and threatens the stability of both individual and *polis*. Poetry plays a vital role in the dynamic interrelationship which P. envisages between the individual and society[52] because it sets up the wrong kind of constitution in the soul (605b–c), just as it does in the city. In the story of political decline which P. tells in book 9, poets are specifically associated with tyrants, the worst of all human types. At 568a–d the tragedians (and we should remember that Homer is described as their 'original master and leader' at 595c1–2) are criticised for celebrating tyranny and praising it as 'god-like'. They will not be acceptable in cities whose constitution is like ours, says S., but doubtless they will go to other states where they will draw the crowds and, through the fine persuasive voices of the actors whom they hire, they will convert them to tyranny or democracy. Poets like these will be particularly acclaimed (and financially rewarded) by tyrannies, and to a lesser degree by democracies, but the higher up the constitutional scale they go, the less acceptable they will be. This passage illustrates the strength of the interdependence between poets and their public, for poets thrive in, and are the products of, degenerate societies, whose wickedness they reinforce, by fostering the worst elements in the souls of the individuals who make up those societies.

P.'s purpose is none other than to reform society by expelling the cause of its corruption: Homer and his fellow poets. If men are now incapable of recognising a good man when they see one (604e2–4), it is because they have been nurtured from earliest childhood on the false images of the poets, which are the source of so much damage, and yet of so much pleasure. P. does not allow us to forget the overwhelming charm of poetry, which, like some magic spell, exerts its lethal influence on all who come into contact with it (601b1–4). But however much we enjoy giving way to the passions which poetry arouses, passions which should be kept firmly under the control of reason if we are truly to live the good life, such temptation must be resisted. In the *polis* ruled by the philosopher king there will be no place for such a dangerous and subversive power.

[52] On this subject see the excellent article by Lear (1992).

P. takes poetry seriously precisely because it represents such a threat to his own philosophical enterprise. His hostility can be partly explained in historical terms, for P.'s desire to replace poetry by philosophy as the highest form of *mousike* must be seen against the background of the paramount importance of poetry in Greek culture, as Havelock demonstrated in his influential book *Preface to Plato* (1963). There Havelock argued that P.'s view of poetry as a kind of encyclopaedia of technical information and ethical values was not idiosyncratic, but indicative of the oral mentality which still persisted in the Greece of P.'s day. P.'s extreme mistrust not just of bad poetry, but of the poetic experience itself could only be explained, Havelock argued, as a reaction to a cultural situation still dominated by oral communication.[53] No doubt Havelock exaggerated his case in claiming that P. was at the centre of a revolution in communications, and that he was himself instrumental in bringing about a transition from an oral to a literate mentality in Greek society. Clearly the concepts of orality and literacy are more flexible, and the interplay between them more complex, than Havelock's analysis suggested.[54] Nevertheless it cannot be denied that P.'s attack on poetry represents a radical break with the past. Greece in many ways continued to be an oral society: historians, for example, regularly recited their works in public, and Greek social and political life was dominated by oratory, a performance art if ever there was one. But after the fifth century, despite the enormous popularity of drama, the performance of poetry was no longer at the centre of Greek culture as it had been in earlier times.

6. THE PLATONIC LEGACY

P.'s attitude to poetry is neither simple nor consistent: when he banishes poetry he does so in terms which suggest the renunciation of a sinful love in the interests of a higher good; equally, when he speaks of the poet as divinely inspired, that image does not carry with it an unambiguous respect for the poet's message. The ambivalence of P.'s presentation of poets and poetry in his dialogues has generated

---

[53] For the further development of this thesis see Gentili (1988).
[54] See Thomas (1992) *passim*, but especially 3–5, 17–28, 102–17.

an extraordinary variety and range of responses; here I shall merely draw attention to some of the most significant ways in which Platonic themes persist in later literature.

(a) The inspired poet

In the *Ion* and *Phaedrus* P. developed a quasi-mythical picture of the poet as a divinely inspired being, which was to remain an archetypal image in European literature for centuries to come. At the end of Coleridge's poem Kubla Khan an inspired figure appears:

> Beware! Beware!
> His flashing eyes, his floating hair!
> Weave a circle round him thrice,
> And close your eyes with holy dread,
> For he on honey-dew hath fed,
> And drunk the milk of Paradise.

This figure, we can see, is a poet, particularly as depicted in P.'s *Ion*, where milk and honey are also associated with poetic inspiration (534a-b).[55] The inspired bard also appears in many eighteenth-century poems on poesy, but perhaps the most famous depiction of this archetypal image is Shakespeare's:

> The poet's eye in a fine frenzy rolling,
> Doth glance from heaven to earth, from earth to heaven;
> And as imagination bodies forth
> The forms of things unknown, the poet's pen
> Turns them to shapes, and gives to airy nothing
> A local habitation and a name.
> (*A Midsummer Night's Dream* 5.1.12-17)

Shakespeare with his 'small Latin and less Greek'[56] would not have read P. But the Platonic notion of the poet's divine frenzy, transmitted through the agency of Latin writers such as Cicero, Horace

---

[55] See J. Bate, *Shakespeare and the English Romantic imagination* (Oxford 1986) 62.

[56] Ben Jonson, 'To the memory of My Beloved, The Author, Mr. William Shakespeare' (1623).

and Seneca, had become a commonplace in European literature.[57] E. R. Curtius discusses this *topos* of *furor poeticus*, remarking that the Middle Ages 'knew the poet's divine frenzy without knowing Plato ... If we now look back at the Middle Ages, we can see that the theory of "poetic madness" – the Platonic interpretation of the doctrine of inspiration and enthusiasm – lived on through the entire millennium which extends from the conquest of Rome by the Goths to the conquest of Constantinople by the Turks'.[58] The Latin Middle Ages knew P. only at second hand. But the great revival of interest in Plato which began in Italy in the age of Petrarch (1304–74) culminated in the translation of the entire Platonic corpus into Latin by the Florentine Neoplatonist, Marsilio Ficino (1484), which made P.'s works accessible to educated Europe.[59] Ficino's own development of the themes of Platonic love and divine inspiration brought new life to the traditional *topos* of *furor poeticus*, which played a prominent role in the literary criticism of the Italian Renaissance, and thereafter in the works of many French and other European writers.[60] In the *Defence of poetry* Sir Philip Sidney, following the lead of many an Italian critic, invoked P.'s account of the poet's *enthousiasmos* in the *Ion* to prove that when he banished poets from the *Republic* he banished 'the abuse, not the thing'.[61]

P.'s account of inspiration also made its impact on literary theory in other ways: in the *Ion* S. describes how the rhapsode inspires his audience with the emotions which he himself feels (535b–e). Poet,

[57] See e.g. Cic. *De or.* 2.46.194 and *De div.* 1.37.80; Hor. *C.* 3.4.5–6, 3.25, *A.P.* 455; Sen. *De tranquillitate animi* 17.10.2. On the importance of these texts for the transmission of P.'s ideas see M. Kemp, 'From "mimesis" to "fantasia": the quattrocento vocabulary of creation, inspiration and genius in the visual arts', *Viator* 8 (1977) 384–6.

[58] Curtius (1953) 474–5; see also J. M. Ziolkowski, 'Classical influences on views of inspiration', in P. Godman and O. Murray (edd.), *Latin poetry and the classical tradition: essays in Medieval and Renaissance literature* (London 1990) 29–31.

[59] See Shorey (1938) 121–2; Hankins (1990) I 300–59. Ficino's translation was still in use many centuries later. Shelley had a copy of it by his side when he was working on his own translation of the *Symposium* in 1818. See R. Holmes, *Shelley: the pursuit* (Harmondsworth 1987) 431.

[60] See Shorey (1938) 137–50; Weinberg (1961) I 250–96; J. M. Cocking, *Imagination: a study in the history of ideas* (London 1991) 228–42.

[61] *A defence of poetry*, ed. J. van Dorsten (Oxford 1966) 58.

rhapsode and audience are all linked together like a chain of iron
rings suspended from the magnet of the Muses (533d3–e5, 535e7–
536b4), which draws the human mind wherever it wills (536a2–3).
This image is the forerunner of the idea which emerges in later
poetic theory, that in order to move his audience the poet must feel
the emotions with which he wishes to inspire them, an idea which is
given its classic expression by Horace, *A.P.* 99–103:

> non satis est pulchra esse poemata; dulcia sunto,
> et quocumque uolent animum auditoris agunto.
> ut ridentibus arrident, ita flentibus adflent
> humani uultus. si uis me flere, dolendum est
> primum ipsi tibi.[62]

In the field of rhetoric too it became a commonplace that the
speaker must feel the emotions he wishes to communicate in order
to be convincing.[63] P.'s influence can be seen directly in Longinus'
development of this notion in connexion with his theory of sub-
limity, τὸ ὕψος, and the effect which inspired utterance has on its
audience or readers.[64] But whereas P.'s principal concern is with the
enthousiasmos of the poet, Longinus focuses on the emotional transport of the listener or reader to whom the passion of the speaker or
writer has been transmitted. Longinus' own enthusiasm for P. is evident,[65] and in a memorable simile he uses the Platonic language of
inspiration to illustrate the influence of the great writers of the past
upon aspiring authors: 'many are possessed by a spirit not their own,

---

[62] 'It is not enough for poems to be beautiful. Let them also be pleasing, so
that they can draw the mind of the listener wherever they want. The human
countenance smiles with those who smile, weeps with those who weep. So
if you want me to weep, you must first feel grief yourself.' This idea had
already been adumbrated by Aristophanes in the *Thesmophoriazusae*, where
Euripides and Mnesilochus visit Agathon, whom they find dressed in woman's
clothes, and in the very throes of creation. Agathon justifies his strange appearance and conduct on the grounds that a poet must take on the characteristics of the characters whom he portrays (*Thesm.* 149–50). Cf. *Ach.* 410–15.
But Ar.'s emphasis is on the composer rather than on the effect which he
produces on his audience.

[63] See e.g. Cic. *Orat.* 132; *De or.* 2.189ff; Quint. 6.2.26ff.

[64] See e.g. 1.4, 8.1, 8.4, 15.1 and Russell (1981) 81–2.

[65] See e.g. 12.3, 13.1, 13.3, 32.5–7, 35.1

in the same way as happens, we are told, when the Pythia sits on her tripod ... and prophesies when inspired ... similarly, the genius of the ancients acts as a kind of oracular cavern, and effluences flow from it into the minds of their imitators'.[66]

In terms of aesthetic theory the significance of P.'s notion of inspiration lies in the distinction that it implies between poetry and knowledge. Before P. poets claimed to be inspired, but that inspiration brought with it knowledge and authority. Pre-Platonic ideas of inspiration were also compatible with claims to craftsmanship, but, as we have seen, the *Ion*, like the *Phaedrus*, drives a wedge between inspiration and *techne*. Though S.'s target in this dialogue is the rhapsode, poets are inevitably implicated in its conclusions. Ion knows nothing about the subjects on which he speaks, nor is he credited with any definable skill. Similarly the poet's inspiration carries with it the corollary of ignorance, even though his product, at any rate in this dialogue, remains valuable. The important question which the dialogue raises is that of what the critic (and by implication the poet) knows. By what means does Ion judge the merits of Homer's poetry? Wherein lies his expertise? The quasi-mythical account of divine inspiration does not answer this question; but it does suggest that poetry cannot be judged by criteria which are applicable to other kinds of activity. The opposition between inspiration and knowledge (both of what the poet makes and how he makes it) sharply demarcates poetry from rational discourse, and suggests the possibility that poetry answers to standards of its own.[67] Schaper (1968) 48–50 points out that P.'s account of inspiration highlights a problem which has been central in the history of aesthetic thought, the problem 'of how to establish, philosophically, the autonomy of art and its independence from other schemes of evaluation'.

(b) *Poetry and* mimesis

Of no less importance was P.'s conception of poetry as *mimesis*, particularly as developed in book 10 of the *Republic*. P.'s was the first theoretical discussion of art in these terms, and thereafter it was taken

---

[66] 13.2. Trans. adapted from Russell's in *Ancient literary criticism*, edd. D. A. Russell and M. Winterbottom (Oxford 1972) 158. Cf. Pl. *Laws* 719c quoted on p. 237 for the image of the poet sitting on the tripod.

[67] See e.g. Annas (1981) 343; Woodruff (1982) 146–7.

for granted in ancient literary criticism that works of art in some sense, and with varying degrees of complexity, imitate the external world.[68] Indeed *mimesis* or imitation (defined, of course, in many different ways) played an important part in theories of literature and art from antiquity right through to the end of the eighteenth century. A standard image used to describe the relationship between a work of art and the world or 'nature', was that of a mirror, an image which P. uses at *Rep.* 596d8–e3, where S. tells Glaucon that he can create anything he likes by holding up a mirror to the external world. For P. this image has strongly negative connotations, but it was not always so. Even before P. the sophist Alcidamas had described the *Odyssey* as 'a beautiful mirror of human life', καλὸν ἀνθρωπίνου βίου κάτοπτρον (Arist. *Rhet.* 1406b). Although Aristotle condemned the metaphor as frigid, it was taken up enthusiastically by later writers. Cicero, for example, is alleged to have called comedy *imitatio uitae, speculum consuetudinis, imago ueritatis* ('an imitation of life, a mirror of custom, an image of truth', Donatus, *De com.* 5.1). The image continued to have a long history, and was still current in the eighteenth century. The highest praise that Johnson could lavish on Shakespeare was that he was above all writers 'the poet of nature; the poet that holds up to his readers a faithful mirror of manners and of life' (*Preface to Shakespeare*, 1759). The legacy of P.'s characterisation of the artist's activity in terms of *mimesis* is discussed in detail by M. H. Abrams in *The mirror and the lamp* (New York, 1953), a book whose very title testifies to the centrality of the image of art as a mirror in European thought.[69]

P.'s characterisation of art as an imitation which is at third remove from reality led him to condemn poetry as simply a form of play.[70] Many later thinkers have agreed with him that aesthetic experience can indeed be likened to play, but have argued nevertheless that works of art have their own intrinsic value: 'of course art is playful, but its play is serious', as Iris Murdoch puts it.[71] P.'s own practice as a writer, and particularly his use of myth, suggest, of

[68] See Russell (1981) 99–113 with bibliography on p. 99 n. 1.

[69] See especially 8–14, 30–5, and on the image of the mirror Curtius (1953) 336.

[70] See on *Rep.* 602b8 and cf. *Soph.* 234a–b, *Pol.* 288c, *Laws* 889c–d.

[71] Murdoch (1977) 84. See also Schaper (1968) 53–4; J. Huizinga, *Homo ludens*, English trans. (London 1970) 141–58, 182–6.

course, that he was well aware of the potentially serious playfulness of literature. But when he refers to the composition of the *Republic* itself as a form of play,[72] and when he speaks of the truth that can be conveyed by *muthoi* (see on 377a5–6), he claims a value for his own work which he denies to the trivial imitations of Homer and his fellow-poets. If myths and stories are to have any value, they must contain some moral or religious truth, but the only people capable of perceiving such truths are philosophers. Hence art must serve the interests of philosophy.

In the *Laws* much emphasis is placed on the importance of poetry in the education of the young and in the cultural life of the citizens as a whole.[73] The tone is less vehement than that of the *Republic*, and it might be argued that we find here a more positive valuation of poetry than in the earlier dialogue. But though poetry has its place, it is to be strictly subordinated to the purposes of the rulers. Like the other mimetic arts, poetry is to be judged according to the criterion of accuracy rather than of pleasure (668a–b), and the judge must be one who understands the object of the imitation so that he may assess not only the accuracy of the copy, but also its moral value (669a–b). On no account are poets to be allowed to compose as they please, since they are incapable of judging their own productions (719c). When poems are performed at public festivals, the Minister of Education will select composers on the basis of the excellence of their conduct in the community rather than on their artistic ability; no one should dare to sing an unauthorised song, 'not even if it were sweeter than the hymns of Thamyras or of Orpheus' (829c–e). Only the morally virtuous will be allowed to compose poetry. Despite the difference in tone, the attitude adopted towards art in the *Laws* is every bit as hostile as that of the *Republic*. For to deprive poets of their autonomy is to deprive them of their power.

(c) The defence of poetry

P.'s views on art resist systematisation, yet there is a discernible continuity in the attitudes expressed towards poetry and poets in the

---

[72] *Rep.* 536c1, cf. 376d9–10 and *Phdr.* 276c–e, and on the dialogues themselves as play see Gadamer (1980) 70–1.
[73] See Ferrari (1989) 103–8.

dialogues. P.'s approach is critical, but ambivalently so. In the *Symposium* (205b8–c2) Diotima explains the meaning of the term *poiesis*, claiming that all creators in whatever sphere should be called *poietai*, 'poets'. A little later on, in a passage which counterbalances the arguments of *Rep.* 599c–d,[74] Homer and Hesiod are held up as examples of mortals who have created spiritual offspring in the form of their poems, and are linked with law-givers such as Lycurgus and Solon, and other creators of beauty and goodness (209d–e). Here the poet is no mere imitator of images, but a creator whose progeny is associated with the upward ascent of the soul from earthly to spiritual beauty, whose ultimate goal is the vision of Beauty itself. This passage, together with the mythical account of the poet's divine frenzy in the *Ion* and *Phaedrus*, provided the impetus for many extravagant claims on the part of creative artists in later writers. Thus the later tradition, and particularly that inspired by Neoplatonism, was able to respond to P.'s provocation by developing a defence of poetry which was constructed out of P.'s own work.

Of all the apologias for poetry elicited by P.'s challenge that which best illustrates this point is Shelley's *Defence of poetry* (1821). Though written as a reply to Thomas Love Peacock's *The four ages of poetry* (1820), in which Peacock condemned poetry as an anachronism in the modern age, Shelley's *Defence* must also be read as a response to P. himself. In a letter to Peacock (15 February 1821) Shelley claimed, like Sidney before him,[75] that the true basis for a defence of poetry was to be found in P.'s *Ion*, which he was reading at the time; and the influence of this dialogue can clearly be seen in Shelley's essay: 'poetry is indeed something divine' (503)[76] and 'is as it were the interpenetration of a diviner nature through our own' (504). Ignoring any hint of Socratic irony which may lurk beneath the surface of P.'s text, he celebrates the irrational nature of the poetic process: 'Poetry is not like reasoning, a power to be exerted

[74] See Asmis (1992) 354.
[75] See above p. 26; J. Roe, 'Italian Neoplatonism and the poetry of Sidney, Shakespeare, Chapman and Donne', in Baldwin and Hutton (1994) 103–6; J. Wallace, 'Shelley, Plato and the political imagination', *ibid.* 235–6.
[76] Page references are to *Shelley's poetry and prose*, ed. D. H. Reiman and S. B. Powers (New York 1977).

according to the determination of the will. A man cannot say, "I will compose poetry". The greatest poet even cannot say it: for the mind in creation is as a fading coal, which some invisible influence, like an inconstant wind, awakens to brightness' (503–4). And Shelley implicitly refutes P.'s arguments against poetry in the *Republic* by substituting imagination for reason, and by making the poet rather than the philosopher the saviour of society.[77] Throughout this essay, like Diotima in the *Symposium*, Shelley uses the term 'poetry' to include the creative faculty in general. And he treats poetry not merely as a literary phenomenon, but as a moral and political force. By using Platonic imagery and Platonic arguments, Shelley thus arrives at a wholly un-Platonic estimate of the poet's value and function in society. And by appropriating for poets the powers which P. had given to philosophers, Shelley restores to poets the authority and status they had once had in early Greece before the coming of philosophy. So he speaks of the imagination as 'the great instrument of moral good' (488) and concludes his essay (508) with the triumphant claim that 'Poets are the unacknowledged legislators of the world'.

7. THE TEXT

The text printed here is based on Burnet's Oxford Classical Text. The abbreviated apparatus, on the model of previous volumes in this series, draws attention to places where the text adopted here differs from Burnet's. For a detailed analysis of the manuscript tradition of the *Republic* see Boter (1989). A new edition of the Oxford Classical Text of the *Republic* is currently being prepared by S. R. Slings, who has published a series of critical notes on the early books in *Mnemosyne* (1988, 1989, 1990). I have taken account of the views and new readings proposed by Slings in these articles, and have also benefited from his advice on several points of difficulty in the text. The following sigla are used:

c   a reading on which there is consensus between the primary
        manuscripts

---

[77] See Wallace, in Baldwin and Hutton (1994) 234–7.

m   a reading found in one or more of the primary sources

(*m*) a reading found in one of the secondary manuscripts, or inserted by a late or uncertain hand in a primary manuscript

t   a reading found in a quotation of the *Ion* or *Republic* by another ancient author

e   a reading proposed by a modern editor.

PLATO
ION; REPUBLIC 376e–398b9;
REPUBLIC 595–608b10

ΙΩΝ

ΣΩ. Τὸν Ἴωνα χαίρειν. πόθεν τὰ νῦν ἡμῖν ἐπιδεδή-
μηκας; ἢ οἴκοθεν ἐξ Ἐφέσου;
ΙΩΝ Οὐδαμῶς, ὦ Σώκρατες, ἀλλ᾽ ἐξ Ἐπιδαύρου ἐκ τῶν
Ἀσκληπιείων.
ΣΩ. Μῶν καὶ ῥαψωιδῶν ἀγῶνα τιθέασιν τῶι θεῶι οἱ 5
Ἐπιδαύριοι;
ΙΩΝ Πάνυ γε, καὶ τῆς ἄλλης γε μουσικῆς.
ΣΩ. Τί οὖν; ἠγωνίζου τι ἡμῖν; καὶ πῶς τι ἠγωνίσω;
ΙΩΝ Τὰ πρῶτα τῶν ἄθλων ἠνεγκάμεθα, ὦ Σώκρατες.   b
ΣΩ. Εὖ λέγεις· ἄγε δὴ ὅπως καὶ τὰ Παναθήναια νική-
σομεν.
ΙΩΝ Ἀλλ᾽ ἔσται ταῦτα, ἐὰν θεὸς ἐθέληι.
ΣΩ. Καὶ μὴν πολλάκις γε ἐζήλωσα ὑμᾶς τοὺς ῥαψωιδούς, 5
ὦ Ἴων, τῆς τέχνης· τὸ γὰρ ἅμα μὲν τὸ σῶμα κεκοσμῆσθαι
ἀεὶ πρέπον ὑμῶν εἶναι τῆι τέχνηι καὶ ὡς καλλίστοις φαίνεσθαι, ἅμα δὲ ἀναγκαῖον εἶναι ἔν τε ἄλλοις ποιηταῖς διατρίβειν πολλοῖς καὶ ἀγαθοῖς καὶ δὴ καὶ μάλιστα ἐν Ὁμήρωι,
τῶι ἀρίστωι καὶ θειοτάτωι τῶν ποιητῶν, καὶ τὴν τούτου διά-   10
νοιαν ἐκμανθάνειν, μὴ μόνον τὰ ἔπη, ζηλωτόν ἐστιν. οὐ   c
γὰρ ἂν γένοιτό ποτε ἀγαθὸς ῥαψωιδός, εἰ μὴ συνείη τὰ
λεγόμενα ὑπὸ τοῦ ποιητοῦ. τὸν γὰρ ῥαψωιδὸν ἑρμηνέα δεῖ
τοῦ ποιητοῦ τῆς διανοίας γίγνεσθαι τοῖς ἀκούουσι· τοῦτο δὲ
καλῶς ποιεῖν μὴ γιγνώσκοντα ὅτι λέγει ὁ ποιητὴς ἀδύνατον.   5
ταῦτα οὖν πάντα ἄξια ζηλοῦσθαι.
ΙΩΝ Ἀληθῆ λέγεις, ὦ Σώκρατες· ἐμοὶ γοῦν τοῦτο
πλεῖστον ἔργον παρέσχεν τῆς τέχνης, καὶ οἶμαι κάλλιστα
ἀνθρώπων λέγειν περὶ Ὁμήρου, ὡς οὔτε Μητρόδωρος ὁ
Λαμψακηνὸς οὔτε Στησίμβροτος ὁ Θάσιος οὔτε Γλαύκων   d
οὔτε ἄλλος οὐδεὶς τῶν πώποτε γενομένων ἔσχεν εἰπεῖν οὕτω
πολλὰς καὶ καλὰς διανοίας περὶ Ὁμήρου ὅσας ἐγώ.
ΣΩ. Εὖ λέγεις, ὦ Ἴων· δῆλον γὰρ ὅτι οὐ φθονήσεις
μοι ἐπιδεῖξαι.   5
ΙΩΝ Καὶ μὴν ἄξιόν γε ἀκοῦσαι, ὦ Σώκρατες, ὡς εὖ

κεκόσμηκα τὸν Ὅμηρον· ὥστε οἶμαι ὑπὸ Ὁμηριδῶν ἄξιος εἶναι χρυσῶι στεφάνωι στεφανωθῆναι.

ΣΩ. Καὶ μὴν ἐγὼ ἔτι ποιήσομαι σχολὴν ἀκροάσασθαί 531 σου, νῦν δέ μοι τοσόνδε ἀπόκριναι· πότερον περὶ Ὁμήρου μόνον δεινὸς εἶ ἢ καὶ περὶ Ἡσιόδου καὶ Ἀρχιλόχου; ΙΩΝ Οὐδαμῶς, ἀλλὰ περὶ Ὁμήρου μόνον· ἱκανὸν γάρ μοι δοκεῖ εἶναι.

5 ΣΩ. Ἔστι δὲ περὶ ὅτου Ὅμηρός τε καὶ Ἡσίοδος ταὐτὰ λέγετον; – ΙΩΝ Οἶμαι ἔγωγε καὶ πολλά. – ΣΩ. Πότερον οὖν περὶ τούτων κάλλιον ἂν ἐξηγήσαιο ἃ Ὅμηρος λέγει ἢ ἃ Ἡσίοδος; – ΙΩΝ Ὁμοίως ἂν περὶ γε τούτων, ὧ b Σώκρατες, περὶ ὧν ταὐτὰ λέγουσιν. – ΣΩ. Τί δὲ ὧν πέρι μὴ ταὐτὰ λέγουσιν; οἷον περὶ μαντικῆς λέγει τι Ὅμηρός τε καὶ Ἡσίοδος. – ΙΩΝ Πάνυ γε. – ΣΩ. Τί οὖν; ὅσα τε ὁμοίως καὶ ὅσα διαφόρως περὶ μαντικῆς 5 λέγετον τὼ ποιητὰ τούτω, πότερον σὺ κάλλιον ἂν ἐξηγήσαιο ἢ τῶν μάντεών τις τῶν ἀγαθῶν; – ΙΩΝ Τῶν μάντεων. – ΣΩ. Εἰ δὲ σὺ ἦσθα μάντις, οὐκ, εἴπερ περὶ τῶν ὁμοίως λεγομένων οἷός τ' ἦσθα ἐξηγήσασθαι, καὶ περὶ τῶν διαφόρως λεγομένων ἠπίστω ἂν ἐξηγεῖσθαι; – ΙΩΝ 10 Δῆλον ὅτι.

c ΣΩ. Τί οὖν ποτε περὶ μὲν Ὁμήρου δεινὸς εἶ, περὶ δὲ Ἡσιόδου οὔ, οὐδὲ τῶν ἄλλων ποιητῶν; ἢ Ὅμηρος περὶ ἄλλων τινῶν λέγει ἢ ὧνπερ σύμπαντες οἱ ἄλλοι ποιηταί; οὐ περὶ πολέμου τε τὰ πολλὰ διελήλυθεν καὶ περὶ ὁμιλιῶν 5 πρὸς ἀλλήλους ἀνθρώπων ἀγαθῶν τε καὶ κακῶν καὶ ἰδιωτῶν καὶ δημιουργῶν, καὶ περὶ θεῶν πρὸς ἀλλήλους καὶ πρὸς ἀνθρώπους ὁμιλούντων, ὡς ὁμιλοῦσι, καὶ περὶ τῶν οὐρανίων παθημάτων καὶ περὶ τῶν ἐν Ἅιδου, καὶ γενέσεις καὶ θεῶν d καὶ ἡρώων; οὐ ταῦτά ἐστι περὶ ὧν Ὅμηρος τὴν ποίησιν πεποίηκεν;

ΙΩΝ Ἀληθῆ λέγεις, ὦ Σώκρατες.

ΣΩ. Τί δὲ οἱ ἄλλοι ποιηταί; οὐ περὶ τῶν αὐτῶν 5 τούτων;

ΙΩΝ Ναί, ἀλλ', ὦ Σώκρατες, οὐχ ὁμοίως πεποιήκασι καὶ Ὅμηρος.

ΣΩ. Τί μήν; κάκιον;

ΙΩΝ Πολύ γε.

ΣΩ. Ὅμηρος δὲ ἄμεινον; 10

ΙΩΝ Ἄμεινον μέντοι νὴ Δία.

ΣΩ. Οὐκοῦν, ὦ φίλη κεφαλὴ Ἴων, ὅταν περὶ ἀριθμοῦ πολλῶν λεγόντων εἷς τις ἄριστα λέγηι, γνώσεται δήπου τις τὸν εὖ λέγοντα; – ΙΩΝ Φημί. – ΣΩ. Πότερον οὖν ὁ αὐτὸς ε ὅσπερ καὶ τοὺς κακῶς λέγοντας, ἢ ἄλλος; – ΙΩΝ Ὁ αὐτὸς δήπου. – ΣΩ. Οὐκοῦν ὁ τὴν ἀριθμητικὴν τέχνην ἔχων οὗτός ἐστιν; – ΙΩΝ Ναί. – ΣΩ. Τί δ'; ὅταν πολλῶν λεγόντων περὶ ὑγιεινῶν σιτίων ὁποῖά ἐστιν, εἷς τις ἄριστα λέγηι, 5 πότερον ἕτερος μέν τις τὸν ἄριστα λέγοντα γνώσεται ὅτι ἄριστα λέγει, ἕτερος δὲ τὸν κάκιον ὅτι κάκιον, ἢ ὁ αὐτός; – ΙΩΝ Δῆλον δήπου, ὁ αὐτός. – ΣΩ. Τίς οὗτος; τί ὄνομα αὐτῶι; – ΙΩΝ Ἰατρός. – ΣΩ. Οὐκοῦν ἐν κεφαλαίωι λέγομεν ὡς ὁ αὐτὸς γνώσεται ἀεί, περὶ τῶν αὐτῶν πολλῶν λεγόν- 10 των, ὅστις τε εὖ λέγει καὶ ὅστις κακῶς· ἢ εἰ μὴ γνώσεται 532 τὸν κακῶς λέγοντα, δῆλον ὅτι οὐδὲ τὸν εὖ, περί γε τοῦ αὐτοῦ. – ΙΩΝ Οὕτως. – ΣΩ. Οὐκοῦν ὁ αὐτὸς γίγνεται δεινὸς περὶ ἀμφοτέρων; – ΙΩΝ Ναί. – ΣΩ. Οὐκοῦν σὺ φὴις καὶ Ὅμηρον καὶ τοὺς ἄλλους ποιητάς, ἐν οἷς καὶ Ἡσίοδος καὶ 5 Ἀρχίλοχός ἐστιν, περί γε τῶν αὐτῶν λέγειν, ἀλλ' οὐχ ὁμοίως, ἀλλὰ τὸν μὲν εὖ γε, τοὺς δὲ χεῖρον; – ΙΩΝ Καὶ ἀληθῆ λέγω. – ΣΩ. Οὐκοῦν, εἴπερ τὸν εὖ λέγοντα γιγνώ-σκεις, καὶ τοὺς χεῖρον λέγοντας γιγνώσκοις ἂν ὅτι χεῖρον b λέγουσιν. – ΙΩΝ Ἔοικέν γε. – ΣΩ. Οὐκοῦν, ὦ βέλτιστε, ὁμοίως τὸν Ἴωνα λέγοντες περὶ Ὁμήρου τε δεινὸν εἶναι καὶ περὶ τῶν ἄλλων ποιητῶν οὐχ ἁμαρτησόμεθα, ἐπειδή γε αὐτὸς ὁμολογῆι τὸν αὐτὸν ἔσεσθαι κριτὴν ἱκανὸν πάντων 5 ὅσοι ἂν περὶ τῶν αὐτῶν λέγωσι, τοὺς δὲ ποιητὰς σχεδὸν ἅπαντας τὰ αὐτὰ ποιεῖν.

ΙΩΝ Τί οὖν ποτε τὸ αἴτιον, ὦ Σώκρατες, ὅτι ἐγώ, ὅταν

μέν τις περὶ ἄλλου του ποιητοῦ διαλέγηται, οὔτε προσέχω
c τὸν νοῦν ἀδυνατῶ τε καὶ ὁτιοῦν συμβαλέσθαι λόγου ἄξιον,
ἀλλ' ἀτεχνῶς νυστάζω, ἐπειδὰν δέ τις περὶ Ὁμήρου μνησθῆι,
εὐθύς τε ἐγρήγορα καὶ προσέχω τὸν νοῦν καὶ εὐπορῶ ὅτι
λέγω;

5 ΣΩ. Οὐ χαλεπὸν τοῦτό γε εἰκάσαι, ὦ ἑταῖρε, ἀλλὰ παντὶ
δῆλον ὅτι τέχνηι καὶ ἐπιστήμηι περὶ Ὁμήρου λέγειν ἀδύνατος
εἶ· εἰ γὰρ τέχνηι οἷός τε ἦσθα, καὶ περὶ τῶν ἄλλων ποιητῶν
ἁπάντων λέγειν οἷός τ' ἂν ἦσθα· ποιητικὴ γάρ πού ἐστιν
τὸ ὅλον. ἢ οὔ;

10 ΙΩΝ Ναί.

d ΣΩ. Οὐκοῦν ἐπειδὰν λάβηι τις καὶ ἄλλην τέχνην ἡντι-
νοῦν ὅλην, ὁ αὐτὸς τρόπος τῆς σκέψεως ἔσται περὶ ἁπασῶν
τῶν τεχνῶν; πῶς τοῦτο λέγω, δέηι τί μου ἀκοῦσαι, ὦ Ἴων;
ΙΩΝ Ναὶ μὰ τὸν Δία, ὦ Σώκρατες, ἔγωγε· χαίρω γὰρ
5 ἀκούων ὑμῶν τῶν σοφῶν.

ΣΩ. Βουλοίμην ἄν σε ἀληθῆ λέγειν, ὦ Ἴων· ἀλλὰ σοφοὶ
μέν πού ἐστε ὑμεῖς οἱ ῥαψωιδοὶ καὶ ὑποκριταὶ καὶ ὧν ὑμεῖς
ἄιδετε τὰ ποιήματα, ἐγὼ δὲ οὐδὲν ἄλλο ἢ τἀληθῆ λέγω,
e οἷον εἰκὸς ἰδιώτην ἄνθρωπον. ἐπεὶ καὶ περὶ τούτου οὗ νῦν
ἠρόμην σε, θέασαι ὡς φαῦλον καὶ ἰδιωτικόν ἐστι καὶ παντὸς
ἀνδρὸς γνῶναι ὃ ἔλεγον, τὴν αὐτὴν εἶναι σκέψιν, ἐπειδάν
τις ὅλην τέχνην λάβηι. λάβωμεν γὰρ τῶι λόγωι· γραφικὴ
5 γάρ τίς ἐστι τέχνη τὸ ὅλον; – ΙΩΝ Ναί. – ΣΩ. Οὐκοῦν
καὶ γραφῆς πολλοὶ καὶ εἰσὶ καὶ γεγόνασιν ἀγαθοὶ καὶ φαῦ-
λοι; – ΙΩΝ Πάνυ γε. – ΣΩ. Ἤδη οὖν τινα εἶδες ὅστις περὶ
μὲν Πολυγνώτου τοῦ Ἀγλαοφῶντος δεινός ἐστιν ἀποφαί-
νειν ἃ εὖ τε γράφει καὶ ἃ μή, περὶ δὲ τῶν ἄλλων γραφέων
533 ἀδύνατος; καὶ ἐπειδὰν μέν τις τὰ τῶν ἄλλων ζωγράφων
ἔργα ἐπιδεικνύηι, νυστάζει τε καὶ ἀπορεῖ καὶ οὐκ ἔχει ὅτι
συμβάληται, ἐπειδὰν δὲ περὶ Πολυγνώτου ἢ ἄλλου ὅτου
βούλει τῶν γραφέων ἑνὸς μόνου δέηι ἀποφήνασθαι γνώμην,
5 ἐγρήγορέν τε καὶ προσέχει τὸν νοῦν καὶ εὐπορεῖ ὅτι εἴπηι; —
ΙΩΝ Οὐ μὰ τὸν Δία, οὐ δῆτα. – ΣΩ. Τί δέ; ἐν ἀνδριαντο-
ποιίαι ἤδη τιν' εἶδες ὅστις περὶ μὲν Δαιδάλου τοῦ Μητίονος

ἢ Ἐπειοῦ τοῦ Πανοπέως ἢ Θεοδώρου τοῦ Σαμίου ἢ ἄλλου **b**
τινὸς ἀνδριαντοποιοῦ ἑνὸς πέρι δεινός ἐστιν ἐξηγεῖσθαι ἃ
εὖ πεποίηκεν, ἐν δὲ τοῖς τῶν ἄλλων ἀνδριαντοποιῶν ἔργοις
ἀπορεῖ τε καὶ νυστάζει, οὐκ ἔχων ὅτι εἴπηι; – ΙΩΝ Οὐ μὰ
τὸν Δία, οὐδὲ τοῦτον ἑώρακα. – ΣΩ. Ἀλλὰ μήν, ὡς γ᾽ ἐγὼ 5
οἶμαι, οὐδ᾽ ἐν αὐλήσει γε οὐδὲ ἐν κιθαρίσει οὐδὲ ἐν κιθαρωιδίαι
οὐδὲ ἐν ῥαψωιδίαι οὐδεπώποτ᾽ εἶδες ἄνδρα ὅστις περὶ μὲν
Ὀλύμπου δεινός ἐστιν ἐξηγεῖσθαι ἢ περὶ Θαμύρου ἢ περὶ
Ὀρφέως ἢ περὶ Φημίου τοῦ Ἰθακησίου ῥαψωιδοῦ, περὶ δὲ **c**
Ἴωνος τοῦ Ἐφεσίου ἀπορεῖ καὶ οὐκ ἔχει συμβαλέσθαι ἅ τε εὖ ῥαψωιδεῖ καὶ ἃ μή.

ΙΩΝ Οὐκ ἔχω σοι περὶ τούτου ἀντιλέγειν, ὦ Σώκρατες·
ἀλλ᾽ ἐκεῖνο ἐμαυτῶι σύνοιδα, ὅτι περὶ Ὁμήρου κάλλιστ᾽ 5
ἀνθρώπων λέγω καὶ εὐπορῶ καὶ οἱ ἄλλοι πάντες μέ φασιν
εὖ λέγειν, περὶ δὲ τῶν ἄλλων οὔ. καίτοι ὅρα τοῦτο τί
ἔστιν.

ΣΩ. Καὶ ὁρῶ, ὦ Ἴων, καὶ ἔρχομαί γέ σοι ἀποφαινό-
μενος ὅ μοι δοκεῖ τοῦτο εἶναι. ἔστι γὰρ τοῦτο τέχνη μὲν **d**
οὐκ ὂν παρὰ σοὶ περὶ Ὁμήρου εὖ λέγειν, ὃ νυνδὴ ἔλεγον,
θεία δὲ δύναμις ἥ σε κινεῖ, ὥσπερ ἐν τῆι λίθωι ἣν Εὐρι-
πίδης μὲν Μαγνῆτιν ὠνόμασεν, οἱ δὲ πολλοὶ Ἡρακλείαν.
καὶ γὰρ αὕτη ἡ λίθος οὐ μόνον αὐτοὺς τοὺς δακτυλίους ἄγει 5
τοὺς σιδηροῦς, ἀλλὰ καὶ δύναμιν ἐντίθησι τοῖς δακτυλίοις
ὥστ᾽ αὖ δύνασθαι ταὐτὸν τοῦτο ποιεῖν ὅπερ ἡ λίθος, ἄλλους
ἄγειν δακτυλίους, ὥστ᾽ ἐνίοτε ὁρμαθὸς μακρὸς πάνυ σιδη- **e**
ρίων καὶ δακτυλίων ἐξ ἀλλήλων ἤρτηται· πᾶσι δὲ τούτοις
ἐξ ἐκείνης τῆς λίθου ἡ δύναμις ἀνήρτηται. οὕτω δὲ καὶ ἡ
Μοῦσα ἐνθέους μὲν ποιεῖ αὐτή, διὰ δὲ τῶν ἐνθέων τούτων
ἄλλων ἐνθουσιαζόντων ὁρμαθὸς ἐξαρτᾶται. πάντες γὰρ οἵ 5
τε τῶν ἐπῶν ποιηταὶ οἱ ἀγαθοὶ οὐκ ἐκ τέχνης ἀλλ᾽ ἔνθεοι
ὄντες καὶ κατεχόμενοι πάντα ταῦτα τὰ καλὰ λέγουσι ποιήματα, καὶ οἱ μελοποιοὶ οἱ ἀγαθοὶ ὡσαύτως, ὥσπερ οἱ κορυβαντιῶντες οὐκ ἔμφρονες ὄντες ὀρχοῦνται, οὕτω καὶ οἱ μελο- **534**

ποιοὶ οὐκ ἔμφρονες ὄντες τὰ καλὰ μέλη ταῦτα ποιοῦσιν,
ἀλλ᾽ ἐπειδὰν ἐμβῶσιν εἰς τὴν ἁρμονίαν καὶ εἰς τὸν ῥυθμόν,
βακχεύουσι καὶ κατεχόμενοι, ὥσπερ αἱ βάκχαι ἀρύονται ἐκ
5 τῶν ποταμῶν μέλι καὶ γάλα κατεχόμεναι, ἔμφρονες δὲ οὖσαι
οὔ, καὶ τῶν μελοποιῶν ἡ ψυχὴ τοῦτο ἐργάζεται, ὅπερ αὐτοὶ
λέγουσι. λέγουσι γὰρ δήπουθεν πρὸς ἡμᾶς οἱ ποιηταὶ ὅτι
b ἀπὸ κρηνῶν μελιρρύτων ἐκ Μουσῶν κήπων τινῶν καὶ ναπῶν
δρεπόμενοι τὰ μέλη ἡμῖν φέρουσιν ὥσπερ αἱ μέλιτται, καὶ
αὐτοὶ οὕτω πετόμενοι· καὶ ἀληθῆ λέγουσι. κοῦφον γὰρ
χρῆμα ποιητής ἐστιν καὶ πτηνὸν καὶ ἱερόν, καὶ οὐ πρότερον
5 οἷός τε ποιεῖν πρὶν ἂν ἔνθεός τε γένηται καὶ ἔκφρων καὶ
ὁ νοῦς μηκέτι ἐν αὐτῶι ἐνῆι· ἕως δ᾽ ἂν τουτὶ ἔχῃ τὸ κτῆμα,
ἀδύνατος πᾶς ποιεῖν ἄνθρωπός ἐστιν καὶ χρησμωιδεῖν. ἅτε
οὖν οὐ τέχνηι ποιοῦντες καὶ πολλὰ λέγοντες καὶ καλὰ περὶ
c τῶν πραγμάτων, ὥσπερ σὺ περὶ Ὁμήρου, ἀλλὰ θείαι μοίραι,
τοῦτο μόνον οἷός τε ἕκαστος ποιεῖν καλῶς ἐφ᾽ ὃ ἡ Μοῦσα
αὐτὸν ὥρμησεν, ὁ μὲν διθυράμβους, ὁ δὲ ἐγκώμια, ὁ δὲ
ὑπορχήματα, ὁ δ᾽ ἔπη, ὁ δ᾽ ἰάμβους· τὰ δ᾽ ἄλλα φαῦλος
5 αὐτῶν ἕκαστός ἐστιν. οὐ γὰρ τέχνηι ταῦτα λέγουσιν ἀλλὰ
θείαι δυνάμει, ἐπεί, εἰ περὶ ἑνὸς τέχνηι καλῶς ἠπίσταντο
λέγειν, κἂν περὶ τῶν ἄλλων ἁπάντων· διὰ ταῦτα δὲ ὁ θεὸς
ἐξαιρούμενος τούτων τὸν νοῦν τούτοις χρῆται ὑπηρέταις καὶ
d τοῖς χρησμωιδοῖς καὶ τοῖς μάντεσι τοῖς θείοις, ἵνα ἡμεῖς οἱ
ἀκούοντες εἰδῶμεν ὅτι οὐχ οὗτοί εἰσιν οἱ ταῦτα λέγοντες
οὕτω πολλοῦ ἄξια, οἷς νοῦς μὴ πάρεστιν, ἀλλ᾽ ὁ θεὸς αὐτός
ἐστιν ὁ λέγων, διὰ τούτων δὲ φθέγγεται πρὸς ἡμᾶς. μέ-
5 γιστον δὲ τεκμήριον τῶι λόγωι Τύννιχος ὁ Χαλκιδεύς, ὃς
ἄλλο μὲν οὐδὲν πώποτε ἐποίησε ποίημα ὅτου τις ἂν ἀξιώ-
σειεν μνησθῆναι, τὸν δὲ παίωνα ὃν πάντες ἄιδουσι, σχεδόν
τι πάντων μελῶν κάλλιστον, ἀτεχνῶς, ὅπερ αὐτὸς λέγει,
e "εὕρημά τι Μοισᾶν." ἐν τούτωι γὰρ δὴ μάλιστά μοι δοκεῖ
ὁ θεὸς ἐνδείξασθαι ἡμῖν, ἵνα μὴ διστάζωμεν, ὅτι οὐκ ἀνθρώ-
πινά ἐστιν τὰ καλὰ ταῦτα ποιήματα οὐδὲ ἀνθρώπων, ἀλλὰ
θεῖα καὶ θεῶν, οἱ δὲ ποιηταὶ οὐδὲν ἀλλ᾽ ἢ ἑρμηνῆς εἰσιν
5 τῶν θεῶν, κατεχόμενοι ἐξ ὅτου ἂν ἕκαστος κατέχηται.
ταῦτα ἐνδεικνύμενος ὁ θεὸς ἐξεπίτηδες διὰ τοῦ φαυλοτάτου

ποιητοῦ τὸ κάλλιστον μέλος ᾖσεν· ἢ οὐ δοκῶ σοι ἀληθῆ 535
λέγειν, ὦ Ἴων;

ΙΩΝ Ναὶ μὰ τὸν Δία, ἔμοιγε· ἅπτει γάρ πώς μου τοῖς
λόγοις τῆς ψυχῆς, ὦ Σώκρατες, καί μοι δοκοῦσι θεῖαι μοίραι
ἡμῖν παρὰ τῶν θεῶν ταῦτα οἱ ἀγαθοὶ ποιηταὶ ἑρμηνεύειν. 5

ΣΩ. Οὐκοῦν ὑμεῖς αὖ οἱ ῥαψῳδοὶ τὰ τῶν ποιητῶν ἑρμη-
νεύετε;

ΙΩΝ Καὶ τοῦτο ἀληθὲς λέγεις.

ΣΩ. Οὐκοῦν ἑρμηνέων ἑρμηνῆς γίγνεσθε;

ΙΩΝ Παντάπασί γε. 10

ΣΩ. Ἔχε δή μοι τόδε εἰπέ, ὦ Ἴων, καὶ μὴ ἀποκρύψῃι b
ὅτι ἄν σε ἔρωμαι· ὅταν εὖ εἴπῃς ἔπη καὶ ἐκπλήξῃς μάλιστα
τοὺς θεωμένους, ἢ τὸν Ὀδυσσέα ὅταν ἐπὶ τὸν οὐδὸν ἐφαλ-
λόμενον ἄιδῃς, ἐκφανῆ γιγνόμενον τοῖς μνηστῆρσι καὶ ἐκ-
χέοντα τοὺς ὀιστοὺς πρὸ τῶν ποδῶν, ἢ Ἀχιλλέα ἐπὶ τὸν 5
Ἕκτορα ὁρμῶντα, ἢ καὶ τῶν περὶ Ἀνδρομάχην ἐλεινῶν τι ἢ
περὶ Ἑκάβην ἢ περὶ Πρίαμον, τότε πότερον ἔμφρων εἶ ἢ ἔξω
σαυτοῦ γίγνῃι καὶ παρὰ τοῖς πράγμασιν οἴεταί σου εἶναι ἡ c
ψυχὴ οἷς λέγεις ἐνθουσιάζουσα, ἢ ἐν Ἰθάκῃι οὖσιν ἢ ἐν
Τροίαι ἢ ὅπως ἂν καὶ τὰ ἔπη ἔχῃι;

ΙΩΝ Ὡς ἐναργές μοι τοῦτο, ὦ Σώκρατες, τὸ τεκμήριον
εἶπες· οὐ γάρ σε ἀποκρυψάμενος ἐρῶ. ἐγὼ γὰρ ὅταν 5
ἐλεινόν τι λέγω, δακρύων ἐμπίμπλανταί μου οἱ ὀφθαλμοί·
ὅταν τε φοβερὸν ἢ δεινόν, ὀρθαὶ αἱ τρίχες ἵστανται ὑπὸ
φόβου καὶ ἡ καρδία πηδᾶι.

ΣΩ. Τί οὖν; φῶμεν, ὦ Ἴων, ἔμφρονα εἶναι τότε τοῦτον d
τὸν ἄνθρωπον, ὃς ἂν κεκοσμημένος ἐσθῆτι ποικίληι καὶ
χρυσοῖσι στεφάνοις κλάηι τ᾽ ἐν θυσίαις καὶ ἑορταῖς, μηδὲν
ἀπολωλεκὼς τούτων, ἢ φοβῆται πλέον ἢ ἐν δισμυρίοις ἀνθρώποις ἑστηκὼς φιλίοις, μηδενὸς ἀποδύοντος μηδὲ ἀδικοῦντος; 5

ΙΩΝ Οὐ μὰ τὸν Δία, οὐ πάνυ, ὦ Σώκρατες, ὥς γε
τἀληθὲς εἰρῆσθαι.

ΣΩ. Οἶσθα οὖν ὅτι καὶ τῶν θεατῶν τοὺς πολλοὺς ταὐτὰ
ταῦτα ὑμεῖς ἐργάζεσθε;

ΙΩΝ Καὶ μάλα καλῶς οἶδα· καθορῶ γὰρ ἑκάστοτε e
αὐτοὺς ἄνωθεν ἀπὸ τοῦ βήματος κλάοντάς τε καὶ δεινὸν

ἐμβλέποντας καὶ συνθαμβοῦντας τοῖς λεγομένοις. δεῖ γάρ
με καὶ σφόδρ' αὐτοῖς τὸν νοῦν προσέχειν· ὡς ἐὰν μὲν
5 κλάοντας αὐτοὺς καθίσω, αὐτὸς γελάσομαι ἀργύριον λαμβά-
νων, ἐὰν δὲ γελῶντας, αὐτὸς κλαύσομαι ἀργύριον ἀπολλύς.
ΣΩ. Οἶσθα οὖν ὅτι οὗτός ἐστιν ὁ θεατὴς τῶν δακτυλίων
ὁ ἔσχατος, ὧν ἐγὼ ἔλεγον ὑπὸ τῆς Ἡρακλειώτιδος λίθου
ἀπ' ἀλλήλων τὴν δύναμιν λαμβάνειν; ὁ δὲ μέσος σὺ ὁ
536 ῥαψωιδὸς καὶ ὑποκριτής, ὁ δὲ πρῶτος αὐτὸς ὁ ποιητής· ὁ δὲ
θεὸς διὰ πάντων τούτων ἕλκει τὴν ψυχὴν ὅποι ἂν βούληται
τῶν ἀνθρώπων, ἀνακρεμαννὺς ἐξ ἀλλήλων τὴν δύναμιν.
καὶ ὥσπερ ἐκ τῆς λίθου ἐκείνης ὁρμαθὸς πάμπολυς ἐξῆρ-
5 τηται χορευτῶν τε καὶ διδασκάλων καὶ ὑποδιδασκάλων, ἐκ
πλαγίου ἐξηρτημένων τῶν τῆς Μούσης ἐκκρεμαμένων δακτυλίων. καὶ ὁ μὲν τῶν ποιητῶν ἐξ ἄλλης Μούσης, ὁ δὲ
ἐξ ἄλλης ἐξήρτηται – ὀνομάζομεν δὲ αὐτὸ κατέχεται, τὸ δέ
b ἐστι παραπλήσιον· ἔχεται γάρ – ἐκ δὲ τούτων τῶν πρώτων
δακτυλίων, τῶν ποιητῶν, ἄλλοι ἐξ ἄλλου αὖ ἠρτημένοι εἰσὶ
καὶ ἐνθουσιάζουσιν, οἱ μὲν ἐξ Ὀρφέως, οἱ δὲ ἐκ Μουσαίου·
οἱ δὲ πολλοὶ ἐξ Ὁμήρου κατέχονταί τε καὶ ἔχονται. ὧν
5 σύ, ὦ Ἴων, εἷς εἶ καὶ κατέχηι ἐξ Ὁμήρου, καὶ ἐπειδὰν μέν
τις ἄλλου του ποιητοῦ ἄιδηι, καθεύδεις τε καὶ ἀπορεῖς ὅτι
λέγηις, ἐπειδὰν δὲ τούτου τοῦ ποιητοῦ φθέγξηταί τις μέλος,
εὐθὺς ἐγρήγορας καὶ ὀρχεῖταί σου ἡ ψυχὴ καὶ εὐπορεῖς ὅτι
c λέγηις· οὐ γὰρ τέχνηι οὐδ' ἐπιστήμηι περὶ Ὁμήρου λέγεις
ἃ λέγεις, ἀλλὰ θείαι μοίραι καὶ κατοκωχῆι, ὥσπερ οἱ κορυβαντιῶντες ἐκείνου μόνου αἰσθάνονται τοῦ μέλους ὀξέως
ὃ ἂν ἦι τοῦ θεοῦ ἐξ ὅτου ἂν κατέχωνται, καὶ εἰς ἐκεῖνο τὸ
5 μέλος καὶ σχημάτων καὶ ῥημάτων εὐποροῦσι, τῶν δὲ ἄλλων
οὐ φροντίζουσιν· οὕτω καὶ σύ, ὦ Ἴων, περὶ μὲν Ὁμήρου
ὅταν τις μνησθῆι, εὐπορεῖς, περὶ δὲ τῶν ἄλλων ἀπορεῖς·
d τούτου δ' ἐστὶ τὸ αἴτιον, ὅ μ' ἐρωτᾶις, δι' ὅτι σὺ περὶ μὲν
Ὁμήρου εὐπορεῖς, περὶ δὲ τῶν ἄλλων οὔ, ὅτι οὐ τέχνηι ἀλλὰ
θείαι μοίραι Ὁμήρου δεινὸς εἶ ἐπαινέτης.
ΙΩΝ Σὺ μὲν εὖ λέγεις, ὦ Σώκρατες· θαυμάζοιμι μεντἂν
5 εἰ οὕτως εὖ εἴποις, ὥστε με ἀναπεῖσαι ὡς ἐγὼ κατεχόμενος
καὶ μαινόμενος Ὅμηρον ἐπαινῶ. οἶμαι δὲ οὐδ' ἂν σοὶ

δόξαιμι, εἴ μου ἀκούσαις λέγοντος περὶ Ὁμήρου.

ΣΩ. Καὶ μὴν ἐθέλω γε ἀκοῦσαι, οὐ μέντοι πρότερον
πρὶν ἄν μοι ἀποκρίνῃ τόδε· ὧν Ὅμηρος λέγει περὶ τίνος e
εὖ λέγεις; οὐ γὰρ δήπου περὶ ἁπάντων γε.

ΙΩΝ Εὖ ἴσθι, ὦ Σώκρατες, περὶ οὐδενὸς ὅτου οὔ.

ΣΩ. Οὐ δήπου καὶ περὶ τούτων ὧν σὺ μὲν τυγχάνεις
οὐκ εἰδώς, Ὅμηρος δὲ λέγει.   5

ΙΩΝ Καὶ ταῦτα ποῖά ἐστιν ἃ Ὅμηρος μὲν λέγει, ἐγὼ
δὲ οὐκ οἶδα;

ΣΩ. Οὐ καὶ περὶ τεχνῶν μέντοι λέγει πολλαχοῦ Ὅμηρος 537
καὶ πολλά; οἷον καὶ περὶ ἡνιοχείας – ἐὰν μνησθῶ τὰ ἔπη,
ἐγώ σοι φράσω.

ΙΩΝ Ἀλλ' ἐγὼ ἐρῶ· ἐγὼ γὰρ μέμνημαι.

ΣΩ. Εἰπὲ δή μοι ἃ λέγει Νέστωρ Ἀντιλόχωι τῶι υἱεῖ, 5
παραινῶν εὐλαβηθῆναι περὶ τὴν καμπὴν ἐν τῆι ἱπποδρομίαι
τῆι ἐπὶ Πατρόκλωι.

ΙΩΝ Κλινθῆναι δέ, φησί, καὶ αὐτὸς ἐυξέστωι ἐνὶ δίφρωι

ἦκ' ἐπ' ἀριστερὰ τοῖιν· ἀτὰρ τὸν δεξιὸν ἵππον   b
κένσαι ὁμοκλήσας, εἶξαί τέ οἱ ἡνία χερσίν.
ἐν νύσσηι δέ τοι ἵππος ἀριστερὸς ἐγχριμφθήτω,
ὡς ἄν τοι πλήμνη γε δοάσσεται ἄκρον ἱκέσθαι
κύκλου ποιητοῖο· λίθου δ' ἀλέασθαι ἐπαυρεῖν.   5

ΣΩ. Ἀρκεῖ. ταῦτα δή, ὦ Ἴων, τὰ ἔπη εἴτε ὀρθῶς λέγει c
Ὅμηρος εἴτε μή, πότερος ἂν γνοίη ἄμεινον, ἰατρὸς ἢ ἡνίοχος; – ΙΩΝ Ἡνίοχος δήπου. – ΣΩ. Πότερον ὅτι τέχνην
ταύτην ἔχει ἢ κατ' ἄλλο τι; – ΙΩΝ Οὔκ, ἀλλ' ὅτι τέχνην.
– ΣΩ. Οὐκοῦν ἑκάστηι τῶν τεχνῶν ἀποδέδοταί τι ὑπὸ τοῦ 5
θεοῦ ἔργον οἵαι τε εἶναι γιγνώσκειν; οὐ γάρ που ἃ κυβερνη-
τικῆι γιγνώσκομεν, γνωσόμεθα καὶ ἰατρικῆι. – ΙΩΝ Οὐ δῆτα.
– ΣΩ. Οὐδέ γε ἃ ἰατρικῆι, ταῦτα καὶ τεκτονικῆι. – ΙΩΝ
Οὐ δῆτα. – ΣΩ. Οὐκοῦν οὕτω καὶ κατὰ πασῶν τῶν τεχνῶν, d
ἃ τῆι ἑτέραι τέχνηι γιγνώσκομεν, οὐ γνωσόμεθα τῆι ἑτέραι;
τόδε δέ μοι πρότερον τούτου ἀπόκριναι· τὴν μὲν ἑτέραν φῂς
εἶναί τινα τέχνην, τὴν δ' ἑτέραν; – ΙΩΝ Ναί. – ΣΩ. Ἆρα
ὥσπερ ἐγὼ τεκμαιρόμενος, ὅταν ἡ μὲν ἑτέρων πραγμάτων ἦι 5

ἐπιστήμη, ἡ δ' ἑτέρων, οὕτω καλῶ τὴν μὲν ἄλλην, τὴν δὲ ἄλλην
e τέχνην, οὕτω καὶ σύ; – ΙΩΝ Ναί. – ΣΩ. Εἰ γάρ που τῶν
αὐτῶν πραγμάτων ἐπιστήμη εἴη τις, τί ἂν τὴν μὲν ἑτέραν
φαῖμεν εἶναι, τὴν δ' ἑτέραν, ὁπότε γε ταὐτὰ εἴη εἰδέναι ἀπ'
ἀμφοτέρων; ὥσπερ ἐγώ τε γιγνώσκω ὅτι πέντε εἰσὶν οὗτοι
5 οἱ δάκτυλοι, καὶ σύ, ὥσπερ ἐγώ, περὶ τούτων ταὐτὰ γιγνώ-
σκεις· καὶ εἴ σε ἐγὼ ἐροίμην εἰ τῆι αὐτῆι τέχνηι γιγνώσκομεν
τῆι ἀριθμητικῆι τὰ αὐτὰ ἐγώ τε καὶ σὺ ἢ ἄλληι, φαίης ἂν
δήπου τῆι αὐτῆι. – ΙΩΝ Ναί.
53ᵇ ΣΩ. Ὃ τοίνυν ἄρτι ἔμελλον ἐρήσεσθαί σε, νυνὶ εἰπέ, εἰ
κατὰ πασῶν τῶν τεχνῶν οὕτω σοι δοκεῖ, τῆι μὲν αὐτῆι τέχνηι
τὰ αὐτὰ ἀναγκαῖον εἶναι γιγνώσκειν, τῆι δ' ἑτέραι μὴ τὰ αὐτά,
ἀλλ' εἴπερ ἄλλη ἐστίν, ἀναγκαῖον καὶ ἕτερα γιγνώσκειν. –
5 ΙΩΝ Οὕτω μοι δοκεῖ, ὦ Σώκρατες. – ΣΩ. Οὐκοῦν ὅστις ἂν
μὴ ἔχηι τινὰ τέχνην, ταύτης τῆς τέχνης τὰ λεγόμενα ἢ
πραττόμενα καλῶς γιγνώσκειν οὐχ οἷός τ' ἔσται; – ΙΩΝ
b Ἀληθῆ λέγεις. – ΣΩ. Πότερον οὖν περὶ τῶν ἐπῶν ὧν εἶπες,
εἴτε καλῶς λέγει Ὅμηρος εἴτε μή, σὺ κάλλιον γνώσηι ἢ
ἡνίοχος; – ΙΩΝ Ἡνίοχος. – ΣΩ. Ῥαψωιδὸς γάρ που εἶ ἀλλ'
οὐχ ἡνίοχος. – ΙΩΝ Ναί. – ΣΩ. Ἡ δὲ ῥαψωιδικὴ τέχνη
5 ἑτέρα ἐστὶ τῆς ἡνιοχικῆς; – ΙΩΝ Ναί. – ΣΩ. Εἰ ἄρα ἑτέρα,
περὶ ἑτέρων καὶ ἐπιστήμη πραγμάτων ἐστίν. – ΙΩΝ Ναί.
ΣΩ. Τί δὲ δὴ ὅταν Ὅμηρος λέγηι ὡς τετρωμένωι τῶι
Μαχάονι Ἑκαμήδη ἡ Νέστορος παλλακὴ κυκεῶνα πίνειν
c δίδωσι; καὶ λέγει πως οὕτως –

οἴνωι πραμνείωι, φησίν, ἐπὶ δ' αἴγειον κνῆ τυρὸν
κνήστι χαλκείηι· παρὰ δὲ κρόμυον ποτῶι ὄψον·

ταῦτα εἴτε ὀρθῶς λέγει Ὅμηρος εἴτε μή, πότερον ἰατρικῆς
5 ἔστι διαγνῶναι καλῶς ἢ ῥαψωιδικῆς;
ΙΩΝ Ἰατρικῆς.
ΣΩ. Τί δέ, ὅταν λέγηι Ὅμηρος –

d ἡ δὲ μολυβδαίνηι ἰκέλη ἐς βυσσὸν ἴκανεν,
ἥ τε κατ' ἀγραύλοιο βοὸς κέρας ἐμμεμαυῖα
ἔρχεται ὠμηστῆισι μετ' ἰχθύσι πῆμα φέρουσα·

ταῦτα πότερον φῶμεν ἁλιευτικῆς εἶναι τέχνης μᾶλλον κρῖναι
ἢ ῥαψωιδικῆς, ἅττα λέγει καὶ εἴτε καλῶς εἴτε μή; 5
ΙωΝ Δῆλον δή, ὦ Σώκρατες, ὅτι ἁλιευτικῆς.
ΣΩ. Σκέψαι δή, σοῦ ἐρομένου, εἰ ἔροιό με· "'Επειδὴ
τοίνυν, ὦ Σώκρατες, τούτων τῶν τεχνῶν ἐν Ὁμήρωι εὑρίσκεις ε
ἃ προσήκει ἑκάστηι διακρίνειν, ἴθι μοι ἔξευρε καὶ τὰ τοῦ
μάντεώς τε καὶ μαντικῆς, ποῖά ἐστιν ἃ προσήκει αὐτῶι οἴωι
τ' εἶναι διαγιγνώσκειν, εἴτε εὖ εἴτε κακῶς πεποίηται" –
σκέψαι ὡς ῥαιδίως τε καὶ ἀληθῆ ἐγώ σοι ἀποκρινοῦμαι. 5
πολλαχοῦ μὲν γὰρ καὶ ἐν Ὀδυσσείαι λέγει, οἷον καὶ ἃ ὁ
τῶν Μελαμποδιδῶν λέγει μάντις πρὸς τοὺς μνηστῆρας,
Θεοκλύμενος –

δαιμόνιοι, τί κακὸν τόδε πάσχετε; νυκτὶ μὲν ὑμέων 539
εἰλύαται κεφαλαί τε πρόσωπά τε νέρθε τε γυῖα,
οἰμωγὴ δὲ δέδηε, δεδάκρυνται δὲ παρειαί·
εἰδώλων τε πλέον πρόθυρον, πλείη δὲ καὶ αὐλὴ
ἱεμένων ἔρεβόσδε ὑπὸ ζόφον· ἤλιος δὲ 5
οὐρανοῦ ἐξαπόλωλε, κακὴ δ' ἐπιδέδρομεν ἀχλύς· b

πολλαχοῦ δὲ καὶ ἐν Ἰλιάδι, οἷον καὶ ἐπὶ τειχομαχίαι· λέγει
γὰρ καὶ ἐνταῦθα –

ὄρνις γάρ σφιν ἐπῆλθε περησέμεναι μεμαῶσιν,
αἰετὸς ὑψιπέτης, ἐπ' ἀριστερὰ λαὸν ἐέργων, 5
φοινήεντα δράκοντα φέρων ὀνύχεσσι πέλωρον, c
ζωιόν, ἔτ' ἀσπαίροντα· καὶ οὔπω λήθετο χάρμης.
κόψε γὰρ αὐτὸν ἔχοντα κατὰ στῆθος παρὰ δειρὴν
ἰδνωθεὶς ὀπίσω, ὁ δ' ἀπὸ ἔθεν ἧκε χαμᾶζε
ἀλγήσας ὀδύνηισι, μέσωι δ' ἐνὶ κάββαλ' ὁμίλωι· 5
αὐτὸς δὲ κλάγξας πέτετο πνοιῆις ἀνέμοιο. d

ταῦτα φήσω καὶ τὰ τοιαῦτα τῶι μάντει προσήκειν καὶ σκο-
πεῖν καὶ κρίνειν.
ΙωΝ Ἀληθῆ γε σὺ λέγων, ὦ Σώκρατες.
ΣΩ. Καὶ σύ γε, ὦ Ἴων, ἀληθῆ ταῦτα λέγεις. ἴθι δὴ καὶ 5
σὺ ἐμοί, ὥσπερ ἐγὼ σοὶ ἐξέλεξα καὶ ἐξ Ὀδυσσείας καὶ ἐξ

Ἰλιάδος ὁποῖα τοῦ μάντεώς ἐστι καὶ ὁποῖα τοῦ ἰατροῦ καὶ
e ὁποῖα τοῦ ἁλιέως, οὕτω καὶ σὺ ἐμοὶ ἔκλεξον, ἐπειδὴ καὶ
ἐμπειρότερος εἶ ἐμοῦ τῶν Ὁμήρου, ὁποῖα τοῦ ῥαψωιδοῦ ἐστιν,
ὦ Ἴων, καὶ τῆς τέχνης τῆς ῥαψωιδικῆς, ἃ τῶι ῥαψωιδῶι προσήκει καὶ σκοπεῖσθαι καὶ διακρίνειν παρὰ τοὺς ἄλλους
5 ἀνθρώπους.
ΙΩΝ Ἐγὼ μέν φημι, ὦ Σώκρατες, ἅπαντα.
ΣΩ. Οὐ σύ γε φήις, ὦ Ἴων, ἅπαντα· ἢ οὕτως ἐπιλήσμων
εἶ; καίτοι οὐκ ἂν πρέποι γε ἐπιλήσμονα εἶναι ῥαψωιδὸν
ἄνδρα.
540 ΙΩΝ Τί δὲ δὴ ἐπιλανθάνομαι;
ΣΩ. Οὐ μέμνησαι ὅτι ἔφησθα τὴν ῥαψωιδικὴν τέχνην
ἑτέραν εἶναι τῆς ἡνιοχικῆς; – ΙΩΝ Μέμνημαι. – ΣΩ. Οὐκοῦν καὶ ἑτέραν οὖσαν ἕτερα γνώσεσθαι ὡμολόγεις; – ΙΩΝ
5 Ναί. – ΣΩ. Οὐκ ἄρα πάντα γε γνώσεται ἡ ῥαψωιδικὴ κατὰ
τὸν σὸν λόγον οὐδὲ ὁ ῥαψωιδός. – ΙΩΝ Πλήν γε ἴσως τὰ
τοιαῦτα, ὦ Σώκρατες.
b ΣΩ. Τὰ τοιαῦτα δὲ λέγεις πλὴν τὰ τῶν ἄλλων τεχνῶν
σχεδόν τι· ἀλλὰ ποῖα δὴ γνώσεται, ἐπειδὴ οὐχ ἅπαντα;
ΙΩΝ Ἃ πρέπει, οἶμαι ἔγωγε, ἀνδρὶ εἰπεῖν καὶ ὁποῖα
γυναικί, καὶ ὁποῖα δούλωι καὶ ὁποῖα ἐλευθέρωι, καὶ ὁποῖα
5 ἀρχομένωι καὶ ὁποῖα ἄρχοντι.
ΣΩ. Ἆρα ὁποῖα ἄρχοντι, λέγεις, ἐν θαλάττηι χειμαζομένου
πλοίου πρέπει εἰπεῖν, ὁ ῥαψωιδὸς γνώσεται κάλλιον ἢ ὁ
κυβερνήτης; – ΙΩΝ Οὔκ, ἀλλὰ ὁ κυβερνήτης τοῦτό γε. –
c ΣΩ. Ἀλλ' ὁποῖα ἄρχοντι κάμνοντος πρέπει εἰπεῖν, ὁ
ῥαψωιδὸς γνώσεται κάλλιον ἢ ὁ ἰατρός; – ΙΩΝ Οὐδὲ
τοῦτο. – ΣΩ. Ἀλλ' οἷα δούλωι πρέπει, λέγεις; – ΙΩΝ
Ναί. – ΣΩ. Οἷον βουκόλωι λέγεις δούλωι ἃ πρέπει εἰπεῖν
5 ἀγριαινουσῶν βοῶν παραμυθουμένωι, ἃ ῥαψωιδὸς γνώσεται
ἀλλ' οὐχ ὁ βουκόλος; – ΙΩΝ Οὐ δῆτα. – ΣΩ. Ἀλλ' οἷα
γυναικὶ πρέποντά ἐστιν εἰπεῖν ταλασιουργῶι περὶ ἐρίων
d ἐργασίας; – ΙΩΝ Οὔ. – ΣΩ. Ἀλλ' οἷα ἀνδρὶ πρέπει εἰπεῖν
γνώσεται στρατηγῶι στρατιώταις παραινοῦντι; – ΙΩΝ Ναί,
τὰ τοιαῦτα γνώσεται ὁ ῥαψωιδός.
ΣΩ. Τί δέ; ἡ ῥαψωιδικὴ τέχνη στρατηγικὴ ἐστιν;

ΙΩΝ Γνοίην γοῦν ἂν ἔγωγε οἷα στρατηγὸν πρέπει εἰπεῖν. 5

ΣΩ. Ἴσως γὰρ εἶ καὶ στρατηγικός, ὦ Ἴων. καὶ γὰρ εἰ
ἐτύγχανες ἱππικὸς ὢν ἅμα καὶ κιθαριστικός, ἔγνως ἂν ἵππους
εὖ καὶ κακῶς ἱππαζομένους· ἀλλ' εἴ σ' ἐγὼ ἠρόμην· "Ποτέραι e
δὴ τέχνηι, ὦ Ἴων, γιγνώσκεις τοὺς εὖ ἱππαζομένους ἵππους;
ἧι ἱππεὺς εἶ ἢ ἧι κιθαριστής;" τί ἄν μοι ἀπεκρίνω; – ΙΩΝ
Ἧι ἱππεύς, ἔγωγ' ἄν. – ΣΩ. Οὐκοῦν εἰ καὶ τοὺς εὖ κιθαρί-
ζοντας διεγίγνωσκες, ὡμολόγεις ἄν, ἧι κιθαριστὴς εἶ, ταύτηι 5
διαγιγνώσκειν, ἀλλ' οὐχ ἧι ἱππεύς. – ΙΩΝ Ναί. – ΣΩ.
Ἐπειδὴ δὲ τὰ στρατιωτικὰ γιγνώσκεις, πότερον ἧι στρατη-
γικὸς εἶ γιγνώσκεις ἢ ἧι ῥαψωιδὸς ἀγαθός; – ΙΩΝ Οὐδὲν
ἔμοιγε δοκεῖ διαφέρειν.

ΣΩ. Πῶς; οὐδὲν λέγεις διαφέρειν; μίαν λέγεις τέχνην 541
εἶναι τὴν ῥαψωιδικὴν καὶ τὴν στρατηγικὴν ἢ δύο; – ΙΩΝ Μία
ἔμοιγε δοκεῖ. – ΣΩ. Ὅστις ἄρα ἀγαθὸς ῥαψωιδός ἐστιν, οὗτος
καὶ ἀγαθὸς στρατηγὸς τυγχάνει ὤν; – ΙΩΝ Μάλιστα, ὦ Σώκρατες. – ΣΩ. Οὐκοῦν καὶ ὅστις ἀγαθὸς στρατηγὸς τυγχάνει 5
ὤν, ἀγαθὸς καὶ ῥαψωιδός ἐστιν. – ΙΩΝ Οὐκ αὖ μοι δοκεῖ
τοῦτο. – ΣΩ. Ἀλλ' ἐκεῖνο μὴν δοκεῖ σοι, ὅστις γε ἀγαθὸς
ῥαψωιδός, καὶ στρατηγὸς ἀγαθὸς εἶναι; – ΙΩΝ Πάνυ γε. – b
ΣΩ. Οὐκοῦν σὺ τῶν Ἑλλήνων ἄριστος ῥαψωιδὸς εἶ; – ΙΩΝ
Πολύ γε, ὦ Σώκρατες. – ΣΩ. Ἦ καὶ στρατηγός, ὦ Ἴων, τῶν
Ἑλλήνων ἄριστος εἶ; – ΙΩΝ Εὖ ἴσθι, ὦ Σώκρατες· καὶ
ταῦτά γε ἐκ τῶν Ὁμήρου μαθών. 5

ΣΩ. Τί δή ποτ' οὖν πρὸς τῶν θεῶν, ὦ Ἴων, ἀμφότερα
ἄριστος ὢν τῶν Ἑλλήνων, καὶ στρατηγὸς καὶ ῥαψωιδός,
ῥαψωιδεῖς μὲν περιιὼν τοῖς Ἕλλησι, στρατηγεῖς δ' οὔ; ἢ
ῥαψωιδοῦ μὲν δοκεῖ σοι χρυσῶι στεφάνωι ἐστεφανωμένου c
πολλὴ χρεία εἶναι τοῖς Ἕλλησι, στρατηγοῦ δὲ οὐδεμία;

ΙΩΝ Ἡ μὲν γὰρ ἡμετέρα, ὦ Σώκρατες, πόλις ἄρχεται
ὑπὸ ὑμῶν καὶ στρατηγεῖται καὶ οὐδὲν δεῖται στρατηγοῦ, ἡ δὲ
ὑμετέρα καὶ ἡ Λακεδαιμονίων οὐκ ἄν με ἕλοιτο στρατηγόν· 5
αὐτοὶ γὰρ οἴεσθε ἱκανοὶ εἶναι.

ΣΩ. Ὦ βέλτιστε Ἴων, Ἀπολλόδωρον οὐ γιγνώσκεις τὸν
Κυζικηνόν;

ΙΩΝ Ποῖον τοῦτον;

ΙΟ ΣΩ. Ὃν Ἀθηναῖοι πολλάκις ἑαυτῶν στρατηγὸν ᾑρηνται
d ξένον ὄντα· καὶ Φανοσθένη τὸν Ἄνδριον καὶ Ἡρακλείδην τὸν
Κλαζομένιον, οὓς ἥδε ἡ πόλις ξένους ὄντας, ἐνδειξαμένους
ὅτι ἄξιοι λόγου εἰσί, καὶ εἰς στρατηγίας καὶ εἰς τὰς ἄλλας
ἀρχὰς ἄγει· Ἴωνα δ᾽ ἄρα τὸν Ἐφέσιον οὐχ αἱρήσεται
5 στρατηγὸν καὶ τιμήσει, ἐὰν δοκῇ ἄξιος λόγου εἶναι; τί δέ;
οὐκ Ἀθηναῖοι μέν ἐστε οἱ Ἐφέσιοι τὸ ἀρχαῖον, καὶ ἡ Ἔφεσος
e οὐδεμιᾶς ἐλάττων πόλεως; ἀλλὰ γὰρ σύ, ὦ Ἴων, εἰ μὲν ἀληθῆ
λέγεις ὡς τέχνῃ καὶ ἐπιστήμῃ οἷός τε εἶ Ὅμηρον ἐπαινεῖν,
ἀδικεῖς, ὅστις ἐμοὶ ὑποσχόμενος ὡς πολλὰ καὶ καλὰ περὶ
Ὁμήρου ἐπίστασαι καὶ φάσκων ἐπιδείξειν, ἐξαπατᾷς με καὶ
5 πολλοῦ δεῖς ἐπιδεῖξαι, ὅς γε οὐδὲ ἄττα ἐστὶ ταῦτα περὶ
ὧν δεινὸς εἶ ἐθέλεις εἰπεῖν, πάλαι ἐμοῦ λιπαροῦντος, ἀλλὰ
ἀτεχνῶς ὥσπερ ὁ Πρωτεὺς παντοδαπὸς γίγνῃ στρεφόμενος
ἄνω καὶ κάτω, ἕως τελευτῶν διαφυγών με στρατηγὸς ἀνεφά-
542 νης, ἵνα μὴ ἐπιδείξῃς ὡς δεινὸς εἶ τὴν περὶ Ὁμήρου σοφίαν.
εἰ μὲν οὖν τεχνικὸς ὤν, ὅπερ νυνδὴ ἔλεγον, περὶ Ὁμήρου
ὑποσχόμενος ἐπιδείξειν ἐξαπατᾷς με, ἄδικος εἶ· εἰ δὲ μὴ
τεχνικὸς εἶ, ἀλλὰ θείᾳ μοίρᾳ κατεχόμενος ἐξ Ὁμήρου μηδὲν
5 εἰδὼς πολλὰ καὶ καλὰ λέγεις περὶ τοῦ ποιητοῦ, ὥσπερ ἐγὼ
εἶπον περὶ σοῦ, οὐδὲν ἀδικεῖς. ἑλοῦ οὖν πότερα βούλει
νομίζεσθαι ὑπὸ ἡμῶν ἄδικος ἀνὴρ εἶναι ἢ θεῖος.
b ΙΩΝ Πολὺ διαφέρει, ὦ Σώκρατες· πολὺ γὰρ κάλλιον τὸ
θεῖον νομίζεσθαι.
ΣΩ. Τοῦτο τοίνυν τὸ κάλλιον ὑπάρχει σοι παρ᾽ ἡμῖν, ὦ
Ἴων, θεῖον εἶναι καὶ μὴ τεχνικὸν περὶ Ὁμήρου ἐπαινέτην.

ΠΟΛΙΤΕΙΑ

Β

Τίς οὖν ἡ παιδεία; ἢ χαλεπὸν εὑρεῖν βελτίω τῆς ὑπὸ
τοῦ πολλοῦ χρόνου ηὑρημένης; ἔστιν δέ που ἡ μὲν ἐπὶ
σώμασι γυμναστική, ἡ δ' ἐπὶ ψυχῆι μουσική.

Ἔστιν γάρ. 5
Ἆρ' οὖν οὐ μουσικῆι πρότερον ἀρξόμεθα παιδεύοντες ἢ
γυμναστικῆι;

Πῶς δ' οὔ;

Μουσικῆς δ', εἶπον, τιθεῖς λόγους, ἢ οὔ;

Ἔγωγε. 10

Λόγων δὲ διττὸν εἶδος, τὸ μὲν ἀληθές, ψεῦδος δ' ἕτερον;

Ναί.

Παιδευτέον δ' ἐν ἀμφοτέροις, πρότερον δ' ἐν τοῖς ψευ- 377
δέσιν;

Οὐ μανθάνω, ἔφη, πῶς λέγεις.

Οὐ μανθάνεις, ἦν δ' ἐγώ, ὅτι πρῶτον τοῖς παιδίοις μύθους
λέγομεν; τοῦτο δέ που ὡς τὸ ὅλον εἰπεῖν ψεῦδος, ἔνι δὲ 5
καὶ ἀληθῆ. πρότερον δὲ μύθοις πρὸς τὰ παιδία ἢ γυμνασίοις
χρώμεθα.

Ἔστι ταῦτα.

Τοῦτο δὴ ἔλεγον, ὅτι μουσικῆς πρότερον ἁπτέον ἢ γυ-
μναστικῆς. 10

Ὀρθῶς, ἔφη.

Οὐκοῦν οἶσθ' ὅτι ἀρχὴ παντὸς ἔργου μέγιστον, ἄλλως
τε δὴ καὶ νέωι καὶ ἁπαλῶι ὁτωιοῦν; μάλιστα γὰρ δὴ τότε b
πλάττεται, καὶ ἐνδύεται τύπος ὃν ἄν τις βούληται ἐνσημήνασθαι ἑκάστωι.

Κομιδῆι μὲν οὖν.

Ἆρ' οὖν ῥαιδίως οὕτω παρήσομεν τοὺς ἐπιτυχόντας ὑπὸ 5
τῶν ἐπιτυχόντων μύθους πλασθέντας ἀκούειν τοὺς παῖδας
καὶ λαμβάνειν ἐν ταῖς ψυχαῖς ὡς ἐπὶ τὸ πολὺ ἐναντίας

δόξας ἐκείναις ἅς, ἐπειδὰν τελεωθῶσιν, ἔχειν οἰησόμεθα δεῖν αὐτούς;

10 Οὐδ' ὁπωστιοῦν παρήσομεν.

Πρῶτον δὴ ἡμῖν, ὡς ἔοικεν, ἐπιστατητέον τοῖς μυθοποιοῖς,

c καὶ ὃν μὲν ἂν καλὸν ποιήσωσιν, ἐγκριτέον, ὃν δ' ἂν μή, ἀποκριτέον. τοὺς δ' ἐγκριθέντας πείσομεν τὰς τροφούς τε καὶ μητέρας λέγειν τοῖς παισίν, καὶ πλάττειν τὰς ψυχὰς αὐτῶν τοῖς μύθοις πολὺ μᾶλλον ἢ τὰ σώματα ταῖς χερσίν·

5 ὧν δὲ νῦν λέγουσι τοὺς πολλοὺς ἐκβλητέον.

Ποίους δή; ἔφη.

Ἐν τοῖς μείζοσιν, ἦν δ' ἐγώ, μύθοις ὀψόμεθα καὶ τοὺς ἐλάττους. δεῖ γὰρ δὴ τὸν αὐτὸν τύπον εἶναι καὶ ταὐτὸν

d δύνασθαι τούς τε μείζους καὶ τοὺς ἐλάττους. ἢ οὐκ οἴει;

Ἔγωγ', ἔφη· ἀλλ' οὐκ ἐννοῶ οὐδὲ τοὺς μείζους τίνας λέγεις.

Οὓς Ἡσίοδός τε, εἶπον, καὶ Ὅμηρος ἡμῖν ἐλεγέτην καὶ

5 οἱ ἄλλοι ποιηταί. οὗτοι γάρ που μύθους τοῖς ἀνθρώποις ψευδεῖς συντιθέντες ἔλεγόν τε καὶ λέγουσι.

Ποίους δή, ἦ δ' ὅς, καὶ τί αὐτῶν μεμφόμενος λέγεις;

Ὅπερ, ἦν δ' ἐγώ, χρὴ καὶ πρῶτον καὶ μάλιστα μέμφεσθαι, ἄλλως τε καὶ ἐάν τις μὴ καλῶς ψεύδηται.

10 Τί τοῦτο;

e Ὅταν εἰκάζῃ τις κακῶς τῶι λόγωι, περὶ θεῶν τε καὶ ἡρώων οἷοί εἰσιν, ὥσπερ γραφεὺς μηδὲν ἐοικότα γράφων οἷς ἂν ὅμοια βουληθῇι γράψαι.

Καὶ γάρ, ἔφη, ὀρθῶς ἔχει τά γε τοιαῦτα μέμφεσθαι.

5 ἀλλὰ πῶς δὴ λέγομεν καὶ ποῖα;

Πρῶτον μέν, ἦν δ' ἐγώ, τὸ μέγιστον καὶ περὶ τῶν μεγίστων ψεῦδος ὁ εἰπὼν οὐ καλῶς ἐψεύσατο ὡς Οὐρανός τε ἠργάσατο ἅ φησι δρᾶσαι αὐτὸν Ἡσίοδος, ὅ τε αὖ Κρόνος

378 ὡς ἐτιμωρήσατο αὐτόν. τὰ δὲ δὴ τοῦ Κρόνου ἔργα καὶ

c1 μῦθον mt: om. mt
e1 κακῶς mt: κακῶς οὐσίαν t: κακῶ οὐσίαν m: οὐσίαν κακῶς m

πάθη ὑπὸ τοῦ ὑέος, οὐδ' ἂν εἰ ἦν ἀληθῆ ὤιμην δεῖν ῥαιδίως
οὕτως λέγεσθαι πρὸς ἄφρονάς τε καὶ νέους, ἀλλὰ μάλιστα
μὲν σιγᾶσθαι, εἰ δὲ ἀνάγκη τις ἦν λέγειν, δι' ἀπορρήτων 5
ἀκούειν ὡς ὀλιγίστους, θυσαμένους οὐ χοῖρον ἀλλά τι μέγα
καὶ ἄπορον θῦμα, ὅπως ὅτι ἐλαχίστοις συνέβη ἀκοῦσαι.
    Καὶ γάρ, ἦ δ' ὅς, οὗτοί γε οἱ λόγοι χαλεποί.   b
    Καὶ οὐ λεκτέοι γ', ἔφην, ὦ Ἀδείμαντε, ἐν τῆι ἡμετέραι
πόλει. οὐδὲ λεκτέον νέωι ἀκούοντι ὡς ἀδικῶν τὰ ἔσχατα
οὐδὲν ἂν θαυμαστὸν ποιοῖ, οὐδ' αὖ ἀδικοῦντα πατέρα κολάζων
παντὶ τρόπωι, ἀλλὰ δρώιη ἂν ὅπερ θεῶν οἱ πρῶτοί τε καὶ 5
μέγιστοι.
    Οὐ μὰ τὸν Δία, ἦ δ' ὅς, οὐδὲ αὐτῶι μοι δοκεῖ ἐπιτήδεια
εἶναι λέγειν.
    Οὐδέ γε, ἦν δ' ἐγώ, τὸ παράπαν ὡς θεοὶ θεοῖς πολεμοῦσί
τε καὶ ἐπιβουλεύουσι καὶ μάχονται – οὐδὲ γὰρ ἀληθῆ – εἴ c
γε δεῖ ἡμῖν τοὺς μέλλοντας τὴν πόλιν φυλάξειν αἴσχιστον
νομίζειν τὸ ῥαιδίως ἀλλήλοις ἀπεχθάνεσθαι – πολλοῦ δεῖ
γιγαντομαχίας τε μυθολογητέον αὐτοῖς καὶ ποικιλτέον, καὶ
ἄλλας ἔχθρας πολλὰς καὶ παντοδαπὰς θεῶν τε καὶ ἡρώων 5
πρὸς συγγενεῖς τε καὶ οἰκείους αὐτῶν – ἀλλ' εἴ πως μέλλομεν πείσειν ὡς οὐδεὶς πώποτε πολίτης ἕτερος ἑτέρωι
ἀπήχθετο οὐδ' ἔστιν τοῦτο ὅσιον, τοιαῦτα λεκτέα μᾶλλον πρὸς
τὰ παιδία εὐθὺς καὶ γέρουσι καὶ γραυσί, καὶ πρεσβυτέροις d
γιγνομένοις καὶ τοὺς ποιητὰς ἐγγὺς τούτων ἀναγκαστέον
λογοποιεῖν. Ἥρας δὲ δεσμοὺς ὑπὸ ὑέος καὶ Ἡφαίστου
ῥίψεις ὑπὸ πατρός, μέλλοντος τῆι μητρὶ τυπτομένηι ἀμυνεῖν,
καὶ θεομαχίας ὅσας Ὅμηρος πεποίηκεν οὐ παραδεκτέον εἰς 5
τὴν πόλιν, οὔτ' ἐν ὑπονοίαις πεποιημένας οὔτε ἄνευ ὑπο-
νοιῶν. ὁ γὰρ νέος οὐχ οἷός τε κρίνειν ὅτι τε ὑπόνοια καὶ
ὃ μή, ἀλλ' ἃ ἂν τηλικοῦτος ὢν λάβηι ἐν ταῖς δόξαις δυσέκ-
νιπτά τε καὶ ἀμετάστατα φιλεῖ γίγνεσθαι· ὧν δὴ ἴσως e
ἕνεκα περὶ παντὸς ποιητέον ἃ πρῶτα ἀκούουσιν ὅτι κάλλιστα
μεμυθολογημένα πρὸς ἀρετὴν ἀκούειν.
    Ἔχει γάρ, ἔφη, λόγον. ἀλλ' εἴ τις αὖ καὶ ταῦτα ἐρω-

5 τώιη ἡμᾶς, ταῦτα ἄττα τ' ἐστὶν καὶ τίνες οἱ μῦθοι, τίνας ἂν
φαῖμεν;

Καὶ ἐγὼ εἶπον· Ὦ Ἀδείμαντε, οὐκ ἐσμὲν ποιηταὶ ἐγώ τε
379 καὶ σὺ ἐν τῶι παρόντι, ἀλλ' οἰκισταὶ πόλεως· οἰκισταῖς δὲ
τοὺς μὲν τύπους προσήκει εἰδέναι ἐν οἷς δεῖ μυθολογεῖν τοὺς
ποιητάς, παρ' οὓς ἐὰν ποιῶσιν οὐκ ἐπιτρεπτέον, οὐ μὴν
αὐτοῖς γε ποιητέον μύθους.

5 Ὀρθῶς, ἔφη· ἀλλ' αὐτὸ δὴ τοῦτο, οἱ τύποι περὶ θεο-
λογίας τίνες ἂν εἶεν;

Τοιοίδε πού τινες, ἦν δ' ἐγώ· οἷος τυγχάνει ὁ θεὸς ὤν,
ἀεὶ δήπου ἀποδοτέον, ἐάντέ τις αὐτὸν ἐν ἔπεσιν ποιῆι ἐάντε
ἐν μέλεσιν ἐάντε ἐν τραγωιδίαι.

10 Δεῖ γάρ.

b Οὐκοῦν ἀγαθὸς ὅ γε θεὸς τῶι ὄντι τε καὶ λεκτέον οὕτω;

Τί μήν;

Ἀλλὰ μὴν οὐδέν γε τῶν ἀγαθῶν βλαβερόν· ἦ γάρ;

Οὔ μοι δοκεῖ.

5 Ἆρ' οὖν ὃ μὴ βλαβερὸν βλάπτει;

Οὐδαμῶς.

Ὃ δὲ μὴ βλάπτει κακόν τι ποιεῖ;

Οὐδὲ τοῦτο.

Ὃ δέ γε μηδὲν κακὸν ποιεῖ οὐδ' ἄν τινος εἴη κακοῦ αἴτιον;

10 Πῶς γάρ;

Τί δέ; ὠφέλιμον τὸ ἀγαθόν;

Ναί.

Αἴτιον ἄρα εὐπραγίας;

Ναί.

15 Οὐκ ἄρα πάντων γε αἴτιον τὸ ἀγαθόν, ἀλλὰ τῶν μὲν εὖ
ἐχόντων αἴτιον, τῶν δὲ κακῶν ἀναίτιον.

c Παντελῶς γ', ἔφη.

Οὐδ' ἄρα, ἦν δ' ἐγώ, ὁ θεός, ἐπειδὴ ἀγαθός, πάντων ἂν
εἴη αἴτιος, ὡς οἱ πολλοὶ λέγουσιν, ἀλλὰ ὀλίγων μὲν τοῖς
ἀνθρώποις αἴτιος, πολλῶν δὲ ἀναίτιος· πολὺ γὰρ ἐλάττω
5 τἀγαθὰ τῶν κακῶν ἡμῖν, καὶ τῶν μὲν ἀγαθῶν οὐδένα

ἄλλον αἰτιατέον, τῶν δὲ κακῶν ἄλλ' ἄττα δεῖ ζητεῖν τὰ
αἴτια, ἀλλ' οὐ τὸν θεόν.

Ἀληθέστατα, ἔφη, δοκεῖς μοι λέγειν.

Οὐκ ἄρα, ἦν δ' ἐγώ, ἀποδεκτέον οὔτε Ὁμήρου οὔτ' ἄλλου d
ποιητοῦ ταύτην τὴν ἁμαρτίαν περὶ τοὺς θεοὺς ἀνοήτως
ἁμαρτάνοντος καὶ λέγοντος –

ὡς δοιοί τε πίθοι κατακείαται ἐν Διὸς οὔδει
κηρῶν ἔμπλειοι, ὁ μὲν ἐσθλῶν, αὐτὰρ ὃ δειλῶν·   5

καὶ ὧι μὲν ἂν μείξας ὁ Ζεὺς δῶι ἀμφοτέρων,

ἄλλοτε μέν τε κακῶι ὃ γε κύρεται, ἄλλοτε δ' ἐσθλῶι·

ὧι δ' ἂν μή, ἀλλ' ἄκρατα τὰ ἕτερα,

τὸν δὲ κακὴ βούβρωστις ἐπὶ χθόνα δῖαν ἐλαύνει·   e

οὐδ' ὡς ταμίας ἡμῖν Ζεὺς –

ἀγαθῶν τε κακῶν τε τέτυκται.

τὴν δὲ τῶν ὅρκων καὶ σπονδῶν σύγχυσιν, ἣν ὁ Πάν-
δαρος συνέχεεν, ἐάν τις φῆι δι' Ἀθηνᾶς τε καὶ Διὸς 5
γεγονέναι, οὐκ ἐπαινεσόμεθα, οὐδὲ θεῶν ἔριν τε καὶ κρίσιν 380
διὰ Θέμιτός τε καὶ Διός, οὐδ' αὖ, ὡς Αἰσχύλος λέγει,
ἐατέον ἀκούειν τοὺς νέους, ὅτι –

θεὸς μὲν αἰτίαν φύει βροτοῖς,
ὅταν κακῶσαι δῶμα παμπήδην θέλῃ.
                                                          5

ἀλλ' ἐάν τις ποιῆι ἐν οἷς ταῦτα τὰ ἰαμβεῖα ἔνεστιν, τὰ τῆς
Νιόβης πάθη, ἢ τὰ Πελοπιδῶν ἢ τὰ Τρωικὰ ἤ τι ἄλλο τῶν
τοιούτων, ἢ οὐ θεοῦ ἔργα ἐατέον αὐτὰ λέγειν, ἢ εἰ θεοῦ,
ἐξευρετέον αὐτοῖς σχεδὸν ὃν νῦν ἡμεῖς λόγον ζητοῦμεν, καὶ b
λεκτέον ὡς ὁ μὲν θεὸς δίκαιά τε καὶ ἀγαθὰ ἠργάζετο, οἱ δὲ
ὠνίναντο κολαζόμενοι· ὡς δὲ ἄθλιοι μὲν οἱ δίκην διδόντες,
ἦν δὲ δὴ ὁ δρῶν ταῦτα θεός, οὐκ ἐατέον λέγειν τὸν ποιητήν. ἀλλ' εἰ μὲν ὅτι ἐδεήθησαν κολάσεως λέγοιεν ὡς

5 ἄθλιοι οἱ κακοί, διδόντες δὲ δίκην ὠφελοῦντο ὑπὸ τοῦ θεοῦ,
ἐατέον· κακῶν δὲ αἴτιον φάναι θεόν τινι γίγνεσθαι ἀγαθὸν
ὄντα, διαμαχετέον παντὶ τρόπωι μήτε τινὰ λέγειν ταῦτα ἐν
τῆι αὑτοῦ πόλει, εἰ μέλλει εὐνομήσεσθαι, μήτε τινὰ ἀκούειν,
c μήτε νεώτερον μήτε πρεσβύτερον, μήτ' ἐν μέτρωι μήτε ἄνευ
μέτρου μυθολογοῦντα, ὡς οὔτε ὅσια ἂν λεγόμενα εἰ λέγοιτο,
οὔτε σύμφορα ἡμῖν οὔτε σύμφωνα αὐτὰ αὑτοῖς.
　　Σύμψηφός σοί εἰμι, ἔφη, τούτου τοῦ νόμου, καὶ μοι
5 ἀρέσκει.
　　Οὗτος μὲν τοίνυν, ἦν δ' ἐγώ, εἷς ἂν εἴη τῶν περὶ θεοὺς
νόμων τε καὶ τύπων, ἐν ὧι δεήσει τούς τε λέγοντας λέγειν
καὶ τοὺς ποιοῦντας ποιεῖν, μὴ πάντων αἴτιον τὸν θεὸν ἀλλὰ
τῶν ἀγαθῶν.
10 Καὶ μάλ', ἔφη, ἀπόχρη.
d Τί δὲ δὴ ὁ δεύτερος ὅδε; ἆρα γόητα τὸν θεὸν οἴει εἶναι
καὶ οἷον ἐξ ἐπιβουλῆς φαντάζεσθαι ἄλλοτε ἐν ἄλλαις ἰδέαις,
τοτὲ μὲν αὐτὸν γιγνόμενον καὶ ἀλλάττοντα τὸ αὑτοῦ εἶδος
εἰς πολλὰς μορφάς, τοτὲ δὲ ἡμᾶς ἀπατῶντα καὶ ποιοῦντα
5 περὶ αὑτοῦ τοιαῦτα δοκεῖν, ἢ ἁπλοῦν τε εἶναι καὶ πάντων
ἥκιστα τῆς ἑαυτοῦ ἰδέας ἐκβαίνειν;
　　Οὐκ ἔχω, ἔφη, νῦν γε οὕτως εἰπεῖν.
　　Τί δὲ τόδε; οὐκ ἀνάγκη, εἴπερ τι ἐξίσταιτο τῆς αὑτοῦ
e ἰδέας, ἢ αὐτὸ ὑφ' ἑαυτοῦ μεθίστασθαι ἢ ὑπ' ἄλλου;
　　Ἀνάγκη.
　　Οὐκοῦν ὑπὸ μὲν ἄλλου τὰ ἄριστα ἔχοντα ἥκιστα ἀλλοι-
οῦταί τε καὶ κινεῖται; οἷον σῶμα ὑπὸ σιτίων τε καὶ ποτῶν
5 καὶ πόνων, καὶ πᾶν φυτὸν ὑπὸ εἱλήσεών τε καὶ ἀνέμων καὶ
τῶν τοιούτων παθημάτων, οὐ τὸ ὑγιέστατον καὶ ἰσχυρότατον
381 ἥκιστα ἀλλοιοῦται;
　　Πῶς δ' οὔ;
　　Ψυχὴν δὲ οὐ τὴν ἀνδρειοτάτην καὶ φρονιμωτάτην ἥκιστ'
ἄν τι ἔξωθεν πάθος ταράξειέν τε καὶ ἀλλοιώσειεν;

---

d3 καὶ ἀλλάττοντα m: τοτὲ δὲ ἐναλλάτοντα m: καὶ secl. Burnet

Ναί.   5

Καὶ μήν που καὶ τά γε σύνθετα πάντα σκεύη τε καὶ
οἰκοδομήματα καὶ ἀμφιέσματα κατὰ τὸν αὐτὸν λόγον τὰ εὖ
εἰργασμένα καὶ εὖ ἔχοντα ὑπὸ χρόνου τε καὶ τῶν ἄλλων
παθημάτων ἥκιστα ἀλλοιοῦται.

Ἔστι δὴ ταῦτα.   10

Πᾶν δὴ τὸ καλῶς ἔχον ἢ φύσει ἢ τέχνηι ἢ ἀμφοτέροις b
ἐλαχίστην μεταβολὴν ὑπ' ἄλλου ἐνδέχεται.

Ἔοικεν.

Ἀλλὰ μὴν ὁ θεός γε καὶ τὰ τοῦ θεοῦ πάντηι ἄριστα ἔχει.

Πῶς δ' οὔ;   5

Ταύτηι μὲν δὴ ἥκιστα ἂν πολλὰς μορφὰς ἴσχοι ὁ θεός.

Ἥκιστα δῆτα.

Ἀλλ' ἄρα αὐτὸς αὑτὸν μεταβάλλοι ἂν καὶ ἀλλοιοῖ;

Δῆλον, ἔφη, ὅτι, εἴπερ ἀλλοιοῦται.

Πότερον οὖν ἐπὶ τὸ βέλτιόν τε καὶ κάλλιον μεταβάλλει 10
ἑαυτὸν ἢ ἐπὶ τὸ χεῖρον καὶ τὸ αἴσχιον ἑαυτοῦ;

Ἀνάγκη, ἔφη, ἐπὶ τὸ χεῖρον, εἴπερ ἀλλοιοῦται· οὐ γάρ c
που ἐνδεᾶ γε φήσομεν τὸν θεὸν κάλλους ἢ ἀρετῆς εἶναι.

Ὀρθότατα, ἦν δ' ἐγώ, λέγεις. καὶ οὕτως ἔχοντος δοκεῖ
ἄν τίς σοι, ὦ Ἀδείμαντε, ἑκὼν αὑτὸν χείρω ποιεῖν ὁπηιοῦν
ἢ θεῶν ἢ ἀνθρώπων;   5

Ἀδύνατον, ἔφη.

Ἀδύνατον ἄρα, ἔφην, καὶ θεῶι ἐθέλειν αὑτὸν ἀλλοιοῦν,
ἀλλ' ὡς ἔοικε, κάλλιστος καὶ ἄριστος ὢν εἰς τὸ δυνατὸν
ἕκαστος αὐτῶν μένει ἀεὶ ἁπλῶς ἐν τῆι αὑτοῦ μορφῆι.

Ἅπασα, ἔφη, ἀνάγκη ἔμοιγε δοκεῖ.   10

Μηδεὶς ἄρα, ἦν δ' ἐγώ, ὦ ἄριστε, λεγέτω ἡμῖν τῶν d
ποιητῶν, ὡς –

        θεοὶ ξείνοισιν ἐοικότες ἀλλοδαποῖσι,
        παντοῖοι τελέθοντες, ἐπιστρωφῶσι πόληας·

μηδὲ Πρωτέως καὶ Θέτιδος καταψευδέσθω μηδείς, μηδ' ἐν 5
τραγωιδίαις μηδ' ἐν τοῖς ἄλλοις ποιήμασιν εἰσαγέτω Ἥραν
ἠλλοιωμένην, ὡς ἱέρειαν ἀγείρουσαν –

Ἰνάχου Ἀργείου ποταμοῦ παισὶν βιοδώροις·

e καὶ ἄλλα τοιαῦτα πολλὰ μὴ ἡμῖν ψευδέσθων. μηδ' αὖ ὑπὸ
τούτων ἀναπειθόμεναι αἱ μητέρες τὰ παιδία ἐκδειματούντων,
λέγουσαι τοὺς μύθους κακῶς, ὡς ἄρα θεοί τινες περιέρχονται
νύκτωρ πολλοῖς ξένοις καὶ παντοδαποῖς ἰνδαλλόμενοι, ἵνα
5 μὴ ἅμα μὲν εἰς θεοὺς βλασφημῶσιν, ἅμα δὲ τοὺς παῖδας
ἀπεργάζωνται δειλοτέρους.
Μὴ γάρ, ἔφη.
Ἀλλ' ἄρα, ἦν δ' ἐγώ, αὐτοὶ μὲν οἱ θεοί εἰσιν οἷοι μὴ
μεταβάλλειν, ἡμῖν δὲ ποιοῦσιν δοκεῖν σφᾶς παντοδαποὺς
10 φαίνεσθαι, ἐξαπατῶντες καὶ γοητεύοντες;
Ἴσως, ἔφη.
382 Τί δέ; ἦν δ' ἐγώ· ψεύδεσθαι θεὸς ἐθέλοι ἂν ἢ λόγωι ἢ
ἔργωι φάντασμα προτείνων;
Οὐκ οἶδα, ἦ δ' ὅς.
Οὐκ οἶσθα, ἦν δ' ἐγώ, ὅτι τό γε ὡς ἀληθῶς ψεῦδος, εἰ
5 οἷόν τε τοῦτο εἰπεῖν, πάντες θεοί τε καὶ ἄνθρωποι μισοῦσιν;
Πῶς, ἔφη, λέγεις;
Οὕτως, ἦν δ' ἐγώ, ὅτι τῶι κυριωτάτωι που ἑαυτῶν ψεύδεσθαι καὶ περὶ τὰ κυριώτατα οὐδεὶς ἑκὼν ἐθέλει, ἀλλὰ
πάντων μάλιστα φοβεῖται ἐκεῖ αὐτὸ κεκτῆσθαι.
10 Οὐδὲ νῦν πω, ἦ δ' ὅς, μανθάνω.
b Οἴει γάρ τί με, ἔφην, σεμνὸν λέγειν· ἐγὼ δὲ λέγω ὅτι
τῆι ψυχῆι περὶ τὰ ὄντα ψεύδεσθαί τε καὶ ἐψεῦσθαι καὶ
ἀμαθῆ εἶναι καὶ ἐνταῦθα ἔχειν τε καὶ κεκτῆσθαι τὸ ψεῦδος
πάντες ἥκιστα ἂν δέξαιντο, καὶ μισοῦσι μάλιστα αὐτὸ ἐν
5 τῶι τοιούτωι.
Πολύ γε, ἔφη.
Ἀλλὰ μὴν ὀρθότατά γ' ἄν, ὃ νυνδὴ ἔλεγον, τοῦτο ὡς
ἀληθῶς ψεῦδος καλοῖτο, ἡ ἐν τῆι ψυχῆι ἄγνοια ἡ τοῦ ἐψευ-
σμένου· ἐπεὶ τό γε ἐν τοῖς λόγοις μίμημά τι τοῦ ἐν τῆι
10 ψυχῆι ἐστὶν παθήματος καὶ ὕστερον γεγονὸς εἴδωλον, οὐ πάνυ
c ἄκρατον ψεῦδος. ἢ οὐχ οὕτω;
Πάνυ μὲν οὖν.

Τὸ μὲν δὴ τῶι ὄντι ψεῦδος οὐ μόνον ὑπὸ θεῶν ἀλλὰ καὶ
ὑπ' ἀνθρώπων μισεῖται.

Δοκεῖ μοι.

Τί δὲ δὴ τὸ ἐν τοῖς λόγοις ψεῦδος; πότε καὶ τῶι χρήσιμον, ὥστε μὴ ἄξιον εἶναι μίσους; ἆρ' οὐ πρός τε τοὺς
πολεμίους καὶ τῶν καλουμένων φίλων, ὅταν διὰ μανίαν ἤ
τινα ἄνοιαν κακόν τι ἐπιχειρῶσιν πράττειν, τότε ἀποτροπῆς
ἕνεκα ὡς φάρμακον χρήσιμον γίγνεται; καὶ ἐν αἷς νυνδὴ 10
ἐλέγομεν ταῖς μυθολογίαις, διὰ τὸ μὴ εἰδέναι ὅπηι τἀληθὲς **d**
ἔχει περὶ τῶν παλαιῶν, ἀφομοιοῦντες τῶι ἀληθεῖ τὸ ψεῦδος
ὅτι μάλιστα, οὕτω χρήσιμον ποιοῦμεν;

Καὶ μάλα, ἦ δ' ὅς, οὕτως ἔχει.

Κατὰ τί δὴ οὖν τούτων τῶι θεῶι τὸ ψεῦδος χρήσιμον; 5
πότερον διὰ τὸ μὴ εἰδέναι τὰ παλαιὰ ἀφομοιῶν ἂν
ψεύδοιτο;

Γελοῖον μεντἂν εἴη, ἔφη.

Ποιητὴς μὲν ἄρα ψευδὴς ἐν θεῶι οὐκ ἔνι.

Οὔ μοι δοκεῖ. 10

Ἀλλὰ δεδιὼς τοὺς ἐχθροὺς ψεύδοιτο;

Πολλοῦ γε δεῖ. **e**

Ἀλλὰ δι' οἰκείων ἄνοιαν ἢ μανίαν;

Ἀλλ' οὐδείς, ἔφη, τῶν ἀνοήτων καὶ μαινομένων θεοφιλής.

Οὐκ ἄρα ἔστιν οὗ ἕνεκα ἂν θεὸς ψεύδοιτο.

Οὐκ ἔστιν. 5

Πάντηι ἄρα ἀψευδὲς τὸ δαιμόνιόν τε καὶ τὸ θεῖον.

Παντάπασι μὲν οὖν, ἔφη.

Κομιδῆι ἄρα ὁ θεὸς ἁπλοῦν καὶ ἀληθὲς ἔν τε ἔργωι καὶ
λόγωι, καὶ οὔτε αὐτὸς μεθίσταται οὔτε ἄλλους ἐξαπατᾶι, οὔτε
κατὰ φαντασίας οὔτε κατὰ λόγους οὔτε κατὰ σημείων πομπάς, 10
ὕπαρ οὐδ' ὄναρ.

Οὕτως, ἔφη, ἔμοιγε καὶ αὐτῶι φαίνεται σοῦ λέγοντος.

383

c6 ψεῦδος *mt*: om. *m*
e11 ὕπαρ οὐδ' ὄναρ *mt*: οὔθ' ὕπαρ οὐδ' ὄναρ *m(m)*

Συγχωρεῖς ἄρα, ἔφην, τοῦτον δεύτερον τύπον εἶναι ἐν ὧι
δεῖ περὶ θεῶν καὶ λέγειν καὶ ποιεῖν, ὡς μήτε αὐτοὺς γόητας
ὄντας τῶι μεταβάλλειν ἑαυτοὺς μήτε ἡμᾶς ψεύδεσι παράγειν
5 ἐν λόγωι ἢ ἐν ἔργωι;
Συγχωρῶ.

Πολλὰ ἄρα Ὁμήρου ἐπαινοῦντες ἄλλα τοῦτο οὐκ ἐπαινεσόμεθα, τὴν τοῦ ἐνυπνίου πομπὴν ὑπὸ Διὸς τῶι Ἀγαμέμνονι·
οὐδὲ Αἰσχύλου, ὅταν φῆι ἡ Θέτις τὸν Ἀπόλλω ἐν τοῖς αὐτῆς
b γάμοις ἄιδοντα ἐνδατεῖσθαι τὰς ἑὰς εὐπαιδίας –

νόσων τ᾽ ἀπείρους καὶ μακραίωνας βίους,
ξύμπαντά τ᾽ εἰπὼν θεοφιλεῖς ἐμὰς τύχας
παιᾶν᾽ ἐπηυφήμησεν, εὐθυμῶν ἐμέ.
5   κἀγὼ τὸ Φοίβου θεῖον ἀψευδὲς στόμα
ἤλπιζον εἶναι, μαντικῆι βρύον τέχνηι·
ὁ δ᾽, αὐτὸς ὑμνῶν, αὐτὸς ἐν θοίνηι παρών,
αὐτὸς τάδ᾽ εἰπών, αὐτός ἐστιν ὁ κτανὼν
τὸν παῖδα τὸν ἐμόν –

c ὅταν τις τοιαῦτα λέγηι περὶ θεῶν, χαλεπανοῦμέν τε καὶ
χορὸν οὐ δώσομεν, οὐδὲ τοὺς διδασκάλους ἐάσομεν ἐπὶ
παιδείαι χρῆσθαι τῶν νέων, εἰ μέλλουσιν ἡμῖν οἱ φύλακες
θεοσεβεῖς τε καὶ θεῖοι γίγνεσθαι, καθ᾽ ὅσον ἀνθρώπωι ἐπὶ
5 πλεῖστον οἷόν τε.
Παντάπασιν, ἔφη, ἔγωγε τοὺς τύπους τούτους συγχωρῶ,
καὶ ὡς νόμοις ἂν χρώιμην.

Γ

386 Τὰ μὲν δὴ περὶ θεούς, ἦν δ᾽ ἐγώ, τοιαῦτ᾽ ἄττα, ὡς ἔοικεν,
ἀκουστέον τε καὶ οὐκ ἀκουστέον εὐθὺς ἐκ παίδων τοῖς θεούς
τε τιμήσουσιν καὶ γονέας τήν τε ἀλλήλων φιλίαν μὴ περὶ
σμικροῦ ποιησομένοις.
5   Καὶ οἶμαί γ᾽, ἔφη, ὀρθῶς ἡμῖν φαίνεσθαι.

a7 ἄλλα m: ἀλλὰ m

Τί δὲ δὴ εἰ μέλλουσιν εἶναι ἀνδρεῖοι; ἆρα οὐ ταῦτά τε
λεκτέον καὶ οἷα αὐτοὺς ποιῆσαι ἥκιστα τὸν θάνατον δεδιέναι;
ἢ ἡγῇ τινά ποτ' ἂν γενέσθαι ἀνδρεῖον ἔχοντα ἐν αὑτῶι τοῦτο **b**
τὸ δεῖμα;
Μὰ Δία, ἦ δ' ὅς, οὐκ ἔγωγε.
Τί δέ; τὰν Ἅιδου ἡγούμενον εἶναί τε καὶ δεινὰ εἶναι οἴει
τινὰ θανάτου ἀδεῆ ἔσεσθαι καὶ ἐν ταῖς μάχαις αἱρήσεσθαι 5
πρὸ ἥττης τε καὶ δουλείας θάνατον;
Οὐδαμῶς.
Δεῖ δή, ὡς ἔοικεν, ἡμᾶς ἐπιστατεῖν καὶ περὶ τούτων τῶν μύ-
θων τοῖς ἐπιχειροῦσιν λέγειν, καὶ δεῖσθαι μὴ λοιδορεῖν ἁπλῶς
οὕτως τὰ ἐν Ἅιδου ἀλλὰ μᾶλλον ἐπαινεῖν, ὡς οὔτε ἀληθῆ 10
ἂν λέγοντας οὔτε ὠφέλιμα τοῖς μέλλουσιν μαχίμοις ἔσεσθαι. **c**
Δεῖ μέντοι, ἔφη.
Ἐξαλείψομεν ἄρα, ἦν δ' ἐγώ, ἀπὸ τοῦδε τοῦ ἔπους
ἀρξάμενοι πάντα τὰ τοιαῦτα –

> βουλοίμην κ' ἐπάρουρος ἐὼν θητευέμεν ἄλλωι   5
> ἀνδρὶ παρ' ἀκλήρωι, ὧι μὴ βίοτος πολὺς εἴη
> ἢ πᾶσιν νεκύεσσι καταφθιμένοισιν ἀνάσσειν

καὶ τὸ –

> οἰκία δὲ θνητοῖσι καὶ ἀθανάτοισι φανείη   **d**
> σμερδαλέ', εὐρώεντα, τά τε στυγέουσι θεοί περ

καὶ –

> ὢ πόποι, ἦ ῥά τις ἔστι καὶ εἰν Ἀΐδαο δόμοισιν
> ψυχὴ καὶ εἴδωλον, ἀτὰρ φρένες οὐκ ἔνι πάμπαν   5

καὶ τὸ –

> οἴωι πεπνῦσθαι, ταὶ δὲ σκιαὶ ἀΐσσουσι

καὶ –

> ψυχὴ δ' ἐκ ῥεθέων πταμένη Ἄϊδόσδε βεβήκει,
> ὃν πότμον γοόωσα, λιποῦσ' ἀνδροτῆτα καὶ ἥβην   10

387 καὶ τὸ –

        ψυχὴ δὲ κατὰ χθονός, ἠΰτε καπνός,
  ᾤχετο τετριγυῖα
καὶ –

5   ὡς δ' ὅτε νυκτερίδες μυχῶι ἄντρου θεσπεσίοιο
τρίζουσαι ποτέονται, ἐπεί κέ τις ἀποπέσηισιν
ὁρμαθοῦ ἐκ πέτρης, ἀνά τ' ἀλλήληισιν ἔχονται,
ὡς αἱ τετριγυῖαι ἅμ' ἤιεσαν.

b ταῦτα καὶ τὰ τοιαῦτα πάντα παραιτησόμεθα Ὅμηρόν τε καὶ
τοὺς ἄλλους ποιητὰς μὴ χαλεπαίνειν ἂν διαγράφωμεν, οὐχ
ὡς οὐ ποιητικὰ καὶ ἡδέα τοῖς πολλοῖς ἀκούειν, ἀλλ' ὅσωι
5 ποιητικώτερα, τοσούτωι ἧττον ἀκουστέον παισὶ καὶ ἀνδράσιν
οὓς δεῖ ἐλευθέρους εἶναι, δουλείαν θανάτου μᾶλλον
πεφοβημένους.
    Παντάπασι μὲν οὖν.
    Οὐκοῦν ἔτι καὶ τὰ περὶ ταῦτα ὀνόματα πάντα τὰ δεινά
10 τε καὶ φοβερὰ ἀποβλητέα, Κωκυτούς τε καὶ Στύγας καὶ
c ἐνέρους καὶ ἀλίβαντας, καὶ ἄλλα ὅσα τούτου τοῦ τύπου
ὀνομαζόμενα φρίττειν δὴ ποιεῖ ὡς οἴεται† πάντας τοὺς
ἀκούοντας. καὶ ἴσως εὖ ἔχει πρὸς ἄλλο τι· ἡμεῖς δὲ ὑπὲρ
τῶν φυλάκων φοβούμεθα μὴ ἐκ τῆς τοιαύτης φρίκης θερμό-
5 τεροι καὶ μαλακώτεροι τοῦ δέοντος γένωνται ἡμῖν.
    Καὶ ὀρθῶς γ', ἔφη, φοβούμεθα.
    Ἀφαιρετέα ἄρα;
    Ναί.
    Τὸν δὲ ἐναντίον τύπον τούτοις λεκτέον τε καὶ ποιητέον;
10 Δῆλα δή.
d Καὶ τοὺς ὀδυρμοὺς ἄρα ἐξαιρήσομεν καὶ τοὺς οἴκτους
τοὺς τῶν ἐλλογίμων ἀνδρῶν;
    Ἀνάγκη, ἔφη, εἴπερ καὶ τὰ πρότερα.
    Σκόπει δή, ἦν δ' ἐγώ, εἰ ὀρθῶς ἐξαιρήσομεν ἢ οὔ.
5 φαμὲν δὲ δὴ ὅτι ὁ ἐπιεικὴς ἀνὴρ τῶι ἐπιεικεῖ, οὗπερ καὶ
ἑταῖρός ἐστιν, τὸ τεθνάναι οὐ δεινὸν ἡγήσεται.
    Φαμὲν γάρ.

Οὐκ ἄρα ὑπέρ γ' ἐκείνου ὡς δεινόν τι πεπονθότος ὀδύροιτ'
ἄν.

Οὐ δῆτα.

Ἀλλὰ μὴν καὶ τόδε λέγομεν, ὡς ὁ τοιοῦτος μάλιστα
αὐτὸς αὑτῶι αὐτάρκης πρὸς τὸ εὖ ζῆν καὶ διαφερόντως τῶν
ἄλλων ἥκιστα ἑτέρου προσδεῖται.   e

Ἀληθῆ, ἔφη.

Ἥκιστα ἄρ' αὑτῶι δεινὸν στερηθῆναι ὑέος ἢ ἀδελφοῦ ἢ
χρημάτων ἢ ἄλλου του τῶν τοιούτων.

Ἥκιστα μέντοι.   5

Ἥκιστ' ἄρα καὶ ὀδύρεσθαι, φέρειν δὲ ὡς πραιότατα, ὅταν
τις αὐτὸν τοιαύτη συμφορὰ καταλάβηι.

Πολύ γε.

Ὀρθῶς ἄρ' ἂν ἐξαιροῖμεν τοὺς θρήνους τῶν ὀνομαστῶν
ἀνδρῶν, γυναιξὶ δὲ ἀποδιδοῖμεν, καὶ οὐδὲ ταύταις σπου-   10
δαίαις, καὶ ὅσοι κακοὶ τῶν ἀνδρῶν, ἵνα ἡμῖν δυσχεραίνωσιν   388
ὅμοια τούτοις ποιεῖν οὓς δή φαμεν ἐπὶ φυλακῆι τῆς χώρας
τρέφειν.

Ὀρθῶς, ἔφη.

Πάλιν δὴ Ὁμήρου τε δεησόμεθα καὶ τῶν ἄλλων ποιητῶν   5
μὴ ποιεῖν Ἀχιλλέα θεᾶς παῖδα –

ἄλλοτ' ἐπὶ πλευρᾶς κατακείμενον, ἄλλοτε δ' αὖτε
ὕπτιον, ἄλλοτε δὲ πρηνῆ,

τοτὲ δ' ὀρθὸν ἀναστάντα πλάζοντ' ἀλύοντ' ἐπὶ
θῖν' ἁλὸς ἀτρυγέτοιο, μηδὲ ἀμφοτέραισιν χερσὶν   b
ἑλόντα κόνιν αἰθαλόεσσαν χευάμενον κὰκ κεφαλῆς,
μηδὲ ἄλλα κλαίοντά τε καὶ ὀδυρόμενον ὅσα καὶ οἷα ἐκεῖνος
ἐποίησε, μηδὲ Πρίαμον ἐγγὺς θεῶν γεγονότα λιτανεύοντά
τε καὶ –   5

κυλινδόμενον κατὰ κόπρον,
ἐξονομακλήδην ὀνομάζοντ' ἄνδρα ἕκαστον.

a9 πλάζοντ' m: πλωΐζοντ' m: πλώζοντ' m

πολὺ δ' ἔτι τούτων μᾶλλον δεησόμεθα μήτοι θεούς γε ποιεῖν
ὀδυρομένους καὶ λέγοντας –

c   ὤμοι ἐγὼ δειλή, μοι δυσαριστοτόκεια·

εἰ δ' οὖν θεούς, μήτοι τόν γε μέγιστον τῶν θεῶν τολμῆσαι
οὕτως ἀνομοίως μιμήσασθαι, ὥστε

       ὦ πόποι, φάναι, ἦ φίλον ἄνδρα διωκόμενον περὶ ἄστυ
5   ὀφθαλμοῖσιν ὁρῶμαι, ἐμὸν δ' ὀλοφύρεται ἦτορ·

καὶ –

       αἲ αἲ ἐγών, ὅ τέ μοι Σαρπηδόνα φίλτατον ἀνδρῶν
d   μοῖρ' ὑπὸ Πατρόκλοιο Μενοιτιάδαο δαμῆναι.

εἰ γάρ, ὦ φίλε Ἀδείμαντε, τὰ τοιαῦτα ἡμῖν οἱ νέοι σπουδῆι
ἀκούοιεν καὶ μὴ καταγελῶιεν ὡς ἀναξίως λεγομένων, σχολῆι
ἂν ἑαυτόν γέ τις ἄνθρωπον ὄντα ἀνάξιον ἡγήσαιτο τούτων
5 καὶ ἐπιπλήξειεν, εἰ καὶ ἐπίοι αὐτῶι τι τοιοῦτον ἢ λέγειν ἢ
ποιεῖν, ἀλλ' οὐδὲν αἰσχυνόμενος οὐδὲ καρτερῶν πολλοὺς ἐπὶ
σμικροῖσιν παθήμασιν θρήνους ἂν ἄιδοι καὶ ὀδυρμούς.

e   Ἀληθέστατα, ἔφη, λέγεις.

Δεῖ δέ γε οὔχ, ὡς ἄρτι ἡμῖν ὁ λόγος ἐσήμαινεν· ὧι
πειστέον, ἕως ἄν τις ἡμᾶς ἄλλωι καλλίονι πείσηι.

Οὐ γὰρ οὖν δεῖ.

5   Ἀλλὰ μὴν οὐδὲ φιλογέλωτάς γε δεῖ εἶναι. σχεδὸν γὰρ
ὅταν τις ἐφιῆι ἰσχυρῶι γέλωτι, ἰσχυρὰν καὶ μεταβολὴν ζητεῖ
τὸ τοιοῦτον.

Δοκεῖ μοι, ἔφη.

Οὔτε ἄρα ἀνθρώπους ἀξίους λόγου κρατουμένους ὑπὸ
389 γέλωτος ἄν τις ποιῆι, ἀποδεκτέον, πολὺ δὲ ἧττον, ἐὰν θεούς.

Πολὺ μέντοι, ἦ δ' ὅς.

Οὐκοῦν Ὁμήρου οὐδὲ τὰ τοιαῦτα ἀποδεξόμεθα περὶ
θεῶν –

5   ἄσβεστος δ' ἄρ' ἐνῶρτο γέλως μακάρεσσι θεοῖσιν,
       ὡς ἴδον Ἥφαιστον διὰ δώματα ποιπνύοντα

οὐκ ἀποδεκτέον κατὰ τὸν σὸν λόγον.

Εἰ σύ, ἔφη, βούλει ἐμὸν τιθέναι· οὐ γὰρ οὖν δὴ
ἀποδεκτέον.   b

Ἀλλὰ μὴν καὶ ἀλήθειάν γε περὶ πολλοῦ ποιητέον. εἰ
γὰρ ὀρθῶς ἐλέγομεν ἄρτι, καὶ τῶι ὄντι θεοῖσι μὲν ἄχρηστον
ψεῦδος, ἀνθρώποις δὲ χρήσιμον ὡς ἐν φαρμάκου εἴδει, δῆλον
ὅτι τό γε τοιοῦτον ἰατροῖς δοτέον, ἰδιώταις δὲ οὐχ ἁπτέον.   5
Δῆλον, ἔφη.

Τοῖς ἄρχουσιν δὴ τῆς πόλεως, εἴπερ τισὶν ἄλλοις, προσήκει ψεύδεσθαι ἢ πολεμίων ἢ πολιτῶν ἕνεκα ἐπ' ὠφελίαι τῆς
πόλεως, τοῖς δὲ ἄλλοις πᾶσιν οὐχ ἁπτέον τοῦ τοιούτου·
ἀλλὰ πρός γε δὴ τοὺς τοιούτους ἄρχοντας ἰδιώτηι ψεύσασθαι   c
ταὐτὸν καὶ μεῖζον ἁμάρτημα φήσομεν ἢ κάμνοντι πρὸς ἰατρὸν
ἢ ἀσκοῦντι πρὸς παιδοτρίβην περὶ τῶν τοῦ αὐτοῦ σώματος
παθημάτων μὴ τἀληθῆ λέγειν, ἢ πρὸς κυβερνήτην περὶ τῆς
νεώς τε καὶ τῶν ναυτῶν μὴ τὰ ὄντα λέγοντι ὅπως ἢ αὐτὸς   5
ἤ τις τῶν συνναυτῶν πράξεως ἔχει.

Ἀληθέστατα, ἔφη.

Ἂν ἄρ' ἄλλον τινὰ λαμβάνηι ψευδόμενον ἐν τῆι πόλει –   d

τῶν οἳ δημιοεργοὶ ἔασι,
μάντιν ἢ ἰητῆρα κακῶν ἢ τέκτονα δούρων,

κολάσει ὡς ἐπιτήδευμα εἰσάγοντα πόλεως ὥσπερ νεὼς
ἀνατρεπτικόν τε καὶ ὀλέθριον.   5

Ἐάνπερ, ἦ δ' ὅς, ἐπί γε λόγωι ἔργα τελῆται.

Τί δέ; σωφροσύνης ἄρα οὐ δεήσει ἡμῖν τοῖς νεανίαις;

Πῶς δ' οὔ;

Σωφροσύνης δὲ ὡς πλήθει οὐ τὰ τοιάδε μέγιστα, ἀρχόν-
των μὲν ὑπηκόους εἶναι, αὐτοὺς δὲ ἄρχοντας τῶν περὶ πότους   e
καὶ ἀφροδίσια καὶ περὶ ἐδωδὰς ἡδονῶν;

Ἔμοιγε δοκεῖ.

Τὰ δὴ τοιάδε φήσομεν οἶμαι καλῶς λέγεσθαι, οἷα καὶ
Ὁμήρωι Διομήδης λέγει –   5

τέττα, σιωπῆι ἧσο, ἐμῶι δ' ἐπιπείθεο μύθωι,

καὶ τὰ τούτων ἐχόμενα, τὰ –

ἴσαν μένεα πνείοντες Ἀχαιοί,
σιγῆι δειδιότες σημάντορας,

10 καὶ ὅσα ἄλλα τοιαῦτα.
Καλῶς.

Τί δέ; τὰ τοιάδε –

οἰνοβαρές, κυνὸς ὄμματ' ἔχων, κραδίην δ' ἐλάφοιο

390 καὶ τὰ τούτων ἑξῆς ἆρα καλῶς, καὶ ὅσα ἄλλα τις ἐν λόγωι
ἢ ἐν ποιήσει εἴρηκε νεανιεύματα ἰδιωτῶν εἰς ἄρχοντας;
Οὐ καλῶς.
Οὐ γὰρ οἶμαι εἴς γε σωφροσύνην νέοις ἐπιτήδεια ἀκούειν·
5 εἰ δέ τινα ἄλλην ἡδονὴν παρέχεται, θαυμαστὸν οὐδέν. ἢ
πῶς σοι φαίνεται;
Οὕτως, ἔφη.
Τί δέ; ποιεῖν ἄνδρα τὸν σοφώτατον λέγοντα ὡς δοκεῖ
αὐτῶι κάλλιστον εἶναι πάντων, ὅταν –

10   παρὰ πλεῖαι ὦσι τράπεζαι
b   σίτου καὶ κρειῶν, μέθυ δ' ἐκ κρητῆρος ἀφύσσων
οἰνοχόος φορέηισι καὶ ἐγχείηι δεπάεσσι,

δοκεῖ σοι ἐπιτήδειον εἶναι πρὸς ἐγκράτειαν ἑαυτοῦ ἀκούειν
νέωι; ἢ τὸ –

5   λιμῶι δ' οἴκτιστον θανέειν καὶ πότμον ἐπισπεῖν;

ἢ Δία, καθευδόντων τῶν ἄλλων θεῶν τε καὶ ἀνθρώπων,
ὡς, μόνος ἐγρηγορὼς ἃ ἐβουλεύσατο, τούτων πάντων ῥαιδίως
c ἐπιλανθανόμενον διὰ τὴν τῶν ἀφροδισίων ἐπιθυμίαν, καὶ
οὕτως ἐκπλαγέντα ἰδόντα τὴν Ἥραν, ὥστε μηδ' εἰς τὸ
δωμάτιον ἐθέλειν ἐλθεῖν, ἀλλ' αὐτοῦ βουλόμενον χαμαὶ
συγγίγνεσθαι, λέγοντα ὡς οὕτως ὑπὸ ἐπιθυμίας ἔχεται,
5 ὡς οὐδ' ὅτε τὸ πρῶτον ἐφοίτων πρὸς ἀλλήλους φίλους
λήθοντε τοκῆας· οὐδὲ Ἄρεώς τε καὶ Ἀφροδίτης ὑπὸ
Ἡφαίστου δεσμὸν δι' ἕτερα τοιαῦτα.
Οὐ μὰ τὸν Δία, ἦ δ' ὅς, οὔ μοι φαίνεται ἐπιτήδειον.

Άλλ' εἴ πού τινες, ἦν δ' ἐγώ, καρτερίαι πρὸς ἅπαντα d
καὶ λέγονται καὶ πράττονται ὑπὸ ἐλλογίμων ἀνδρῶν, θεατέον
τε καὶ ἀκουστέον, οἷον καὶ τὸ –

στῆθος δὲ πλήξας κραδίην ἠνίπαπε μύθωι·
τέτλαθι δή, κραδίη· καὶ κύντερον ἄλλο ποτ' ἔτλης.   5

Παντάπασι μὲν οὖν, ἔφη.
Οὐ μὲν δὴ δωροδόκους γε ἐατέον εἶναι τοὺς ἄνδρας οὐδὲ
φιλοχρημάτους.
Οὐδαμῶς.
Οὐδ' ἀιστέον αὐτοῖς ὅτι –   e

δῶρα θεοὺς πείθει, δῶρ' αἰδοίους βασιλῆας·

οὐδὲ τὸν τοῦ Ἀχιλλέως παιδαγωγὸν Φοίνικα ἐπαινετέον
ὡς μετρίως ἔλεγε συμβουλεύων αὐτῶι δῶρα μὲν λαβόντι   5
ἐπαμύνειν τοῖς Ἀχαιοῖς, ἄνευ δὲ δώρων μὴ ἀπαλλάττεσθαι
τῆς μήνιος. οὐδ' αὐτὸν τὸν Ἀχιλλέα ἀξιώσομεν οὐδ'
ὁμολογήσομεν οὕτω φιλοχρήματον εἶναι, ὥστε παρὰ τοῦ
Ἀγαμέμνονος δῶρα λαβεῖν, καὶ τιμὴν αὖ λαβόντα νεκροῦ
ἀπολύειν, ἄλλως δὲ μὴ 'θέλειν.   391
Οὔκουν δίκαιόν γε, ἔφη, ἐπαινεῖν τὰ τοιαῦτα.
Ὀκνῶ δέ γε, ἦν δ' ἐγώ, δι' Ὅμηρον λέγειν ὅτι οὐδ' ὅσιον
ταῦτά γε κατὰ Ἀχιλλέως φάναι καὶ ἄλλων λεγόντων
πείθεσθαι, καὶ αὖ ὡς πρὸς τὸν Ἀπόλλω εἶπεν –   5

ἔβλαψάς μ' ἑκάεργε, θεῶν ὀλοώτατε πάντων·
ἦ σ' ἂν τισαίμην, εἴ μοι δύναμίς γε παρείη·

καὶ ὡς πρὸς τὸν ποταμόν, θεὸν ὄντα, ἀπειθῶς εἶχεν καὶ   b
μάχεσθαι ἕτοιμος ἦν, καὶ αὖ τὰς τοῦ ἑτέρου ποταμοῦ Σπερ-
χειοῦ ἱερὰς τρίχας Πατρόκλωι ἥρωϊ, ἔφη, κόμην ὀπά-
σαιμι φέρεσθαι, νεκρῶι ὄντι, καὶ ὡς ἔδρασεν τοῦτο, οὐ
πειστέον· τάς τε αὖ Ἕκτορος ἕλξεις περὶ τὸ σῆμα τὸ Πα-   5
τρόκλου καὶ τὰς τῶν ζωγρηθέντων σφαγὰς εἰς τὴν πυράν,
σύμπαντα ταῦτα οὐ φήσομεν ἀληθῆ εἰρῆσθαι, οὐδ' ἐάσομεν
πείθεσθαι τοὺς ἡμετέρους ὡς Ἀχιλλεύς, θεᾶς ὢν παῖς καὶ   c

Πηλέως, σωφρονεστάτου τε καὶ τρίτου ἀπὸ Διός, καὶ ὑπὸ
τῶι σοφωτάτωι Χείρωνι τεθραμμένος, τοσαύτης ἦν ταραχῆς
πλέως, ὥστ' ἔχειν ἐν αὑτῶι νοσήματε δύο ἐναντίω ἀλλήλοιν,
5 ἀνελευθερίαν μετὰ φιλοχρηματίας καὶ αὖ ὑπερηφανίαν θεῶν
τε καὶ ἀνθρώπων.
Ὀρθῶς, ἔφη, λέγεις.
Μὴ τοίνυν, ἦν δ' ἐγώ, μηδὲ τάδε πειθώμεθα μηδ' ἐῶμεν
λέγειν, ὡς Θησεὺς Ποσειδῶνος ὑὸς Πειρίθους τε Διὸς
d ὥρμησαν οὕτως ἐπὶ δεινὰς ἁρπαγάς, μηδέ τιν' ἄλλον θεοῦ
παῖδά τε καὶ ἥρω τολμῆσαι ἂν δεινὰ καὶ ἀσεβῆ ἐργάσασθαι,
οἷα νῦν καταψεύδονται αὐτῶν· ἀλλὰ προσαναγκάζωμεν τοὺς
ποιητὰς ἢ μὴ τούτων αὐτὰ ἔργα φάναι ἢ τούτους μὴ εἶναι
5 θεῶν παῖδας, ἀμφότερα δὲ μὴ λέγειν, μηδὲ ἡμῖν ἐπιχειρεῖν
πείθειν τοὺς νέους ὡς οἱ θεοὶ κακὰ γεννῶσιν, καὶ ἥρωες
ἀνθρώπων οὐδὲν βελτίους· ὅπερ γὰρ ἐν τοῖς πρόσθεν ἐλέ-
e γομεν, οὔθ' ὅσια ταῦτα οὔτε ἀληθῆ· ἐπεδείξαμεν γάρ που
ὅτι ἐκ θεῶν κακὰ γίγνεσθαι ἀδύνατον.
Πῶς γὰρ οὔ;
Καὶ μὴν τοῖς γε ἀκούουσιν βλαβερά· πᾶς γὰρ ἑαυτῶι
5 συγγνώμην ἕξει κακῶι ὄντι, πεισθεὶς ὡς ἄρα τοιαῦτα πράτ-
τουσίν τε καὶ ἔπραττον καὶ –

οἱ θεῶν ἀγχίσποροι,
⟨οἳ⟩Ζηνὸς ἐγγύς, ὧν κατ' Ἰδαῖον πάγον
Διὸς πατρώιου βωμός ἐστ' ἐν αἰθέρι,

10 καὶ –

οὔ πώ σφιν ἐξίτηλον αἷμα δαιμόνων.

ὧν ἕνεκα παυστέον τοὺς τοιούτους μύθους, μὴ ἡμῖν πολλὴν
392 εὐχέρειαν ἐντίκτωσι τοῖς νέοις πονηρίας.
Κομιδῆι μὲν οὖν, ἔφη.
Τί οὖν, ἦν δ' ἐγώ, ἡμῖν ἔτι λοιπὸν εἶδος λόγων πέρι
ὁριζομένοις οἵους τε λεκτέον καὶ μή; περὶ γὰρ θεῶν ὡς δεῖ
5 λέγεσθαι εἴρηται, καὶ περὶ δαιμόνων τε καὶ ἡρώων καὶ τῶν
ἐν Ἅιδου.

Πάνυ μὲν οὖν.

Οὐκοῦν καὶ περὶ ἀνθρώπων τὸ λοιπὸν εἴη ἄν;

Δῆλα δή.

Ἀδύνατον δή, ὦ φίλε, ἡμῖν τοῦτό γε ἐν τῶι παρόντι 10
τάξαι.

Πῶς;

Ὅτι οἶμαι ἡμᾶς ἐρεῖν ὡς ἄρα καὶ ποιηταὶ καὶ λογοποιοὶ
κακῶς λέγουσιν περὶ ἀνθρώπων τὰ μέγιστα, ὅτι εἰσὶν ἄδικοι b
μὲν εὐδαίμονες πολλοί, δίκαιοι δὲ ἄθλιοι, καὶ ὡς λυσιτελεῖ τὸ ἀδικεῖν, ἐὰν λανθάνηι, ἡ δὲ δικαιοσύνη ἀλλότριον
μὲν ἀγαθόν, οἰκεία δὲ ζημία· καὶ τὰ μὲν τοιαῦτα ἀπερεῖν
λέγειν, τὰ δ᾽ ἐναντία τούτων προστάξειν ἄιδειν τε καὶ 5
μυθολογεῖν. ἢ οὐκ οἴει;

Εὖ μὲν οὖν, ἔφη, οἶδα.

Οὐκοῦν ἐὰν ὁμολογῆις ὀρθῶς με λέγειν, φήσω σε ὡμο-
λογηκέναι ἃ πάλαι ἐζητοῦμεν;

Ὀρθῶς, ἔφη, ὑπέλαβες.   10

Οὐκοῦν περί γε ἀνθρώπων ὅτι τοιούτους δεῖ λόγους c
λέγεσθαι, τότε διομολογησόμεθα, ὅταν εὕρωμεν οἷόν ἐστιν
δικαιοσύνη καὶ ὡς φύσει λυσιτελοῦν τῶι ἔχοντι, ἐάντε δοκῆι
ἐάντε μὴ τοιοῦτος εἶναι;

Ἀληθέστατα, ἔφη.   5

Τὰ μὲν δὴ λόγων πέρι ἐχέτω τέλος· τὸ δὲ λέξεως, ὡς
ἐγὼ οἶμαι, μετὰ τοῦτο σκεπτέον, καὶ ἡμῖν ἅ τε λεκτέον καὶ
ὡς λεκτέον παντελῶς ἐσκέψεται.

Καὶ ὁ Ἀδείμαντος, Τοῦτο, ἦ δ᾽ ὅς, οὐ μανθάνω ὅτι
λέγεις.   10

Ἀλλὰ μέντοι, ἦν δ᾽ ἐγώ, δεῖ γε· ἴσως οὖν τῆιδε μᾶλλον d
εἴσηι. ἆρ᾽ οὐ πάντα ὅσα ὑπὸ μυθολόγων ἢ ποιητῶν λέγεται
διήγησις οὖσα τυγχάνει ἢ γεγονότων ἢ ὄντων ἢ μελλόντων;

Τί γάρ, ἔφη, ἄλλο;

Ἀρ᾽ οὖν οὐχὶ ἤτοι ἁπλῆι διηγήσει ἢ διὰ μιμήσεως γιγνο- 5
μένηι ἢ δι᾽ ἀμφοτέρων περαίνουσιν;

b9 ἐζητοῦμεν c: ζητοῦμεν e

Καὶ τοῦτο, ἦ δ' ὅς, ἔτι δέομαι σαφέστερον μαθεῖν.

Γελοῖος, ἦν δ' ἐγώ, ἔοικα διδάσκαλος εἶναι καὶ ἀσαφής· ὥσπερ οὖν οἱ ἀδύνατοι λέγειν, οὐ κατὰ ὅλον ἀλλ' ἀπολαβὼν e μέρος τι πειράσομαί σοι ἐν τούτωι δηλῶσαι ὃ βούλομαι. καὶ μοι εἰπέ· ἐπίστασαι τῆς Ἰλιάδος τὰ πρῶτα, ἐν οἷς ὁ ποιητής φησι τὸν μὲν Χρύσην δεῖσθαι τοῦ Ἀγαμέμνονος ἀπολῦσαι τὴν θυγατέρα, τὸν δὲ χαλεπαίνειν, τὸν δέ, ἐπειδὴ 393 οὐκ ἐτύγχανεν, κατεύχεσθαι τῶν Ἀχαιῶν πρὸς τὸν θεόν; Ἔγωγε.

Οἶσθ' οὖν ὅτι μέχρι μὲν τούτων τῶν ἐπῶν –

καὶ ἐλίσσετο πάντας Ἀχαιούς,
5   Ἀτρείδα δὲ μάλιστα δύω, κοσμήτορε λαῶν

λέγει τε αὐτὸς ὁ ποιητὴς καὶ οὐδὲ ἐπιχειρεῖ ἡμῶν τὴν διά- νοιαν ἄλλοσε τρέπειν ὡς ἄλλος τις ὁ λέγων ἢ αὐτός· τὰ δὲ μετὰ ταῦτα ὥσπερ αὐτὸς ὢν ὁ Χρύσης λέγει καὶ πειρᾶται b ἡμᾶς ὅτι μάλιστα ποιῆσαι μὴ Ὅμηρον δοκεῖν εἶναι τὸν λέγοντα ἀλλὰ τὸν ἱερέα, πρεσβύτην ὄντα. καὶ τὴν ἄλλην δὴ πᾶσαν σχεδόν τι οὕτω πεποίηται διήγησιν περί τε τῶν ἐν Ἰλίωι καὶ περὶ τῶν ἐν Ἰθάκηι καὶ ὅληι Ὀδυσσείαι παθη- 5 μάτων.

Πάνυ μὲν οὖν, ἔφη.

Οὐκοῦν διήγησις μέν ἐστιν καὶ ὅταν τὰς ῥήσεις ἑκάστοτε λέγηι καὶ ὅταν τὰ μεταξὺ τῶν ῥήσεων;

Πῶς γὰρ οὔ;

c   Ἀλλ' ὅταν γέ τινα λέγηι ῥῆσιν ὥς τις ἄλλος ὤν, ἆρ' οὐ τότε ὁμοιοῦν αὐτὸν φήσομεν ὅτι μάλιστα τὴν αὑτοῦ λέξιν ἑκάστωι ὃν ἂν προείπηι ὡς ἐροῦντα;

Φήσομεν· τί γάρ;

5   Οὐκοῦν τό γε ὁμοιοῦν ἑαυτὸν ἄλλωι ἢ κατὰ φωνὴν ἢ κατὰ σχῆμα μιμεῖσθαί ἐστιν ἐκεῖνον ὧι ἄν τις ὁμοιοῖ;

Τί μήν;

Ἐν δὴ τῶι τοιούτωι, ὡς ἔοικεν, οὗτός τε καὶ οἱ ἄλλοι ποιηταὶ διὰ μιμήσεως τὴν διήγησιν ποιοῦνται.

10   Πάνυ μὲν οὖν.

Εἰ δέ γε μηδαμοῦ ἑαυτὸν ἀποκρύπτοιτο ὁ ποιητής, πᾶσα
ἂν αὐτῶι ἄνευ μιμήσεως ἡ ποίησίς τε καὶ διήγησις γεγονυῖα **d**
εἴη. ἵνα δὲ μὴ εἴπηις ὅτι οὐκ αὖ μανθάνεις, ὅπως ἂν τοῦτο
γένοιτο ἐγὼ φράσω. εἰ γὰρ Ὅμηρος εἰπὼν ὅτι ἦλθεν
ὁ Χρύσης τῆς τε θυγατρὸς λύτρα φέρων καὶ ἱκέτης τῶν
Ἀχαιῶν, μάλιστα δὲ τῶν βασιλέων, μετὰ τοῦτο μὴ ὡς 5
Χρύσης γενόμενος ἔλεγεν ἀλλ' ἔτι ὡς Ὅμηρος, οἶσθ' ὅτι
οὐκ ἂν μίμησις ἦν ἀλλὰ ἁπλῆ διήγησις. εἶχε δ' ἂν ὧδε
πως – φράσω δὲ ἄνευ μέτρου· οὐ γάρ εἰμι ποιητικός – Ἐλθὼν
ὁ ἱερεὺς ηὔχετο ἐκείνοις μὲν τοὺς θεοὺς δοῦναι ἑλόντας τὴν **e**
Τροίαν αὐτοὺς σωθῆναι, τὴν δὲ θυγατέρα οἱ λῦσαι δεξα-
μένους ἄποινα καὶ τὸν θεὸν αἰδεσθέντας. ταῦτα δὲ εἰπόντος
αὐτοῦ οἱ μὲν ἄλλοι ἐσέβοντο καὶ συνῄνουν, ὁ δὲ Ἀγαμέμνων
ἠγρίαινεν ἐντελλόμενος νῦν τε ἀπιέναι καὶ αὖθις μὴ ἐλθεῖν, 5
μὴ αὐτῶι τό τε σκῆπτρον καὶ τὰ τοῦ θεοῦ στέμματα οὐκ
ἐπαρκέσοι· πρὶν δὲ λυθῆναι αὐτοῦ τὴν θυγατέρα, ἐν Ἄργει
ἔφη γηράσειν μετὰ οὗ· ἀπιέναι δ' ἐκέλευεν καὶ μὴ ἐρεθίζειν,
ἵνα σῶς οἴκαδε ἔλθοι. ὁ δὲ πρεσβύτης ἀκούσας ἔδεισέν τε **394**
καὶ ἀπήιει σιγῆι, ἀποχωρήσας δὲ ἐκ τοῦ στρατοπέδου πολλὰ
τῶι Ἀπόλλωνι ηὔχετο, τάς τε ἐπωνυμίας τοῦ θεοῦ ἀνακαλῶν
καὶ ὑπομιμνήισκων καὶ ἀπαιτῶν, εἴ τι πώποτε ἢ ἐν ναῶν
οἰκοδομήσεσιν ἢ ἐν ἱερῶν θυσίαις κεχαρισμένον δωρήσαιτο· 5
ὧν δὴ χάριν κατηύχετο τεῖσαι τοὺς Ἀχαιοὺς τὰ ἃ δάκρυα
τοῖς ἐκείνου βέλεσιν. οὕτως, ἦν δ' ἐγώ, ὦ ἑταῖρε, ἄνευ
μιμήσεως ἁπλῆ διήγησις γίγνεται. **b**

Μανθάνω, ἔφη.

Μάνθανε τοίνυν, ἦν δ' ἐγώ, ὅτι ταύτης αὖ ἐναντία γίγνεται, ὅταν τις τὰ τοῦ ποιητοῦ τὰ μεταξὺ τῶν ῥήσεων
ἐξαιρῶν τὰ ἀμοιβαῖα καταλείπηι. 5

Καὶ τοῦτο, ἔφη, μανθάνω, ὅτι ἔστιν τὸ περὶ τὰς τραγωιδίας
τοιοῦτον.

Ὀρθότατα, ἔφην, ὑπέλαβες, καὶ οἶμαί σοι ἤδη δηλοῦν
ὃ ἔμπροσθεν οὐχ οἷός τ' ἦ, ὅτι τῆς ποιήσεώς τε καὶ μυθο-
λογίας ἡ μὲν διὰ μιμήσεως ὅλη ἐστίν, ὥσπερ σὺ λέγεις, **c**
τραγωιδία τε καὶ κωμωιδία, ἡ δὲ δι' ἀπαγγελίας αὐτοῦ τοῦ

ποιητοῦ – εὕροις δ' ἂν αὐτὴν μάλιστά που ἐν διθυράμβοις –
ἢ δ' αὖ δι' ἀμφοτέρων ἔν τε τῆι τῶν ἐπῶν ποιήσει, πολλαχοῦ
5 δὲ καὶ ἄλλοθι, εἴ μοι μανθάνεις.

Ἀλλὰ συνίημι, ἔφη, ὃ τότε ἐβούλου λέγειν.

Καὶ τὸ πρὸ τούτου δὴ ἀναμνήσθητι, ὅτι ἔφαμεν ἃ μὲν
λεκτέον ἤδη εἰρῆσθαι, ὡς δὲ λεκτέον ἔτι σκεπτέον εἶναι.

Ἀλλὰ μέμνημαι.

d   Τοῦτο τοίνυν αὐτὸ ἦν ὃ ἔλεγον, ὅτι χρείη διομολογήσασθαι πότερον ἐάσομεν τοὺς ποιητὰς μιμουμένους ἡμῖν
τὰς διηγήσεις ποιεῖσθαι ἢ τὰ μὲν μιμουμένους, τὰ δὲ μή,
καὶ ὁποῖα ἑκάτερα, ἢ οὐδὲ μιμεῖσθαι.

5   Μαντεύομαι, ἔφη, σκοπεῖσθαί σε εἴτε παραδεξόμεθα
τραγωιδίαν τε καὶ κωμωιδίαν εἰς τὴν πόλιν, εἴτε καὶ οὔ.

Ἴσως, ἦν δ' ἐγώ, ἴσως δὲ καὶ πλείω ἔτι τούτων· οὐ γὰρ
δὴ ἔγωγέ πω οἶδα, ἀλλ' ὅπηι ἂν ὁ λόγος ὥσπερ πνεῦμα
φέρηι, ταύτηι ἰτέον.

10 Καὶ καλῶς γ', ἔφη, λέγεις.

e   Τόδε τοίνυν, ὦ Ἀδείμαντε, ἄθρει, πότερον μιμητικοὺς
ἡμῖν δεῖ εἶναι τοὺς φύλακας ἢ οὔ· ἢ καὶ τοῦτο τοῖς ἔμπροσθεν ἕπεται, ὅτι εἷς ἕκαστος ἓν μὲν ἂν ἐπιτήδευμα
καλῶς ἐπιτηδεύοι, πολλὰ δ' οὔ, ἀλλ' εἰ τοῦτο ἐπιχειροῖ,
5 πολλῶν ἐφαπτόμενος πάντων ἀποτυγχάνοι ἄν, ὥστ' εἶναί
που ἐλλόγιμος;

Τί δ' οὐ μέλλει;

Οὐκοῦν καὶ περὶ μιμήσεως ὁ αὐτὸς λόγος, ὅτι πολλὰ ὁ
αὐτὸς μιμεῖσθαι εὖ ὥσπερ ἓν οὐ δυνατός;

10 Οὐ γὰρ οὖν.

395 Σχολῆι ἄρα ἐπιτηδεύσει γέ τι ἅμα τῶν ἀξίων λόγου
ἐπιτηδευμάτων καὶ πολλὰ μιμήσεται καὶ ἔσται μιμητικός,
ἐπεί που οὐδὲ τὰ δοκοῦντα ἐγγὺς ἀλλήλων εἶναι δύο μιμήματα δύνανται οἱ αὐτοὶ ἅμα εὖ μιμεῖσθαι, οἷον κωμωιδίαν
5 καὶ τραγωιδίαν ποιοῦντες. ἢ οὐ μιμήματε ἄρτι τούτω
ἐκάλεις;

Ἔγωγε· καὶ ἀληθῆ γε λέγεις, ὅτι οὐ δύνανται οἱ αὐτοί.

Οὐδὲ μὴν ῥαψωιδοί γε καὶ ὑποκριταὶ ἅμα.

Ἀληθῆ.

Ἀλλ' οὐδέ τοι ὑποκριταὶ κωμωδοῖς τε καὶ τραγωδοῖς οἱ 10
αὐτοί· πάντα δὲ ταῦτα μιμήματα. ἢ οὔ;   b

Μιμήματα.

Καὶ ἔτι γε τούτων, ὦ Ἀδείμαντε, φαίνεταί μοι εἰς
σμικρότερα κατακεκερματίσθαι ἡ τοῦ ἀνθρώπου φύσις, ὥστε
ἀδύνατος εἶναι πολλὰ καλῶς μιμεῖσθαι ἢ αὐτὰ ἐκεῖνα πράττειν 5
ὧν δὴ καὶ τὰ μιμήματά ἐστιν ἀφομοιώματα.

Ἀληθέστατα, ἦ δ' ὅς.

Εἰ ἄρα τὸν πρῶτον λόγον διασώσομεν, τοὺς φύλακας
ἡμῖν τῶν ἄλλων πασῶν δημιουργιῶν ἀφειμένους δεῖν εἶναι
δημιουργοὺς ἐλευθερίας τῆς πόλεως πάνυ ἀκριβεῖς καὶ μηδὲν c
ἄλλο ἐπιτηδεύειν ὅτι μὴ εἰς τοῦτο φέρει, οὐδὲν δὴ δέοι ἂν
αὐτοὺς ἄλλο πράττειν οὐδὲ μιμεῖσθαι· ἐὰν δὲ μιμῶνται,
μιμεῖσθαι τὰ τούτοις προσήκοντα εὐθὺς ἐκ παίδων, ἀνδρείους,
σώφρονας, ὁσίους, ἐλευθέρους, καὶ τὰ τοιαῦτα πάντα, τὰ δὲ 5
ἀνελεύθερα μήτε ποιεῖν μήτε δεινοὺς εἶναι μιμήσασθαι, μηδὲ
ἄλλο μηδὲν τῶν αἰσχρῶν, ἵνα μὴ ἐκ τῆς μιμήσεως τοῦ εἶναι
ἀπολαύσωσιν. ἢ οὐκ ᾔσθησαι ὅτι αἱ μιμήσεις, ἐὰν ἐκ νέων d
πόρρω διατελέσωσιν, εἰς ἔθη τε καὶ φύσιν καθίστανται καὶ
κατὰ σῶμα καὶ φωνὰς καὶ κατὰ τὴν διάνοιαν;

Καὶ μάλα, ἦ δ' ὅς.

Οὐ δὴ ἐπιτρέψομεν, ἦν δ' ἐγώ, ὧν φαμὲν κήδεσθαι καὶ 5
δεῖν αὐτοὺς ἄνδρας ἀγαθοὺς γενέσθαι, γυναῖκα μιμεῖσθαι
ἄνδρας ὄντας, ἢ νέαν ἢ πρεσβυτέραν, ἢ ἀνδρὶ λοιδορουμένην
ἢ πρὸς θεοὺς ἐρίζουσάν τε καὶ μεγαλαυχουμένην, οἰομένην
εὐδαίμονα εἶναι, ἢ ἐν συμφοραῖς τε καὶ πένθεσιν καὶ θρήνοις e
ἐχομένην· κάμνουσαν δὲ ἢ ἐρῶσαν ἢ ὠδίνουσαν, πολλοῦ καὶ
δεήσομεν.

Παντάπασι μὲν οὖν, ἦ δ' ὅς.

Οὐδέ γε δούλας τε καὶ δούλους πράττοντας ὅσα δούλων. 5

Οὐδὲ τοῦτο.

Οὐδέ γε ἄνδρας κακούς, ὡς ἔοικεν, δειλούς τε καὶ τὰ
ἐναντία πράττοντας ὧν νυνδὴ εἴπομεν, κακηγοροῦντάς τε καὶ
κωμωδοῦντας ἀλλήλους καὶ αἰσχρολογοῦντας, μεθύοντας ἢ

396 καὶ νήφοντας, ἢ καὶ ἄλλα ὅσα οἱ τοιοῦτοι καὶ ἐν λόγοις καὶ
ἐν ἔργοις ἁμαρτάνουσιν εἰς αὑτούς τε καὶ εἰς ἄλλους, οἶμαι
δὲ οὐδὲ μαινομένοις ἐθιστέον ἀφομοιοῦν αὑτοὺς ἐν λόγοις
οὐδὲ ἐν ἔργοις· γνωστέον μὲν γὰρ καὶ μαινομένους καὶ
5 πονηροὺς ἄνδρας τε καὶ γυναῖκας, ποιητέον δὲ οὐδὲν τούτων
οὐδὲ μιμητέον.

Ἀληθέστατα, ἔφη.

Τί δέ; ἦν δ᾽ ἐγώ· χαλκεύοντας ἤ τι ἄλλο δημιουργοῦντας,
b ἢ ἐλαύνοντας τριήρεις ἢ κελεύοντας τούτοις, ἤ τι ἄλλο τῶν
περὶ ταῦτα μιμητέον;

Καὶ πῶς; ἔφη, οἷς γε οὐδὲ προσέχειν τὸν νοῦν τούτων
οὐδενὶ ἐξέσται;

5 Τί δέ; ἵππους χρεμετίζοντας καὶ ταύρους μυκωμένους καὶ
ποταμοὺς ψοφοῦντας καὶ θάλατταν κτυποῦσαν καὶ βροντὰς
καὶ πάντα αὖ τὰ τοιαῦτα ἦ μιμήσονται;

Ἀλλ᾽ ἀπείρηται αὐτοῖς, ἔφη, μήτε μαίνεσθαι μήτε μαινομένοις ἀφομοιοῦσθαι.

10 Εἰ ἄρα, ἦν δ᾽ ἐγώ, μανθάνω ἃ σὺ λέγεις, ἔστιν τι εἶδος
λέξεώς τε καὶ διηγήσεως ἐν ὧι ἂν διηγοῖτο ὁ τῶι ὄντι καλὸς
c κἀγαθός, ὁπότε τι δέοι αὐτὸν λέγειν, καὶ ἕτερον αὖ ἀνόμοιον
τούτωι εἶδος, οὗ ἂν ἔχοιτο ἀεὶ καὶ ἐν ὧι διηγοῖτο ὁ ἐναντίως
ἐκείνωι φύς τε καὶ τραφείς.

Ποῖα δή, ἔφη, ταῦτα;

5 Ὁ μέν μοι δοκεῖ, ἦν δ᾽ ἐγώ, μέτριος ἀνήρ, ἐπειδὰν ἀφίκηται ἐν τῆι διηγήσει ἐπὶ λέξιν τινὰ ἢ πρᾶξιν ἀνδρὸς ἀγαθοῦ,
ἐθελήσειν ὡς αὐτὸς ὢν ἐκεῖνος ἀπαγγέλλειν καὶ οὐκ αἰσχυνεῖσθαι ἐπὶ τῆι τοιαύτηι μιμήσει, μάλιστα μὲν μιμούμενος
d τὸν ἀγαθὸν ἀσφαλῶς τε καὶ ἐμφρόνως πράττοντα, ἐλάττω δὲ
καὶ ἧττον ἢ ὑπὸ νόσων ἢ ὑπὸ ἐρώτων ἐσφαλμένον ἢ καὶ ὑπὸ
μέθης ἤ τινος ἄλλης συμφορᾶς· ὅταν δὲ γίγνηται κατά τινα
ἑαυτοῦ ἀνάξιον, οὐκ ἐθελήσειν σπουδῆι ἀπεικάζειν ἑαυτὸν τῶι
5 χείρονι, εἰ μὴ ἄρα κατὰ βραχύ, ὅταν τι χρηστὸν ποιῆι, ἀλλ᾽
αἰσχυνεῖσθαι, ἅμα μὲν ἀγύμναστος ὢν τοῦ μιμεῖσθαι τοὺς
τοιούτους, ἅμα δὲ καὶ δυσχεραίνων αὑτὸν ἐκμάττειν τε καὶ

ἐνιστάναι εἰς τοὺς τῶν κακιόνων τύπους, ἀτιμάζων τῆι διανοίαι, e
ὅτι μὴ παιδιᾶς χάριν.

Εἰκός, ἔφη.

Οὐκοῦν διηγήσει χρήσεται οἵαι ἡμεῖς ὀλίγον πρότερον
διήλθομεν περὶ τὰ τοῦ Ὁμήρου ἔπη, καὶ ἔσται αὐτοῦ ἡ λέξις 5
μετέχουσα μὲν ἀμφοτέρων, μιμήσεώς τε καὶ τῆς ἄλλης διηγήσεως, σμικρὸν δέ τι μέρος ἐν πολλῶι λόγωι τῆς μιμήσεως; ἢ
οὐδὲν λέγω;

Καὶ μάλα, ἔφη, οἷόν γε ἀνάγκη τὸν τύπον εἶναι τοῦ
τοιούτου ῥήτορος.   10

Οὐκοῦν, ἦν δ᾽ ἐγώ, ὁ μὴ τοιοῦτος αὖ, ὅσωι ἂν φαυλότερος 397
ἦι, πάντα τε μᾶλλον διηγήσεται καὶ οὐδὲν ἑαυτοῦ ἀνάξιον
οἰήσεται εἶναι, ὥστε πάντα ἐπιχειρήσει μιμεῖσθαι σπουδῆι τε
καὶ ἐναντίον πολλῶν, καὶ ἃ νυνδὴ ἐλέγομεν, βροντάς τε καὶ
ψόφους ἀνέμων τε καὶ χαλαζῶν καὶ ἀξόνων τε καὶ τροχιλιῶν, 5
καὶ σαλπίγγων καὶ αὐλῶν καὶ συρίγγων καὶ πάντων ὀργάνων
φωνάς, καὶ ἔτι κυνῶν καὶ προβάτων καὶ ὀρνέων φθόγγους·
καὶ ἔσται δὴ ἡ τούτου λέξις ἅπασα διὰ μιμήσεως φωναῖς τε b
καὶ σχήμασιν, ἢ σμικρόν τι διηγήσεως ἔχουσα;

Ἀνάγκη, ἔφη, καὶ τοῦτο.

Ταῦτα τοίνυν, ἦν δ᾽ ἐγώ, ἔλεγον τὰ δύο εἴδη τῆς λέξεως.

Καὶ γὰρ ἔστιν, ἔφη.   5

Οὐκοῦν αὐτοῖν τὸ μὲν σμικρὰς τὰς μεταβολὰς ἔχει, καὶ
ἐάν τις ἀποδιδῶι πρέπουσαν ἁρμονίαν καὶ ῥυθμὸν τῆι λέξει,
ὀλίγου πρὸς τὴν αὐτὴν γίγνεται λέγειν τῶι ὀρθῶς λέγοντι καὶ
ἐν μιᾶι ἁρμονίαι – σμικραὶ γὰρ αἱ μεταβολαί – καὶ δὴ καὶ ἐν
ῥυθμῶι ὡσαύτως παραπλησίωι τινί;   c

Κομιδῆι μὲν οὖν, ἔφη, οὕτως ἔχει.

Τί δὲ τὸ τοῦ ἑτέρου εἶδος; οὐ τῶν ἐναντίων δεῖται,
πασῶν μὲν ἁρμονιῶν, πάντων δὲ ῥυθμῶν, εἰ μέλλει αὖ
οἰκείως λέγεσθαι, διὰ τὸ παντοδαπὰς μορφὰς τῶν μεταβολῶν 5
ἔχειν;

Καὶ σφόδρα γε οὕτως ἔχει.

Ἆρ᾽ οὖν πάντες οἱ ποιηταὶ καὶ οἵ τι λέγοντες ἢ τῶι ἑτέρωι

τούτων ἐπιτυγχάνουσιν τύπωι τῆς λέξεως ἢ τῶι ἑτέρωι ἢ ἐξ
10 ἀμφοτέρων τινὶ συγκεραννύντες;
Ἀνάγκη, ἔφη.

d Τί οὖν ποιήσομεν; ἦν δ' ἐγώ· πότερον εἰς τὴν πόλιν
πάντας τούτους παραδεξόμεθα ἢ τῶν ἀκράτων τὸν ἕτερον ἢ
τὸν κεκραμένον;
Ἐὰν ἡ ἐμή, ἔφη, νικᾶι, τὸν τοῦ ἐπιεικοῦς μιμητὴν
5 ἄκρατον.
Ἀλλὰ μήν, ὦ Ἀδείμαντε, ἡδύς γε καὶ ὁ κεκραμένος,
πολὺ δὲ ἥδιστος παισί τε καὶ παιδαγωγοῖς ὁ ἐναντίος οὗ σὺ
αἱρῆι καὶ τῶι πλείστωι ὄχλωι.
Ἥδιστος γάρ.

10 Ἀλλ' ἴσως, ἦν δ' ἐγώ, οὐκ ἂν αὐτὸν ἁρμόττειν φαίης τῆι
e ἡμετέραι πολιτείαι, ὅτι οὐκ ἔστιν διπλοῦς ἀνὴρ παρ' ἡμῖν οὐδὲ
πολλαπλοῦς, ἐπειδὴ ἕκαστος ἓν πράττει.
Οὐ γὰρ οὖν ἁρμόττει.

Οὐκοῦν διὰ ταῦτα ἐν μόνηι τῆι τοιαύτηι πόλει τόν τε
5 σκυτοτόμον σκυτοτόμον εὑρήσομεν καὶ οὐ κυβερνήτην πρὸς
τῆι σκυτοτομίαι, καὶ τὸν γεωργὸν γεωργὸν καὶ οὐ δικαστὴν
πρὸς τῆι γεωργίαι, καὶ τὸν πολεμικὸν πολεμικὸν καὶ οὐ
χρηματιστὴν πρὸς τῆι πολεμικῆι, καὶ πάντας οὕτω;
Ἀληθῆ, ἔφη.

398 Ἄνδρα δή, ὡς ἔοικε, δυνάμενον ὑπὸ σοφίας παντοδαπὸν
γίγνεσθαι καὶ μιμεῖσθαι πάντα χρήματα, εἰ ἡμῖν ἀφίκοιτο
εἰς τὴν πόλιν αὐτός τε καὶ τὰ ποιήματα βουλόμενος ἐπιδείξασθαι, προσκυνοῖμεν ἂν αὐτὸν ὡς ἱερὸν καὶ θαυμαστὸν καὶ
5 ἡδύν, εἴποιμεν δ' ἂν ὅτι οὐκ ἔστιν τοιοῦτος ἀνὴρ ἐν τῆι πόλει
παρ' ἡμῖν οὔτε θέμις ἐγγενέσθαι, ἀποπέμποιμέν τε εἰς ἄλλην
πόλιν μύρον κατὰ τῆς κεφαλῆς καταχέαντες καὶ ἐρίωι στέψαντες, αὐτοὶ δ' ἂν τῶι αὐστηροτέρωι καὶ ἀηδεστέρωι ποιητῆι
b χρώιμεθα καὶ μυθολόγωι ὠφελίας ἕνεκα, ὃς ἡμῖν τὴν
τοῦ ἐπιεικοῦς λέξιν μιμοῖτο καὶ τὰ λεγόμενα λέγοι ἐν ἐκείνοις
τοῖς τύποις οἷς κατ' ἀρχὰς ἐνομοθετησάμεθα, ὅτε τοὺς
στρατιώτας ἐπεχειροῦμεν παιδεύειν.

Καὶ μάλ', ἔφη, οὕτως ἂν ποιοῖμεν, εἰ ἐφ' ἡμῖν εἴη.   5
Νῦν δή, εἶπον ἐγώ, ὦ φίλε, κινδυνεύει ἡμῖν τῆς μουσικῆς
τὸ περὶ λόγους τε καὶ μύθους παντελῶς διαπεπεράνθαι· ἅ τε
γὰρ λεκτέον καὶ ὡς λεκτέον εἴρηται.
Καὶ αὐτῶι μοι δοκεῖ, ἔφη.

I

Καὶ μήν, ἦν δ' ἐγώ, πολλὰ μὲν καὶ ἄλλα περὶ αὐτῆς 595
ἐννοῶ, ὡς παντὸς ἄρα μᾶλλον ὀρθῶς ὠικίζομεν τὴν πόλιν,
οὐχ ἥκιστα δὲ ἐνθυμηθεὶς περὶ ποιήσεως λέγω.
Τὸ ποῖον; ἔφη.
Τὸ μηδαμῆι παραδέχεσθαι αὐτῆς ὅση μιμητική· παντὸς 5
γὰρ μᾶλλον οὐ παραδεκτέα νῦν καὶ ἐναργέστερον, ὡς ἐμοὶ
δοκεῖ, φαίνεται, ἐπειδὴ χωρὶς ἕκαστα διήιρηται τὰ τῆς ψυχῆς
εἴδη.   b
Πῶς λέγεις;
Ὡς μὲν πρὸς ὑμᾶς εἰρῆσθαι – οὐ γάρ μου κατερεῖτε πρὸς
τοὺς τῆς τραγωιδίας ποιητὰς καὶ τοὺς ἄλλους ἅπαντας τοὺς
μιμητικούς – λώβη ἔοικεν εἶναι πάντα τὰ τοιαῦτα τῆς τῶν 5
ἀκουόντων διανοίας, ὅσοι μὴ ἔχουσι φάρμακον τὸ εἰδέναι
αὐτὰ οἷα τυγχάνει ὄντα.
Πῆι δή, ἔφη, διανοούμενος λέγεις;
Ῥητέον, ἦν δ' ἐγώ· καίτοι φίλια γέ τίς με καὶ αἰδὼς ἐκ
παιδὸς ἔχουσα περὶ Ὁμήρου ἀποκωλύει λέγειν. ἔοικε μὲν 10
γὰρ τῶν καλῶν ἁπάντων τούτων τῶν τραγικῶν πρῶτος διδά- c
σκαλός τε καὶ ἡγεμὼν γενέσθαι. ἀλλ' οὐ γὰρ πρό γε τῆς
ἀληθείας τιμητέος ἀνήρ, ἀλλ', ὃ λέγω, ῥητέον.
Πάνυ μὲν οὖν, ἔφη.
Ἄκουε δή, μᾶλλον δὲ ἀποκρίνου.   5
Ἐρώτα.
Μίμησιν ὅλως ἔχοις ἄν μοι εἰπεῖν ὅτι ποτ' ἐστίν; οὐδὲ
γάρ τοι αὐτὸς πάνυ τι συννοῶ τί βούλεται εἶναι.

Ἦ που ἄρ', ἔφη, ἐγὼ συννοήσω.

10 Οὐδέν γε, ἦν δ' ἐγώ, ἄτοπον, ἐπεὶ πολλά τοι ὀξύτερον
596 βλεπόντων ἀμβλύτερον ὁρῶντες πρότεροι εἶδον.

Ἔστιν, ἔφη, οὕτως· ἀλλὰ σοῦ παρόντος οὐδ' ἂν προθυμη-
θῆναι οἷός τε εἴην εἰπεῖν, εἴ τί μοι καταφαίνεται, ἀλλ'
αὐτὸς ὅρα.

5 Βούλει οὖν ἐνθένδε ἀρξώμεθα ἐπισκοποῦντες, ἐκ τῆς
εἰωθυίας μεθόδου; εἶδος γάρ πού τι ἓν ἕκαστον εἰώθαμεν
τίθεσθαι περὶ ἕκαστα τὰ πολλά, οἷς ταὐτὸν ὄνομα ἐπιφέρομεν.
ἢ οὐ μανθάνεις;

Μανθάνω.

10 Θῶμεν δὴ καὶ νῦν ὅτι βούλει τῶν πολλῶν. οἷον, εἰ
b 'θέλεις, πολλαί πού εἰσι κλῖναι καὶ τράπεζαι.

Πῶς δ' οὔ;

Ἀλλὰ ἰδέαι γέ που περὶ ταῦτα τὰ σκεύη δύο, μία μὲν
κλίνης, μία δὲ τραπέζης.

5 Ναί.

Οὐκοῦν καὶ εἰώθαμεν λέγειν ὅτι ὁ δημιουργὸς ἑκατέρου
τοῦ σκεύους πρὸς τὴν ἰδέαν βλέπων οὕτω ποιεῖ ὁ μὲν τὰς
κλίνας, ὁ δὲ τὰς τραπέζας, αἷς ἡμεῖς χρώμεθα, καὶ τἆλλα
κατὰ ταὐτά; οὐ γάρ που τήν γε ἰδέαν αὐτὴν δημιουργεῖ
10 οὐδεὶς τῶν δημιουργῶν· πῶς γάρ;

Οὐδαμῶς.

Ἀλλ' ὅρα δὴ καὶ τόνδε τίνα καλεῖς τὸν δημιουργόν.

c Τὸν ποῖον;

Ὃς πάντα ποιεῖ, ὅσαπερ εἷς ἕκαστος τῶν χειροτεχνῶν.

Δεινόν τινα λέγεις καὶ θαυμαστὸν ἄνδρα.

Οὔπω γε, ἀλλὰ τάχα μᾶλλον φήσεις. ὁ αὐτὸς γὰρ οὗτος
5 χειροτέχνης οὐ μόνον πάντα οἷός τε σκεύη ποιῆσαι, ἀλλὰ
καὶ τὰ ἐκ τῆς γῆς φυόμενα ἅπαντα ποιεῖ καὶ ζῷα πάντα
ἐργάζεται, τά τε ἄλλα καὶ ἑαυτόν, καὶ πρὸς τούτοις γῆν καὶ
οὐρανὸν καὶ θεοὺς καὶ πάντα τὰ ἐν οὐρανῶι καὶ τὰ ἐν Ἅιδου
ὑπὸ γῆς ἅπαντα ἐργάζεται.

d Πάνυ θαυμαστόν, ἔφη, λέγεις σοφιστήν.

Ἀπιστεῖς; ἦν δ' ἐγώ. καί μοι εἰπέ, τὸ παράπαν οὐκ ἂν σοι δοκεῖ εἶναι τοιοῦτος δημιουργός, ἤ τινὶ μὲν τρόπωι γενέσθαι ἂν τούτων ἁπάντων ποιητής, τινὶ δὲ οὐκ ἄν; ἢ οὐκ αἰσθάνηι ὅτι κἂν αὐτὸς οἷός τ' εἴης πάντα ταῦτα ποιῆσαι 5 τρόπωι γέ τινι;

Καὶ τίς, ἔφη, ὁ τρόπος οὗτος;

Οὐ χαλεπός, ἦν δ' ἐγώ, ἀλλὰ πολλαχῆι καὶ ταχὺ δημιουργούμενος, τάχιστα δέ που, εἰ 'θέλεις λαβὼν κάτοπτρον περιφέρειν πανταχῆι· ταχὺ μὲν ἥλιον ποιήσεις καὶ τὰ ἐν τῶι e οὐρανῶι, ταχὺ δὲ γῆν, ταχὺ δὲ σαυτόν τε καὶ τἆλλα ζῶια καὶ σκεύη καὶ φυτὰ καὶ πάντα ὅσα νυνδὴ ἐλέγετο.

Ναί, ἔφη, φαινόμενα, οὐ μέντοι ὄντα γέ που τῆι ἀληθείαι.

Καλῶς, ἦν δ' ἐγώ, καὶ εἰς δέον ἔρχηι τῶι λόγωι. τῶν 5 τοιούτων γὰρ οἶμαι δημιουργῶν καὶ ὁ ζωγράφος ἐστίν. ἤ γάρ;

Πῶς γὰρ οὔ;

Ἀλλὰ φήσεις οὐκ ἀληθῆ οἶμαι αὐτὸν ποιεῖν ἃ ποιεῖ. καίτοι τρόπωι γέ τινι καὶ ὁ ζωγράφος κλίνην ποιεῖ· ἢ οὔ; 10

Ναί, ἔφη, φαινομένην γε καὶ οὗτος.

Τί δὲ ὁ κλινοποιός; οὐκ ἄρτι μέντοι ἔλεγες ὅτι οὐ τὸ 597 εἶδος ποιεῖ, ὃ δή φαμεν εἶναι ὃ ἔστι κλίνη, ἀλλὰ κλίνην τινά;

Ἔλεγον γάρ.

Οὐκοῦν εἰ μὴ ὃ ἔστιν ποιεῖ, οὐκ ἂν τὸ ὂν ποιοῖ, ἀλλά τι τοιοῦτον οἷον τὸ ὄν, ὂν δὲ οὔ· τελέως δὲ εἶναι ὂν τὸ τοῦ 5 κλινουργοῦ ἔργον ἢ ἄλλου τινὸς χειροτέχνου εἴ τις φαίη, κινδυνεύει οὐκ ἂν ἀληθῆ λέγειν;

Οὔκουν, ἔφη, ὥς γ' ἂν δόξειεν τοῖς περὶ τοὺς τοιούσδε λόγους διατρίβουσιν.

Μηδὲν ἄρα θαυμάζωμεν εἰ καὶ τοῦτο ἀμυδρόν τι τυγχάνει 10 ὂν πρὸς ἀλήθειαν.

Μὴ γάρ.   b

Βούλει οὖν, ἔφην, ἐπ' αὐτῶν τούτων ζητήσωμεν τὸν μιμητὴν τοῦτον, τίς ποτ' ἐστίν;

Εἰ βούλει, ἔφη.

5 Οὐκοῦν τριτταί τινες κλῖναι αὗται γίγνονται· μία μὲν ἡ
ἐν τῆι φύσει οὖσα, ἣν φαῖμεν ἄν, ὡς ἐγῷιμαι, θεὸν ἐργάσασθαι. ἢ τίν' ἄλλον;
Οὐδένα, οἶμαι.
Μία δέ γε ἦν ὁ τέκτων.
10 Ναί, ἔφη.
Μία δὲ ἦν ὁ ζωγράφος. ἢ γάρ;
Ἔστω.
Ζωγράφος δή, κλινοποιός, θεός, τρεῖς οὗτοι ἐπιστάται
τρισὶν εἴδεσι κλινῶν.
15 Ναὶ τρεῖς.
c Ὁ μὲν δὴ θεός, εἴτε οὐκ ἐβούλετο, εἴτε τις ἀνάγκη ἐπῆν
μὴ πλέον ἢ μίαν ἐν τῆι φύσει ἀπεργάσασθαι αὐτὸν κλίνην,
οὕτως ἐποίησεν μίαν μόνον αὐτὴν ἐκείνην ὃ ἔστιν κλίνη·
δύο δὲ τοιαῦται ἢ πλείους οὔτε ἐφυτεύθησαν ὑπὸ τοῦ θεοῦ
5 οὔτε μὴ φυῶσιν.
Πῶς δή; ἔφη.
Ὅτι, ἦν δ' ἐγώ, εἰ δύο μόνας ποιήσειεν, πάλιν ἂν μία
ἀναφανείη ἧς ἐκεῖναι ἂν αὖ ἀμφότεραι τὸ εἶδος ἔχοιεν, καὶ
εἴη ἂν ὃ ἔστιν κλίνη ἐκείνη ἀλλ' οὐχ αἱ δύο.
10 Ὀρθῶς, ἔφη.
d Ταῦτα δὴ οἶμαι εἰδὼς ὁ θεός, βουλόμενος εἶναι ὄντως
κλίνης ποιητὴς ὄντως οὔσης, ἀλλὰ μὴ κλίνης τινὸς μηδὲ
κλινοποιός τις, μίαν φύσει αὐτὴν ἔφυσεν.
Ἔοικεν.
Βούλει οὖν τοῦτον μὲν φυτουργὸν τούτου προσαγορεύω-
5 μεν,
ἤ τι τοιοῦτον;
Δίκαιον γοῦν, ἔφη, ἐπειδήπερ φύσει γε καὶ τοῦτο καὶ
τἆλλα πάντα πεποίηκεν.
Τί δὲ τὸν τέκτονα; ἆρ' οὐ δημιουργὸν κλίνης;
10 Ναί.
Ἦ καὶ τὸν ζωγράφον δημιουργὸν καὶ ποιητὴν τοῦ τοιούτου;
Οὐδαμῶς.

Ἀλλὰ τί αὐτὸν κλίνης φήσεις εἶναι;

Τοῦτο, ἦ δ' ὅς, ἔμοιγε δοκεῖ μετριώτατ' ἂν προσαγορεύ- e
εσθαι, μιμητὴς οὗ ἐκεῖνοι δημιουργοί.

Εἶεν, ἦν δ' ἐγώ· τὸν τοῦ τρίτου ἄρα γεννήματος ἀπὸ τῆς
φύσεως μιμητὴν καλεῖς;

Πάνυ μὲν οὖν, ἔφη.   5

Τοῦτ' ἄρα ἔσται καὶ ὁ τραγωιδοποιός, εἴπερ μιμητής ἐστι,
τρίτος τις ἀπὸ βασιλέως καὶ τῆς ἀληθείας πεφυκώς, καὶ
πάντες οἱ ἄλλοι μιμηταί.

Κινδυνεύει.

Τὸν μὲν δὴ μιμητὴν ὡμολογήκαμεν. εἰπὲ δέ μοι περὶ   10
τοῦ ζωγράφου τόδε· πότερα ἐκεῖνο αὐτὸ τὸ ἐν τῆι φύσει 598
ἕκαστον δοκεῖ σοι ἐπιχειρεῖν μιμεῖσθαι ἢ τὰ τῶν δημιουργῶν
ἔργα;

Τὰ τῶν δημιουργῶν, ἔφη.

Ἆρα οἷα ἔστιν ἢ οἷα φαίνεται; τοῦτο γὰρ ἔτι διόρισον.   5

Πῶς λέγεις; ἔφη.

Ὧδε· κλίνη, ἐάντε ἐκ πλαγίου αὐτὴν θεᾶι ἐάντε καταντικρὺ
ἢ ὁπηιοῦν, μή τι διαφέρει αὐτὴ ἑαυτῆς, ἢ διαφέρει μὲν οὐδέν,
φαίνεται δὲ ἀλλοία; καὶ τἆλλα ὡσαύτως;

Οὕτως, ἔφη· φαίνεται, διαφέρει δ' οὐδέν.   10

Τοῦτο δὴ αὐτὸ σκόπει· πρὸς πότερον ἡ γραφικὴ πεποίηται b
περὶ ἕκαστον; πότερα πρὸς τὸ ὄν, ὡς ἔχει, μιμήσασθαι, ἢ
πρὸς τὸ φαινόμενον, ὡς φαίνεται, φαντάσματος ἢ ἀληθείας
οὖσα μίμησις;

Φαντάσματος, ἔφη.   5

Πόρρω ἄρα που τοῦ ἀληθοῦς ἡ μιμητική ἐστιν καί, ὡς
ἔοικεν, διὰ τοῦτο πάντα ἀπεργάζεται, ὅτι σμικρόν τι ἑκάστου
ἐφάπτεται, καὶ τοῦτο εἴδωλον. οἷον ὁ ζωγράφος, φαμέν,
ζωγραφήσει ἡμῖν σκυτοτόμον, τέκτονα, τοὺς ἄλλους δημιουρ-
γούς, περὶ οὐδενὸς τούτων ἐπαΐων τῶν τεχνῶν· ἀλλ' ὅμως c
παῖδάς γε καὶ ἄφρονας ἀνθρώπους, εἰ ἀγαθὸς εἴη ζωγράφος,
γράψας ἂν τέκτονα καὶ πόρρωθεν ἐπιδεικνὺς ἐξαπατῶι ἂν τῶι
δοκεῖν ὡς ἀληθῶς τέκτονα εἶναι.

Τί δ' οὔ;   5

Ἀλλὰ γὰρ οἶμαι ὦ φίλε, τόδε δεῖ περὶ πάντων τῶν τοιούτων διανοεῖσθαι· ἐπειδάν τις ἡμῖν ἀπαγγέλληι περί του,
ὡς ἐνέτυχεν ἀνθρώπωι πάσας ἐπισταμένωι τὰς δημιουργίας
καὶ τἄλλα πάντα ὅσα εἰς ἕκαστος οἶδεν, οὐδὲν ὅτι οὐχὶ
d ἀκριβέστερον ὁτουοῦν ἐπισταμένωι, ὑπολαμβάνειν δεῖ τῶι
τοιούτωι ὅτι εὐήθης τις ἄνθρωπος, καί, ὡς ἔοικεν, ἐντυχὼν
γόητί τινι καὶ μιμητῆι ἐξηπατήθη, ὥστε ἔδοξεν αὐτῶι πάσσοφος εἶναι, διὰ τὸ αὐτὸς μὴ οἷός τ' εἶναι ἐπιστήμην καὶ
5 ἀνεπιστημοσύνην καὶ μίμησιν ἐξετάσαι.

Ἀληθέστατα, ἔφη.

Οὐκοῦν, ἦν δ' ἐγώ, μετὰ τοῦτο ἐπισκεπτέον τήν τε
τραγωιδίαν καὶ τὸν ἡγεμόνα αὐτῆς Ὅμηρον, ἐπειδή τινων
e ἀκούομεν ὅτι οὗτοι πάσας μὲν τέχνας ἐπίστανται, πάντα δὲ
τὰ ἀνθρώπεια τὰ πρὸς ἀρετὴν καὶ κακίαν, καὶ τά γε θεῖα·
ἀνάγκη γὰρ τὸν ἀγαθὸν ποιητήν, εἰ μέλλει περὶ ὧν ἂν ποιῆι
καλῶς ποιήσειν, εἰδότα ἄρα ποιεῖν, ἢ μὴ οἷόν τε εἶναι
5 ποιεῖν. δεῖ δὴ ἐπισκέψασθαι πότερον μιμηταῖς τούτοις
οὗτοι ἐντυχόντες ἐξηπάτηνται καὶ τὰ ἔργα αὐτῶν ὁρῶντες
599 οὐκ αἰσθάνονται τριττὰ ἀπέχοντα τοῦ ὄντος καὶ ῥάιδια ποιεῖν
μὴ εἰδότι τὴν ἀλήθειαν – φαντάσματα γὰρ ἀλλ' οὐκ ὄντα
ποιοῦσιν – ἤ τι καὶ λέγουσιν καὶ τῶι ὄντι οἱ ἀγαθοὶ ποιηταὶ
ἴσασιν περὶ ὧν δοκοῦσιν τοῖς πολλοῖς εὖ λέγειν.

5 Πάνυ μὲν οὖν, ἔφη, ἐξεταστέον.

Οἴει οὖν, εἴ τις ἀμφότερα δύναιτο ποιεῖν, τό τε μιμηθησόμενον καὶ τὸ εἴδωλον, ἐπὶ τῆι τῶν εἰδώλων δημιουργίαι
ἑαυτὸν ἀφεῖναι ἂν σπουδάζειν καὶ τοῦτο προστήσασθαι τοῦ
b ἑαυτοῦ βίου ὡς βέλτιστον ἔχοντα;

Οὐκ ἔγωγε.

Ἀλλ' εἴπερ γε οἶμαι ἐπιστήμων εἴη τῆι ἀληθείαι τούτων
πέρι ἅπερ καὶ μιμεῖται, πολὺ πρότερον ἐν τοῖς ἔργοις ἂν
5 σπουδάσειεν ἢ ἐπὶ τοῖς μιμήμασι, καὶ πειρῶιτο ἂν πολλὰ καὶ
καλὰ ἔργα ἑαυτοῦ καταλιπεῖν μνημεῖα, καὶ εἶναι προθυμοῖτ'
ἂν μᾶλλον ὁ ἐγκωμιαζόμενος ἢ ὁ ἐγκωμιάζων.

Οἶμαι, ἔφη· οὐ γὰρ ἐξ ἴσου ἥ τε τιμὴ καὶ ἡ ὠφελία.

Τῶν μὲν τοίνυν ἄλλων πέρι μὴ ἀπαιτῶμεν λόγον Ὅμηρον ἢ ἄλλον ὀντινοῦν τῶν ποιητῶν, ἐρωτῶντες εἰ ἰατρικὸς c
ἦν τις αὐτῶν ἀλλὰ μὴ μιμητὴς μόνον ἰατρικῶν λόγων, τίνας
ὑγιεῖς ποιητής τις τῶν παλαιῶν ἢ τῶν νέων λέγεται πεποι-
ηκέναι, ὥσπερ Ἀσκληπιός, ἢ τίνας μαθητὰς ἰατρικῆς κατε-
λίπετο, ὥσπερ ἐκεῖνος τοὺς ἐκγόνους, μηδ' αὖ περὶ τὰς 5
ἄλλας τέχνας αὐτοὺς ἐρωτῶμεν, ἀλλ' ἐῶμεν· περὶ δὲ ὧν
μεγίστων τε καὶ καλλίστων ἐπιχειρεῖ λέγειν Ὅμηρος, πολέμων τε πέρι καὶ στρατηγιῶν καὶ διοικήσεων πόλεων, καὶ
παιδείας πέρι ἀνθρώπου, δίκαιόν που ἐρωτᾶν αὐτὸν πυνθα- d
νομένους· Ὦ φίλε Ὅμηρε, εἴπερ μὴ τρίτος ἀπὸ τῆς ἀληθείας
εἶ ἀρετῆς πέρι, εἰδώλου δημιουργός, ὃν δὴ μιμητὴν ὡρισάμεθα, ἀλλὰ καὶ δεύτερος, καὶ οἷός τε ἦσθα γιγνώσκειν ποῖα
ἐπιτηδεύματα βελτίους ἢ χείρους ἀνθρώπους ποιεῖ ἰδίαι καὶ 5
δημοσίαι, λέγε ἡμῖν τίς τῶν πόλεων διὰ σὲ βέλτιον ὤικησεν,
ὥσπερ διὰ Λυκοῦργον Λακεδαίμων καὶ δι' ἄλλους πολλοὺς
πολλαὶ μεγάλαι τε καὶ σμικραί; σὲ δὲ τίς αἰτιᾶται πόλις e
νομοθέτην ἀγαθὸν γεγονέναι καὶ σφᾶς ὠφεληκέναι; Χαρώνδαν μὲν γὰρ Ἰταλία καὶ Σικελία, καὶ ἡμεῖς Σόλωνα· σὲ δὲ
τίς; ἕξει τινὰ εἰπεῖν;
Οὐκ οἶμαι, ἔφη ὁ Γλαύκων· οὔκουν λέγεταί γε οὐδ' ὑπ' 5
αὐτῶν Ὁμηριδῶν.
Ἀλλὰ δή τις πόλεμος ἐπὶ Ὁμήρου ὑπ' ἐκείνου ἄρχοντος 600
ἢ συμβουλεύοντος εὖ πολεμηθεὶς μνημονεύεται;
Οὐδείς.
Ἀλλ' οἷα δὴ εἰς τὰ ἔργα σοφοῦ ἀνδρὸς πολλαὶ ἐπίνοιαι
καὶ εὐμήχανοι εἰς τέχνας ἢ τινας ἄλλας πράξεις λέγονται, 5
ὥσπερ αὖ Θάλεώ τε πέρι τοῦ Μιλησίου καὶ Ἀναχάρσιος
τοῦ Σκύθου;
Οὐδαμῶς τοιοῦτον οὐδέν.
Ἀλλὰ δὴ εἰ μὴ δημοσίαι, ἰδίαι τισὶν ἡγεμὼν παιδείας
αὐτὸς ζῶν λέγεται Ὅμηρος γενέσθαι, οἳ ἐκεῖνον ἠγάπων ἐπὶ 10
συνουσίαι καὶ τοῖς ὑστέροις ὁδόν τινα παρέδοσαν βίου b
Ὁμηρικήν, ὥσπερ Πυθαγόρας αὐτός τε διαφερόντως ἐπὶ

τούτωι ἠγαπήθη, καὶ οἱ ὕστεροι ἔτι καὶ νῦν Πυθαγόρειον
τρόπον ἐπονομάζοντες τοῦ βίου διαφανεῖς πηι δοκοῦσιν εἶναι
5 ἐν τοῖς ἄλλοις;
Οὐδ' αὖ, ἔφη, τοιοῦτον οὐδὲν λέγεται. ὁ γὰρ Κρεώφυλος,
ὦ Σώκρατες, ἴσως, ὁ τοῦ Ὁμήρου ἑταῖρος, τοῦ ὀνόματος ἂν
γελοιότερος ἔτι πρὸς παιδείαν φανείη, εἰ τὰ λεγόμενα περὶ
Ὁμήρου ἀληθῆ. λέγεται γὰρ ὡς πολλή τις ἀμέλεια περὶ
c αὐτὸν ἦν ἐπ' αὐτοῦ ἐκείνου, ὅτε ἔζη.
Λέγεται γὰρ οὖν, ἦν δ' ἐγώ. ἀλλ' οἴει, ὦ Γλαύκων, εἰ
τῶι ὄντι οἷός τ' ἦν παιδεύειν ἀνθρώπους καὶ βελτίους ἀπ-
εργάζεσθαι Ὅμηρος, ἅτε περὶ τούτων οὐ μιμεῖσθαι ἀλλὰ
5 γιγνώσκειν δυνάμενος, οὐκ ἄρ' ἂν πολλοὺς ἑταίρους ἐποιή-
σατο καὶ ἐτιμᾶτο καὶ ἠγαπᾶτο ὑπ' αὐτῶν, ἀλλὰ Πρωταγόρας
μὲν ἄρα ὁ Ἀβδηρίτης καὶ Πρόδικος ὁ Κεῖος καὶ ἄλλοι πάμ-
πολλοι δύνανται τοῖς ἐφ' ἑαυτῶν παριστάναι ἰδίαι συγγιγνό-
d μενοι ὡς οὔτε οἰκίαν οὔτε πόλιν τὴν αὐτῶν διοικεῖν οἷοί τ'
ἔσονται, ἐὰν μὴ σφεῖς αὐτῶν ἐπιστατήσωσιν τῆς παιδείας,
καὶ ἐπὶ ταύτηι τῆι σοφίαι οὕτω σφόδρα φιλοῦνται, ὥστε μόνον
οὐκ ἐπὶ ταῖς κεφαλαῖς περιφέρουσιν αὐτοὺς οἱ ἑταῖροι·
5 Ὅμηρον δ' ἄρα οἱ ἐπ' ἐκείνου, εἴπερ οἷός τ' ἦν πρὸς ἀρετὴν
ὀνῆσαι ἀνθρώπους, ἢ Ἡσίοδον ῥαψωιδεῖν ἂν περιιόντας εἴων,
καὶ οὐχὶ μᾶλλον ἂν αὐτῶν ἀντείχοντο ἢ τοῦ χρυσοῦ καὶ
e ἠνάγκαζον παρὰ σφίσιν οἴκοι εἶναι, ἢ εἰ μὴ ἔπειθον, αὐτοὶ ἂν
ἐπαιδαγώγουν ὅπηι ἦισαν, ἕως ἱκανῶς παιδείας μεταλάβοιεν;
Παντάπασιν, ἔφη, δοκεῖς μοι, ὦ Σώκρατες, ἀληθῆ λέγειν.
Οὐκοῦν τιθῶμεν ἀπὸ Ὁμήρου ἀρξαμένους πάντας τοὺς
5 ποιητικοὺς μιμητὰς εἰδώλων ἀρετῆς εἶναι καὶ τῶν ἄλλων
περὶ ὧν ποιοῦσιν, τῆς δὲ ἀληθείας οὐχ ἅπτεσθαι, ἀλλ' ὥσπερ
νυνδὴ ἐλέγομεν, ὁ ζωγράφος σκυτοτόμον ποιήσει δοκοῦντα
601 εἶναι, αὐτός τε οὐκ ἐπαΐων περὶ σκυτοτομίας καὶ τοῖς μὴ
ἐπαΐουσιν, ἐκ τῶν χρωμάτων δὲ καὶ σχημάτων θεωροῦσιν;
Πάνυ μὲν οὖν.
Οὕτω δὴ οἶμαι καὶ τὸν ποιητικὸν φήσομεν χρώματα ἄττα
5 ἑκάστων τῶν τεχνῶν τοῖς ὀνόμασι καὶ ῥήμασιν ἐπιχρωματί-

ζειν αὐτὸν οὐκ ἐπαΐοντα ἀλλ' ἢ μιμεῖσθαι, ὥστε ἑτέροις
τοιούτοις ἐκ τῶν λόγων θεωροῦσι δοκεῖν, ἐάντε περὶ σκυτοτομίας τις λέγηι ἐν μέτρωι καὶ ῥυθμῶι καὶ ἁρμονίαι, πάνυ εὖ
δοκεῖν λέγεσθαι, ἐάντε περὶ στρατηγίας ἐάντε περὶ ἄλλου
ὁτουοῦν· οὕτω φύσει αὐτὰ ταῦτα μεγάλην τινὰ κήλησιν b
ἔχειν. ἐπεὶ γυμνωθέντα γε τῶν τῆς μουσικῆς χρωμάτων
τὰ τῶν ποιητῶν, αὐτὰ ἐφ' αὑτῶν λεγόμενα, οἶμαί σε εἰδέναι
οἷα φαίνεται. τεθέασαι γάρ που.

Ἔγωγ', ἔφη.   5

Οὐκοῦν, ἦν δ' ἐγώ, ἔοικεν τοῖς τῶν ὡραίων προσώποις,
καλῶν δὲ μή, οἷα γίγνεται ἰδεῖν ὅταν αὐτὰ τὸ ἄνθος προλίπηι;

Παντάπασιν, ἦ δ' ὅς.

Ἴθι δή, τόδε ἄθρει· ὁ τοῦ εἰδώλου ποιητής, ὁ μιμητής,
φαμέν, τοῦ μὲν ὄντος οὐδὲν ἐπαΐει, τοῦ δὲ φαινομένου· οὐχ 10
οὕτως;   c

Ναί.

Μὴ τοίνυν ἡμίσεως αὐτὸ καταλίπωμεν ῥηθέν, ἀλλ' ἱκανῶς
ἴδωμεν.

Λέγε, ἔφη.   5

Ζωγράφος, φαμέν, ἡνίας τε γράψει καὶ χαλινόν;

Ναί.

Ποιήσει δέ γε σκυτοτόμος καὶ χαλκεύς;

Πάνυ γε.

Ἆρ' οὖν ἐπαΐει οἵας δεῖ τὰς ἡνίας εἶναι καὶ τὸν χαλινὸν 10
ὁ γραφεύς; ἢ οὐδ' ὁ ποιήσας, ὅ τε χαλκεὺς καὶ ὁ σκυτεύς,
ἀλλ' ἐκεῖνος ὅσπερ τούτοις ἐπίσταται χρῆσθαι, μόνος ὁ
ἱππικός;

Ἀληθέστατα.

Ἆρ' οὖν οὐ περὶ πάντα οὕτω φήσομεν ἔχειν;   15

Πῶς;

Περὶ ἕκαστον ταύτας τινὰς τρεῖς τέχνας εἶναι, χρησομένην, d
ποιήσουσαν, μιμησομένην;

Ναί.

Οὐκοῦν ἀρετὴ καὶ κάλλος καὶ ὀρθότης ἑκάστου σκεύους
5 καὶ ζώιου καὶ πράξεως οὐ πρὸς ἄλλο τι ἢ τὴν χρείαν ἐστίν,
πρὸς ἣν ἂν ἕκαστον ἦι πεποιημένον ἢ πεφυκός;
Οὕτως.

Πολλὴ ἄρα ἀνάγκη τὸν χρώμενον ἑκάστωι ἐμπειρότατόν
τε εἶναι καὶ ἄγγελον γίγνεσθαι τῶι ποιητῆι οἷα ἀγαθὰ ἢ κακὰ
10 ποιεῖ ἐν τῆι χρείαι ὧι χρῆται· οἷον αὐλητής που αὐλοποιῶι
e ἐξαγγέλλει περὶ τῶν αὐλῶν, οἳ ἂν ὑπηρετῶσιν ἐν τῶι αὐλεῖν,
καὶ ἐπιτάξει οἵους δεῖ ποιεῖν, ὁ δ' ὑπηρετήσει.

Πῶς δ' οὔ;

Οὐκοῦν ὁ μὲν εἰδὼς ἐξαγγέλλει περὶ χρηστῶν καὶ πονηρῶν
5 αὐλῶν, ὁ δὲ πιστεύων ποιήσει;

Ναί.

Τοῦ αὐτοῦ ἄρα σκεύους ὁ μὲν ποιητὴς πίστιν ὀρθὴν ἕξει
περὶ κάλλους τε καὶ πονηρίας, συνὼν τῶι εἰδότι καὶ ἀναγκα-
602 ζόμενος ἀκούειν παρὰ τοῦ εἰδότος, ὁ δὲ χρώμενος ἐπιστήμην.

Πάνυ γε.

Ὁ δὲ μιμητὴς πότερον ἐκ τοῦ χρῆσθαι ἐπιστήμην ἕξει
περὶ ὧν ἂν γράφηι, εἴτε καλὰ καὶ ὀρθὰ εἴτε μή, ἢ δόξαν
5 ὀρθὴν διὰ τὸ ἐξ ἀνάγκης συνεῖναι τῶι εἰδότι καὶ ἐπιτάττεσθαι
οἷα χρὴ γράφειν;

Οὐδέτερα.

Οὔτε ἄρα εἴσεται οὔτε ὀρθὰ δοξάσει ὁ μιμητὴς περὶ ὧν
ἂν μιμῆται πρὸς κάλλος ἢ πονηρίαν.

10 Οὐκ ἔοικεν.

Χαρίεις ἂν εἴη ὁ ἐν τῆι ποιήσει μιμητικὸς πρὸς σοφίαν
περὶ ὧν ἂν ποιῆι.

Οὐ πάνυ.

b Ἀλλ' οὖν δὴ ὅμως γε μιμήσεται, οὐκ εἰδὼς περὶ ἑκάστου
ὅπηι πονηρὸν ἢ χρηστόν· ἀλλ', ὡς ἔοικεν, οἷον φαίνεται
καλὸν εἶναι τοῖς πολλοῖς τε καὶ μηδὲν εἰδόσιν, τοῦτο
μιμήσεται.

5 Τί γὰρ ἄλλο;

Ταῦτα μὲν δή, ὥς γε φαίνεται, ἐπιεικῶς ἡμῖν διωμολόγηται,
τόν τε μιμητικὸν μηδὲν εἰδέναι ἄξιον λόγου περὶ ὧν μιμεῖται,

ἀλλ' εἶναι παιδιάν τινα καὶ οὐ σπουδὴν τὴν μίμησιν, τούς
τε τῆς τραγικῆς ποιήσεως ἁπτομένους ἐν ἰαμβείοις καὶ ἐν
ἔπεσι πάντας εἶναι μιμητικοὺς ὡς οἷόν τε μάλιστα.   10
Πάνυ μὲν οὖν.
Πρὸς Διός, ἦν δ' ἐγώ, τὸ δὲ δὴ μιμεῖσθαι τοῦτο οὐ περὶ c
τρίτον μέν τί ἐστιν ἀπὸ τῆς ἀληθείας; ἦ γάρ;
Ναί.
Πρὸς δὲ δὴ ποῖόν τί ἐστιν τῶν τοῦ ἀνθρώπου ἔχον τὴν
δύναμιν ἣν ἔχει;   5
Τοῦ ποίου τινὸς πέρι λέγεις;
Τοῦ τοιοῦδε· ταὐτόν που ἡμῖν μέγεθος ἐγγύθεν τε καὶ
πόρρωθεν διὰ τῆς ὄψεως οὐκ ἴσον φαίνεται.
Οὐ γάρ.
Καὶ ταὐτὰ καμπύλα τε καὶ εὐθέα ἐν ὕδατί τε θεωμένοις 10
καὶ ἔξω, καὶ κοῖλά τε δὴ καὶ ἐξέχοντα διὰ τὴν περὶ τὰ
χρώματα αὖ πλάνην τῆς ὄψεως, καὶ πᾶσά τις ταραχὴ δήλη
ἡμῖν ἐνοῦσα αὕτη ἐν τῆι ψυχῆι· ὧι δὴ ἡμῶν τῶι παθήματι d
τῆς φύσεως ἡ σκιαγραφία ἐπιθεμένη γοητείας οὐδὲν ἀπολείπει, καὶ ἡ θαυματοποιία καὶ αἱ ἄλλαι πολλαὶ τοιαῦται
μηχαναί.
Ἀληθῆ.   5
Ἆρ' οὖν οὐ τὸ μετρεῖν καὶ ἀριθμεῖν καὶ ἱστάναι βοήθειαι
χαριέσταται πρὸς αὐτὰ ἐφάνησαν, ὥστε μὴ ἄρχειν ἐν ἡμῖν
τὸ φαινόμενον μεῖζον ἢ ἔλαττον ἢ πλέον ἢ βαρύτερον, ἀλλὰ
τὸ λογισάμενον καὶ μετρῆσαν ἢ καὶ στῆσαν;
Πῶς γὰρ οὔ;   10
Ἀλλὰ μὴν τοῦτό γε τοῦ λογιστικοῦ ἂν εἴη τοῦ ἐν ψυχῆι e
ἔργον.
Τούτου γὰρ οὖν.
Τούτωι δὲ πολλάκις μετρήσαντι καὶ σημαίνοντι μείζω
ἄττα εἶναι ἢ ἐλάττω ἕτερα ἑτέρων ἢ ἴσα τἀναντία φαίνεται 5
ἅμα περὶ ταὐτά.
Ναί.
Οὐκοῦν ἔφαμεν τῶι αὐτῶι ἅμα περὶ ταὐτὰ ἐναντία δοξάζειν
ἀδύνατον εἶναι;

10 Καὶ ὀρθῶς γ' ἔφαμεν.

603 Τὸ παρὰ τὰ μέτρα ἄρα δοξάζον τῆς ψυχῆς τῶι κατὰ τὰ μέτρα οὐκ ἂν εἴη ταὐτόν.

Οὐ γὰρ οὖν.

Ἀλλὰ μὴν τὸ μέτρωι γε καὶ λογισμῶι πιστεῦον βέλτιστον
5 ἂν εἴη τῆς ψυχῆς.

Τί μήν;

Τὸ ἄρα τούτωι ἐναντιούμενον τῶν φαύλων ἄν τι εἴη ἐν ἡμῖν.

Ἀνάγκη.

10 Τοῦτο τοίνυν διομολογήσασθαι βουλόμενος ἔλεγον ὅτι ἡ γραφικὴ καὶ ὅλως ἡ μιμητικὴ πόρρω μὲν τῆς ἀληθείας ὂν τὸ αὑτῆς ἔργον ἀπεργάζεται, πόρρω δ' αὖ φρονήσεως ὄντι τῶι
b ἐν ἡμῖν προσομιλεῖ τε καὶ ἑταίρα καὶ φίλη ἐστὶν ἐπ' οὐδενὶ ὑγιεῖ οὐδ' ἀληθεῖ.

Παντάπασιν, ἦ δ' ὅς.

Φαύλη ἄρα φαύλωι συγγιγνομένη φαῦλα γεννᾶι ἡ μιμητική.
5 Ἔοικεν.

Πότερον, ἦν δ' ἐγώ, ἡ κατὰ τὴν ὄψιν μόνον, ἢ καὶ κατὰ τὴν ἀκοήν, ἣν δὴ ποίησιν ὀνομάζομεν;

Εἰκός γ', ἔφη, καὶ ταύτην.

Μὴ τοίνυν, ἦν δ' ἐγώ, τῶι εἰκότι μόνον πιστεύσωμεν ἐκ
10 τῆς γραφικῆς, ἀλλὰ καὶ ἐπ' αὐτὸ αὖ ἔλθωμεν τῆς διανοίας
c τοῦτο ὧι προσομιλεῖ ἡ τῆς ποιήσεως μιμητική, καὶ ἴδωμεν φαῦλον ἢ σπουδαῖόν ἐστιν.

Ἀλλὰ χρή.

Ὧδε δὴ προθώμεθα· πράττοντας, φαμέν, ἀνθρώπους
5 μιμεῖται ἡ μιμητικὴ βιαίους ἢ ἑκουσίας πράξεις, καὶ ἐκ τοῦ πράττειν ἢ εὖ οἰομένους ἢ κακῶς πεπραγέναι, καὶ ἐν τούτοις δὴ πᾶσιν ἢ λυπουμένους ἢ χαίροντας. μή τι ἄλλο ἦι παρὰ ταῦτα;

Οὐδέν.

10 Ἆρ' οὖν ἐν ἅπασι τούτοις ὁμονοητικῶς ἄνθρωπος διάκει-

c7 ἦι m: ἦ m: ἦν e

ται; ἢ ὥσπερ κατὰ τὴν ὄψιν ἐστασίαζεν καὶ ἐναντίας εἶχεν d
ἐν ἑαυτῶι δόξας ἅμα περὶ τῶν αὐτῶν, οὕτω καὶ ἐν ταῖς
πράξεσι στασιάζει τε καὶ μάχεται αὐτὸς αὑτῶι; ἀναμιμνῄ-
σκομαι δὲ ὅτι τοῦτό γε νῦν οὐδὲν δεῖ ἡμᾶς διομολογεῖσθαι·
ἐν γὰρ τοῖς ἄνω λόγοις ἱκανῶς πάντα ταῦτα διωμολογησά- 5
μεθα, ὅτι μυρίων τοιούτων ἐναντιωμάτων ἅμα γιγνομένων ἡ
ψυχὴ γέμει ἡμῶν.
    Ὀρθῶς, ἔφη.
    Ὀρθῶς γάρ, ἦν δ᾽ ἐγώ· ἀλλ᾽ ὃ τότε ἀπελίπομεν, νῦν μοι
δοκεῖ ἀναγκαῖον εἶναι διεξελθεῖν.   e
    Τὸ ποῖον; ἔφη.
    Ἀνήρ, ἦν δ᾽ ἐγώ, ἐπιεικὴς τοιᾶσδε τύχης μετασχών, ὑὸν
ἀπολέσας ἤ τι ἄλλο ὧν περὶ πλείστου ποιεῖται, ἐλέγομέν
που καὶ τότε ὅτι ῥᾷστα οἴσει τῶν ἄλλων.   5
    Πάνυ γε.
    Νῦν δέ γε τόδ᾽ ἐπισκεψώμεθα, πότερον οὐδὲν ἀχθέσεται,
ἢ τοῦτο μὲν ἀδύνατον, μετριάσει δέ πως πρὸς λύπην.
    Οὕτω μᾶλλον, ἔφη, τό γε ἀληθές.
    Τόδε νῦν μοι περὶ αὐτοῦ εἰπέ· πότερον μᾶλλον αὐτὸν 604
οἴει τῆι λύπηι μαχεῖσθαί τε καὶ ἀντιτείνειν, ὅταν ὁρᾶται ὑπὸ
τῶν ὁμοίων, ἢ ὅταν ἐν ἐρημίαι μόνος αὐτὸς καθ᾽ αὑτὸν
γίγνηται;
    Πολύ που, ἔφη, διοίσει, ὅταν ὁρᾶται.   5
    Μονωθεὶς δέ γε οἶμαι πολλὰ μὲν τολμήσει φθέγξασθαι,
ἃ εἴ τις αὐτοῦ ἀκούοι αἰσχύνοιτ᾽ ἄν, πολλὰ δὲ ποιήσει, ἃ οὐκ
ἂν δέξαιτό τινα ἰδεῖν δρῶντα.
    Οὕτως ἔχει, ἔφη.
    Οὐκοῦν τὸ μὲν ἀντιτείνειν διακελευόμενον λόγος καὶ νόμος 10
ἐστίν, τὸ δὲ ἕλκον ἐπὶ τὰς λύπας αὐτὸ τὸ πάθος;   b
    Ἀληθῆ.
    Ἐναντίας δὲ ἀγωγῆς γιγνομένης ἐν τῶι ἀνθρώπωι περὶ τὸ
αὐτὸ ἅμα, δύο φαμὲν ἐν αὐτῶι ἀναγκαῖον εἶναι.
    Πῶς δ᾽ οὔ;   5

Οὐκοῦν τὸ μὲν ἕτερον τῶι νόμωι ἕτοιμον πείθεσθαι, ἧι ὁ νόμος ἐξηγεῖται;

Πῶς;

Λέγει που ὁ νόμος ὅτι κάλλιστον ὅτι μάλιστα ἡσυχίαν 10 ἄγειν ἐν ταῖς συμφοραῖς καὶ μὴ ἀγανακτεῖν, ὡς οὔτε δῆλου ὄντος τοῦ ἀγαθοῦ τε καὶ κακοῦ τῶν τοιούτων, οὔτε εἰς τὸ πρόσθεν οὐδὲν προβαῖνον τῶι χαλεπῶς φέροντι, οὔτε τι τῶν c ἀνθρωπίνων ἄξιον ὂν μεγάλης σπουδῆς, ὅ τε δεῖ ἐν αὐτοῖς ὅτι τάχιστα παραγίγνεσθαι ἡμῖν, τούτωι ἐμποδὼν γιγνόμενον τὸ λυπεῖσθαι.

Τίνι, ἦ δ' ὅς, λέγεις;

5 Τῶι βουλεύεσθαι, ἦν δ' ἐγώ, περὶ τὸ γεγονὸς καὶ ὥσπερ ἐν πτώσει κύβων πρὸς τὰ πεπτωκότα τίθεσθαι τὰ αὑτοῦ πράγματα, ὅπηι ὁ λόγος αἱρεῖ βέλτιστ' ἂν ἔχειν, ἀλλὰ μὴ προσπταίσαντας καθάπερ παῖδας ἐχομένους τοῦ πληγέντος ἐν τῶι βοᾶν διατρίβειν, ἀλλ' ἀεὶ ἐθίζειν τὴν ψυχὴν ὅτι d τάχιστα γίγνεσθαι πρὸς τὸ ἰᾶσθαί τε καὶ ἐπανορθοῦν τὸ πεσόν τε καὶ νοσῆσαν, ἰατρικῆι θρηνωιδίαν ἀφανίζοντα.

Ὀρθότατα γοῦν ἄν τις, ἔφη, πρὸς τὰς τύχας οὕτω προσφέροιτο.

5 Οὐκοῦν, φαμέν, τὸ μὲν βέλτιστον τούτωι τῶι λογισμῶι ἐθέλει ἕπεσθαι.

Δῆλον δή.

Τὸ δὲ πρὸς τὰς ἀναμνήσεις τε τοῦ πάθους καὶ πρὸς τοὺς ὀδυρμοὺς ἄγον καὶ ἀπλήστως ἔχον αὐτῶν ἆρ' οὐκ ἀλόγιστόν 10 τε φήσομεν εἶναι καὶ ἀργὸν καὶ δειλίας φίλον;

Φήσομεν μὲν οὖν.

e Οὐκοῦν τὸ μὲν πολλὴν μίμησιν καὶ ποικίλην ἔχει, τὸ ἀγανακτητικόν, τὸ δὲ φρόνιμόν τε καὶ ἡσύχιον ἦθος, παραπλήσιον ὂν ἀεὶ αὐτὸ αὑτῶι, οὔτε ῥάιδιον μιμήσασθαι οὔτε μιμουμένου εὐπετὲς καταμαθεῖν, ἄλλως τε καὶ πανηγύρει καὶ 5 παντοδαποῖς ἀνθρώποις εἰς θέατρα συλλεγομένοις· ἀλλοτρίου γάρ που πάθους ἡ μίμησις αὐτοῖς γίγνεται.

605 Παντάπασι μὲν οὖν.

Ὁ δὴ μιμητικὸς ποιητὴς δῆλον ὅτι οὐ πρὸς τὸ τοιοῦτον
τῆς ψυχῆς πέφυκέ τε καὶ ἡ σοφία αὐτοῦ τούτωι ἀρέσκειν
πέπηγεν, εἰ μέλλει εὐδοκιμήσειν ἐν τοῖς πολλοῖς, ἀλλὰ
πρὸς τὸ ἀγανακτητικόν τε καὶ ποικίλον ἦθος διὰ τὸ εὐμί- 5
μητον ἔναι.

Δῆλον.

Οὐκοῦν δικαίως ἂν αὐτοῦ ἤδη ἐπιλαμβανοίμεθα, καὶ τιθεῖμεν ἀντίστροφον αὐτὸν τῶι ζωγράφωι· καὶ γὰρ τῶι φαῦλα
ποιεῖν πρὸς ἀλήθειαν ἔοικεν αὐτῶι, καὶ τῶι πρὸς ἕτερον τοι- 10
οῦτον ὁμιλεῖν τῆς ψυχῆς ἀλλὰ μὴ πρὸς τὸ βέλτιστον, καὶ b
ταύτηι ὡμοίωται. καὶ οὕτως ἤδη ἂν ἐν δίκηι οὐ παραδεχοίμεθα εἰς μέλλουσαν εὐνομεῖσθαι πόλιν, ὅτι τοῦτο ἐγείρει
τῆς ψυχῆς καὶ τρέφει καὶ ἰσχυρὸν ποιῶν ἀπόλλυσι τὸ
λογιστικόν, ὥσπερ ἐν πόλει ὅταν τις μοχθηροὺς ἐγκρατεῖς 5
ποιῶν παραδιδῶι τὴν πόλιν, τοὺς δὲ χαριεστέρους φθείρηι·
ταὐτὸν καὶ τὸν μιμητικὸν ποιητὴν φήσομεν κακὴν πολιτείαν ἰδίαι ἑκάστου τῆι ψυχῆι ἐμποιεῖν, τῶι ἀνοήτωι αὐτῆς
χαριζόμενον καὶ οὔτε τὰ μείζω οὔτε τὰ ἐλάττω διαγιγνώ- c
σκοντι, ἀλλὰ τὰ αὐτὰ τοτὲ μὲν μεγάλα ἡγουμένωι, τοτὲ δὲ
σμικρά, εἴδωλα εἰδωλοποιοῦντα, τοῦ δὲ ἀληθοῦς πόρρω πάνυ
ἀφεστῶτα.

Πάνυ μὲν οὖν. 5

Οὐ μέντοι πω τό γε μέγιστον κατηγορήκαμεν αὐτῆς. τὸ
γὰρ καὶ τοὺς ἐπιεικεῖς ἱκανὴν εἶναι λωβᾶσθαι, ἐκτὸς πάνυ
τινῶν ὀλίγων, πάνδεινόν που.

Τί δ᾽ οὐ μέλλει, εἴπερ γε δρᾶι αὐτό;

Ἀκούων σκόπει. οἱ γάρ που βέλτιστοι ἡμῶν ἀκροώ- 10
μενοι Ὁμήρου ἢ ἄλλου τινὸς τῶν τραγωιδοποιῶν μιμουμένου
τινὰ τῶν ἡρώων ἐν πένθει ὄντα καὶ μακρὰν ῥῆσιν ἀποτεί- d
νοντα ἐν τοῖς ὀδυρμοῖς ἢ καὶ ἀιδοντάς τε καὶ κοπτομένους,
οἶσθ᾽ ὅτι χαίρομέν τε καὶ ἐνδόντες ἡμᾶς αὐτοὺς ἑπόμεθα
συμπάσχοντες καὶ σπουδάζοντες ἐπαινοῦμεν ὡς ἀγαθὸν
ποιητήν, ὃς ἂν ἡμᾶς ὅτι μάλιστα οὕτω διαθῆι. 5

Οἶδα· πῶς δ᾽ οὔ;

Ὅταν δὲ οἰκεῖόν τινι ἡμῶν κῆδος γένηται, ἐννοεῖς αὖ ὅτι
ἐπὶ τῶι ἐναντίωι καλλωπιζόμεθα, ἂν δυνώμεθα ἡσυχίαν ἄγειν
e καὶ καρτερεῖν, ὡς τοῦτο μὲν ἀνδρὸς ὄν, ἐκεῖνο δὲ γυναικός,
ὃ τότε ἐπηινοῦμεν.
Ἐννοῶ, ἔφη.
Ἦ καλῶς οὖν, ἦν δ' ἐγώ, οὗτος ὁ ἔπαινος ἔχει, τὸ ὁρῶντα
5 τοιοῦτον ἄνδρα, οἷον ἑαυτόν τις μὴ ἀξιοῖ εἶναι ἀλλ' αἰσχύνοιτο
ἄν, μὴ βδελύττεσθαι ἀλλὰ χαίρειν τε καὶ ἐπαινεῖν;
Οὐ μὰ τὸν Δί', ἔφη, οὐκ εὐλόγωι ἔοικεν.
606 Ναί, ἦν δ' ἐγώ, εἰ ἐκείνηι γ' αὐτὸ σκοποίης.
Πῆι;
Εἰ ἐνθυμοῖο ὅτι τὸ βίαι κατεχόμενον τότε ἐν ταῖς οἰκείαις
συμφοραῖς καὶ πεπεινηκὸς τοῦ δακρῦσαί τε καὶ ἀποδύρασθαι
5 ἱκανῶς καὶ ἀποπλησθῆναι, φύσει ὃν τοιοῦτον οἷον τούτων ἐπιθυμεῖν, τότ' ἐστὶν τοῦτο τὸ ὑπὸ τῶν ποιητῶν πιμπλάμενον
καὶ χαῖρον· τὸ δὲ φύσει βέλτιστον ἡμῶν, ἅτε οὐχ ἱκανῶς
πεπαιδευμένον λόγωι οὐδὲ ἔθει, ἀνίησιν τὴν φυλακὴν τοῦ
b θρηνώδους τούτου, ἅτε ἀλλότρια πάθη θεωροῦν καὶ ἑαυτῶι
οὐδὲν αἰσχρὸν ὃν εἰ ἄλλος ἀνὴρ ἀγαθὸς φάσκων εἶναι ἀκαί-
ρως πενθεῖ, τοῦτον ἐπαινεῖν καὶ ἐλεεῖν, ἀλλ' ἐκεῖνο κερδαίνειν
ἡγεῖται, τὴν ἡδονήν, καὶ οὐκ ἂν δέξαιτο αὐτῆς στερηθῆναι
5 καταφρονήσας ὅλου τοῦ ποιήματος. λογίζεσθαι γὰρ οἶμαι
ὀλίγοις τισὶν μέτεστιν ὅτι ἀπολαύειν ἀνάγκη ἀπὸ τῶν ἀλλο-
τρίων εἰς τὰ οἰκεῖα· θρέψαντα γὰρ ἐν ἐκείνοις ἰσχυρὸν τὸ
ἐλεινὸν οὐ ῥάιδιον ἐν τοῖς αὑτοῦ πάθεσι κατέχειν.
c Ἀληθέστατα, ἔφη.
Ἆρ' οὖν οὐχ ὁ αὐτὸς λόγος καὶ περὶ τοῦ γελοίου; ὅτι,
ἂν αὐτὸς αἰσχύνοιο γελωτοποιῶν, ἐν μιμήσει δὲ κωμωιδικῆι ἢ
καὶ ἰδίαι ἀκούων σφόδρα χαρῆις καὶ μὴ μισῆις ὡς πονηρά,
5 ταὐτὸν ποιεῖς ὅπερ ἐν τοῖς ἐλέοις; ὃ γὰρ τῶι λόγωι αὖ
κατεῖχες ἐν σαυτῶι βουλόμενον γελωτοποιεῖν, φοβούμενος
δόξαν βωμολοχίας, τότ' αὖ ἀνίης καὶ ἐκεῖ νεανικὸν ποιήσας

c7 ἀνίης (m): ἂν εἴης m: ἀνείης m

ἔλαθες πολλάκις ἐν τοῖς οἰκείοις ἐξενεχθεὶς ὥστε κωμωιδοποιὸς γενέσθαι.
     Καὶ μάλα, ἔφη.   10
     Καὶ περὶ ἀφροδισίων δὴ καὶ θυμοῦ καὶ περὶ πάντων τῶν d
ἐπιθυμητικῶν τε καὶ λυπηρῶν καὶ ἡδέων ἐν τῆι ψυχῆι, ἃ δή
φαμεν πάσηι πράξει ἡμῖν ἕπεσθαι, ὅτι τοιαῦτα ἡμᾶς ἡ
ποιητικὴ μίμησις ἐργάζεται· τρέφει γὰρ ταῦτα ἄρδουσα, δέον
αὐχμεῖν, καὶ ἄρχοντα ἡμῖν καθίστησιν, δέον ἄρχεσθαι αὐτὰ 5
ἵνα βελτίους τε καὶ εὐδαιμονέστεροι ἀντὶ χειρόνων καὶ
ἀθλιωτέρων γιγνώμεθα.
     Οὐκ ἔχω ἄλλως φάναι, ἦ δ᾽ ὅς.
     Οὐκοῦν, εἶπον, ὦ Γλαύκων, ὅταν Ὁμήρου ἐπαινέταις e
ἐντύχηις λέγουσιν ὡς τὴν Ἑλλάδα πεπαίδευκεν οὗτος ὁ
ποιητὴς καὶ πρὸς διοίκησίν τε καὶ παιδείαν τῶν ἀνθρωπίνων
πραγμάτων ἄξιος ἀναλαβόντι μανθάνειν τε καὶ κατὰ τοῦτον
τὸν ποιητὴν πάντα τὸν αὑτοῦ βίον κατασκευασάμενον ζῆν, 5
φιλεῖν μὲν χρὴ καὶ ἀσπάζεσθαι ὡς ὄντας βελτίστους εἰς 607
ὅσον δύνανται, καὶ συγχωρεῖν Ὅμηρον ποιητικώτατον εἶναι
καὶ πρῶτον τῶν τραγωιδοποιῶν, εἰδέναι δὲ ὅτι ὅσον μόνον
ὕμνους θεοῖς καὶ ἐγκώμια τοῖς ἀγαθοῖς ποιήσεως παραδεκτέον
εἰς πόλιν· εἰ δὲ τὴν ἡδυσμένην Μοῦσαν παραδέξηι ἐν μέλεσιν 5
ἢ ἔπεσιν, ἡδονή σοι καὶ λύπη ἐν τῆι πόλει βασιλεύσετον
ἀντὶ νόμου τε καὶ τοῦ κοινῆι ἀεὶ δόξαντος εἶναι βελτίστου
λόγου.
     Ἀληθέστατα, ἔφη.
     Ταῦτα δή, ἔφην, ἀπολελογήσθω ἡμῖν ἀναμνησθεῖσιν περὶ b
ποιήσεως, ὅτι εἰκότως ἄρα τότε αὐτὴν ἐκ τῆς πόλεως ἀπε-
στέλλομεν τοιαύτην οὖσαν· ὁ γὰρ λόγος ἡμᾶς ἥιρει. προσεί-
πωμεν δὲ αὐτῆι, μὴ καί τινα σκληρότητα ἡμῶν καὶ ἀγροικίαν
καταγνῶι, ὅτι παλαιὰ μέν τις διαφορὰ φιλοσοφίαι τε καὶ 5
ποιητικῆι· καὶ γὰρ ἡ "λακέρυζα πρὸς δεσπόταν κύων"
ἐκείνη "κραυγάζουσα" καὶ "μέγας ἐν ἀφρόνων κενε-
αγορίαισι" καὶ ὁ "τῶν διασόφων ὄχλος κρατῶν" c
καὶ οἱ "λεπτῶς μεριμνῶντες," ὅτι ἄρα "πένονται",
καὶ ἄλλα μυρία σημεῖα παλαιᾶς ἐναντιώσεως τούτων. ὅμως

δὲ εἰρήσθω ὅτι ἡμεῖς γε, εἴ τινα ἔχοι λόγον εἰπεῖν ἡ πρὸς
5 ἡδονὴν ποιητικὴ καὶ ἡ μίμησις, ὡς χρὴ αὐτὴν εἶναι ἐν πόλει
εὐνομουμένηι, ἄσμενοι ἂν καταδεχοίμεθα, ὡς σύνισμέν γε ἡμῖν
αὐτοῖς κηλουμένοις ὑπ᾽ αὐτῆς· ἀλλὰ γὰρ τὸ δοκοῦν ἀληθὲς
οὐχ ὅσιον προδιδόναι. ἢ γάρ, ὦ φίλε, οὐ κηλῆι ὑπ᾽ αὐτῆς
d καὶ σύ, καὶ μάλιστα ὅταν δι᾽ Ὁμήρου θεωρῆις αὐτήν;
   Πολύ γε.
   Οὐκοῦν δικαία ἐστὶν οὕτω κατιέναι, ἀπολογησαμένη ἐν
μέλει ἤ τινι ἄλλωι μέτρωι;
5 Πάνυ μὲν οὖν.
   Δοῖμεν δέ γέ που ἂν καὶ τοῖς προστάταις αὐτῆς, ὅσοι μὴ
ποιητικοί, φιλοποιηταὶ δέ, ἄνευ μέτρου λόγον ὑπὲρ αὐτῆς
εἰπεῖν, ὡς οὐ μόνον ἡδεῖα ἀλλὰ καὶ ὠφελίμη πρὸς τὰς πολιτείας καὶ τὸν βίον τὸν ἀνθρώπινόν ἐστιν· καὶ εὐμενῶς ἀκου-
e σόμεθα. κερδανοῦμεν γάρ που ἐὰν μὴ μόνον ἡδεῖα φανῆι ἀλλὰ
καὶ ὠφελίμη.
   Πῶς δ᾽ οὐ μέλλομεν, ἔφη, κερδαίνειν;
   Εἰ δέ γε μή, ὦ φίλε ἑταῖρε, ὥσπερ οἱ ποτέ του ἐρα-
5 σθέντες, ἐὰν ἡγήσωνται μὴ ὠφέλιμον εἶναι τὸν ἔρωτα, βίαι
μέν, ὅμως δὲ ἀπέχονται, καὶ ἡμεῖς οὕτως, διὰ τὸν ἐγγεγονότα
μὲν ἔρωτα τῆς τοιαύτης ποιήσεως ὑπὸ τῆς τῶν καλῶν πολι-
608 τειῶν τροφῆς, εὖνοι μὲν ἐσόμεθα φανῆναι αὐτὴν ὡς βελτί-
στην καὶ ἀληθεστάτην, ἕως δ᾽ ἂν μὴ οἶά τ᾽ ἦι ἀπολογήσασθαι,
ἀκροασόμεθ᾽ αὐτῆς ἐπάιδοντες ἡμῖν αὐτοῖς τοῦτον τὸν λόγον,
ὃν λέγομεν, καὶ ταύτην τὴν ἐπωιδήν, εὐλαβούμενοι πάλιν
5 ἐμπεσεῖν εἰς τὸν παιδικόν τε καὶ τὸν τῶν πολλῶν ἔρωτα.
ἀισόμεθα δ᾽ οὖν ὡς οὐ σπουδαστέον ἐπὶ τῆι τοιαύτηι ποιήσει
ὡς ἀληθείας τε ἁπτομένηι καὶ σπουδαίαι, ἀλλ᾽ εὐλαβητέον
b αὐτὴν ὂν τῶι ἀκροωμένωι, περὶ τῆς ἐν αὐτῶι πολιτείας δεδιότι,
καὶ νομιστέα ἅπερ εἰρήκαμεν περὶ ποιήσεως.
   Παντάπασιν, ἦ δ᾽ ὅς, σύμφημι.
   Μέγας γάρ, ἔφην, ὁ ἀγών, ὦ φίλε Γλαύκων, μέγας,
5 οὐχ ὅσος δοκεῖ, τὸ χρηστὸν ἢ κακὸν γενέσθαι, ὥστε οὔτε
τιμῆι ἐπαρθέντα οὔτε χρήμασιν οὔτε ἀρχῆι οὐδεμιᾶι οὐδέ γε

ποιητικῆι ἄξιον ἀμελῆσαι δικαιοσύνης τε καὶ τῆς ἄλλης
ἀρετῆς.

Σύμφημί σοι, ἔφη, ἐξ ὧν διεληλύθαμεν· οἶμαι δὲ καὶ
ἄλλον ὁντινοῦν.   10

COMMENTARY

Ion

The *Ion*, P.'s shortest work, probably belongs to his early period. In the past there have been doubts as to its authenticity: Goethe's reading of the dialogue as nothing more than a satirical attack on a rather dim rhapsode, which had nothing to do with poetry, initiated a scholarly debate concerning its authenticity which lasted until well into this century. It was felt, for example, that the ironic caricature of the rhapsode and the farcical arguments deployed against him by S. were unworthy of P., and that the dialogue as a whole lacked a coherent structure. But in fact there are no objective reasons for regarding it as un-Platonic. Details of the controversy are discussed by e.g. Méridier (1931) 17–22; Tigerstedt (1969) 18–20; Moore (1974) 421–4. Although we cannot be certain of its date of composition, it bears many of the hallmarks of the early dialogues, and most scholars now assign it to the period after S.'s death in 399, when P. embarked upon his literary career. See e.g. Méridier (1931) 23–8; Guthrie (1962–81) IV 199; G. R. Ledger, *Re-counting Plato: a computer analysis of Plato's style* (Oxford 1989) 81–2, 157, 218–19.

The dialogue consists of a conversation between S. and Ion, who is apparently the finest rhapsode in all Greece (541b3–4 cf. 530b1), at a date which is probably sometime before 412 (see on 541c3–4). Rhapsodes (ῥαψωιδοί = lit. 'song-stitchers') were professional reciters of poetry, particularly the poetry of Homer (but for other poets see on 531a2), who travelled round Greece, competing at contests and festivals such as those discussed on pp. 19–20 above. At first there seems to have been no distinction made between bards who performed their own poetry, and rhapsodes who recited other people's. Thus Hesiod (fr. dub. 357), in the earliest occurrence of the word ῥάπτειν in the context of poetry, claims that he and Homer sang at Delos, ῥάψαντες ἀοιδήν ('stitching song'), whereas Pindar begins *Nem.* 2 with our earliest reference to the Homeridae, a guild of singers on Chios who claimed descent from Homer and who were dedicated to the preservation and propagation of his poetry (see on 530d7), as ῥαπτῶν ἐπέων ... ἀοιδοί ('singers of stitched words').

96

Similarly Herodotus (5.67.1) uses the term ῥαψωιδός of reciters of Homer's poetry, but Sophocles (*O.T.* 391) describes the sphinx, who presumably composed her own riddles, as ῥαψωιδός. Xenophanes, according to Diog. Laert. (9.18), ἐρραψώιδει his own poems, and P. himself refers to the bard Phemius as a ῥαψωιδός (*Ion* 533c1), and describes Homer and Hesiod as ῥαψωιδοί (*Rep.* 600d6). The use of the terms ῥάπτειν and ῥαψωιδός to characterise both oral bards who performed their own poetry, and rhapsodes who recited the poetry of others, suggests that we should not press the distinction between the two groups of people too closely, at any rate during the early period. For further discussion see Sealey (1957) 312–18; G. S. Kirk, *The songs of Homer* (Cambridge 1962) 312–15; M. L. West (1981) 113–15.

Ion, however, is obviously a professional reciter of Homer's poetry, who declaimed his texts in histrionic manner, rather than accompanying himself on the lyre like an old fashioned bard (see on 532d6–7 and d7–8), and the dialogue that bears his name provides us with the most detailed evidence that we have about the nature of rhapsodic performances in the classical period. P.'s dialogue suggests that rhapsodes not only recited the works of poets, but also commented on them. At 530b S. envies Ion his profession, because he has to immerse himself in the best and most inspired of poets, Homer, and not only to learn his poetry, but also to understand his thought, so that he can interpret it for the audience. Ion agrees that this is the most difficult part of his job, but he is nevertheless confident that he can talk about Homer better than anyone else, and is eager to show S. how well he has embellished Homer (530d6–7). But unfortunately we never get a chance to hear Ion displaying his talent for commenting on Homer. Twice he offers to show off his skills (530d9 and 536d8), but on both occasions S. professes not to have time to listen. For P.'s purposes in this dialogue, the precise nature of the rhapsode's comments are evidently not important.

We get a much clearer idea of the kind of thing that rhapsodes probably did do from Isocrates (*Panathenaicus* 18), who describes certain sophists who were 'talking about poets, and especially about the poetry of Hesiod and Homer; they were saying nothing original, but were reciting (ῥαψωιδοῦντες) their verses, and repeating from memory (μνημονεύοντες) the cleverest things that other people had said about them in the past'. This example well describes the combined activity of reciting and commenting which Ion and his fellow rhapsodes evidently performed, and it is presumably this kind of recitation which Xenophon's Niceratus attended almost every day (*Symp.* 3.6, discussed above on p. 20). It is significant that Isocrates describes these people as sophists, for rhapsodes and sophists had much in common: both gave displays before large audiences (see on 530d4), and both concerned themselves with poetry. The sophists Hippias and Gorgias apparently wore purple robes, like rhapsodes, as if to lay claim to the authority of poets in earlier times (Gorgias 82 A 9 D–K, and see Kerferd (1981(b) 28–9). Indeed P., not without irony, likens Protagoras to Orpheus: 'he draws people from every city that he passes through, charming them with his voice like Orpheus, and they follow spellbound' (*Prot.* 315a–b), and Protagoras himself claims that his art is a continuation of the poet's ancient art (316d–e; see also on *Rep.* 600c6–d4). As we have seen (above p. 18), the interpretation of early poetry played an important part in sophistic education. It would be very surprising if, in this milieu, rhapsodes, whose profession consisted in reciting the works of the poets, particularly Homer, had not also become involved in the interpretation of that poetry.

However, the view put forward by Flashar (1958), that the *Ion* is largely an attack on the sophistic interpretation of poetry, and that Ion is little more than a cover for the sophists, is hardly convincing, and has been refuted by Tigerstedt (1969) 22–5. Ion does indeed compare himself with certain authorities on Homer who should probably be called sophists – Metrodorus of Lampsacus, Stesimbrotus of Thasos, Glaucon (530c9–d1) – but it would be very curious to attack a method of criticising poetry of which we are given no examples in the dialogue. Besides, rhapsodes apparently had a reputation for stupidity (see on 539e7), and Ion himself is so stupid that he is not worth attacking; the target of the dialogue must be something other than this proverbially silly rhapsode.

Indeed the reason why this little dialogue has attracted so much attention is because it is concerned with the subject of poetry, and in particular with the nature of the poet's inspiration. In it P. manages to combine an attack on the authority of poets, albeit a veiled one, and one that is lightly done, with a eulogy of the poet's creative powers. The ambivalence which characterises P.'s attitude to poets and poetry throughout his career is already evident in the *Ion*, and the dialogue raises many of the issues which remained central to P.'s thinking about poetry in his later works.

530a–530b4: Prologue

S. meets Ion, congratulates him on his success in the rhapsodic contest at Epidaurus and wishes him luck for the Panathenaea.

530a1 Τὸν Ἴωνα χαίρειν sc. κέλευω. The first two words neatly constitute the title of the dialogue. Nothing is known about Ion apart from what P. tells us.   **τὰ νῦν**, like τὸ νῦν, is regularly used by P. for νῦν. Cf. e.g. *Phlb.* 31a2, 63c4, *Laws* 625a6, 635a3. At *Rep.* 506e1 we find τὸ νῦν followed by τὰ νῦν at e3.   **a1–2 ἡμῖν ἐπιδεδήμηκας** 'have come to visit us'. Cf. *Prot.* 309d3 Ὦ τί λέγεις; Πρωταγόρας ἐπιδεδήμηκεν;   **a2 ἐξ Ἐφέσου** explains οἴκοθεν 'from your home at Ephesus'.   **a3 Οὐδαμῶς:** the negative might sound unexpectedly emphatic, unless the nuance is 'you'll never guess where I've been'. S.'s surprise at a5 indicates that this may be the case.   **ἐξ Ἐπιδαύρου ἐκ τῶν Ἀσκληπιείων** 'from the festival of Asclepius at Epidaurus'. Epidaurus was a centre for the worship of Asclepius, god of healing, in whose honour a festival was held which included athletic and musical contests. Athletic contests were already established there in Pindar's time (*Nem.* 3.84, 5.52; *Isthm.* 8.68), but it is uncertain when musical competitions were first introduced. See further E. J. and L. Edelstein, *Asclepius* (Baltimore 1945) II 208–11.   **a5 Μῶν** = μὴ οὖν expecting a negative answer.   **καὶ ῥαψῳδῶν** 'rhapsodes too'. Not all μουσικοὶ ἀγῶνες included rhapsodic performances, but we know that these took place at the Panathenaea (see b2 n.), at Sicyon (Hdt. 5.67.1) and possibly at Delos (Hes. fr. dub. 357 M–W). See further Herington (1985) 7–9, 161–6. S.'s surprise at the inclusion of rhapsodic contests at the festival of Asclepius may suggest that this was a recent innovation, but we have no independent evidence as to when rhapsodes first performed there. See Moore (1974) 428–30. The alternative, and more likely possibility, is that S.'s surprise is ironic.   **a7 καὶ τῆς ἄλλης γε μουσικῆς** 'and of the musical arts in general'. The term μουσική refers, of

course, to any art over which the Muses preside, and therefore includes poetry and dance as well as vocal and instrumental music. Cf.
Rep. 376e4, and see Introduction p. 15.   **a8 ἠγωνίζου ... ἠγωνίσω**
'Did you compete then? How did you get on?' The imperfect expresses the process, the aorist the result of the action. τι 'in any way'
is somewhat deprecatory in tone. ἡμῖν 'tell me', ethic dative, indicating the interest of the speaker in the thing spoken, also contains
a hint of irony. S.'s tone towards Ion seems rather teasing throughout, cf. b2 n.

b2 ὅπως καὶ τὰ Παναθήναια νικήσομεν 'Mind we win the Panathenaea too.' Supply ὅρα. Again there is irony in the way that S.
associates himself with Ion through his patronising use of the first
person plural. But despite their apparent rapport, a basic contrast
has already been established between Ion as a much travelled man
of the world, and S. as one who knows little of what goes on outside
his own city. For S.'s indifference to the outside world see e.g. *Cri.*
52b–53a, where it is said that he never travelled abroad for any purpose other than to take part in military campaigns. Cf. *Phdr.* 230c–e
where it is unusual for Socrates even to go outside the city walls. By
contrast S.'s interlocutors are typically foreigners who travel from
city to city professing a wide knowledge of worldly affairs. See e.g.
Hipp. Maj. 281a–b; *Apol.* 19e with Burnet's note *ad loc.*; *Prot.* 315a–b.
The Panathenaea was celebrated annually by the Athenians in honour of their patron goddess, but once every four years the ceremony
was held on a grander scale and included contests in music and
athletics, on the model of the great quadrennial festivals at Olympia,
Delphi, Nemea and the Isthmus. A distinctive feature of this en-
larged festival, the Great Panathenaea, was the contest between
Homeric rhapsodes, to which S. here refers. But when were these
rhapsodic contests introduced? Evidence on the early history of the
festival is confused. A scholium on Aristides, *Panathenaicus* (111.323
Dindorf) records that it was Peisistratus who established the Great
Panathenaea. But according to Marcellinus, *Vit. Thuc.* 3–4, the festival was reorganised in the archonship of Hippocleides (on whom
see Hdt. 6.127.4), generally dated to the year 566/5. Jerome (Euseb.
Chron., Ol. 53.3–4) gives 565 as the date when athletic contests were
first introduced, and archaeological evidence provided by Pan-

athenaic prize amphoras (on which see J. Boardman, *Athenian Black Figure Vases* (London 1974) 167–70) confirms that such contests had become established by about 560. In the case of musical competitions the evidence is less clear: according to Plutarch (*Pericles* 13.7–12) it was Pericles who instituted them, but evidence from vases suggests that musical contests were already in existence at the Panathenaea by the middle of the sixth century. Rhapsodic recitation seems to have become a feature of the festival during the Peisistratid period. The author of the pseudo-Platonic *Hipparchus* (thought to have been written in the fourth century B.C.) states that Peisistratus' son first brought Homer's poems to Attica and 'compelled the rhapsodes at the Panathenaea to go through them taking up the cue in turn (ἐξ ὑπολήψεως ἐφεξῆς), as they still do now' (228b). The fourth-century orator, Lycurgus, also refers to this Panathenaic regulation, implying that it was established in the distant past (*In Leocr.* 102). Cf. Isoc. *Paneg.* 159; Diog. Laert. 1.57. In the Hellenistic period it was generally believed that Peisistratus had been responsible for standardising the text of Homer, a belief which must reflect the tradition linking the house of Peisistratus with the introduction of rhapsodic recitations of Homer at the Great Panathenaea. On the 'Peisistratean recension' of Homer, see R. Merkelbach, 'Die pisistratische Redaktion der homerischen Gedichte', *Rh. M.* 95 (1952) 23–47; M. Skafte Jensen, *The Homeric question and the oral formulaic theory* (Copenhagen 1980) 128–58; S. West (1988) 36–8. On the history and development of the festival see further J. A. Davison, 'Notes on the Panathenaea', *J.H.S.* 78 (1958) 23–42 and Herington (1985) 84–7.

b4 ἐὰν θεὸς ἐθέλῃι: Ion's conventionally pious phrase is given a quite literal interpretation by S. during the course of the dialogue.

530b5–d8

S. envies rhapsodes their profession, particularly because of their expertise in Homer.

530b5 Καὶ μήν here, as often, introduces a new point.   **b6 τῆς τέχνης** here means something like 'profession' or 'métier'. The emphatic positioning of this key word, repeated in the following line, and its juxtaposition with Ion's name, are clearly ironical. But the full significance of S.'s apparently casual remark only emerges later (532c6ff), as it beomes clear that one of the main purposes of the dialogue is to deny the rhapsode τέχνη. **b6–c1 τὸ γὰρ ἅμα μὲν ... ζηλωτόν ἐστιν** 'For the fact that it is always appropriate to your art that you should dress up in fine clothes and look as splendid as possible, and that at the same time it is necessary for you to occupy yourself with, the works of many excellent poets ... is enviable.' **τὸ σῶμα κεκοσμῆσθαι:** cf. 535d2. S.'s emphasis on the rhapsode's appearance, repeated in the words καλλίστοις φαίνεσθαι, suggests Ion's vanity and also hints at the superficiality of his τέχνη. Cf. *Hipp. Maj.* 291a where Hippias' reputation for wisdom, which similarly proves to be unfounded, is associated with his fine appearance. **b7 καλλίστοις** sc. ὑμῖν understood from ὑμῶν ... τῆι τέχνηι. **b8 ἐν ... ποιηταῖς διατρίβειν:** a phrase more often used of a life spent in philosophy as e.g. at *Hipp. Min.* 363a, *Phaed.* 63e, *Rep.* 561d, *Theaet.* 172c, 173c. **b9 Ὁμήρωι ... θειοτάτωι τῶν ποιητῶν:** no doubt the epithet θεῖος which is regularly applied to bards in the *Odyssey* influenced the characterisation of Homer himself as 'divine'. But the centrality of the Homeric poems in Greek education and culture generally (see Introduction p. 19), ensured the special status of their supposed author. Cf. *Phaed.* 95a1–2; *Rep.* 607a2–3; Ar. *Frogs* 1034 and see further Buffière (1956) 10–13, 25–31. **b10–11 διάνοιαν:** here and at c4 = 'meaning' or 'thought', as opposed to form of expression (τὰ ἔπη), but διανοίας at d3 = 'opinions'.

c2 ἀγαθὸς ῥαψωιδός: ῥαψωιδός is the subject, ἀγαθός the predicate. **c2–3 εἰ μὴ συνείη ... τοῦ ποιητοῦ:** cf. *Prot.* 339a where expertise in poetry is described as the ability to understand the differences between good and bad poetry, and to give reasons for one's judgements when asked. **c3 ἑρμηνέα:** this key word, like τέχνη, is introduced at a very early stage in the dialogue. The rhapsode is the interpreter of the poet's meaning just as at 534e poets are the interpreters of the gods. But P.'s use of the term ἑρμηνεύς is ambiguous: here it clearly implies knowledge and participation on the part of the rhapsode, but at 534e (see below) it is used in a context which shows that the poet is merely the unconscious instrument of the divine. **c4–5 τοῦτο δὲ καλῶς ποιεῖν ... ἀδύνατον:** cf. *Rep.* 598e where S. says that a good poet must understand his subject-matter if he is to compose well.   **c6 ζηλοῦσθαι:** S.'s repetition of this idea (cf. ἐζήλωσα at 530b5 and ζηλωτόν at 530c1) is heavily ironical, as later becomes clear.   **c7 ἐμοὶ γοῦν** suggests that what follows applies specifically to Ion rather than to rhapsodes in general.   **c8 τῆς τέχνης:** partitive genitive with τοῦτο. 'This is the aspect of my profession which has given me most trouble'.   **c9 ὡς** 'since' is causal.   **Μητρόδωρος:** Metrodorus of Lampsacus was a follower of Anaxagoras who allegorised Homer, interpreting both gods and heroes as representations of physical substances. Thus, for example, Agamemnon represented the aether, Achilles the sun, Hector the moon. He also seems to have considered grammatical questions. See D–K 61, Diog. Laert. 11.3.7 and Pfeiffer (1968) 35.

d1 Στησίμβροτος: Stesimbrotus of Thasos (*fl.* late fifth century) wrote a book on Homer, and is quoted in the scholia to the *Iliad* on 11.636 and 15.193. There is no firm evidence that he used the same allegorical methods as Metrodorus, but a passage in Xenophon (*Symp.* 3.6) implies that his teaching involved the interpretation of Homer's ὑπόνοιαι ('hidden meanings'). Whether this concern with Homer's ὑπόνοιαι involved allegorical criticism in the strict sense of the word it is impossible to tell, since the term ὑπόνοια could be used in a general sense to refer to any interpretation which penetrated below the surface meaning of a text. See further Richardson (1975) 65–81.   **Γλαύκων:** it is not possible to identify Glaucon with certainty, although he may be the commentator on Homer mentioned by Aristotle at *Po.* 1461b. Some scholars suggest that this Glaucon is identical with Glaucos of Rhegium, the late fifth-century writer of a work Περὶ τῶν ἀρχαίων ποιητῶν καὶ μουσικῶν (see Diog. Laert. 9.38; Plut. *De mus.* 4.1132e). In that case we would have to assume that the latter is referred to as Glaucon in both the *Ion* and the *Poetics*, a mistake which, though possible, seems unlikely. See further Richardson (1975) 76–7. By comparing himself with these individuals Ion implies that his task as a rhapsode was not merely to recite the works of Homer, but also to comment on them. But in fact the nature of his comments on Homer is left teasingly vague. At 530d2 Ion claims to have πολλὰς καὶ καλὰς διανοίας concerning Homer, and S. twice refers to him as Ὁμήρου ἐπαινέτης

(536d3 and 542b4), but we are given no examples to illustrate these claims. See further Tigerstedt (1969) 22–4. **d3 καλὰς διανοίας:** Ion's opinions about Homer may be 'fine', but they may not necessarily be true. The ambiguity in the meaning of the word καλός is exploited throughout the dialogue. See further on 533e7. **d4–5 οὐ φθονήσεις μοι ἐπιδεῖξαι:** when Ion twice offers to show off his skills, S. professes not to have time to listen (530d9 and 536d8), but later complains (541e) that Ion has not displayed the many fine things he knows about Homer. For ἐπιδεῖξαι cf. *Prot.* 320c, 347b; *Gorg.* 447a6 (with Dodds *ad loc.*), b2, b8 and *Rep.* 398a. The ἐπίδειξις or display lecture was part of the standard repertoire of sophists such as Hippias, Gorgias, Prodicus and Protagoras, who earned large sums by dazzling audiences with their oratorical skills (*Hipp. Maj.* 282b–d). Surviving examples of such performances are Gorgias' *Helen* and *Palamedes* and Prodicus' tale of the choice of Heracles (Xen. *Mem.* 2.1.21). See further Kerferd (1981(b)) 28–9. S.'s mistrust of these superficial displays is clear from e.g. *Hipp. Min.* 363a–364b or *Prot.* 329a where he objects that the listener cannot ask questions of the speaker. **d6–7 ὡς εὖ κεκόσμηκα** 'how well I embellish'. Some commentators (e.g. Méridier (1931) 11) take this to mean that Ion's comments on Homer were designed to bring out the beauties of the poetry. Cf. S.'s description of Ion as Ὁμήρου ἐπαινέτης (536d, 542b, *Prot.* 309a6, *Rep.* 606e1). But in the absence of any specific examples we cannot be sure. κεκόσμηκα does, however, pick up τὸ σῶμα κεκοσμῆσθαι at b6 above, suggesting the superficiality of the rhapsode's activity. On the significance of the term κοσμεῖν in pre-Platonic poetry see Velardi (1989) 20–3. **d7 Ὁμηριδῶν:** A guild of reciters known in Chios by the sixth century and claiming descent from Homer. See Strab. 14.1.35; Pi. *Nem.* 2.1; Pl. *Rep.* 599e6 and *Phdr.* 252b4; Isoc. *Hel.* 65; Sealey (1957) 312–17; Pfeiffer (1968) 11–12. **d8 χρυσῶι στεφάνωι στεφανωθῆναι:** the exaggerated repetition emphasises Ion's naiveté and vanity. Cf. 535d3, and 541c1 where Ion's phrase is ironically echoed by S.

530d9–533c9

S. questions Ion and establishes that the rhapsode's expertise should apply to poetry as a whole. Ion asks why it is, in that case, that he can only speak well about Homer.

530d9 Καὶ μήν: S. picks up Ion's words, with a hint of mockery at his naive desire to show off.   **ἔτι** is almost the equivalent of 'later'. Cf. 530d4n.

531a1 τοσόνδε 'just this'. This small question, on an apparently minor matter, is in fact the starting point of S.'s elenchus. Cf. *Hipp. Maj.* 286c, *Euthyd.* 274d, *Euthyphr.* 6c, *Prot.* 329b5–7.   **a2 Ἡσιόδου καὶ Ἀρχιλόχου:** for rhapsodic performances of Hesiod see Hes. fr. dub. 357; Pl. *Laws.* 658d. Isoc. *Panathenaicus* 18, quoted above, p. 97. Rhapsodic performances of Archilochus are mentioned in Athenaeus, 14.620c: 'Clearchus in the first of his two books *On riddles* says, "Simonides of Zacynthus used to recite (ἐρραψῴδει) the poems of Archilochus in the theatres, seated on a chair".' The date of this Simonides is not known, but Clearchus of Soli flourished around 300 B.C.   **a5 Ἔστι δὲ περὶ ὅτου** 'is there anything about which' : the antecedent of the relative is omitted.   **a7 ἐξηγήσαιο** 'expound'. In what follows it is clear that S. is questioning Ion's ability to interpret and comment on Homer rather than criticising him as a performer.   **a8 ἤ** 'or', the alternative to πότερον, not 'than' after the comparative κάλλιον.

b2 λέγει: for a singular verb with a compound subject cf. 532a6, and see Goodwin (1894) 198.   **b6 ἢ τῶν μάντεών τις τῶν ἀγαθῶν** 'one of the seers, one of the good ones'; the word order places the emphasis on τῶν ἀγαθῶν. The argument that the practitioner of a craft is a better judge of poetic descriptions of his craft than the rhapsode is at the heart of S.'s critique of the rhapsode's claim to knowledge, and is further developed at 537. The same argument is also used against poets in *Rep.* 599.   **b7 Εἰ δὲ σὺ ἦσθα μάντις:** the implication is that a good seer would understand his craft as a whole and would therefore be able to judge all aspects of it, as in the cases of arithmetic (531d12) and medicine (531e5) below. Both here and at 538e2–3 prophecy is used as an example of a τέχνη, but in the middle section of the dialogue at 534d1, the μάντις is the recipient of ἐνθουσιασμός and is out of his mind. This is not as much of a paradox as it might appear in view of *Phdr.* 244b–d, where a distinction is made between prophecy which depends on technique, and prophecy which is divinely inspired. Cf. Paus. 1.34.4. Nevertheless, we may suspect a certain playfulness in the choice of this particular example to illustrate S.'s point.

c1 Τί οὖν ποτε 'Why on earth, then': S.'s mock surprise is a further example of his ironic treatment of Ion.   **c4–d1 οὐ περὶ πολέμου ... καὶ ἡρώων:** S. lists warfare, the dealings of men and gods, what goes on in the heavens and in Hades, and the genealogies of gods and men, as typical subjects on which Homer and the other poets compose. With this summary compare *Rep.* 598e1–2 and 599c7–9. That Homer was an authority on warfare seems to have been something of a *topos*, hence Ion's claim at 540d5–541b5 that knowledge of Homer makes him a good general. Cf. Xen. *Symp.* 4.6, and Ar. *Frogs* 1034–6 where Aeschylus says that Homer's glory and fame arose from the fact that he taught useful things, such as 'marshalling of troops, deeds of bravery, the arming of men'. Dover (1993) points out *ad loc.* that 'despite considerable differences between Homeric and fifth-century warfare, it was still conventional in some quarters to regard Homer as the source of wisdom on tactics'. Even Alexander the Great, if we are to believe Plutarch (*Alex.* 8.2–3) took a text of the *Iliad* with him on campaign, and always kept it with his dagger beneath his pillow.   **c5–6 ἰδιωτῶν καὶ δημιουργῶν:** the contrast is between laymen and professionals. For ἰδιώτης see below on 532d8–e1; for δημιουργός see Hom. *Od.* 17.383–5 with Stanford (1947) *ad loc.* and 19.135.   **c6–7 περὶ θεῶν ... ὁμιλούντων, ὡς ὁμιλοῦσι:** an example of prolepsis, when the subject of a subordinate clause is anticipated in the sentence on which that clause depends, as in the sentence 'I know thee, who thou art'. Cf. 531e5.   **c7–8 οὐρανίων παθημάτων:** either 'what goes on in the heavens', i.e. the scenes on Olympus, or 'the phenomena of the heavens' (cf. *Hipp. Maj.* 285c1; *Phaed.* 96b9–c1), in which case the phrase must refer to Homer's descriptions of sunrise, sunset and the stars (as e.g. at *Il.* 4.75–7, 5.5–6, 22.317–18). The parallelism with the phrase τῶν ἐν Ἅιδου, 'what goes on in Hades', as described in *Od.* 11, supports the first interpretation rather than the second.

d6 ὁμοίως: Ion understands this as a distinction between good and bad, whereas S. had earlier used this term to contrast sameness and difference (531b4 above). Ion's claim that it is Homer's treatment of his subject-matter rather than the subject-matter itself which distinguishes Homer from other poets is completely ignored by S., who persistently views poetry simply in terms of its factual content. Cf.

540b3. Ladrière (1951) 29 points out that the problem of value first enters the discussion here, and remains a central issue throughout. Ion values Homer above all other poets, but on what basis does he make that judgement?   **διₐ ὦ φίλη κεφαλή** 'my dear chap', with the use of the proper name as well, is clearly ironic in tone. Cf. *Gorg.* 513c2, *Phdr.* 264a8, *Euthyd.* 293e4.   **ἀριθμοῦ** 'arithmetic'. Cf. 537e4–8 where S. returns to the example of arithmetic.

e5 περὶ ὑγιεινῶν ... ὁποῖά ἐστιν: prolepsis. Cf. 531c7n. For the example of medicine cf. 538c4–5.   **e9 Οὐκοῦν:** each of the next five sentences spoken by S. begins with this word, and together they include all the premises for the conclusion that Ion is incapable of speaking about Homer with knowledge and understanding. The steps in the argument are as follows: 1. In relation to any given subject the same man will know who speaks well and who speaks badly. 2. The same man will be an expert on both the good and the bad speaker. 3. Ion has already agreed that Homer and the other poets speak about the same things, but not in the same way, because Homer speaks well, the others badly. 4. If he understands one who speaks well, he will also understand those who speak badly. 5. Ion must know not only about Homer but also about the other poets too, since he himself agrees that the same man will be an adequate judge of all those who speak about the same things, and practically all poets deal with the same subject-matter. Conclusion (532c6–8): since Ion can only speak about Homer, his ability to do so cannot depend on τέχνη. On S.'s method in this section, see Robinson (1953) 20–2.   **e10–532a1** ὁ αὐτὸς γνώσεται ... ὅστις κακῶς states the fundamental principle applicable to any τέχνη, that he who has knowledge in a given field will know it as a whole. Cf. *Charm.* 166e7–8, *Phaed.* 97d1–5, *Rep.* 334a, 409d8–10 and *Symp.* 223d3 where S. compels his listeners to agree that the same man ought to understand how to write both tragedy and comedy. There, in marked contrast to what is said elsewhere in P.'s work (see e.g. *Rep.* 395), S. appears to attribute τέχνη to poets. But the fact that he produces no examples to illustrate this point, combined with the fact that his listeners are Agathon and Aristophanes, a tragic and a comic poet respectively, suggests that the argument is purely hypothetical. If composing poetry were indeed a τέχνη, then it would be the case that the same poet could compose both tragedy and comedy. Since no such poet exists, we are left to infer that poetry is not in fact a τέχνη. See further on *Rep.* 601d1–2.

532a6 ἐστιν: for a singular verb with a compound subject cf. 531b2.

b2 ὦ βέλτιστε 'excellent fellow' ironically underlines Ion's inability to see where S.'s argument is leading. For the expression cf. 541c7 and e.g. *Cri.* 48a5, *Euthyd.* 300c5, *Gorg.* 515d9.   **b9 διαλέγηται:** again the emphasis is on the discussion rather than the recital of Homer.

c2 ἀτεχνῶς 'simply', to be distinguished from ἀτέχνως 'artlessly', plays on the etymological connexion between the two words.   **c2–3 νυστάζω ... ἐγρήγορα** introduces the significant metaphor of sleeping and waking. Cf. 533a2, 536b6–8.   **c3 εὐπορῶ:** there is an unwitting irony in Ion's use of this word precisely at the point in the dialogue where he has been reduced to ἀπορία.   **c6 τέχνηι καὶ ἐπιστήμηι:** these words are virtually synonymous in this dialogue. Cf. 536c1 and 537d6–e. Despite S.'s references to the rhapsode's τέχνη at the beginning of the dialogue (530b6–7), it now emerges that he has none, since, on his own admission, he is quite unable to apply his knowledge of Homer to any other poet. A τέχνη must be based on rational principles and be able to give an account of its procedure, as is clear from the discussion of rhetoric at *Gorg.* 462–3, where τέχνη is contrasted with ἐμπειρία, a kind of empirical knack. Anything which is irrational (ἄλογον) cannot be called a τέχνη, as S. says at *Gorg.* 465a5–6. See further Sprague (1976) 1–14; T. Irwin, *Plato's moral theory* (Oxford 1977) 71–5.   **c8–9 ποιητικὴ ... τὸ ὅλον** 'for the whole thing is poetry, isn't it?' With this deceptively simple question S. broadens the discussion to include not only the rhapsode's activity, but also the poet's. But it is significant that he makes no clear distinction between the two. Ion might reasonably argue that being a good rhapsode is not the same thing as being a good poet, for the skills of the two are different, the one being concerned with performance and interpretation, the other with composition. But S. deliberately obscures the differences so that the two activities become indistinguishable. In an oral culture these differences may not be as clear-cut as they are to us, but in any case it is part of S.'s strategy to treat the production, transmission and enjoyment of poetry as a single process. See Velardi (1989) 45. S. appears to imply here that there *is* an art of poetry, which covers poetry as a whole; but he then proceeds to demonstrate that there is no such thing. If poetry were a τέχνη, poets would understand their subject-matter and be able to give an account of what they do. Similarly if there were such a thing as rhapsodic τέχνη, (1) Ion would be able to exercise his skill on all poets, not just on Homer, and (2) his τέχνη would be different from all other τέχναι (538bff). But in fact neither poets nor rhapsodes fulfil the requirements necessary for the practitioner of a τέχνη. S. thus raises the possibility of there being an art of poetry, but only in order to deny it. For a similar strategy see *Symp.* 223d3 discussed at 531e10 above. Janaway (1992) rightly points out that there is no explicit denial of rhapsodic or poetic τέχνη *per se* in the dialogue. But his conclusion that P. therefore genuinely assumes the existence of poetic and rhapsodic τέχνη, and that it is the *fineness* of the rhapsode's performance and the poet's productions which cannot be explained by τέχνη, fails to take account of the irony with which P. treats the subject. Cf. 538b4.

d2–3 ὁ αὐτὸς τρόπος ... τῶν τεχνῶν 'there will be the same method of enquiry in all τέχναι'. S. here repeats the point made at 531e10–532a1, that a practitioner of a τέχνη will have knowledge of the whole of a given subject area, on the basis of which he will be able to judge between good and bad in individual cases. **d5 τῶν σοφῶν:** the term σοφός meaning 'wise', 'intelligent' or 'clever' could be applied to anyone who possessed a specialised skill ranging from carpenters and shoe-makers to poets, philosophers and teachers of rhetoric. But the question of who was truly σοφός became a central issue in fifth-century literature and thought. See e.g. Goldhill (1986) 222–43. For S.'s reputation as a σοφός see *Apol.* 23a. On the history and significance of the term see B. Snell, *Die Ausdrücke für den Begriff des Wissens in der vor-platonischen Philosophie* (Berlin 1924); B. Gladigow, *Sophia und Kosmos* (Hildesheim 1965). **d6–7 σοφοὶ ... ῥαψῳδοὶ καὶ ὑποκριταί:** with characteristic self-deprecation, and not a little irony, S. rejects the title of σοφός for himself, insisting that it is Ion and his colleagues who really deserve it. What has up until now been applied specifically to Ion is now generalised to include all rhapsodes and actors. For the connexion between rhapsodes and actors see 536a1, *Rep.* 373b7, 395a8; Alcidamas, *De Sophistis* 14 Blass; Arist. *Po.* 1462a, *Rhet.* 1403b22. The description of Ion's own performances of Homeric epic at 535b1–e6 shows clearly that the rhapsode was no mere passive reciter, but threw himself into his part in much the same way as an actor. Hence the term ὑποκριτής, normally used of the dramatic actor, could also be used of the rhapsode. See further, H. Koller, 'Hypokrisis und Hypokrites', *Mus. Helv.* 14 (1957) 100ff.; Flashar (1958) 47; Herington (1985) 12–13, 51; Velardi (1989) 14. **d7–8: ὧν ὑμεῖς ... ποιήματα:** poets were, of course, traditionally characterised as σοφοί. Cf. 542a1 where S. refers to Homer's σοφία. ἀιδειν and λέγειν are used interchangeably of the rhapsode's delivery, (see e.g. below 535b2–4, c2, c6, e3, 537a5, [Pl.] *Eryx.* 403d and cf. *Tim.* 21b–c), just as ἀείδειν and ἐνέπειν are used indiscriminately of poetic performance by Homer and Hesiod. But whereas bards in Homeric epic sang or chanted to the accompaniment of a lyre, rhapsodes in the classical period normally recited without musical accompaniment, holding instead a staff. See M. L. West (1981) 113–15; Herington (1985) 12–13; Nagy (1989) 4–8.   **d8–e1 τἀληθῆ λέγω ... ἰδιώτην:** typically S. says that he is merely an amateur, disclaiming any technical expertise or professional skill. For the contrast between the layman's concern with simple truth and the spurious wisdom of the σοφοί see *e.g. Hipp. Maj.*, 288d4–5, *Hipp. Min.* 372a6–c1, 376c4, *Gorg.* 462e6, *Symp.* 198d3–4, 199a6–b1. For ἰδιώτης used of prose as opposed to poetry see *Symp.* 178b3, *Phdr.* 258d10–11, *Rep.* 366e7–8.

e1 περὶ τούτου οὗ: the relative is attracted into the case of its antecedent.   **e2–3 παντὸς ἀνδρός** 'within the power of any man'.   **e4 τῶι λόγωι:** by reasoning or argument, as opposed to fact. Cf. *Rep.* 369c9 Ἴθι δή ... τῶι λόγωι ἐξ ἀρχῆς ποιῶμεν πόλιν.   **e4–5 γραφικὴ γάρ ... τὸ ὅλον;** 'is there an art of painting as a whole?' The inclusion of the word τέχνη here makes the nuance of this sentence slightly different from that at 532c8–9. Having made the general statement at 532d2–3 that the same method of enquiry will apply to all τέχναι, S. now takes painting as an example of a τέχνη to see how the general principles underlying all τέχναι apply in a particular case. For P.'s fondness for references to painting see Keuls

(1978) 33–47, and for painting as a τέχνη see e.g. *Gorg.* 448b–c, 450c, 503e; *Prot.* 312c–d, 318b–c, and Demand (1975) 3–4. Contrast *Rep.* 597e2 where the implication is that the painter is simply a μιμητής whose skill amounts to very little. It is significant that all the τέχναι referred to in this section – painting, sculpture, pipe playing, lyre playing, singing to the lyre and rhapsodic performance – are arts involving μίμησις. Cf. *Rep.* 373b5–8.   **e6 καὶ γραφῆς:** painters as well as an art of painting.   **e8 Πολυγνώτου:** one of the most famous painters working in Athens in the middle of the fifth century, born in Thasos and later given Athenian citizenship. According to Aristotle, he idealised his figures (*Po.* 1448a5), but was good at depicting character (*Po.* 1450a27, *Pol.* 1340a37–8).

533a2 ἐπιδεικνύηι implies commenting on paintings as well as showing them. See on 530d4 above.   **a3–4 ὅτου βούλει:** the relative is attracted into the case of its antecedent. Cf. 532e1 above.   **a4 ἑνὸς μόνου** emphasises the putative critic's expertise in one painter alone.   **a7 Δαιδάλου τοῦ Μητίονος:** a legendary character who personified skill in craftsmanship, as his name indicates. He was famous amongst other things for his exceptionally life-like statues. Cf. *Euthyphr.* 11c, *Men.* 97d–e and in general see F. Frontisi-Ducroux, *Dédale. Mythologie de l'artisan en Grèce ancienne* (Paris 1975).

b1 Ἐπειοῦ τοῦ Πανοπέως: Epeius, with the help of Athena, made the famous wooden horse of Troy (*Od.* 8.493).   **Θεοδώρου τοῦ Σαμίου:** a celebrated craftsman of the middle of the sixth century B.C., maker of a silver bowl which Croesus sent as a votive offering to Delphi (Hdt. 1.51) and of Polycrates' emerald seal (Hdt. 3.41).   **b2 ἑνὸς πέρι** cf. ἑνὸς μόνου at 533a4 above.   **b6–7 αὐλήσει … ῥαψωιδίαι:** these are all branches of μουσική as opposed to painting and sculpture. For the difference between κιθάρισις, playing the lyre, and κιθαρωιδία, singing to the lyre, see e.g. *Laws.* 669e. According to Heraclides Ponticus (Plut. *De mus.* 1132c) Terpander was an outstanding exponent of the citharode's art, which involved setting the work of Homer and other poets to music, rather than chanting or reciting like a rhapsode. See further M. L. West (1981) 113–14; Barker (1984) 207–9.   **b8–c1 Ὀλύμπου … Φημίου τοῦ Ἰθακησίου:** legendary exponents of the four types of μουσική just mentioned. Olympus was a mythical pipe player, said to have been taught by Marsyas (*Symp.* 215c) and an inventor of μουσική (*Laws.* 677d). See further Barker (1984) 92. Thamyras was the Thracian bard who challenged the Muses to a contest and was blinded as a punishment for his presumptuousness (Hom. *Il.* 2.595–600, cf. Eur. *Rhes.* 924–5, Plut. *De mus.* 1132b–c and Barker (1984) 21–2). He is mentioned together with Orpheus at *Rep.* 620a, where his soul chooses the form of a nightingale, cf. *Laws.* 829d–e. He also appears with Orpheus in the famous painting of the underworld by Polygnotus, described at Paus. 10.30.8. Ὀρφέως is the mythical Thracian musician who charmed nature itself with his singing and is chosen here as the archetype of κιθαρωιδία. On the numerous legends concerning him see W. K. C. Guthrie, *Orpheus and Greek religion* (London 1935); I. M. Linforth, *The arts of Orpheus* (Berkeley and Los Angeles 1941); M. L. West (1983) 1–38.

c1 Φημίου τοῦ Ἰθακησίου: the bard forced to sing for the entertainment of the suitors in the *Odyssey* (1.154, 22.331). Homer calls him an ἀοιδός, but later tradition described him as a rhapsode, like Homer himself (*Rep.* 600d; *Laws.* 658b; *Cert. Hom. et Hes.* 5 and 17). See further M. L. West (1981) 113–14. There is more than a little irony in comparing Ion with these great masters of the past.   **c7–9 ὅρα ... καὶ ὁρῶ:** the nuance of these words is practically, '*you* explain it (if you can)', to which S. answers, 'Yes, I can and will'.

533c9–536d7

S. explains that Ion's ability does not depend on skill or knowledge, but on inspiration, which derives ultimately from the Muses. As a magnet exerts power over a chain of iron rings, so the Muses' inspiration extends from poet to rhapsode to audience.

533c9–d1 ἔρχομαί γέ σοι ἀποφαινόμενος 'I am going to show you'. There is no need to reject the reading of the MSS here in view of *Phaed.* 100b3, where ἔρχομαι is similarly followed by a present participle.   **d1–2 ἔστι ... οὐκ ὄν = οὐκ ἔστι:** 'this ability of yours to speak well about Homer is not a skill'.   **d2 ὃ νυνδὴ ἔλεγον:** cf. 532c6.   **d3–4 ὥσπερ ἐν τῆι λίθωι ... Ἡρακλείαν:** Delatte (1934) 59–62 points out that Democritus is said to have written a work περὶ τῆς λίθου (68 B 11k), and considers the possible influence of Democritus on P. here. The application of the magnet image to poetry was probably P.'s invention, but Harriott (1969) 81 notes that the power of attraction is associated with music in the legends of Orpheus and of the Sirens. λίθος is feminine when used of a special kind of stone. For the reference to Euripides see fr. 567 Nauck τὰς βροτῶν | γνώμας σκοπῶν ὥστε Μαγνῆτις λίθος | τὴν δόξαν ἕλκει καὶ μεθίησιν πάλιν. Cf. Lucr. *D.R.N.* 6.906–9 with C. Bailey, *Titi Lucreti Cari: de rerum natura libri sex* (Oxford 1947) *ad loc.* There was a Magnesia in Caria on the river Maeander in Asia Minor and a Heraclea to the south of it. But Magnesia was also the name of a region of Thessaly and a town in Lydia, and there were many places called Heraclea. Pliny (*N.H.* 36.127), citing Nicander, says that the stone was named after its discoverer, Magnes, a herdsman who found the nails of his boots sticking to his crook. Pliny also says that there were five kinds of magnet, the worst of which was the stone from Asia Minor. The adjective Ἡρακλείαν (cf. 533e below and *Tim.* 80c) may refer to the stone's physical force, i.e. like that of Heracles, rather than to the place from which it came.   **d6 δύναμιν ἐντίθ-ησι:** contrast *Tim.* 80c where Plato says that there is no attraction in amber or lodestone.

e1–2 σιδηρίων 'pieces of iron'.   **e2 ἤρτηται:** contrast the use of the perfect tense here ('a chain hangs in a state of suspension') with ἐξαρτᾶται ('a chain is strung out') at 533e5. The passage as a whole is imitated by Lucretius (*D.R.N.* 6.910–16):

> hunc homines lapidem mirantur; quippe catenam
> saepe ex anellis reddit pendentibus ex se.
> quinque etenim licet interdum pluresque uidere
> ordine demissos leuibus iactarier auris,
> unus ubi ex uno dependet subter adhaerens
> ex alioque alius lapidis uim uinclaque noscit:
> usque adeo permananter uis perualet eius.

e3–5 οὕτω δὲ καὶ ἡ Μοῦσα ... ὁρμαθὸς ἐξαρτᾶται: with the image of the magnet P. shifts the focus of the dialogue away from the specific question of Ion's skill (or lack of it) as a rhapsode and moves on to the larger subject of poetic inspiration in general. Although he emphasises that all those who experience the Muses' inspiration are in a similar state of enthusiasm, it is significant that his speech in fact concentrates for the most part on poets. The idea that poets are inspired is, of course, age-old, but the notion of ἐνθουσιασμός which P. here introduces is strikingly new. The word ἐνθουσιασμός first occurs in Democritus, fr. 18 ποιητὴς δὲ ἄσσα μὲν ἂν γράφηι μετ' ἐνθουσιασμοῦ καὶ ἱεροῦ πνεύματος, καλὰ κάρτα ἐστίν, and both Cicero (De or. 2.194) and Horace (A.P. 295–7) attribute the idea of inspiration as a form of frenzied enthusiasm to him. But Democritus, fr. 21 suggests that he did not regard inspiration and technique as incompatible: Ὅμηρος φύσεως λαχὼν θεαζούσης ἐπέων κόσμον ἐτεκτήνατο παντοίων. No doubt P. was influenced by his predecessor; but whereas Democritus appears to combine the notions of inspiration and craft, P. consistently opposes them. This opposition became central to discussions of poetry in antiquity, and was expressed in Latin by the standard antithesis between ars and ingenium. For an attempt to reconstruct Democritus' views see Delatte (1934). For Democritus' influence on P. see Flashar (1958) 56–8 and Tigerstedt (1969) 72–6. On the differences between P. and his predecessors see Tigerstedt (1970), Murray (1981) and (1992).   **e5–6 οἵ τε τῶν ἐπῶν ποιηταί:** S. begins with epic poets, since it is Homer by whom Ion is inspired.   **e6 οἱ ἀγαθοί:** For the word order cf. 531b6 above, and 533e8 below. Lack of τέχνη is not the sign of a bad poet, for it is specifically good poets who are devoid of skill, cf. *Phdr.* 245a5–8. Paradoxically, therefore, the better the poetry, the less skill the poet has. Ion himself is, of course, a particularly good rhapsode, having carried off first prize at Epidaurus (above 530b, cf. 530c8–d3).   **e7 κατεχόμενοι** 'possessed', but also 'held'. The pun reinforces the comparison between the chain of iron rings held (literally) by the magnet, and poets possessed (metaphorically) by the Muse. Cf. 536a8–b1.   **καλὰ λέγουσι ποιήματα:** throughout this section the emphasis is on poems which are 'fine' or 'beautiful'. Cf. 534a2, b8, c2, c6, d8, e3 and 535a1. But it is quite possible for poetry to be beautiful without being factually accurate or true. Cf. *Symp.* 198b–d where S. praises the beauty of Agathon's speech about Love, whilst pointing out that its contents are false. For the implications of P.'s use of the word καλός and its cognates in the *Ion* see further Dorter (1973) 74–7. For λέγουσι see on 532d7–8. The fact that P. uses this verb of both composition and recitation suggests that he is not interested in distinguishing between the poet as composer and the rhapsode as reciter.   **e8 οἱ μελοποιοί** 'composers of lyric poetry'. This word, used by P. only here and at *Prot.* 326a, emphasises the musical aspects of lyric composition (cf. Ar. *Frogs*. 1250). The repetition of the word at 534a1–2 and a6 suggests that the comparison with Corybants and Bacchants applies specifically to lyric poets, with music providing the link between them.   **e8–534a1 οἱ κορυβαντιῶντες ... ὀρχοῦνται:** the Corybantes were mythical attendants of the Phrygian mother-goddess, Cybele, whose cult involved wild orgiastic dancing to the music of pipes and drums. In classical Athens Corybantic ritual was believed to be therapeutic in the treatment of madness. Like their mythical counterparts, participants in the rites danced in frenzy, their hearts pounding, their eyes filled with tears (*Symp.* 215e; cf. *Phdr.* 228b, *Laws* 790d; Ar. *Wasps* 8 and 119). See further Linforth (1946), Dodds (1951) 77–80 and below on 536c2.

534a2 οὐκ ἔμφρονες ... ποιοῦσιν is almost a contradiction in terms since ποιεῖν and its cognates generally refer to the craft elements in poetic composition. See e.g. Harriott (1969) 93–4; Nagy (1989) 23–4.   **a3 ἐμβῶσιν** continues the idea of dancing.   **a4 βακχεύουσι** picks up the dancing of the Corybants, but also broadens the picture of frenzied ecstasy. Cf. *Phdr.* 228b, 234d and *Laws* 790d–e for a similar shift from Corybantic to Bacchic ecstasy. Though P. implies that the image of the poet as Bacchant is traditional, there is little evidence to suggest that this was the case. Archilochus, fr. 120 brings together Dionysus, wine and poetic inspiration: ὡς Διωνύσου ἄνακτος καλὸν ἐξάρξαι μέλος | οἶδα διθύραμβον οἴνωι συγκεραυνωθεὶς φρένας, and the association between wine and song was, of course, age-old. But P. significantly makes no mention of wine in the *Ion*. The connexion between poetic inspiration and wineless Bacchic ecstasy (cf. e.g. Hor. *C.* 2.19 with N–H *ad loc.*, and *C.* 3.25) seems to have begun here. See further Tigerstedt (1970) 175–6; Murray (1992) 29–30.   **κατεχόμενοι** refers back to οἱ μελοποιοί, but after the parenthetical ὥσπερ clause, the subject is changed to τῶν μελοποιῶν ἡ ψυχή, which leaves the participle κατεχόμενοι without any grammatical construction (anacoluthon). The sentence as a whole enacts its own meaning, as the clauses are piled up one on top of the

other and the reader is caried away by the stream of words.   **a4–
5 αἱ Βάκχαι ... γάλα:** Aeschines Socraticus (fr. 11c Dittmar) puts
the same image into the mouth of Socrates to describe his love for
Alcibiades: ἐγὼ δὲ διὰ τὸν ἔρωτα ὃν ἐτύγχανον ἐρῶν Ἀλκιβιάδου
οὐδὲν διάφορον τῶν βακχῶν ἐπεπόνθειν. καὶ γὰρ αἱ βάκχαι ἐπειδὰν
ἔνθεοι γένωνται, ὅθεν οἱ ἄλλοι ἐκ τῶν φρεάτων οὐδὲ ὕδωρ δύνανται ὑδρεύεσθαι, ἐκεῖναι μέλι καὶ γάλα ἀρύονται. P.'s more original comparison of poets to Bacchants exploits traditional associa-
tions in order to highlight the irrationality of the poetic process. On
the significance of milk and honey in ancient culture generally see
H. Usener, 'Milch und Honig', *Rh. M.* 57 (1902) 177–95. Honey, the
food of the gods (Porph. *Antr.* 16), was first discovered by Dionysus
(Ovid, *Fast.* 3.736–62), who transmits his miraculous powers over
nature to his frenzied followers. See Eur. *Ba.* 142, 704–11 (with
Dodds (1960) *ad loc.*); Eur. *Hyps.* fr. 57 Bond; Hor. *C.* 2.19.9–12 with
N–H *ad loc.* P.'s words also recall Pi. *Nem.* 3.76–9 where milk and
honey are used as a metaphor for poetry: ἐγὼ τόδε τοι | πέμπω
μεμιγμένον μέλι λευκῶι | σὺν γάλακτι ... πόμ' ἀοίδιμον Αἰολίσσιν
ἐν πνοαῖσιν αὐλῶν. He thus brings together two different types of
experience, Bacchic ecstasy and poetic inspiration. It is striking that
P. makes no mention of wine here, despite its special association
with Dionysus (see in particular *h. Hom.* 7.35–6, where its miraculous
production is described) and with poetry.   **a7 λέγουσι ... οἱ
ποιηταί:** P. validates his picture of poetic enthusiasm by referring to
the language which poets themselves use. Although he does not
quote directly, there are many reminiscences of earlier poetry in
what follows. δήπουθεν 'of course' perhaps contains a hint of irony.
πρὸς ἡμᾶς with ἡμῖν at b2 emphasises the recipients of the poets'
words, reminding us of the importance of the audience in the chain
of poetic communication.

b1–2 ἀπὸ κρηνῶν μελιρρύτων ... ὥσπερ αἱ μέλιτται: κρηνῶν picks
up ποταμῶν at 534a5, underlining the parallelism between poets
and Bacchants. A whole complex of traditional imagery lies behind
P.'s words. See Harriott (1969) 83–6; Velardi (1989) 106–10. The
comparison of flowing speech to a river goes back to Homer, as does
the association between honey and eloquence (see e.g. Hom. *Il.*
1.247–9, *Od.* 8.170–3; Hes. *Th.* 39–40, 83–4 with West *ad loc.*, 96–7).

For the phrase μελίγηρυν ἀοιδήν see *h. Hom.* 3.519, 19.18 and cf. *Od.* 12.187 μελίγηρυν ... ὄπα of the Sirens' voice; Alcm. fr. 26.1 μελιγάρυες ἱαρόφωνοι; Pi. *Ol.* 11.4 μελιγάρυες ὕμνοι, *Pae.* 5.47 συν μελιγάρυι ... ὀμφᾶι). For the metaphor of poets drinking from springs see e.g. Pi. *Ol.* 6.85–6, *Isthm.* 6.74–5; Callim. *h. Ap.* 110–12; Lucr. *D.R.N.* 4.2–3; Hor. *Epist.* 1.3.10–11; Prop.3.1.6, 3.3.5–6, 51–2; Kambylis (1965) 113–16, 125–33. In the lyric poets, particularly in Pindar, honey is a symbol for poetry, and compounds with μελι- are often used of poetry and song. See e.g. Pi. *Ol.* 7.7–8, 10.98–9, *Nem.* 3.76–8, *Pae.* 6.58–9; Pi. *Nem.* 11.18 μελιγδούποισι ... ἀοιδαῖς; *Isthm.* 2.7–8 μελιφθόγγου ... Τερψιχόρας; 32 μελικόμπων ἀοιδᾶν; *Isthm.* 6.9 μελιφθόγγοις ἀοιδαῖς; fr. 122.14 μελίφρονος ... σκολίου; Bacch. fr. 4.63 μελιγλώσσαν ἀοιδᾶν. But P.'s compound μελιρρύτων appears to have no parallel. Honey, of course, suggests sweetness, as is reflected in the anecdotes about bees smearing the infant lips of Pindar with honey (see e.g. Paus. 9.23.2; Ael. *V.H.* 12.45; M. R. Lefkowitz, *The lives of the Greek poets* (London 1981) 59). For the same story about P. see Riginos (1976) 17–21 and cf. Ar. fr. 581 on Sophocles. But it is also associated with prophecy, as e.g. at *h. Hom.* 4.560–3 where the bee maidens of Mount Parnassus can only speak the truth when inspired by feeding on honey. See further Scheinberg (1979). For the motif of poets culling their songs from the gardens and glades of the Muses see Pi. *Ol.* 9.26 ἐξαίρετον Χαρίτων νέμομαι κᾶπον; Ar. *Frogs.* 1300 λειμῶνα Μουσῶν ἱερὸν ... δρέπων.   **ὥσπερ αἱ μέλιτται** brings together the various strands of imagery with a play on words: μελιρρύτων ... μέλη ... μέλιτται. For the poet as bee see e.g. Pi. *Pyth.* 10.53–4; Bacch. 10.10; Ar. *Birds* 748–50; Callim. *h. Ap.* 110; Hor. *C.* 4.27–32. And on the symbolism of bees and honey in ancient poetry generally see Waszink (1974) and Scheinberg (1979).   **b2–3 καὶ αὐτοὶ οὕτω πετόμενοι** 'and they too [like bees] are on the wing'. P. introduces a new point of comparison here, leading from bees to birds. For bees as birds of the Muses see Varro, *De re rust.* 3.16.7 *cum Musarum esse dicantur uolucres.* P.'s words recall Ar. *Birds* 1373–96 where Cinesias comes in quoting Anacreon (*PMG* 378) ἀναπέτομαι δὴ πρὸς Ὄλυμπον πτερύγεσσι κούφαις. Cf. *Peace* 827–31. For the poet as eagle see Pi. *Nem.* 5.20–1, 3.80, *Ol.* 2.88; Bacch. 5.16–30. Cf. Hor. *C.* 2.20 with N-H *ad loc.* and 4.2.25 for the poet as swan.   **b3 καὶ ἀληθῆ λέγουσι** P., like Aristophanes,

mischievously takes poetic metaphor literally.   **b3–4 κοῦφον ...**
ἱερόν spells out the implications of the imagery, but not without
irony: κοῦφον suggests emptiness as well as lightness. The association
of wings and words goes back to Homer in the formulaic phrase
ἔπεα πτερόεντα, on which see Heubeck (1988) on *Od.* 1.122. For the
wings of fame conferred by poetry see Theogn. 237–54; Pi. *Isthm.*
1.64–7. Poets, of course, traditionally claimed to be divinely inspired
and sacred to the Muses. See Sperduti (1950) 209–40. For bees as
sacred see e.g. Pi. fr. 123.11; Virg. *Georg.* 4.219–21.   **b5–6 ἔνθεός**
... ἐν αὐτῶι ἐνῆι: a corollary of being filled with the god (ἔνθεος =
lit. 'having a god in one') is that the poet's own mind is elsewhere, a
point strongly emphasised by the play on ἔνθεος ... ἔκφρων ... ἐν ...
ἐνῆι. Cf. Ar. *Ach.* 395–400 Δι. ἔνδον ἔστ' Εὐριπίδης; | Κη. οὐκ ἔνδον,
ἔνδον ἐστίν, εἰ γνώμην ἔχεις. | Δι. πῶς ἔνδον εἶτ' οὐκ ἔνδον; Κη. ὀρ-
θῶς ὦ γέρον. | ὁ νοῦς μὲν ἔξω ξυλλέγων ἐπύλλια | οὐκ ἔνδον, αὐτὸς
δ' ἔνδον ἀναβάδην ποιεῖ | τραγωιδίαν.   **b7 πᾶς ποιεῖν ...**
χρησμωιδεῖν: cf. *Men.* 99c–d. The notion of enthusiasm which has
been developed in relation to epic and lyric poets is now generalised
to include everyone who composes or prophesies. Characteristically
P. introduces a new point here at the end of the sentence. For prophetic μανία see e.g. Heraclit. fr. 92 where the sibyl speaks μαιν-
ομένωι στόματι; Aesch. *Ag.* 1140 where Cassandra is described as
φρενομανής and θεοφόρητος. Cf. Eur. *Ba.* 298–301 μάντις δ' ὁ
δαίμων ὅδε· τὸ γὰρ Βακχεύσιμον | καὶ τὸ μανιῶδες μαντικὴν
πολλὴν ἔχει· | ὅταν γὰρ ὁ θεὸς ἐς τὸ σῶμ' ἔλθηι πολύς, | λέγειν
τὸ μέλλον τοὺς μεμηνότας ποιεῖ. For the etymological connexion
between μανία and μαντική see Pl. *Phdr.* 244b–c. P. exploits the age-
old association between poetry and prophecy in order to give cre-
dence to his picture of the frenzied poet. See N. K. Chadwick, *Poetry
and prophecy* (Cambridge 1942); J. L. Kugel (ed.), *Poetry and prophecy*
(Ithaca and London 1990). For the *topos* of the poet as prophet see
Pi. fr. 150 μαντεύεο, Μοῖσα, προφατεύσω δ' ἐγώ; *Pae.* 6.6 ἀοίδιμον
Πιερίδων προφάταν; Bacch. 9.3 Μουσᾶν γε ἰοβλεφάρων θεῖος προ-
φ[άτ]ας.   **b8 ποιοῦντες ... λέγοντες:** these participles lead us to
expect a plural subject, instead of which we have ἕκαστος at c2.

c1 ὥσπερ σὺ περὶ Ὁμήρου sc. πολλὰ λέγεις καὶ καλά: for the emphasis on καλά cf. 533e7, 534a2. The sudden inclusion of Ion as a

divinely inspired being at this point is not without irony. But P. also signals that there is no distinction to be made between poet and rhapsode: what he says applies equally to both.   **θεῖαι μοῖραι** 'by divine dispensation'. Cf. 535a4, 536c2, d3, 542a4, and for a discussion of the phrase in P.'s work in general see J. Souilhé, 'La θεία μοῖρα chez Platon', *Philosophia perennis* 1 (1930) 11–25. In the *Apology* (33c6) Socrates defends himself on the grounds that he has always acted under the influence of θεία μοῖρα, but there is no suggestion that his reason was therefore impaired or that he was behaving irrationally. But here the contrast between θεία μοῖρα and τέχνη lays heavy emphasis on the poet's (and rhapsode's) lack of νοῦς. Cf. *Men.* 99e6, with Bluck (1961) 434–6, 424–7; *Phdr.* 244c3; Aeschin. Socr. frr. 11a and b Dittmar. There is undoubtedly irony in ascribing Ion's ability to speak well about Homer to θεία μοῖρα, particularly in view of his revelations at 535e1–6, and that irony must also extend to P.'s treatment of poets. Even if we were to take seriously the idea that poets are divinely inspired, that inspiration is strictly limited (534c2); and it confers no authority on poets or their interpreters themselves, because it deprives them of all understanding.   **c2–3 ἡ Μοῦσα ... ὥρμησεν:** a reminiscence of Hom. *Od.* 8.499 ὁ δ' [Δημόδοκος] ὁρμηθεὶς θεοῦ ἄρχετο, as recognised by Proclus (*In Rep.* 1, p. 184, 27–8 Kroll), who comments: ταύτηι τὸν Ὅμηρον ζηλῶν.   **c3–4 διθυράμβους ... ἰάμβους:** it is striking that P. emphasises the genres of choral lyric, iambic and epic, but makes no reference to dramatic poetry. Perhaps this is in order to sustain the close identification of poet and performer. The dithyramb was a choral song in honour of Dionysus (*Laws* 700b4–5), first mentioned by Archilochus, fr. 120. According to Herodotus (1.23) Arion was the first man to compose and name the dithyramb, but its origins and early nature are obscure. See further Pickard-Cambridge (1962) 1–59; Zimmermann (1992).   **ἐγκώμια:** songs of praise in honour of men, as opposed to ὕμνοι in honour of gods. At *Rep.* 607a3–5 the only kinds of poetry which will be allowed in the state are ὕμνους θεοῖς καὶ ἐγκώμια τοῖς ἀγαθοῖς. Cf. Arist. *Po.* 1448b27. The victory odes of Pindar and Bacchylides are described as ἐγκώμια by P. at e.g. *Lysis* 205c–e, *Laws* 822b5–7, and cf. Ar. fr. 491.   **ὑπορχήματα:** dancing songs. The word occurs first here. See also Dion. Hal. *Dem.* 7; Luc. *Salt.* 16.   **ἔπη:** the normal term for hexameter poetry. See e.g. *Rep.*

379a8; Pi. *Nem.* 2.2; Hdt. 2.117; Thuc. 1.3; Xen. *Mem.* 1.4.3. **ἰάμ-βους:** the only kind of poetry in this list to be designated by metre. Presumably the reference is to the genre of iambic invective rather than to the iambic dialogue and speeches of tragedy, which does not feature in the *Ion*. Arist. *Po.* 1448b attributes the earliest known iambics to Homer in the *Margites*, but it was Archilochus (mentioned at 531a2) who was particularly associated with the development of the genre. See Hdt. 1.12; Arist. *Rhet.* 1418b; H. D. Rankin, *L'Antiquité classique* 46 (1977) 165–8. **c5–7 οὐ γὰρ τέχνηι ... τῶν ἄλλων ἁπάντων:** cf. 533d1–3, 532c7–8. It would not be difficult to refute P.'s argument: of the genres mentioned, Pindar, for example, composed dithyrambs, encomia and ὑπορχήματα. **c8 ὑπηρέταις:** predicative, 'as servants'. It was conventional to describe the poet as 'servant of the Muses' in the phrase Μουσῶν θεράπων (see e.g. Hes. *Th.* 100; *h. Hom.* 32.20; Theogn. 769; Ar. *Birds*. 909, 913), but θερ-άπων suggests an active relationship between poet and Muse (see Murray (1981) 97). Possibly P.'s choice of the word ὑπηρέτης places more emphasis on the poet's dependence on the Muse.

d1 τοῖς χρησμωιδοῖς ... μάντεσι τοῖς θείοις: cf. χρησμωιδεῖν at 534b7. Again P. plays on the close association between poetry and prophecy in order to emphasise the complete passivity of the poet. χρησμωιδοί and θεομάντεις appear together in the same kind of context at *Ap.* 22c1–2 and *Men.* 99c2. Bluck (1961) 427 suggests that the word θεομάντις may refer to an inspired seer as opposed to a μάντις who interpreted dreams or omens, and this may well be the implication of the epithet θείοις here. See further on 531b7 and cf. *Tim.* 71e–72b5, with Taylor (1928) *ad loc.*, where P. distinguishes between μάντεις who are inspired, and προφῆται who interpret their inspired utterances: οὐδεὶς γὰρ ἔννους ἐφάπτεται μαντικῆς ἐνθέου καὶ ἀληθοῦς ... ὅθεν δὴ καὶ τὸ τῶν προφητῶν γένος ἐπὶ ταῖς ἐνθέοις μαντείαις κριτὰς ἐπικαθιστάναι νόμος. **d1–2 ἡμεῖς οἱ ἀκούοντες** with d4 πρὸς ἡμᾶς: cf. 534a7 and b2. P. does not allow us to forget the audience as the final link in the chain. **d4 φθέγγε-ται:** cf. 536b7. **d5 Τύννιχος ὁ Χαλκιδεύς:** Porphyry, *De abstinentia* 2.18 relates that when the Delphians asked Aeschylus to write a paean, he said that Tynnichus had already done that to perfection. But nothing else is known about him. **d8 ἀτεχνῶς:** see on 532c2.

e4 ἑρμηνῆς 'mouthpieces'. Here and at 535a–b the words ἑρμηνεύς and ἑρμηνεύειν convey the idea of passive transmission (cf. *Rep.* 524b1; *Symp.* 202e3), whereas at 530c3 the emphasis is on active interpretation. See Schaper (1968) 24; Guthrie (1962–81) IV 203n.1.

535a3–4 ἅπτει ... ψυχῆς: ἅπτει (2nd sing.), like other verbs of touching, governs the genitive, and μου is possessive genitive depending on τῆς ψυχῆς.   **a4 θείαι μοίραι:** cf. 534c1.   **a9 ἑρμηνέων ἑρμηνῆς:** these words underline the parallelism between poets and rhapsodes, but also imply that rhapsodes are further away from the source of inspiration than poets. Cf. the hierarchy at *Rep.* 597e, where it is the poet who is at third remove from the source of truth.

b1 Ἔχε δή 'Hold on, then'. S. now moves on to question Ion about his emotional state during his recitals of Homeric poetry, in order to show that he is out of his mind when performing. But earlier (533d1–3) he had introduced the notion of ἐνθουσιασμός in relation to Ion's ability to comment on Homer. For the similarity between rhapsodes and actors see on 532d6–7.   **b2 εἴπηις ἔπη:** S. continues to use εἴπειν / λέγειν and ἀίδειν interchangeably of the rhapsode's delivery. Cf. b4, c2, c6, e3 and see on 532d7–8.   **ἐκπλήξηις** 'stun' or 'amaze'. Cf. Arist. *Po.* 1455a17 (with Lucas (1968) *ad loc.*), and 1454a4 where ἔκπληξις is also associated with recognition. The only other occurrence of the word in the *Poetics* is at 1460b25, in connexion with Achilles' pursuit of Hector in *Il.* 22, as here.   **b3–5 τὸν Ὀδυσσέα ... πρὸ τῶν ποδῶν:** these words refer to the opening of *Od.* 22, the climax of the story, when Odysseus strips off his rags and leaps on to the threshold, about to wreak vengeance on the hapless suitors.   **b5–6 Ἀχιλλέα ... ὁρμῶντα:** Achilles rushes on Hector at a similarly climactic point in the story of the *Iliad* (22.312), in the pursuit round the walls of Troy, which culminates in Hector's death.   **b6–7 τῶν περὶ Ἀνδρομάχην ... Πρίαμον:** examples of heart-rending passages in the *Iliad* include the farewell scene between Hector and Andromache at *Il.* 6.390–502, the grief of Priam, Hecuba and Andromache as they see Hector's body maltreated by Achilles at 22.405–515, and the lamentations of Hecuba and Andromache over Hector's body at 24.710–59.   **b7–c2 ἔμφρων ... ἐνθουσιάζουσα:** cf. 534b5–6 where the same language is used of poets.

c2 οἷς λέγεις: the relative is attracted into the case of its antecedent. Cf. 532e1.   **c3 ὅπως ἂν ... ἔχηι** 'wherever the epic sets the scene'. **c5 ἀποκρυψάμενος:** Ion obediently complies with S.'s request at 535b1.   **c5–8 ὅταν ἐλεινόν τι λέγω ... ἡ καρδία πηδᾶι:** for hair standing on end see *Il.* 24.359, where the hair on Priam's body stands out in fear, and for the heart beating with fear see *Il.* 22.461 of Andromache's premonition of Hector's death; Aesch. *Cho.* 167: ὀρχεῖται δὲ καρδία φόβωι.   **c7–8 ὑπὸ φόβου** 'under the influence of fear'. The emotions of pity and fear described here, and the physical symptoms which they generate, recall Gorgias' description (*Hel.* 9) of the effects of poetry on its listeners, who feel 'the shudders of fear and tears full of pity' (φρίκη περίφοβος καὶ ἔλεος πολύδακρυς). For the influence of Gorgias on P. and perhaps also on Aristotle's theory of κάθαρσις see Flashar (1958) 68–72; Segal (1962) 131–5. For the phenomenon which the passage as a whole describes cf. Hamlet's words (Act 2, scene 2): 'Is it not monstrous, that this player here, | But in a fiction, in a dream of passion, | Could force his soul so to his whole conceit, | That, from her working, all his visage wann'd; | Tears in his eyes, distraction in's aspect, | A broken voice, and his whole function suiting, | With forms to his conceit? and all for nothing. | For Hecuba! | What's Hecuba to him, or he to Hecuba, | that he should weep for her?' The identification of the performer with his subject-matter, described here, is of central importance to the notion of μίμησις developed in *Rep.* 3. See Havelock (1963) 44–5 and *Rep.* 393c5–6n. below.

d2–3 κεκοσμημένος ... στεφάνοις: cf. 530b6–8, d8, 541c1. **d3–4 μηδὲν ἀπολωλεκώς** like μηδενὸς ἀποδύοντος at d5 hints at Ion's materialistic concerns.   **d4 δισμυρίοις ἀνθρώποις:** we have no other evidence for the numbers attending rhapsodic performances, so it is difficult to determine the accuracy and significance of this figure. Cf. *Symp.* 175e6–7 where Agathon's plays were performed before πλέον ἢ τρισμυρίοις, the traditional number of Athenian citizens at this time.   **d8–9 τοὺς πολλοὺς ... ἐργάζεσθε:** double accusative after ἐργάζομαι. ὑμεῖς ('you and your fellow rhapsodes') generalises what has up until now applied specifically to Ion.

e2 ἀπὸ τοῦ βήματος: rhapsodes evidently stood on a raised platform for their performances.   **e2–3 κλάοντάς ... συνθαμβοῦν-**

τας: cf. 535b2. Ion inspires his audience with the same emotions as he professes to feel himself at 535c5–8. συνθαμβοῦντας occurs only here, but for the same idea cf. συμπάσχοντες at *Rep.* 605d4. P.'s emphasis on the powerful emotional effects of poetry is nothing new. Already in the *Odyssey* Penelope weeps as she listens to Phemius' song (1.336), and Odysseus himself is reduced to tears by the songs of Demodocus (8.83–95, 521–34). According to Herodotus (6.21), the tragic poet Phrynichus dramatised the capture of Miletus so graphically that the whole audience was moved to tears, and fined him for reminding him of their misfortunes. Gorgias' *Helen* (see on 535c7–8) can be seen as an attempt to rationalise and analyse the emotive power of poetry. See also on *Rep.* 605d3–5. What is different in P. is that it is not just the audience who are carried away as they listen to the poetry, but the performer too. And there is the basic assumption running through the dialogue that the *poet's* mental state when composing is exactly analogous to that of the rhapsode when reciting. P.'s preoccupation with the psychology of poetic performance is interestingly discussed by Havelock (1963) 145–64.   **e4 τὸν νοῦν προσέχειν:** in contrast with the inspired poet, who can only compose when he is out of his mind (534b4–6).   **e4–6 ἐὰν μὲν κλάοντας ... ἀργύριον ἀπολύῃς:** for a similar concern with financial rewards cf. *Hipp. Maj.* 282b–283b, where Hippias boasts about the vast amounts of money he has acquired from his sophistic displays. Arist. *Ath. Pol.* 60.3 states that prizes of silver and gold were awarded to victors in the musical competitions at the Panathenaea, and that testimony is confirmed by a fourth-century prize list. See *IG* ɪɪ² 2311. Ion's words show that, despite his emotional transport, he is nevertheless in control of his faculties, a paradox which is not as inconceivable as it sounds if we think in terms of theatrical performance. Actors are both absorbed in the parts they are playing and yet aware of the effects they are having on an audience. See further Dortèr (1973) 72–3; Ferrari (1989) 96. But the readiness with which Ion reveals the true object of his concern, viz. money, and the flippant manner in which he makes his point undercuts any idea of the rhapsode being divinely inspired.   **e7–8 τῶν δακτυλίων ... ὧν ἐγὼ ἔλεγον:** the relative is attracted into the case of its antecedent. cf. 535c2, 532e1. Having ridiculed the nature of the rhapsode's 'enthusiasm', S. now re-establishes the connexion between audience, rhapsode and poet by returning to the image of the magnet. In spelling out the implications of this image, S. makes it clear that he is concerned with the whole process of poetic communication, involving the poet as composer, the rhapsode as transmitter and the audience as recipients. But the question of how far we should press the analogy between poet and rhapsode is left open. Since the middle link in the chain has been shown to be fraudulent, how can we be sure that the inspiration of the others is genuine? **e8 ὑπό** 'under the influence of'. Cf. 535c7.

536a1 ῥαψῳδὸς καὶ ὑποκριτής: see on 532d7. **a1–2 ὁ δὲ θεὸς ... τὴν ψυχήν:** this image anticipates the idea of ψυχαγωγία in rhetoric. See e.g. *Phdr.* 261a7–8, 271c10 and J. de Romilly, *Magic and rhetoric in ancient Greece* (Cambridge, Mass. 1975) 13. **a3 ἀνακρεμαννὺς ἐξ ἀλλήλων τὴν δύναμιν** 'making the power of one depend upon the other'. Cf. 535e9, and for δύναμις cf. 533d3, d6, e3. **a5 χορευτῶν** 'singers and dancers'. Cf. the emphasis on dancing at 534a–b and at 536c5. See also *Rep.* 373b7 οἱ περὶ μουσικήν, ποιηταί τε καὶ τούτων ὑπηρέται, ῥαψῳδοί, ὑποκριταί, χορευταί. **διδασκάλων** for χοροδιδασκάλων, 'chorus trainers'. Cf. *Euthyd.* 276b6 ὥσπερ ὑπὸ διδασκάλου χορός. **ὑποδιδασκάλων** 'assistant trainers'. **a5– 7 ἐκ πλαγίου ... δακτυλίων** 'attached sideways to the rings that hang from the Muse'. The magnet's power exerts itself not just vertically, but also horizontally, so that the image is extended to include not just performers of poetry, but also their trainers. **a8–b1 ὀνομάζομεν δὲ αὐτὸ κατέχεται ... ἔχεται γάρ** 'We call that "being possessed", which is more or less the case, for he is held'. The pun exploits the etymological connexion between the two verbs. Cf. 533e7.

b3 Ὀρφέως ... Μουσαίου: on Orpheus see 533c1. Musaeus was a legendary singer and priest, often associated with Orpheus as e.g. at *Rep.* 364e3 and Ar. *Frogs* 1032–3. Many religious poems and collections of oracles were attributed to him (see e.g. Hdt. 7.6 and 8.96). Pausanias (1.22.7) regarded all of these as spurious apart from a *Hymn to Demeter*. See further M. L. West (1983) 39–44. **b6 ἄλλου του ποιητοῦ:** the genitive depends on μέλος at the end of the following line. **καθεύδεις τε καὶ ἀπορεῖς:** 532c2–3, 533a2 and a5, and 536b8.   **b8 ὀρχεῖται:** the image of dancing leads on to the comparison with Corybants at c2–6, which itself refers back to 534a1.

c1–2 περὶ Ὁμήρου λέγεις ἃ λέγεις: having concentrated exclusively on the nature of Ion's performances of Homer, S. now slips back into talking about Ion's ability to comment on the poetry, picking up his earlier words at 532c6.   **c2 θείαι μοίραι καὶ κατοκωχῆι:** see on 534c1. κατοκωχή occurs in P. only here and at *Phdr.* 245a1–2, in a similar context: ἀπὸ Μουσῶν κατοκωχή τε καὶ μανία.   **c2–6 ὥσπερ οἱ κορυβαντιῶντες ... τῶν δὲ ἄλλων οὐ φροντίζουσιν:** see on 533e8. This passage suggests that Corybantic ritual involved the use of different types of music for diagnostic purposes, since participants would only respond to the music of the god by whom they were possessed. See further Dodds (1951) 79 and 98, n. 102.   **c5 σχημάτων καὶ ῥημάτων:** the rhyming suggests rhythmical dancing.

536d1 ὅ μ' ἐρωτᾶις: cf. 532b8.   **d3 ἐπαινέτης:** cf. 542b4, and for ἐπαίνω see 536d6, 541e2. Clearly this word must signify more than simply an 'admirer' or 'praiser' of Homer (the sense in which it seems to be used at *Prot.* 309a6; *Rep.* 606e1 and Xen. *Mem.* 1.3.3). Presumably, like κοσμεῖν at 530d7, it relates to Ion's combined activity of reciting and commenting on Homer, on which see Velardi (1989) 31–6. But the vagueness of P.'s description makes it impossible for us to be more specific.   **d4 Σὺ μὲν ... θαυμάζοιμι μεντἄν:** the use of μέντοι rather than δέ emphasises the contrast.   **d6–7 οἶμαι δὲ οὐδ' ἂν σοὶ ... περὶ Ὁμήρου:** Ion's naive assertion is double-edged, for S. might well agree that he was not inspired if he heard him speaking about Homer. Ion's rejection of the notion that he is inspired concludes this section of the dialogue, and we move back again to a discussion of the nature of the rhapsode's τέχνη.

536d8–539d4

S. now questions Ion about the subject-matter of Homer's poetry, and forces him to agree that, in the case of each of the specialised arts about which Homer speaks, e.g. chariot driving, medicine, prophecy, the practitioner of those arts will be a better judge of the poet's words than the rhapsode.

536d8–9 Καὶ μὴν ἐθέλω γε ἀκοῦσαι ... ἀποκρίνηι corresponds to 530d9–10 where S. similarly professes a desire to listen to Ion, but only after he has answered a specific question. In the earlier discussion, S. established that anyone who speaks about Homer on the basis of τέχνη must be able to speak about all other poets too. He now goes on to argue that such a person must also understand all the subjects which the poet treats. Both the opening and closing sections of the dialogue, which consider the question of Ion's τέχνη, focus on his ability as a commentator on Homer. But the central section, in which S. gives his quasi-mythical account of inspiration, ignores this aspect of the rhapsode's activity and concentrates exclusively on performance.

e1 ὧν for τούτων ἅ.   **e3 περὶ οὐδενὸς ὅτου οὔ** 'about everything'.   **e4 περὶ τούτων ὧν:** the relative is attracted into the case of its antecedent. Cf. 532e1, 535e8.   **e6 καὶ ταῦτα ποῖά ἐστιν:** καί before the interrogative expresses surprise or indignation. For ποῖα cf. 541c9.

537a4 Ἀλλ' ἐγὼ ἐρῶ ... μέμνημαι: Ion at last gets a chance to show off his skills. For the memorising abilities of rhapsodes see on 539e7–540a1.   **a6–7 ἐν τῆι ἱπποδρομίαι ... Πατρόκλωι** 'in the chariot race in honour of Patroclus'. This was probably the title of this part of the *Iliad*, which was not divided into books until the Alexandrian period. In P.'s day sections of the poem were identified according to their subject-matter. See e.g. τειχομαχία, 539b2 below; Λιταί, *Hipp. Min.* 364e8, *Crat.* 428c3; Ἀλκίνου ἀπόλογος, *Rep.* 614b2.   **a8–b5 Κλινθῆναι ... ἐπαυρεῖν:** Hom. *Il.* 23.335–40, where Nestor gives advice to his son, Antilochus, about how best to drive his chariot round the turning-point of the course and win the race. Xenophon quotes the same passage at *Symp.* 4.6 as an example of the technical information that knowledge of Homer can impart. See Introduction p. 20. The first line differs slightly from the received text, which is as follows: αὐτὸς δὲ κλινθῆναι ἐυπλέκτωι ἐνὶ δίφρωι. κλινθῆναι is infinitive used as imperative, cf. κένσαι, εἶξαι and ἀλέασθαι. φησί is Ion's parenthesis.   **b1 ἦκ' ἐπ' ἀριστερὰ τοῖιν** 'slightly to the left of them' (sc. the horses). See further Labarbe (1949) 90–101; Van der Valk (1963–4) II 315.

c1 Ἀρκεῖ suggests that Ion could go on indefinitely unless stopped. **c3–4 τέχνην ταύτην:** sc. ἡνιοχείαν.   **c5–6 Οὐκοῦν ἑκάστηι …
γιγνώσκειν** 'So has the god given to each skill the ability to under-
stand a particular activity?' The activities which S. lists as examples
of τέχναι are the traditional ones of chariot-driving, piloting, medicine, carpentry, arithmetic, fishing and prophecy. Cf. Homer *Od.*
17.383–5 where seer, physician, carpenter and 'divinely inspired'
bard are listed as δημιοεργοί. The latter is, of course, omitted from
S.'s list here. Cicero, when looking for parallels to the art of divination, speaks of the physician, the pilot, the general and the states-
man as typical examples of craftsmen. See *De div.* 1.24 with A. S.
Pease, *Ciceronis: de divinatione libri duo* (Darmstadt 1973) *ad loc.* and cf.
De nat. deor. 3.76.

d1 κατὰ πασῶν τῶν τεχνῶν 'in the case of all skills'.   **d3–4 τὴν
μὲν ἑτέραν … τὴν δ' ἑτέραν:** lit. 'Do you say that one skill is of one
sort, and another another?' ἑτέραν is predicative.   **d4–e1 Ἆρα
ὥσπερ ἐγώ … οὕτω καὶ σύ** 'Do you judge as I do and differentiate
between skills when their knowledge is of different objects?'

e1–4 Εἰ γάρ που τῶν αὐτῶν πραγμάτων … ἀπ' ἀμφοτέρων 'For
if there were some knowledge which dealt with the same subject-
matter, how could we say that there are two different skills involved,
since it would be possible to know the same things from both?'

538a1 Ὃ τοίνυν ἄρτι ἔμελλον ἐρήσεσθαί σε: cf. 537d.

b1 τῶν ἐπῶν ὧν εἶπες: ὧν for ἅ. Cf. 536e4.   **b2 εἴτε καλῶς …
εἴτε μή:** cf. 531e10–11, 537c1–2.   **b4 Ἡ δὲ ῥαψωιδικὴ τέχνη:** S.
appears to concede that there is such a thing as rhapsodic skill. But
since he rejects all Ion's attempts to define it (540b3–5) and offers no
account of it himself, we are left to conclude that the rhapsode's activity in fact cannot properly be called a τέχνη.   **b8 Μαχάονι …
παλλακή:** Machaon was a son of Asclepius and doctor to the Greek
army at Troy (*Il.* 11.518). Hecamede was given to Nestor as a prize
after the sack of Tenedos (*Il.* 11.624–7).

c1 λέγει πως οὕτως 'says something like this'. The quotation is a
conflation of three lines, *Il.* 11.639–40 and 630, with παρὰ δὲ κρόμυον for ἐπὶ δὲ κρόμυον. Cf. Xen. *Symp.* 4.7 and see further Labarbe

(1949) 101–8. At *Rep.* 405e–406a3 P. refers to the same episode, but substitutes Eurypylus and Patroclus for Machaon and Hecamede. **c4–5 ἰατρικῆς ... ῥαψωιδικῆς;** sc. τέχνης. According to *Rep.* 406a1 contemporary doctors would have regarded the drink as highly unsuitable treatment for a wounded man. For the argument that the doctor, not the rhapsode, knows about medicine cf. *Rep.* 599c1–5, where Homer himself is similarly contrasted with the doctor.

d1–3 ἡ δὲ μολυβδαίνηι ... πῆμα φέρουσα: these lines describe Iris' descent from Olympus at *Il.* 24.80–2 with the following variations from the received text: ἵκανεν for ὄρουσεν, ἐμμεμαυῖα for ἐμβεβαυῖα, μετ' ἰχθύσι for ἐπ' ἰχθύσι and πῆμα for κῆρα. See further Labarbe (1949) 108–20; Van der Valk (1963–4) II 323–4.   **d5 ἄττα λέγει ... εἴτε μή:** the expert must first decide on the meaning of the poet's words, and then judge whether they are well (i.e. accurately) said or not. Ion could argue that it is the rhapsode's task to evaluate their beauty or appropriateness, as he tries to do at 540b3.   **d7 σοῦ ἐρομένου, εἰ ἔροιό με** 'if you were questioning me and were to ask me'. The conditional reinforces the genitive absolute. S.'s technique of imagining questions that might be put to him by Ion allows him to take complete control of the argument.

e2 ἴθι μοι ἔξευρε: μοι is ethic dative. Cf. ἡμῖν at 530a8.   **e2–3 τὰ τοῦ μάντεως:** see on 531b7.   **e6 πολλαχοῦ ... ἐν 'Οδυσσείαι** is balanced by πολλαχοῦ ... ἐν 'Ιλιάδι at 539b2.   **e6–8 ὁ τῶν Μελαμποδιδῶν ... Θεοκλύμενος:** Melampus was a legendary seer, whose descendants inherited his prophetic gifts. The genealogy of Theoclymenus is given at *Od.* 15.225–56, on which see Heubeck and Hoekstra (1989) *ad loc.*

539a1–b1 δαιμόνιοι ... ἀχλύς: *Od.* 20.351–7 with the following variations from the received text: δαίμονιοι for ἆ δειλοί; γυῖα for γοῦνα; εἰδώλων τε for εἰδώλων δέ. Line 354 is omitted in P.'s text. See further Labarbe (1949) 120–30. It is striking that S. chooses the only passage in Homer which describes ecstatic prophecy, as Stanford (1947) notes *ad loc.* Elsewhere divination is practised by the more rational means of interpreting omens and portents. See on 531b7, 534d1 and 539b4–d1 below.   **b2 ἐπὶ τειχομαχίαι:** the title of *Iliad* 12, which describes the Trojan attack on the Achaean wall. See on

537a6.   **b4–d1 ὄρνις . . . ἀνέμοιο:** the quotation is of *Il.* 12.200–7, where a portent of an eagle carrying a snake in its claws appears before Hector and the Trojans, as they hesitate to storm the wall and set fire to the Achaean ships. The portent is interpreted by the seer, Polydamas. S.'s point is that it will take a prophet rather than a rhapsode to evaluate the correctness or otherwise of the seer's interpretation. See further Labarbe (1949) 130–6; Van der Valk (1963–4) II 310–11.

539d5–541d6

Given that all skills are best understood by their respective practitioners, S. asks Ion to pick out those parts of Homer's poems which are best understood by the rhapsode. After several attempts to pin-point the rhapsode's particular expertise, Ion is manoeuvred into identifying the rhapsode's skill with that of the general's. S. points out that, since he is the best rhapsode in Greece, he must also be the best general. But why, in that case, has he not been appointed general?

539d5 Καὶ σύ . . . λέγεις: S. ironically echoes Ion's words.

e2 ἐμπειρότερος . . . Ὁμήρου: cf. 532d6–e1 where S. in a similarly ironic way contrasts Ion's expertise with his own layman's knowledge of Homer.   **e4 παρά** 'beyond' i.e. 'better than'.   **e6 ἅπαντα:** with this one word Ion refutes himself, as S. demonstrates at 540a.   **e7–540a1 ἐπιλήσμων . . . ἐπιλήσμονα . . . ἐπιλανθάνομαι:** the heavy emphasis on Ion's forgetfulness ridicules his eager desire to show off at 537a4, and ironically exposes the superficiality of his memory. Cf. *Hipp. Min.* 369a where the sophist Hippias, who prides himself on his memory, is similarly chided by S. for his forgetfulness. Rhapsodes were particularly noted for their memorising abilities, but also for their stupidity. See e.g. Xen. *Symp.* 3.6, *Mem.* 4.2.10. S.'s ironic treatment of Ion here underlines the point that simple memorising does not involve understanding. Cf. *Phdr.* 277e8–9 where rhapsodes are described as speaking persuasively, but without questioning or teaching.

540a2–5 Οὐ μέμνησαι . . . Οὐκοῦν . . . ἄρα: an example of syllogism, 'the moment when Socrates, having obtained his premises separately, explicitly brings them together so that their joint implication becomes evident to the answerer' (Robinson (1953) 21).   **a6–b2**

Πλήν γε ἴσως τὰ τοιαῦτα ... σχεδόν τι 'Except such things as these, Socrates. By "such things as these", you mean more or less [that the rhapsode will understand everything] except what belongs to other skills'. **b2 ἀλλὰ ... γνώσεται:** for ἀλλὰ δή after a rejected suggestion cf. *Rep.* 600a1 and Denniston (1954) 241–2. **b3 ἃ πρέπει:** Ion's claim that the rhapsode will know the kinds of things that it is appropriate for different characters to say shows some awareness that knowledge of poetry might be something other than knowledge about its factual content. But, as before, S. refuses to recognise the distinction between content and expression which Ion is tentatively trying to formulate. Cf. 531d6 and see further Flashar (1958) 82–3; Schaper (1968) 20–33.

c4 βουκόλωι specifies a particular type of δοῦλος. S. chooses examples of each kind of character listed by Ion at 540b3–5.

d5 Γνοίην γοῦν ἂν ἔγωγε ... εἰπεῖν 'At any rate *I* would know'. The pronoun is emphatic. Ion does not answer S.'s question, but defiantly insists that he knows what sort of things a general would say. He chooses this particular expertise because of the prominence of warfare in Homer's poetry. Cf. 541b4–5, 531c4, *Rep.* 599c7–8; Ar. *Frogs*, 1034–6. **d6 Ἴσως ... καὶ στρατηγικός** 'Perhaps you are good at generalship too', i.e. as well as being a good rhapsode.

541b2–4 σὺ τῶν Ἑλλήνων ... ἄριστος εἶ: Ion's vanity remains unpunctured, despite S.'s attack. **b8 ῥαψωιδεῖς μὲν περιιών:** cf. *Rep.* 600d5–6 where S. says that their contemporaries would never have allowed Homer and Hesiod to go round reciting poetry (ῥαψωιδεῖν ... περιιόντας) if they could have really made men better.

c1 χρυσῶι στεφάνωι ἐστεφανωμένου: an ironic reference to Ion's boast at 530d8, exposing the worthlessness of such external trappings. **c3–4 Ἡ μὲν γὰρ ἡμετέρα ... ὑμῶν:** Ephesus was part of the Delian league, and would have been under Athenian control until the general Ionian uprising against Athens in 412 (Thuc. 8.14ff). Ion's words indicate that the dramatic date of the dialogue is sometime before 412, during the Peloponnesian War. See further Moore (1974) 431–2. **c7 Ὦ βέλτιστε:** clearly ironic in tone. Cf. 532b2. **c7–8 Ἀπολλόδωρον ... Κυζικηνόν:** nothing more is known about him, although Aelian (*V.H.* 14.5) repeats what is said here, as does

Athenaeus (11.506a), who refers to the passage as an example of
Plato's malignity: 'That Plato was in fact hostile towards everyone is
clear from the *Ion*, in which he first abuses all the poets (κακολογεῖ
πάντας τοὺς ποιητάς), and then also the men promoted by the
people, Phanosthenes of Andros, Apollodorus of Cyzicus, and Heracleides of Clazomenae.'   **c9 Ποῖον τοῦτον:** contemptuous in
tone.

d1–2 Φανοσθένη … Κλαζομένιον: according to Xenophon (*Hell.*
1.5.18) Phanosthenes was sent by the Athenians to replace Conon
at Andros in 408–407. Heracleides of Clazomenae is mentioned by
Aristotle (*Ath. Pol.* 41.3) as having raised the payment for attendance
at the assembly to two obols, probably during the mid-390s, and
certainly before 392 (Ar. *Eccl.* 102, schol.183, 380). There is no direct
evidence as to when he became an Athenian citizen, and the reference to him here may be anachronistic. Alternatively we can take
P.'s words at their face value and assume that he was granted citizenship at some earlier stage in return for services rendered during the
Peloponnesian War. See further Moore (1974) 427–8, 433–7.
d6 οὐκ Ἀθηναῖοι … τὸ ἀρχαῖον: according to tradition Ephesus
was founded by Androclus, son of Codrus, king of Athens (Strab.
14.1.3; Paus. 7.2.5). His tomb could still be seen there in Pausanias'
day (7.2.6).

541e1–542b4

*S. chides Ion for not demonstrating the many fine things he claims to know about
Homer. Either he is being unfair, or he praises Homer not through skill
(τέχνη), but by divine dispensation. Offered the choice between being unfair or
being inspired, Ion chooses to be thought inspired.*

e1 ἀλλὰ γὰρ σύ 'but the fact is that you'. S. here breaks off the discussion, and we move towards the final denouement of the dialogue.
e5 πολλοῦ δεῖς ἐπιδεῖξαι 'you are far from giving a display'. See
on 530d4–5.   **e7 ἀτεχνῶς:** for the pun cf. 532c2.   **e7–8 ὁ
Πρωτεὺς … ἄνω καὶ κάτω:** Proteus was a sea god with prophetic
knowledge which he would only reveal when caught. To avoid capture he transformed himself into all sorts of different shapes, so that
his capacity for metamorphosis became proverbial. See Hom. *Od.*

4.384–461 with S. West (1988) *ad loc.*; Virg. *Georg.* 4.387–414. For Proteus as an example of sophistic slipperiness cf. *Euthyd.* 288b–c, and see Richardson (1975) 79–80. The word παντοδαπός occurs at *Rep.* 398a1 to describe the poet's specious ability to transform himself into different characters. The phrase στρέφειν ἄνω καὶ κάτω is used both of the ἀπορία which S. induces in his interlocutors (*Lach.* 196b1–2) and as an accusation against S.'s method of argument (*Gorg.* 511a4–5). Cf. *Phdr.* 278d9 with Rowe (1986) *ad loc.*, where the phrase is used of poets and speech writers.

542a4–5 τεχνικὸς ... ποιητοῦ: this sentence summarises the main argument of the dialogue, resuming its key terms.

b1–2 Πολὺ ... νομίζεσθαι: Ion's vanity remains unassailable. Right to the end he is simply concerned with appearances, and seems to have learnt nothing from S.'s cross-questioning. **b3 παρ' ἡμῖν** 'in our eyes' ironically suggests that the idea of Ion being inspired is merely a convenient hypothesis on S.'s part. **b4 μὴ τεχνικὸν ... ἐπαινέτην;** these words present us with the real conclusion of the dialogue. The question of whether Ion is inspired or not is neither here nor there. What really matters is the demonstration that the rhapsode's activity does not depend on τέχνη.

Republic 376e–398b

The *Republic* is P.'s most ambitious work, and belongs to his so-called middle period. The dialogue is set in the house of Polemarchus in the Piraeus, where a group of friends are gathered together, and the conversation turns towards the nature of δικαιοσύνη, justice. Various definitions of justice are put forward, and in particular, the sophist Thrasymachus argues forcibly that justice is nothing but the interest of the stronger. S., in the customary manner, poses a series of penetrating questions to his interlocutor, who is speedily reduced to ἀπορία, and thereupon retires from the discussion. The argument is then taken up by P.'s brothers, Glaucon and Adeimantus, who challenge S. to prove that living a just life is not merely an expedient way of gaining external rewards, but intrinsically beneficial to the individual. Is the just life really better than the unjust life? This is the question which the *Republic* as a whole is designed to answer.

But S. points out that, in order to answer this question, it will first of all be necessary to discover what justice actually is. He suggests, therefore, that they should look for justice on a large scale, that is, justice in the *polis*, the community, before considering the nature of justice in the individual (368d; see on 605b5–6 and 7–8). 'Let us build a city in words', says S. at 369c9, as a prelude to his construction of the ideal state. The city which S. envisages is based on the principles of specialisation, and division of labour: each person will do only one job, and that job will be the one to which he is particularly suited by nature. Justice is the harmony which exists when each class in society performs its proper function for the benefit of the community as a whole. One of the most important tasks will be that of defending the state from attack. Hence it will be necessary to have a class of citizens specialising in warfare, who will act as guardians of the state (374c–e). These guardians will need to be brave and spirited against the enemy, but gentle towards their fellow-citizens; in addition they will need to be temperamentally disposed towards philosophy. The reason for this apparently bizarre combination of qualities is explained later on (412b–414b), when we learn that the guardians will be divided into two classes, rulers and auxiliaries; the top class will be trained in philosophy and are destined to become philosopher kings, whose special task will be to rule the state. But to begin with, S. is concerned with the nature of the guardian class as a whole.

Having decided on the natural qualities which will be required in potential guardians, the question then arises as to what sort of education they should receive in order to equip them for their task. We should remember, therefore, that the primary purpose of the educational programme outlined in books 2 and 3 of the *Republic* is to produce efficient guardians. See further Gill (1985). But P.'s assault on the traditional system of education in these books is also part of the wider struggle between poetry and philosophy discussed above (Introduction pp. 14–24). P.'s passionate belief in the power of education to change society is one of the central themes of the *Republic*, as Rousseau observed: 'If you want to know what is meant by public education, read Plato's *Republic*. Those who merely judge books by their titles take this as a treatise on politics, but it is the finest treatise on education ever written' (*Emile*, book 1. Flammarian edn (Paris 1966) p. 40).

376e–378e3

S. is discussing with Adeimantus the question of how the guardians of the pro-
jected state should be educated. In this section he is concerned essentially with
their moral education. The intellectual training of the select number of guardians
who will rule the state as philosopher kings is discussed later on at 502d–541b.
He begins with literature, pointing out that, since the minds of young children
are highly impressionable, it is essential that they should be told suitable stories
from their earliest years. Ideas about the gods and their mythology derive pri-
marily from the poets, but most existing poetry misrepresents the nature of the
divine.

376e2–3 Τίς οὖν ... ηὑρημένης: the education of Athenian boys in
P.'s day was the responsibility of the family rather than the state,
and took place on a private basis. Traditionally it consisted of physical education, reading and writing, and the study of literature.
Learning and reciting poetry, playing music, singing and dancing
were thus at the heart of the Athenian system of education. Cf. *Prot.*
325a–326b; *Laws* 654a; Ar. *Clouds* 961ff, 1353–90; Isoc. *Antidosis* 266–
8, and see further Introduction pp. 15–16. For the evidence from
vase painting see F. A. Beck, *Album of Greek education* (Sydney 1975).
P. takes this existing model as a basis for his discussion, but modifies
it, removing those elements which he regards as damaging to the
formation of character. The answer to the question raised here concludes at 412b2 with the words οἱ μὲν δὴ τύποι τῆς παιδείας τε καὶ
τροφῆς οὗτοι ἂν εἶεν. **e3–4 ἡ μὲν ἐπὶ σώμασι ... μουσική:** for
this traditional view see e.g. Ar. *Frogs* 729; Isoc. 15.180–5. Later on,
at 410c, S. rejects this division, claiming that the main purpose of
both μουσική and γυμναστική is to educate the soul. Μουσική com-
prises all the arts over which the Muses preside, including poetry,
song, music and dance. **e9 Μουσικῆς ... λόγους:** 'Under music
do you include stories?' Μουσικῆς is partitive genitive. λόγους
denotes 'stories' in a wide sense, including 'tales, legends, myths,
narratives in poetry or prose' (Cornford (1941) 66). **e11 Λόγων**
... ἕτερον: the distinction which S. makes here between two forms

of discourse, one true, the other false, is at least as old as Hesiod, *Th.* 27–8. But the word ψεῦδος has a wide semantic range covering lies, falsehood, deceit and fiction, and the question of how far P. (and the Greeks in general) distinguished between these different modern categories is highly debatable. Cf. 382d9 and in general see Rösler (1980); Gill and Wiseman (1993); Pratt (1993). The innovative nature of P.'s treatment of this topic is signalled by the perplexity of Adeimantus' response.

377a1 Παιδευτέον: P.'s use of the verbal adjective throughout this section (cf. e.g. a9, b11, c1, c5, 378b1, c8, d2, d5, e2) underlines the importance he attaches to the task in hand. Cf. 595c3.   **a5–6 ὡς τὸ ὅλον ... ἀληθῆ:** ὡς τὸ ὅλον εἰπεῖν 'to speak generally'. This definition of μῦθοι as being for the most part false, yet nevertheless containing some truth does not apply to the traditional stories told by the poets, which, from 377d5 onwards, are criticised as being wholly false. But it does apply to P.'s own myths. See e.g. *Phaed.* 114d where S. says of the account he has just given of the soul's life after death: 'to insist that these things are exactly as I have described them would not befit a man of intelligence. But to think that this or something like it is true ... seems to me both reasonable and a risk worth taking.' Cf. S.'s comment on his own mythical description of erotic μανία at *Phdr.* 265b–c: 'perhaps we hit upon some truth, though maybe we went astray in some respects, mixing together a not wholly unconvincing speech (οὐ παντάπασιν ἀπίθανον λόγον)'. In these examples and throughout the present discussion P. is less concerned with the factual or literal veracity of myth than with its value as a means of conveying ethical or religious truths. The usefulness of ψεῦδος is explicitly emphasised at 382c6–d3, 459c8–d2 and particularly in connexion with the so-called 'noble lie' at 414b8–415d4, where an avowedly false account of the origins of the city is invented in order to persuade its citizens to live in harmony with each other. Cf. *Laws* 663d6–664c2 and see further Page (1991) 21–6; Gill (1993) 52–4. On Plato's use of myth in general see e.g. Brisson (1982); Edelstein (1949); Friedländer (1958) 1 171–210; Segal (1978); Smith (1986); Stewart (1960). It is clear to us, of course, that P.'s myths are in fact fictions, which are neither true nor false in any literal sense; but P. himself does not speak in terms of fiction, nor does he distinguish between fiction and falsehood. Rather his concern is with truthful and untruthful lies. See on d9 below and in general Gill (1993). **a6–7 πρότερον δὲ μύθοις ... χρώμεθα:** S. reiterates the point made above at 376e6–7 that training in poetry and music takes precedence over gymnastics. Cf. *Prot.* 325e–326c; *Laws* 654a6–7 where it is assumed that the earliest education is that which comes through the Muses and Apollo. See further Nehamas (1982) 71 n. 17.   **a9 Τοῦτο δὴ ἔλεγον** 'This is what I meant by saying'.   **a12 ἀρχὴ ... μέγιστον** appears to be a proverbial expression. Cf. *Laws* 753e6–7: ἀρχὴ γὰρ λέγεται μὲν ἥμισυ παντὸς ἐν ταῖς παροιμίαις ἔργου, and 775e2.

b1–3 μάλιστα γὰρ ... ἐνσημήνασθαι ἑκάστωι 'for then it is most easily moulded, and takes on any impression which one wishes to stamp on it'. Slings (1989) 394–5 points out that there are two distinct, but closely related metaphors here: the first (πλάττεται) is that of moulding a shape in e.g. wax or clay (cf. 377c3), the second (ἐνδύεται τύπος) of imprinting an impression upon it. For a similar image see *Theaet.* 191d6–7 where it is suggested that the mind receives sensations and perceptions like a block of wax stamped with the impressions of signet rings (ὥσπερ δακτυλίων σημεῖα ἐνσημαινομένους).   **b5–6 Ἆρ' οὖν ... τοὺς παῖδας** 'shall we then carelessly (ῥαιδίως οὕτω) allow the children to listen to any stories made up by anyone?' For ῥαιδίως οὕτω cf. 378a2–3. The phrase πλάττειν λόγους is regularly used of telling stories which are false. See e.g. *Ap.* 17c5; Gorg. *Hel.* 11, and LSJ s.v. πλάσσειν V.

c1 καλόν sc. μῦθον, which some MSS insert. For μῦθον understood from μυθοποιοῖς cf. 399d3–4 where αὐλός is understood from αὐλοποιούς. καλόν refers primarily to the suitability of the content of stories, rather than to their aesthetic qualities. Cf. 598e4 and for the implications of the term καλός see on *Ion* 533e7.   **c2–3 τὰς τροφούς ... παισίν:** for stories told by nurses and mothers cf. *Laws* 887d, and for story-telling as a female preserve see Marrou (1965) 218–19; Buxton (1994) 18–21, and 378d1 below.   **c3–4 πλάττειν ... ταῖς χερσίν:** for πλάττειν of moulding character cf. *Gorg.* 483e4, *Laws* 671c1 where the educational benefits of symposia are discussed: when the souls of the drinkers become warm they grow softer and younger so that the law-giver can educate and mould them (παιδεύειν τε καὶ πλάττειν) as when they were young. For the physical massage of young children cf. *Laws* 789e where mothers are told to mould their infants like wax (πλάττειν ... οἷον κήρινον), and *Alc.* 121d6–7 for the same instructions: προστέτακται ἐπιμέλεσθαι τοῦ γενομένου ... ἀναπλάττοντας τὰ μέλη τοῦ παιδός. Cf. Plut. *Mor.* 3e–f. S. reiterates the point made at 377a6–7 that the education of the soul is more important than that of the body.   **c5 ὧν δὲ νῦν** for τούτων δὲ οὓς νῦν.   **c7–d1 Ἐν τοῖς μείζοσιν ... τοὺς ἐλάττους:** lit. 'in the greater stories we shall also see the lesser. For both the greater and the lesser must be cast in the same mould (τύπον cf. 377b2 above) and have the same effect (ταὐτὸν δύνασθαι).' The same principle of moving from the larger to the smaller scale underlies the construction of the story of the ideal state itself (ἴθι δή ... τῶι λόγωι ἐξ ἀρχῆς ποιῶμεν πόλιν 369c9): if they want to discover what justice is in the individual, they must first discover what justice is in the state, like short-sighted men who need to read large letters first and then compare them with the smaller to see if the letters are indeed the same (368c7–369b4). On the image used here see M. Tecusan, 'Speaking about the unspeakable: Plato's use of imagery', in Barker and Warner (1992) 83–5; on the analogy between *polis* and psyche see Lear (1992).

d2–3 ἀλλ' οὐκ ἐννοῶ ... λέγεις 'but I don't understand what you mean by the bigger ones'.   **d4 Ἡσίοδός ... ἐλεγέτην:** the dual emphasises the joint importance of Hesiod and Homer in forming the canon of Greek mythology. Cf. Herodotus' comment (2.53) that it was they who created the genealogy of the gods, giving them their names and apportioning their prerogatives and skills, as well as describing their appearance. Xenophanes too held Homer and Hesiod responsible for Greek views of the gods (fr. B 11 D–K): πάντα θεοῖς ἀνέθηκαν Ὅμηρός θ' Ἡσίοδός τε | ὅσσα παρ' ἀνθρώποισιν ὀνείδεα καὶ ψόγος ἐστίν, | κλέπτειν μοιχεύειν τε καὶ ἀλλήλους ἀπατεύειν. Cf. fr. B 12 and Diog. Laert. 9.18 γέγραφε [Ξενοφάνης] δὲ ἐν ἔπεσι καὶ ἐλεγείας καὶ ἰάμβους καθ' Ἡσιόδου καὶ Ὁμήρου, ἐπικόπτων αὐτῶν τὰ περὶ θεῶν εἰρημένα. Xenophanes' criticism anticipates the arguments developed by P. in the following section. See further on 380d5–6; D. Babut, 'Xénophane critique des poètes', *A.C.* (1974) 83–117; Pratt (1993) 136–40. For the view that human know-

ledge of the gods is derived traditionally from the poets see *Rep.*
365e1–3 where Adeimantus says that if the gods do exist and care
about what we do our knowledge of them is derived ἔκ τε τῶν
νόμων (from tradition) καὶ τῶν γενεαλογησάντων ποιητῶν.   **d7**
τί αὐτῶν: partitive genitive.   **d9** ἐάν τις ... ψεύδηται 'if someone tells an ugly lie', i.e. a story which is 'ugly and immoral as well
as false' (Cornford). Cf. 377c1 above. All myths are for the most part
false (377a5–6), but some myths are more false than others. P.'s objection to the stories of Hesiod and Homer is that they misrepresent
the gods, like portraits which bear no resemblance to their originals.
Hence the μῦθοι which they tell contain no element of truth what-
soever. Contrast Arist. *Po.* 1460a18–19 which praises Homer because
δεδίδαχεν δὲ ... καὶ τοὺς ἄλλους ψευδῆ λέγειν ὡς δεῖ.

e1–3 Ὅταν εἰκάζῃ ... γράψαι 'When someone makes a bad likeness of gods and heroes in words, like a painter whose painting bears
no resemblance to the things he wants to portray'. περὶ θεῶν τε καὶ
ἡρώων οἷοί εἰσιν is an example of prolepsis, on which see *Ion* 531c6–
7. The assumption is that the aim of story-tellers is to produce a likeness to an original in the same way as a representational painter. Cf.
Laws 668b9–c1 where it is stated that all μουσική is concerned with
imitation and representation: καὶ μὴν τοῦτό γε πᾶς ἂν ὁμολογοῖ
περὶ τῆς μουσικῆς, ὅτι πάντα τὰ περὶ αὐτήν ἐστιν ποιήματα μίμ-
ησίς τε καὶ ἀπεικασία. καὶ τοῦτό γε μῶν οὐκ ἂν σύμπαντες ὁμολο-
γοῖεν ποιηταί τε καὶ ἀκροαταὶ καὶ ὑποκριταί; But it is striking that
P. does not use the term μιμεῖσθαι of the poet's activity here, even
though the notion of likeness and copying dominates the subsequent
argument, and despite the fact that later on in book 10 (596e6,
598b8) the analogy between poetry and painting is central to the
concept of μίμησις which is formulated there. Else (1986) 19–28
plausibly suggests that the omission of μιμεῖσθαι and its cognates at
this stage is deliberate, because P. wants to use them in a different
and more innovative sense in the section which begins at 392d5. The
concept of a false copy introduced here implies that P. himself has
knowledge of the original (οἷοί εἰσιν cf. οὐδὲ γὰρ ἀληθῆ at 378c1),
which the poets whom he is criticising do not. Cf. 379a7–8.   **e7–
8** Οὐρανός ... Ἡσίοδος: at *Theogony* 154–82 Hesiod tells the primi-
tive myth of how Kronos castrated his father Ouranos (the sky) in

order to separate him from Gaia (the earth). For details of the myth see further M. L. West (1966) *ad loc.*

378a1–2 τὰ δὲ δὴ ... ὑέος: Kronos himself swallowed his own children through fear of being usurped, but Zeus escaped this fate and eventually deposed his father (Hes. *Th.* 453–506 with M. L. West (1966) *ad loc.*). This myth is emphasised in particular because it portrays Zeus, father of gods and men, in such a bad light, and could be used to justify immoral behaviour on the part of human beings. See e.g. Aesch. *Eum.* 641; Ar. *Clouds* 904–6; Eur. *H.F.* 1317–19, and Pl. *Euthyphr.* 5e–6a where Euthyphro justifies his own prosecution of his father by referring to this succession myth, pointing out the paradox that people acknowledge Zeus as the best and most just of the gods, and yet accept the tales that are told about his wicked conduct towards his father. Burnet (1924) *ad loc.* points out that this argument was clearly used in fifth-century debates about νόμος and φύσις. The corrupting influence of these particular stories is also discussed in the *Laws* at 886c and at 941b where it is said that no one should be deceived by poets and story-tellers into believing their tales of theft and violence amongst the gods.   **a2–3 οὐδ' ἂν ... νέους:** S. is more concerned at this point with the harmful moral effects that such stories will have on the young than with the question of whether they are true or false.   **a2 οὐδ' ἂν ... ὤιμην:** ἂν should be taken with ὤιμην.   **a2–3 ῥαιδίως οὕτως:** cf. 377b5.   **a4 δι' ἀπορρήτων** 'in secrecy'. The word suggests the esoteric doctrines of the mysteries. Cf. e.g. *Phaed.* 62b3; Eur. *Rhes.* 943; Ar. *Eccl.* 442.   **a5–6 θυσαμένους ... θῦμα:** initiates at the Eleusinian mysteries sacrificed a pig (cf. Ar. *Ach.* 764 χοίρως ... μυστικάς), but S. advocates some less easily available and more expensive sacrifice in order that these secrets may be divulged to as few people as possible.

b2–5 οὐδὲ λεκτέον ... μέγιστοι: cf. *Euthyphr.* 6a8 (with Burnet (1924) *ad loc.*) where S. says that he cannot accept stories about crimes committed by the gods, for the same reasons as are given here. **b8 Οὐδέ γε ... πολεμοῦσι:** again the principal objection to such stories is that they set a bad example for human beings.

c1–3 εἴ γε δεῖ ἡμῖν ... νομίζειν 'if we want our future guardians to believe ...'.   **ἡμῖν** is ethic dative, lit. 'those intending to guard the city for us'.   **c3–4 πολλοῦ δεῖ … ποικιλτέον** 'far less must they be told tales about the battles of giants or have them embroidered on robes'. ποικίλλειν denotes decorative works in general (cf. 557c4–9), but there is probably a specific reference here to the πέπλος woven for the statue of Athena at the Great Panathenaea, which depicted the battle of the gods and the giants. Cf. *Euthyphr.* 6b7–c3, and see further E. J. W. Barber, 'The peplos of Athena', in J. Neils, *Goddess and polis: the Panathenaic festival in ancient Athens* (Princeton 1992) 103–17.   **c6–8 εἴ πως μέλλομεν … ὅσιον:** πως 'somehow', together with the alliteration, indicates the difficulty of P.'s project. The desire to persuade people that enmity between citizens is unholy anticipates the 'noble lie' at 414b8–415d5, which is designed to promote unity within the ideal state.

d1 καὶ γέρουσι καὶ γραυσί: nurses and mothers have already been referred to as story-tellers at 377c2–3, and for old women cf. *Rep.* 530e2, *Gorg.* 527a5, *Hipp. Maj.* 286a1–2, *Lysis* 205d, *Theaet.* 176b7. Buxton (1994) 21 notes that female story-tellers are usually invoked in a disparaging way, as in the expression 'old wives' tales'. Old men are less commonly regarded as putative story-tellers.   **d1–3 καὶ πρεσβυτέροις … λογοποιεῖν** 'and we must compel poets too to tell stories of this kind to them as they grow older'. Cf. Ar. *Frogs* 1053–5 where Aeschylus says that poets should keep quiet about wickedness and only deal with χρηστά, for 'children have a teacher to educate them, whereas grown-ups have the poets'. The importance of poetry for the inculcation of morality is also emphasised at *Prot.* 325e–326a, quoted in the Introduction p. 15.   **d3 Ἥρας … ὑέος:** for the story of how Hera was bound to her throne by Hephaestus see Alcaeus fr. 349 (Lobel–Page); D. L. Page, *Sappho and Alcaeus* (Oxford 1955) 258–61; Paus. 1.20.3.   **d3–4 Ἡφαίστου … ἀμυνεῖν:** the story is told at Hom. *Il.* 1.586–94.   **d5 θεομαχίας … πεποίηκεν:** Hom. *Il.* 20.1–74, 21.385–513.   **d6–7 ἐν ὑπονοίαις** 'allegorically'. Criticism of the Homeric poems was at least as old as Xenophanes, who in the sixth century complained that Homer and Hesiod attributed to the gods all the reproaches and faults of men, including theft, adultery and deception (fr. B 11 D–K, quoted above at 377d4; see also on 380d5–6). Heraclitus, too, censured Homer and Hesiod for their lack of knowledge (frr. B 40, B 42, B 57, B 106 D–K). It was probably in response to such criticisms of immorality that others rose to Homer's defence. The first of such defenders was said to have been Theagenes of Rhegium, who allegedly initiated the allegorical interpretation of the poems, explaining, for instance, that the battles of the gods represented the opposition of elements or qualities such as dry and wet, hot and cold, heavy and light, fire and water. Apollo, Helios and Hephaestus symbolise fire, Poseidon and Scamander water, Artemis the moon, Hera the air. Similarly with abstract qualities, Athena represents wisdom, Ares folly, Aphrodite desire and Hermes reason (8 A 1, 8 A 2 D–K, and see further Pfeiffer (1968) 8–11). In the fifth century Metrodorus of Lampsacus (on whom see *Ion* 530c9) was known for his allegorical interpretations of Homer. An example of the kind of interpretation of traditional tales favoured by οἱ σοφοί is given by S. at *Phdr.* 229c–d. See further J. Tate, 'Plato and allegorical interpretation', *C.Q.* 23 (1929) 142–54; Richardson (1975).   **d8–e1 δυσέκνιπτα:** lit. 'hard to wash out'. The metaphor is further developed in book 4 (429d4–430b2) where S. says that the legislator in the ideal state must use education to imbue the soldier class with courage, like a dye that cannot be washed out.

e1–3 ὧν δὴ ... ἀκούειν 'for these reasons everything must be done to ensure that the first stories they hear are as suitable as possible for the encouragement of virtue'.

378e4–383c7

If the young are to be educated correctly from their earliest years, the founders of the state must issue guidelines to the poets about the kinds of μῦθοι they should compose. Concerning the gods two principles are to be established: first (379b1–380c10) that god is good, and can only be responsible for good; second (380d1–383c7) that god is unchanging and totally without deceit.

378e4 Ἔχει γάρ ... λόγον 'Yes, indeed, that's reasonable.' For this use of γάρ to imply assent see Denniston (1954) 73–4.   **e5 ταῦτα ἅττα τ' ἐστίν** 'what these are'. As becomes clear in the following discussion, the programme for the education of potential guardians includes replacing the traditional tales of the poets with myths invented on Platonic lines.   **e7 οὐκ ἐσμὲν ποιηταί:** contrast 369c9 where S. says, Ἴθι δή ... τῶι λόγωι ἐξ ἀρχῆς ποιῶμεν πόλιν or 376d9–10: Ἴθι οὖν, ὥσπερ ἐν μύθωι μυθολογοῦντές τε καὶ σχολὴν ἄγοντες λόγωι παιδεύωμεν τοὺς ἄνδρας. There is a certain irony in the way that P. draws attention to the status of his own text.

379a2 τοὺς ... τύπους 'patterns', an important word in this section. Cf. a5, 383a2, c6, 396e1, 398b3.   **a3** παρ' οὓς ἐὰν ποιῶσιν οὐκ ἐπιτρεπτέον 'outside which they must not be allowed to compose'. **a7–8** οἷος τυγχάνει ... ἀποδοτέον 'the divine must surely always be represented as it really is'. The implication of these words is that S. himself, unlike the poets, knows what the true nature of the divine is. Cf. 377e1–3 and 379b1 below. The change from θεοί to θεός is not in itself significant, since P., in common with many other writers, uses the singular elsewhere without making any particular theological point (see e.g. *Ap.* 19a6, 42a5, *Ion* 534e2–5, *Phdr.* 246d3, *Rep.* 597b6, c1. For singular θεός cf. e.g. Hom. *Il.* 13.727, *Od.* 8.170; Sol. fr. 33.2; Semon. fr. 7.25; Soph. *Aj.* 765; Hdt. 7.10; Ar. *Wasps* 261, *Peace* 1141; Thuc. 7.77.4). Cornford's translation of θεός as 'the divine' is perhaps less misleading than 'God' with its implications of Christian monotheism. But the attributes of divinity which S. goes on to describe are quite unlike the traditional Greek conception of the gods. See on c2–4 and 380d5–6 below; Bloom (1991) 352–3; Gould (1992) 18–19.   **a8–9** ἐν ἔπεσιν ... τραγωιδίαι: the genres of poetry which particularly concern him are epic, lyric and tragedy, presumably because these are the traditional genres of poetry which the young are given to learn in school, and those to which most people would be most exposed, both at public performances and at symposia.

b1 ἀγαθός ... τῶι ὄντι: that god is in reality good is assumed as a self-evident truth rather than demonstrated by argument.   **b3–9** Ἀλλὰ μὴν οὐδέν γε τῶν ἀγαθῶν ... κακοῦ αἴτιον: in book 1 (335b–336a) S. argued that the just man, who is by definition good, will never harm anyone, since to harm a person is to make him morally worse, and a good man will never use his ἀρετή to make others bad. Similarly here it is assumed that what is good cannot be harmful; therefore god, since he is good, cannot be the cause of evil. S. does not distinguish between being good and doing good, indeed the latter is assumed to be a consequence of the former.   **b11** ὠφέλιμον τὸ ἀγαθόν: we are not told what constitutes τὸ ἀγαθόν here, but the passage anticipates the detailed treatment of the theme at 505ff, on which see e.g. White (1979) *ad loc.*; Annas (1981) 242–71. For the identification of the good with the useful cf. Xen. *Mem.* 4.6.8.   **b15–16 Οὐκ ἄρα πάντων . . . ἀναίτιον:** the idea, put forward here in a theological context, that good can only be the cause of good, is further explored in relation to the theory of Forms in book 6, particularly in the analogy between the sun and the Form of the Good at 507a–509c. Cf. the view of causation put forward at *Phaed.* 100b–101b.

c2–7 Οὐδ' ἄρα . . . ἀλλ' οὐ τὸν θεόν: though S. here accepts the time-honoured view that the evils in the world outnumber its blessings, he insists that we must look for some other cause of evil than god. Cf. 380a7–b1. The argument that god, since he is good, can only be the cause of good, is a radical departure from the traditional belief, often expressed in poetry, that the gods are responsible for both good and evil. Apart from the examples which S. himself cites see e.g. Hom. *Il.* 19.86–9, *Od.* 1.32–3; Sol. frr. 4 and 11 (West); Aesch. *Pers.* 93–4, *Ag.* 1485. S. reiterates his own belief at the climactic point in the myth of Er through the words of Lachesis at 617e4–5: αἰτία ἑλομένου· θεὸς ἀναίτιος, on which see Halliwell *ad loc.* Others before S. had, of course, expressed the view that the gods, and Zeus in particular, were concerned with human morality. See e.g. H. Lloyd-Jones, *The justice of Zeus* (California 1971) *passim*, and for the gods as punishers of human wickedness, Saunders (1991) 33–76. But S.'s insistence that the gods cannot be the cause of evil contradicts centuries of popular belief. See Else (1986) 21; Saunders, *ibid.* 301–2.

d3–8 ὡς δοιοί . . . ἐλαύνει: the passage referred to is *Il.* 24.527–32, which in the received text runs as follows: δοιοὶ γάρ τε πίθοι κατακείαται ἐν Διὸς οὔδει | δώρων οἷα δίδωσι, κακῶν, ἕτερος δὲ ἑάων· | ὧι μέν κ' ἀμμείξας δώηι Ζεὺς τερπικέραυνος, | ἄλλοτε μέν τε κακῶι ὅ γε κύρεται, ἄλλοτε δ' ἐσθλῶι· | ὧι δέ κε τῶν λυγρῶν δώηι, λωβητὸν ἔθηκε, | καί ἑ κακὴ βούβρωστις ἐπὶ χθόνα δῖαν ἐλαύνει. The most plausible explanation for the differences between the Homeric text and P.'s version is that P. quotes from memory and adapts the passage to fit into the context he requires. For example, Homer mentions first the bad things, then the good (lines 528 and 530), but P. reverses that order because he wants to show that god is the cause of good. The line κηρῶν ἔμπλειοι, ὁ μὲν ἐσθλῶν, αὐτὰρ ὁ δειλῶν is un-Homeric, but fits in well with the pessimistic view expressed by Achilles, and has presumably been adapted by P. from another author. Cf. e.g. the story of Pandora at Hes. *Op.* 90–5 where the words κῆρας and πίθου occur. The passage as a whole demonstrates P.'s method of citing poetic material to illustrate particular views and arguments, without being bound by the concept of verbatim accuracy. Cf. 398e8 and see further Van der Valk (1963–4) II 356–8; Lohse (1964) 10–17. This is the first of a number of passages quoted by, or referring to, Achilles, on whose importance see below on 386c5–7. The lines summarise the tragic world-view of the *Iliad*, which P. regards as fundamentally flawed, both in its portrayal of the gods, and in the ethical consequences that ensue for human beings. See further Halliwell (1984).   **d7 ἄκρατα τὰ ἕτερα** 'the one kind, unmixed'.

e1–2 ταμίας ... τέτυκται: again P. adapts Homeric material for his own purposes. No single line of the sort Ζεὺς ἡμῖν ταμίης ἀγαθῶν τε κακῶν τε τέτυκται exists in our text of Homer. But at *Il.* 4.84 we have Ζεύς, ὅς τ' ἀνθρώπων ταμίης πολέμοιο τέτυκται and at *Od.* 4.237 Ζεὺς ἀγαθόν τε κακόν τε διδοῖ δύναται γὰρ ἅπαντα. P. has evidently conflated the two lines to produce an appropriate quotation for this context. See further Lohse (1964) 17–18.   **e3–4 σπονδῶν σύγχυσιν ... Διός:** *Il.* 4.69–104, an episode which is elaborately motivated on the divine level.   **e5–380a1 θεῶν ἔριν ... Διός:** the battle of the gods at *Il.* 20.1–74 begins with Zeus bidding Themis to summon the gods to a council. It has been argued, however, that the reference is to the *Cypria*, which deals with the judgement of Paris and the deliberations of Zeus and Themis: Ζεὺς βουλεύεται μετὰ τῆς Θέμιδος περὶ τοῦ Τρωικοῦ πολέμου (*EGF* 31). See further Adam *ad loc.*

380a3–4 Θεός ... θέληι: Aesch. fr. 154a 15–16 Radt. The *Niobe*, one of Aeschylus' most famous plays, depicted the grief of Niobe over the death of her children. See Ar. *Frogs* 911–12 with Dover (1993) *ad loc.*   **a5–6 ἀλλ' ἐάν τις ... πάθη** 'but if anyone does write about the sufferings of Niobe, in which these iambics occur'. The words ἐν οἷς ταῦτα τὰ ἰαμβεῖα ἔνεστιν were deleted by Platt (for details see Adam *ad loc.*), but all the MSS contain them, and I follow Burnet in retaining them. **a8 ἐξευρετέον … ζητοῦμεν** 'they must find some such account as the one we are now seeking'. P. alternates between singular (ἐάν τις ποιῆι a5, ἐατέον λέγειν τὸν ποιητήν b3–4) and plural (ἐξευρετέον αὐτοῖς a8).

b1–6 λεκτέον … ἐατέον: either god is not the cause of human misery, or the misfortunes which mortals suffer are not really evils at all, but punishments inflicted by the gods to make them better. Poets therefore should not say that god makes men miserable by punishing them; rather that the wicked are wretched because they need punishment, which god supplies in order to benefit them. For this remedial view of punishment see *Gorg.* 476–77 with Dodds (1959) *ad loc.*; Mackenzie (1981) 183–95; Saunders (1991) 162–78. **b8 τῆι αὐτοῦ πόλει** 'in one's own city'. The reflexive refers back to διαμαχετέον. With the words εἰ μέλλει εὐνομήσεσθαι S. casually introduces a new, political dimension to the argument for censoring traditional mythology which will be further developed at 382c8–10, 389b7–9, and 414b.

c3 οὔτε σύμφωνα … αὐτοῖς 'self-contradictory'. Robinson (1953) 29 points out that the preceding discussion has given no evidence to support this claim that the tales of Greek mythology are self-contradictory – they merely contradict the notion of divinity which S. has put forward. **c8–9 μὴ πάντων … ἀγαθῶν:** this use of μή with the infinitive in indirect discourse is unusual, though not unparalleled. Cf. *Ap.* 37a5, *Phaed.* 94c3–4, *Rep.* 346e8, and for further examples see Goodwin (1929) 269–70. The effect here, reinforced by the repetition of μήτε at b7–c1 above, is to emphasise the negative. These words conclude the discussion of the first principle to be laid down about the nature of the gods.

d1 Τί δὲ δὴ … γόητα τὸν θεόν: the second principle, that god is incapable of change or deceit is designed to combat the familiar stories of gods appearing to mortals in different guises, like wizards or magicians, in order to deceive them. Later on (398a) we learn that it is not god, but the poet who transforms himself into all sorts of different identities: it is not god who is the deceiver, therefore, but the poet (cf. 382d9). Deception and bewitchment are closely associated here (cf. 381e10) and at 413a–c where S. argues that people never relinquish true beliefs willingly; they only do so when forced or bewitched (γοητευθέντες). See esp. 413c4: ἔοικε γάρ ... γοητεύειν πάντα ὅσα ἀπατᾶι. See further De Romilly (1975) 27–32, and on the negative connotations of the word γόης see W. Burkert, 'ΓΟΗΣ: zum griechischen Schamanismus', *Rh. Mus.* 105 (1962) 36–55. For the association between poetry, magic and deception see on 382c10, 601b1 and cf. 598d3. **d2 ἐξ ἐπιβουλῆς** 'deliberately': the emphasis is on deliberate deceit. **d3–5 τοτὲ μὲν ... δοκεῖν:** 'sometimes turning himself into different shapes and changing his form, sometimes deceiving us and making us think such things about himself'. The contrast is between the god actually transforming himself, and giving the appearance of having done so. γιγνόμενον should be taken with εἰς πολλὰς μορφάς. Cf. *Tim.* 27a εἰς ἄλλο τι γιγνόμενον, and see further Adam *ad loc.* **d5–6 ἁπλοῦν ... ἐκβαίνειν:** lit. 'do you think that he is simple and least of all things departs from his form?' This notion that god is unchanging and simple or single (as opposed to complex and multiform), though completely at odds with the polytheism of traditional Greek religion, had to some extent been anticipated by Xenophanes. He ridiculed the anthropomorphic conception of deity, pointing out that each race attributes to such gods their own characteristics ('The Ethiopians say that their gods are snub-nosed and dark, the Thracians that theirs have blue eyes and red hair', fr. B 16 D–K), and that animals would do the same if they had the ability ('But if cows and horses or lions had hands, or were able to draw with their hands and make the things that men can make, then horses would draw the forms of the gods like horses, cows like cows, and they would make their bodies like those which each had themselves', fr. B 15 D–K). For his other criticisms see above on 377d4. He asserted, on the contrary, that there is a single non-anthropomorphic deity (εἷς θεός, ἔν τε θεοῖσι καὶ ἀνθρώποισι μέγιστος, | οὔτι δέμας θνητοῖσιν ὁμοίιος οὐδὲ νόημα, fr. B 23 D–K), and that this deity remains always in the same place not moving, since it is not fitting (οὐδὲ ... ἐπιπρέπει) for him to go to different places at different times (fr. B 26 D–K). Despite the precedent of Xenophanes, however, Adeimantus' perplexed response at d7 makes it clear that S. is no longer discussing popular beliefs about the gods, but introducing new philosophical ideas, which go far beyond the conceptions of his predecessors. In fact the view of divinity put forward here prefigures the Forms, whose pure and unchanging existence is contrasted with the shifting plurality of appearances in the world of becoming. The use of the words ἰδέαις (d2), εἶδος (d3), ἰδέας (d6 and e1) to describe the god's shape or form underlines the link between this passage and the later development of the theory of Forms at 476–480 and 523–525. See further White (1979) 93–4, 30–4; Annas (1981) 217–41 with bibliographies there given. The importance of singleness or simplicity runs as a leitmotiv throughout the *Republic* in relation both to the state, in which one person will do one job (370b–c, 374a–d, 433a–434d), and (analogously) to the individual, whose soul will be in harmony when each part performs its proper function (441e–444e). The unified and unchanging divinity which P. postulates thus reflects the type of human character which his educational system is designed to foster (383c3–5; cf. 500c–d). Adam points out that in this respect P. adheres to the standard practice in Greek theology of making god in the image of man.   **d7 Οὐκ ἔχω … εἰπεῖν** 'I cannot say at the moment'.

ει ἢ αὐτὸ … ἢ ὑπ' ἄλλου: change is of two kinds, either self generated, or produced from outside.   **e3–4 τὰ ἄριστα … κινεῖται** 'things that are in the best condition are least moved …'   **ἄριστα** is an adverb, not an adjective agreeing with τά. Cf. 381b4. Stability and immunity to change from outside are taken to be characteristic of what is good (cf. 381b1–2), whereas susceptibility to external influences is a sign of inferiority. This principle is applied equally to the body, plants, the human soul and also to artefacts. Changelessness will also be a standard property of the Forms (see e.g. 479a, 484b, 485a–b, 500c, 527b, 585c–d; *Phaed.* 78d cf. 80b; *Symp.* 211a–b).

381a3–4 Ψυχὴν … ἀλλοιώσειεν: cf. 387d5–e8.   **a6 καὶ τά γε σύνθετα:** even in the case of composites, which might be thought to disintegrate more easily than living things, the principle still holds that those which are in the best condition will least be affected by time and change.   **a7 κατὰ τὸν αὐτὸν λόγον** 'according to the same principle'.

b4 Ἀλλὰ μὴν … ἄριστα ἔχει: for ἄριστα see on 380e3–4. That god is perfect is taken as a self-evident truth, even though it is difficult to square this view with the standard portrayal of the gods in poetry.

Cf. 379b1.   **b6 Ταύτηι** 'in this way' i.e. through external influence. Since god is perfect in every way, he will be totally resistant to change from outside.   **b8–9 Ἀλλ' ἄρα αὐτὸς ... ἀλλοιοῦται:** since god cannot be changed from outside, in order to undergo change he would have to change himself.

c1–2 Ἀνάγκη ... ἀρετῆς εἶναι: since god is perfect in beauty and virtue (again a description which hardly applies to the gods of myth and legend, who may be beautiful, but are certainly not virtuous), he could only change for the worse. This is one of the rare moments when Adeimantus is allowed to say something which shows that he really is taking the argument in.   **c4 ἄν** should be taken with ποιεῖν.   **τίς σοι:** τις is indefinite, the accent being thrown back from σοί.   **c4–5 ἑκὼν ... ἀνθρώπων:** cf. the idea that no one goes wrong willingly, on which see below, 382a7–9.   **c7–9 Ἀδύνατον ἄρα ... μορφῆι** summarises the argument which has provided the answer to the question which perplexed Adeimantus at 380d5–6. Since god is perfect it is impossible for god to want to change himself, therefore each of the gods must remain simply in his own shape. The use of the plural (θεῶν at c5 and αὐτῶν at c9) leads us deftly back to the anthropomorphic gods of the Homeric poems.

d3–4 θεοὶ ... πόληας: Hom. *Od.* 17.485–6.   **d5 μηδὲ Πρωτέως ... μηδείς** 'let no one tell false tales against Proteus and Thetis'. P. himself was not averse to referring to the transformations of Proteus when it suited him. See on *Ion* 542e7–8. Aeschylus had written a satyr play on the subject of Proteus, frr. 210–15 Radt. Pi. *Nem.* 4.62–8 alludes to the story of Thetis' capture by Peleus, who had to fight with her whilst she assumed all sorts of different shapes to try and elude him. Cf. Soph. fr. 618 Radt; Apollod. *Bibl.* 3.13.5. The subject was depicted on the chest of Cypselus (Paus. 5.18.5) and was popular in the art of the sixth and fifth centuries. See Brommer (1973) 321–9.   **d8 Ἰνάχου ... βιοδώροις:** Aesch. fr. 168.17 Radt. The line comes from the lost play Ξαντρίαι. It is not known why Hera was disguised as a priestess.

e3 λέγουσαι ... κακῶς: cf. 377e1 κακῶς and e7 οὐ καλῶς. These are examples of false myths.   **e3 ὡς ἄρα θεοί:** ἄρα 'if you please' expresses disagreement with the view being put forward. Cf. e.g.

358c5, 364b3, 391e5.   **e4 πολλοῖς . . . ἰνδαλλόμενοι** 'taking on all sorts of strange shapes'. An example of such frightening creatures is Empousa, described at Ar. *Frogs* 288–95, where she appears as an ox, a mule, a beautiful woman and then a dog, and is characterised as παντοδαπόν (289). See further Dover (1993) *ad loc.* For other examples of frightening mythical figures see Strab. 1.2.8, and on female bogey figures in Greek mythology see Buxton (1994) 18–19.   **e8–10 αὐτοὶ μὲν οἱ θεοί . . . γοητεύοντες:** 'but though the gods themselves do not change, do they make us think that they appear in different forms, deceiving and bewitching us?' i.e. they might delude us into thinking that they change, even though they don't.   **e11 Ἴσως:** the uncertainty of the replies here and in the following section indicates the unfamiliarity of the arguments that are being put forward.

382a1–2 ψεύδεσθαι . . . προτείνων: lit. 'would a god want to deceive us, offering us an illusion, either in word or in deed?' φάντασμα refers to deception in general, not just to physical apparitions. The φάντασμα λόγωι is the spoken lie, the φάντασμα ἔργωι the kind of unreal vision referred to at 382e10–11.   **a4 τό γε ὡς ἀληθῶς ψεῦδος:** for the oxymoron cf. *Theaet.* 189c7 and 11.   **a7–9 τῶι κυριωτάτωι . . . κεκτῆσθαι** 'no one willingly wants to be deceived in the most important part of himself about the most important things, but is especially afraid to have deception there.'   **a10 Οὐδὲ νῦν πω . . . μανθάνω** signals the need for further explanation, which is given in the following sentence. τῶι κυριωτάτωι ἑαυτῶν and ἐκεῖ are explained by τῆι ψυχῆι, περὶ τὰ κυριώτατα by περὶ τὰ ὄντα, αὐτό by τὸ ψεῦδος. Cf. 412e10–413a10 where the same point is made that no one wants to be deceived about the truth (τὰ ὄντα). The argument rests on the assumption that there are objective truths about 'the most important things', and that human beings have an innate desire to know these truths. Cf. the familiar Socratic paradox, οὐδεὶς ἑκὼν ἁμαρτάνει, discussed by e.g. J. Gould, *The development of Plato's ethics* (Cambridge 1955) 47–55; Mackenzie (1981) 134–57; Gill (1993) 52–4.

b2–3 περὶ τὰ ὄντα . . . τὸ ψεῦδος: lit. 'to be deceived and to be in a state of having been deceived and to be ignorant about the truth'. ἔχειν τὸ ψεῦδος balances ψεύδεσθαι, whilst κεκτῆσθαι τὸ ψεῦδος corresponds to ἐψεῦσθαι. The progression underlines the close connexion between deception and ignorance: to be ignorant is to be in a state of delusion, and no one would want that.   **b4–b5 ἐν τῶι τοιούτωι** 'in such a thing' refers back to τῆι ψυχῆι, indicating that the ψυχή is special.   **b7–c1 Ἀλλὰ μὴν … ἄκρατον ψεῦδος** 'But, as I was saying, it is ignorance in the soul of the deceived that is rightly called true falsehood. Since spoken falsehood is a representation of the state of the soul, a subsequent image, not pure unmixed falsehood.' This might be taken to suggest that a lie or spoken falsehood is an image of the falsehood in the soul of the liar, in which case spoken falsehood would not be true falsehood simply because an image is by definition less real than the object of which it is an image. But that would imply that the liar is himself ignorant of the falsehood of his lie, which seems unlikely in view of the context, which is the deliberate use of spoken falsehood. A more plausible explanation of the lie as a μίμημα of the state of the soul is simply that it is 'the expression of a previously conceived false thought' (Nettleship (1901) 91). Certainly the distinction between true and spoken falsehood paves the way for the theme of the usefulness of ψεῦδος in the following section. Spoken falsehood can be used in an educational way for the inculcation of the right kinds of values and attitudes, as in the case of the 'noble lie' at 414b8 (see above on 377a5–6). Indeed P. there stresses that lying is one of the best ways of persuading people of the truth. Spoken falsehood is therefore less harmful than ignorance about τὰ ὄντα because it involves the deliberate use of lies for the purposes of propagating the truth (what we would call propaganda), whereas falsehood in the soul arises through believing what is in fact false. See further Reeve (1988) 208–13; Gill (1993) 45–55.

c6–7 πότε καὶ … μίσους: lit. 'is it not sometimes useful to someone, so that it is not deserving of hatred?' τῶι is for τινί. Cf. Xen. *Mem.* 4.2.15–17 where lying is justified in the following situations: deceiving an enemy in war; a general encouraging a dispirited army; a father tricking his son into taking medicine that will cure him; removing weapons from a suicidal friend. S.'s justification of lying in certain circumstances is not as radical as has sometimes been supposed. See further Page (1991); Pratt (1993) 56–63 on the ethics of lying in archaic Greek poetry.   **c7–10 ἄρ' οὐ πρός τε τοὺς πο-λεμίους** ... **γίγνεται** 'isn't it useful against our enemies and as a kind of preventive medicine for those we call our friends, when they try to do something bad through madness or folly?' **τῶν καλουμένων φίλων** is dependent on **φάρμακον**. This passage recalls the discussion in book 1 of the view that δικαιοσύνη consists in telling the truth and giving back what we have borrowed (331c–332b). There S. argues that it would not be right to give back a weapon borrowed from a friend if that friend had subsequently gone mad, nor would it be right to tell the whole truth to a madman. In speaking about enemies S. here expands the scope of the discussion to open up the possibility of lying not only on pedagogical, but also on political grounds. See further on 389b. For ψεῦδος as a φάρμακον cf. 389b4. But P. also uses the word φάρμακον for the 'medicine' of truth. See further on 595b6–7. Of particular relevance to the present passage is Gorgias' *Helen*, in which the magical powers traditionally associated with poetry (see on 601b1), and especially its power to deceive, are attributed to λόγος in general. Gorgias draws an analogy between soul and body, λόγος being to the soul what φάρμακα are to the body: τὸν αὐτὸν δὲ λόγον ἔχει ἥ τε τοῦ λόγου δύναμις πρὸς τὴν τῆς ψυχῆς τάξιν ἥ τε τῶν φαρμάκων τάξις πρὸς τὴν τῶν σωμάτων φύ-σιν. ὥσπερ γὰρ τῶν φαρμάκων ἄλλους ἄλλα χυμοὺς ἐκ τοῦ σώμα-τος ἐξάγει, καὶ τὰ μὲν νόσου τὰ δὲ βίου παύει, οὕτω καὶ τῶν λόγων οἱ μὲν ἐλύπησαν, οἱ δὲ ἔτερψαν, οἱ δὲ ἐφόβησαν, οἱ δὲ εἰς θάρσος κατέστησαν τοὺς ἀκούοντας, οἱ δὲ πειθοῖ τινι κακῆι τὴν ψυχὴν ἐφαρμάκευσαν καὶ ἐξεγοήτευσαν (*Hel.* 14). See further Segal (1962) 106; W. J. Verdenius, 'Gorgias' doctrine of deception', in Kerferd (1981(a)) 116–28. But whereas Gorgias emphasises the double-edged nature of φάρμακα, which can either cure or kill, P.'s medical ana-logy stresses the therapeutic function of ψεῦδος as a φάρμακον. Cf. 389b5.   **c10–d1 ἐν αἷς** ... **μυθολογίαις** refers back to the begin-ning of the discussion of the kind of μῦθοι poets should compose at 378e4ff.

d2 ἀφομοιοῦντες ... **τὸ ψεῦδος:** cf. the words of the Muses at Hes. *Th.* 27–8 ἴδμεν ψεύδεα πολλὰ λέγειν ἐτύμοισιν ὁμοῖα, | ἴδμεν δ' εὖτ' ἐθέλωμεν ἀληθέα γηρύσασθαι. But there it is the Muses who produce lies which resemble the truth, and they, being goddesses, know what is true. S. says here that human beings *cannot* know the truth about the past: how then can they create falsehood which resembles the truth as much as possible? 'Truth' here clearly means something other than factual knowledge about the past: it is the truth of myth, rather than of history, an example of which is given at 414b–415d when P. invents the foundation myth for his ideal state, the so-called 'noble lie'. For P. the primary purpose of myth is not to provide an accurate account of past events, but to inculcate religious or ethical truths. See above on 377a5–6 and Belfiore (1985). His view that myths about the past must of necessity be factually false runs counter to the prevailing attitude in Greek culture that the traditional myths related by the poets were substantially true, and also that (good) poets somehow had access to the truth. At 414c1–7, for example, S. says that poets have always been able to persuade people of the truth of their myths, and at 415d1–2 he expresses the desire that in time the 'noble lie' will become an established myth, believed by everyone. See further Gill (1993) 53 and 46. Scepticism about traditional tales was from time to time expressed. Hecataeus of Miletus, for example, in an early attempt to disentangle myth from history proclaimed in the opening sentence of his *Genealogies*: 'Hecataeus the Milesian speaks (μυθεῖται) thus: I write these things as they seem to me to be true; for the stories (λόγοι) of the Greeks are many and, in my opinion, absurd' (*FGH* I fr. 1). But a basic belief in the historicity of myth persisted. Despite the recognition that poets did not always tell the truth (on which see d9 below) it is clear that in general the Homeric epics were treated as though they were in some sense history: even Thucydides, though he criticises Homer (as e.g. at 1.10.3 cf. 1.21.1) nevertheless uses his poetry as a source of evidence about past societies and events. See further, J. Moles, 'Truth and untruth in Herodotus and Thucydides' in Gill and Wiseman (1993) 88–121; Pratt (1993) 33–43, 144–6; P. Veyne, *Did the Greeks believe their myths?*, trans. P. Wissing (Chicago 1988).   **d6 ἀφομοιῶν** sc. τῶι ἀληθεῖ.   **d9 Ποιητὴς … οὐκ ἔνι** 'So there is no false poet in god.' The idea that poets lie, epitomised in Solon's blunt statement: πολλὰ ψεύδονται ἀοιδοί (fr. 29 West), is almost as old as the idea that they tell the truth. From Homer onwards poets claimed to have special knowledge vouchsafed to them by the Muses (see e.g. Hom. *Il.* 2.484–92; *Od.* 8.487–91; Hes. *Th.* 32; Pi. *Pae.* 6.51–8 and for further references Murray (1981) 90–2). But the existence of variant legends made it clear that the truth could vary from poet to poet. See e.g. *h. Hom.* 1.1–6; Pi. *O.* 1.28–9, *Nem.* 7.20–4. So at a basic level poets could be perceived as liars because the stories which they told were factually incorrect. But when the Muses tell Hesiod that they 'know how to say many falsehoods that are like the truth' (quoted above at d2) they seem to be referring not just to factual falsehood, but to plausible falsehood, possibly even to a category of utterance that we would call fictional. How far Greeks in this early period (and indeed later) distinguished between lying and fiction is a complex question; but it would be difficult to maintain that they showed *no* awareness of the fictional status of some poetry at least. Already in the *Odyssey* Odysseus' lying tales are likened to the plausible ψεύδεα of a poet in words which resemble those of Hesiod's Muses: Ἴσκε ψεύδεα πολλὰ λέγων ἐτύμοισιν ὁμοῖα (*Od.* 19.203, with Russo (1992) *ad loc.* Cf. *Od.* 11.368, 14.387, 17.518–21, 21.406–9). The self-reflexive nature of the poem, with its bard-like hero and its emphasis on story-telling, suggest that the *Odyssey* poet was well aware of the fictional nature of his own composition. See further Goldhill (1991) 1–68; Bowie (1993) 20–2 and *passim* on the subject of lies and fiction in early Greek poetry; Pratt (1993). However that may be, we do not need the concept of fiction in order to grasp S.'s point here: poets, since they cannot know the truth, can only tell lies, and it is they who deceive us with their tales of the gods changing shape, not god himself. Cf. 380d1. Else (1986) 22–3 points out that the implied contrast between god and the poet becomes almost explicit in this phrase. Perhaps also there is a play on the word ἔνθεος: so far from god (inspiration) being in the poet, there is no poet in god.

e3 Ἀλλ' οὐδείς ... θεοφιλής: at 352b1–2 S. argued that the just man is a friend to the gods, the unjust man their enemy. Later on, in the discussion of the tyrannical man in book 9 the worst human type is characterised as one who is ruled by lust, drink and madness (573c–d, 577d–e). Since justice is defined as a harmony in the soul with each part performing its proper function under the control of reason (441c3–444e6), a man who is a slave to passion and madness will be the antithesis of the just man. The madman must therefore be un-just, and for this reason he will not be a friend of the gods.   **e6 τὸ δαιμόνιόν ... θεῖον** 'the spiritual and the divine'. In Homer the term δαίμων covers the whole range of supernatural phenomena and reli-gious experience which cannot be attributed to or explained in terms of the Olympian gods. '*Daimon* does not designate a specific class of divine beings, but a peculiar mode of activity' (Burkert (1985) 180). But in Hes. *Op.* 121–6 δαίμονες are more precisely categorised as dead men of the Golden Age who act as beneficent guardians of men on earth. In the *Symposium* P. describes δαίμονες as inter-mediaries between gods and men (202d–203a), and τὸ δαιμόνιον is defined as being midway between god and mortal: πᾶν τὸ δαιμόνιον μεταξύ ἐστι θεοῦ τε καὶ θνητοῦ (*Symp.* 202d13–e1). But elsewhere he is rather more vague, particularly in relation to S.'s 'divine sign', which is described variously as θεῖόν τι καὶ δαιμόνιον (*Ap.* 31d, cf. 27b–e), τὸ τοῦ θεοῦ σημεῖον (*Ap.* 40b), τὸ εἰωθὸς σημεῖον τὸ δαι-μόνιον (*Euthyd.* 272e), τὸ δαιμόνιον σημεῖον (*Rep.* 496c). See further Friedländer (1958) 32–44. τὸ δαιμόνιον is, therefore, sometimes syn-onymous with τὸ θεῖον and sometimes differentiated from it, but both terms refer to what is spiritual and divine as opposed to what is mortal, τὸ ἀνθρώπινον.   **e8–9 ὁ θεὸς ἁπλοῦν ... μεθίσταται** summarises the argument from 380d–381e.   **e9–11 οὔτε ἄλλους ... οὐδ' ὄναρ** 'neither does he deceive others through visions or words or the sending of signs, when awake or when asleep'. These words refer back to 382a–d, echoing in particular the language of 382a1–2. On the text see Adam *ad loc.*, and Slings (1988) 395–6.

383a2–5 Συγχωρεῖς ἄρα ... ἐν ἔργωι: lit. 'Do you agree, then, that this is the second pattern according to which it is necessary to speak and compose about the gods, that they are neither magicians who transform themselves, nor do they mislead us with lies either in word or in deed?' At a4 we would expect παράγοντας, parallel to ὄντας, but the construction changes. Instead of ὡς with the participle after ποιεῖν ('that they are neither magicians who transform themselves') we have the infinitive after λέγειν ('nor do they mislead us with lies'). Both ποιεῖν and λέγειν affect the construction, as explained by Adam *ad loc.* This concludes the discussion of the second principle, which began at 380d1.   **a7 Πολλὰ ... ἄλλα:** on the text printed here see Slings (1989) 396.   **a8 τὴν τοῦ ἐνυπνίου ... Ἀγαμέμνονι** refers to the false dream sent by Zeus to Agamemnon at *Il.* 2.1–34.

b2–9 νόσων ... τὸν ἐμόν: Thetis says that Apollo sang at her wedding, celebrating the happiness of her future offspring, 'their long life, free from sickness; telling everything he sang of my good fortune, blessed by the gods, cheering my heart. And I thought the divine mouth of Phoebus, full of prophetic skill, could speak no falsehood. But he who sang the hymn, he who was present at the feast, he who said these things, is the one who killed my child.' (Aesch. fr. 350 Radt). It is not known from which play these lines are taken, but Thetis' bitterness against Apollo for the death of her son prepares us for the emphasis on Achilles in the following section.

c2 χορὸν ... τῶν νέων: when a poet wanted to compete at a dramatic festival he applied to the archon to grant him a chorus, which would be financed by a choregos. We do not know how the archon made his choice but P. *Laws* 817d4–8 implies that he judged between dramatists on the basis of hearing parts of their work read to him. For the phrase χορὸν διδόναι cf. Cratin. fr. 15; Arist. *Po.* 1449b1–2, and see further Pickard-Cambridge (1988) 84. In the ideal state dramatists will be prevented from putting on plays which contain passages of the sort quoted above, and teachers will not be allowed to use them for the education of the young. Cf. 378d1–3.   **c4–5 καθ' ὅσον ... οἷόν τε** 'as far as it is possible for man to be'. For the view that man should strive to be as god-like as possible see 500c–d, 501b–c, 613a7–b1; *Theaet.* 176b–177a; *Laws* 716b–d. Here too P. is at odds with the poetic tradition which insisted on the unbridgeable gap between gods and men, as epitomised in Apollo's words to Diomedes at *Il.* 5.440–2: φράζεο, Τυδεΐδη, καὶ χάζεο, μηδὲ θεοῖσιν | ἶσ' ἔθελε φρονέειν, ἐπεὶ οὔ ποτε φῦλον ὁμοῖον | ἀθανάτων τε θεῶν χαμαὶ ἐρχομένων τ' ἀνθρώπων.

386a1–392a2

A further reason for excluding most existing poetry is that it is morally harmful in content, encouraging cowardice and lack of self-control. The emphasis placed on these particular moral defects anticipates the discussion of the qualities which will be needed in the ideal state, beginning at 427e10. There it is stated that the perfect city is σοφή ... καὶ ἀνδρεία καὶ σώφρων καὶ δικαία. *Hence the insistence in this section on the importance of inculcating courage and self-control in the young right from their earliest years.*

386a3–4 τιμήσουσιν καὶ γονέας ... ποιησομένοις 'if they are to honour the gods and their parents, and to value their friendship with each other'. The participles stand for a conditional clause. These words refer back to 378a–d where S. condemns many of the traditional stories about the gods committing violent crimes against parents and fighting amongst themselves.   **a6–7** ἄρα ... δεδιέναι 'shouldn't they be told stories such as will make them least afraid of death?' καὶ οἷα is for καὶ τοιαῦτα ὥστε. The importance of courage (one of the four cardinal virtues defined in the *Republic*, 427d10) was emphasised in the discussion of the qualities which would be required in the guardians of the state at 374e. Here S. is clearly thinking of courage in the traditional manner, as a virtue displayed on the battlefield. Hence the concentration on Achilles, the embodiment of heroic courage, in what follows (see on 386c5–7). Later on, in book 4 (429a8–430c7), a different definition of courage as steadfastness of purpose is proposed, and at 442b11–c3, after the introduction of the tripartite theory of the soul, the courageous man is described as one whose spirited part (τὸ θυμοειδές) clings to the dictates of reason about what he should or should not fear, in spite of pain and pleasure. This definition recalls S.'s view as stated in the *Apology* (28d6–10) that when a man has taken up a stand, either because he believes it to be right, or in obedience to orders, he should not waver from his purpose, even in the face of death. Cf. Alcibiades' description of S.'s indifference to bodily desires, which is also called ἀνδρεία at *Symp.* 219d–e. The analysis of courage, which begins with a critique of Achilles, thus culminates in an allusion to the type of courage exemplified by S. Such a re-definition is necessary because, traditionally interpreted, courage such as that of Achilles leads to the rejection of reason and to a refusal to bow to authority, behaviour which must be eradicated in the ideal state. In more general terms part of P.'s purpose in constructing his educational programme is to replace Achilles as a role model for the young with that of the philosopher as the highest human type. See further

Bloom (1991) 354–8, and, for a detailed and illuminating discussion of P.'s re-working of heroic values, Hobbs (1990), especially chapters 3 and 4.

b4–5 τὰν Ἄιδου ... οἴει τινά 'do you think that anyone who believes in the existence of Hades and its terrors'. **b9–10 ἁπλῶς οὕτως** 'simply'. **b10–c1 ὡς ...** λέγοντας: ὡς with accusative of the participle, rather than the genitive, which we might have expected after δεῖσθαι sc. αὐτῶν.

c3 ἀπὸ τοῦδε τοῦ ἔπους: for the singular used of a passage, or group of verses cf. Hdt. 7.143. **c5–7 βουλοίμην ... ἀνάσσειν:** the famous words spoken by the shade of Achilles to Odysseus in Hades at *Od.* 11.489–91. Despite S.'s disapproval, the view of death expressed here does not make Achilles himself less brave; on the contrary, his acute awareness of the transience of human life makes him place all the more value on the honour and glory to be won on the battlefield. See further Bloom (1991) 354; Hobbs (1990) 157–61. Indeed Achilles' self-sacrifice in avenging the death of his companion, Patroclus, was widely regarded as a paradigm of heroic courage. See e.g. *Ap.* 28c–d where S. identifies himself with Achilles; *Symp.* 179e–180a2; Aeschin. *In Tim.* 145; Arist. *Rhet.* 1359a4–5. Bloom (1991) 354–8 suggests that P. focuses on Achilles at this point in the argument precisely in order to undermine his traditional status as a role model for the young: he is courageous, but his is not the sort of courage which is conducive to the harmonious society envisaged in the ideal state. If the guardians, whose education is under discussion, are to fulfil their task of defending their city and subordinating themselves to the the good of the community as a whole, a new model of the heroic will be required, exemplifying a different kind of courage. See above on 386a6–7.

d1–2 οἰκία ... θεοί περ: *Il.* 20.64–5, where Hades is afraid that Poseidon will break open the earth and reveal his dreaded abode. The words quoted here are dependent on δείσας μή in Homer's text. **d4–5 ὦ πόποι ... πάμπαν:** *Il.* 23.103–4. Achilles speaks these words after trying to clasp the shade of Patroclus, who disappears beneath the earth like smoke. **d5 ἔνι** for ἔνεστι. **d7 οἴωι ... ἀΐσσουσι:**

Od. 10.495 referring to Teiresias, who alone of the dead has his φρένες ἔμπεδοι (493) and to whom Persephone has granted reason so that he 'alone has understanding, but the others flit about like shadows'. P. also alludes to this passage at *Men.* 100a5.　**e9–10 ψυχὴ ... ἥβην:** *Il.* 16.856–7 of Patroclus.

387a2–3 ψυχὴ ... τετριγυῖα: *Il.* 23.100–1 of Patroclus.　**a5–8 ὡς δ᾽ ὅτε ... ἥιεσαν** 'as when bats flit about gibbering in the corner of a wondrous cave, when one of the colony (ὁρμαθοῦ, lit. 'chain') falls from the rock face, and the others hold on to each other above, so these (sc. souls) went with him gibbering', *Od.* 24.6–9 of Hermes conducting the souls of the suitors down to Hades.

b1–2 Ὅμηρόν ... μὴ χαλεπαίνειν: for the deference shown to Homer cf. 383a7, 391a3–5.　**b2–4 οὐχ ὡς οὐ ποιητικὰ ... ἀκουστέον:** the pleasure of listening to poetry (the emphasis on listening, of course, reflects the oral nature of Greek culture) is a central feature of Greek attitudes to poetry from Homer onwards. See e.g. Hom. *Od.* 1.347, 368–71, 422; 8.45, 91, 368; 12.188; 17.385, 606; 18.305; Hes. *Th.* 37, 40, 51 and in general Havelock (1963) 152–4, 207–8; Walsh (1984); Gentili (1988) 54–5; Goldhill (1991) 57–64, 168–9, 174–5. S. does not deny that the passages he has quoted give pleasure, but insists that they must be suppressed in the interests of educating men to be free from the fear of death. In saying that the more poetic they are, the less suitable they are for the ears of the young, the implication is that the more poetic they are, the more pleasurable they are; indeed it is because they give pleasure that they must be censored. Poetry is dangerous precisely in proportion to the pleasure it gives. See further on 397d6 and 601b1.　**b9–c1 Κωκυτούς ... ἀλίβαντας:** Κωκυτός, the River of Wailing, was a tributary of the Στύξ, the Hateful. The plurals 'Cocytuses' and 'Styxes' imply 'names like Cocytus and Styx'. The word ἔνεροι (used at *Il.* 15.188 and 20.61; Hes. *Th.* 850; *h. Dem.* 357) was thought to derive from the fact that dead bodies lay ἐν τῆι ἔραι (in the earth). ἀλίβας is not found in Homer or Hesiod, but Plut. *Mor.* 736a explains that the words ἀλίβας (dropless) and σκελετός (dried) are used of the dead because dead bodies are dry. On all these etymologies see Chantraine (1968–80).

c1–3 καὶ ἄλλα ὅσα ... ἀκούοντας: lit. 'and other names as many as there are of this type, which make all who hear them shudder – as he thinks'. ἄλλα ὅσα τούτου τοῦ τύπου ὀνομαζόμενα is the equivalent of ἄλλα ὀνόματα ὅσα τούτου τοῦ τύπου ὄντα, as explained by Adam *ad loc.*   **ὡς οἴεται:** many editors omit these undoubtedly corrupt words, assuming that they are a gloss. But Slings (1990) 341–2 argues persuasively that they should be retained, pointing out that what probably lies behind them is a qualification of πάντας.   **c3 καὶ ἴσως ... ἄλλο τι** 'perhaps they are good for other purposes', i.e. for the purposes of pleasure; cf. 390a5. For the pleasure induced by the emotion of fear cf. Gorg. *Hel.* 8–10 and Segal (1962); *Ion* 535b1–e6.   **c4–5 ἐκ ... φρίκης ... μαλακώτεροι:** φρίκη, like φρίττειν at c2 above, denotes the shuddering induced by fear, cf. in particular Gorg. *Hel.* 9 φρίκη περίφοβος. But it can also be used of the cold fit of a fever, as e.g. at Hippocr. *Aph.* 5.61; Theophr. *Lass.* 17 cf. *Ign.* 74. Hence the connexion between shuddering and becoming hotter (θερμότεροι). For the same idea cf. *Phdr.* 251a7–b1, where the effect of the beloved on the lover is described; ἰδόντα δ' αὐτὸν οἷον ἐκ τῆς φρίκης μεταβολή τε καὶ ἱδρὼς καὶ θερμότης ἀήθης λαμβάνει. But with μαλακώτεροι the metaphor changes to one of softening, as of iron by fire. Cf. 411a ὥσπερ σίδηρον ἐμάλαξεν and *Laws* 671b8–10 καθάπερ τινὰ σίδηρον τὰς ψυχὰς τῶν πινόντων διαπύρους γιγνομένας μαλθακωτέρας γίγνεσθαι.

d1–2 τοὺς ὀδυρμοὺς ... τῶν ἐλλογίμων ἀνδρῶν: cf. 605 d–e.   **d5–6 οὗπερ καὶ ἑταῖρός ἐστιν** 'whose friend he is'. The implication is that a good man will only be friends with one who is like himself. Cf. 382c8–10; *Lysis* 214c–d.   **d6 τὸ τεθνάναι ... ἡγήσεται:** cf. 603e. The point here, that the good man will not regard the death of his friend as an evil to be lamented, anticipates the discussion of the nature of the philosopher in book 6, where S. says that such a man will not think of death as something terrible (486b1). For the idea that death will not be feared by the good man see *Ap.* 41c8–d2; *Phaed.* 117c1–5. The description of S.'s death there, and especially the way in which he restrains his friends from weeping, is an example of how the good man should behave in the face of death. This indifference to death depends, of course, on a very different view of the after-life from that depicted in Homer. Not only is death not to be feared, it is even to be welcomed by the philosopher, whose life is spent preparing himself for the final separation of his soul from his body (*Phaed.* 67b8–68b6). See further Halliwell (1984) 53–8.   **d12** αὐτὸς αὑτῶι αὐτάρκης: for the self-sufficiency of the good man cf. *Lysis* 215a–c, and for S. as an exemplar of self-sufficiency see Xen. *Mem.* 1.2.14, 4.8.11 and cf. 4.7.1.

e6 ὀδύρεσθαι, φέρειν δέ: these infinitives (like δεινόν at e3) are best explained as dependent on λέγομεν at d11 above.   **e10–388a1** γυναιξὶ ... σπουδαίαις: for lamentations being characteristic of women cf. 398e, 605e1, *Ap.* 35b3, *Phaed.* 117d–e1 with 60a–b; and women played an important part in Greek funerary ritual and lamentation. See M. Alexiou, *The ritual lament in Greek tradition* (Cambridge 1974) ch. 1, esp. 21–3; H. Foley, 'The politics of tragic lamentation', in A. Sommerstein *et al.* (edd.) *Tragedy, comedy and the polis* (Bari 1993) 101–43. Lack of self-control was a standard attribute of women as represented in Athenian classical literature. See e.g. *Rep.* 431b–c and in general R. Just, *Women in Athenian law and life* (London 1989) 153–217. The idea that some women can be exempted from the stereotype is in keeping with the general view, expressed at 540c5–9, that women can in principle have the same natural capacities as men. On the subject of Plato's attitude to women see e.g. Annas (1981) 181–5, 188–9; Halliwell (1993) 9–16.

388a1 ὅσοι κακοὶ τῶν ἀνδρῶν for ἀνδράσιν ὅσοι κακοί εἰσιν. **a1–3** ἵνα ἡμῖν ... τρέφειν 'so that those whom we say we are educating as guardians of the country will be ashamed to act like these'. ἡμῖν is ethic dative. ὅμοια τούτοις ποιεῖν brings in the notion of likeness and imitation, the idea that literature can encourage imitative behaviour.   **a7–b1** ἄλλοτ ... ἀτρυγέτοιο: at *Il.* 24.10–13 Homer describes Achilles mourning for Patroclus thus: ἄλλοτ' ἐπὶ πλευρὰς κατακείμενος, ἄλλοτε δ' αὖτε | ὕπτιος, ἄλλοτε δὲ πρηνής· τοτὲ δ' ὀρθὸς ἀναστὰς | δινεύεσκ' ἀλύων παρὰ θῖν' ἁλός· οὐδέ μιν ἠὼς | φαινομένη λήθεσκεν ὑπεὶρ ἅλα τ' ἠϊόνας τε. Since P.'s quotation depends on ποιεῖν, he has to make certain grammatical changes, which in turn affect the metre of the passage. The original nominatives become accusatives, leading to the substitution of πλάζοντ' for δινεύεσκ' and ἐπί for παρά, whilst ἀτρυγέτοιο is added to complete the sense of the line. See further Lohse (1965) 279–81.

b1–2 μηδὲ ἀμφοτέραισιν . . . κεφαλῆς: *Il.* 18.23–4, again of Achilles' reaction to Patroclus' death. The quotation is adapted grammatically to fit in with P.'s sentence. In both cases Achilles' uncontrollable grief contrasts tellingly with the restraint that should be shown by the good man when confronting death, whether his own of that of a loved one.   **b3 ἐκεῖνος:** i.e. Homer.   **b4 Πρίαμον . . . γεγονότα** lit. 'Priam, begotten near the gods', i.e. closely related to them. He was descended from Zeus through Dardanus. See *Il.* 20.215ff. with Edwards (1991) *ad loc.*   **b6–7 κυλινδόμενον . . . ἕκαστον:** the quotation is from *Il.* 22.414–15, when Priam sees Achilles maltreating Hector's body. Athenian legislation controlling funerals (for which see on 604a10) suggests that P. was not alone in regarding such uninhibited displays of grief as inappropriate behaviour for a civilised Greek. See further K. J. Dover, *Greek popular morality in the time of Plato and Aristotle* (Oxford 1974) 167–8, and for excessive mourning as characteristic of barbarians see E. Hall, *Inventing the barbarian* (Oxford 1989) 44.

c1 ὤμοι ἐγὼ δειλή, ὤμοι δυσαριστοτόκεια: the words of Thetis at *Il.* 18.54.   **c2–3 εἰ δ᾽ οὖν θεούς κτλ.** sc. ὀδυρομένους ποιοῦσι. 'If they do show the gods lamenting, at least they should not dare to misrepresent the greatest of the gods'. μιμήσασθαι makes explicit the idea implied by the painting analogy at 377e, i.e. that the task of poets and story-tellers is to produce a likeness to an original in the same way as a representational painter.   **c4–5 ὦ πόποι . . . ἦτορ:** Zeus says these words at *Il.* 22.168–9 as he looks down on Hector being pursued by Achilles. φάναι is P.'s parenthesis. The received text of Homer has τεῖχος for P.'s ἄστυ.   **c7–d1 αἶ αἶ . . . δαμῆναι:** Zeus' words at *Il.* 16.433–4, as he laments the impending death of his son, Sarpedon, with αἶ αἶ for the ὤ μοι of the received text. Both here and in the previous case the most plausible explanation for the variations is that P. is quoting from memory. See further Lohse (1965) 282–4.

d2 σπουδῆι: cf. 396d4.   **d3–6 σχολῆι . . . ποιεῖν** 'hardly would he, being a man, think himself unworthy of these things and rebuke himself if it should occur to him too [i.e. as it occurs to the gods in Homer] to say or do anything of this sort'.   **d6–7 ἐπὶ σμικροῖσιν παθήμασιν:** if gods are shown weeping and wailing, human beings who are by definition less able to control themselves, will be encouraged to lament at the slightest provocation. Throughout this section it is assumed that gods should be portrayed as examples of good behaviour for humans to imitate.

e2 ὁ λόγος ἐσήμαινεν refers back to 387d4–388a3.   **e5 Ἀλλὰ μήν** introduces a new point.   **e5–7 σχεδὸν γὰρ ... τὸ τοιοῦτον** 'whenever anyone gives way to violent laughter it tends to provoke a violent change'. Laughter brings about physical change, and since change of any sort is inimical to the divine (381b, 383a) it should be to good men also. Later on we learn that laughter is associated with the lowest part of the soul, τὸ ἐπιθυμητικόν, and should therefore be avoided. See further on 606c2–5, and for the persistence of the idea cf. Lord Chesterfield's remark in a letter to his son, 9 March 1748: 'In my mind there is nothing so illiberal, and so ill-bred, as audible laughter'. I owe this reference to Prof. E. J. Kenney.

389a5–6 ἄσβεστος ... ποιπνύοντα: *Il.* 1.599–600.   **a8 Εἰ σύ ... τιθέναι** 'if you want to consider it mine', a somewhat wry comment on the passive role of the interlocutor in this discussion. For the punctuation adopted here see Slings (1990) 344–5.

b2 Ἀλλὰ μήν introduces another new point, namely the importance of truth.   **b2–4 εἰ γὰρ ὀρθῶς ... ἐν φαρμάκου εἴδει:** this refers back to the discussion at 382c6–e7.   **b5 ἰατροῖς ... ἰδιώταις:** the image of falsehood as a medicine to be administered by doctors implies an analogy between body and soul which is central to P.'s thought. Cf. 382c8–10, 444c5–e2, and see further Mackenzie (1981) 146–51, 175–8. When the idea of ψεῦδος as a φάρμακον was first introduced at 382c10 the implication was that anyone might use it in order to help a friend, but the medical analogy here suggests that ψεῦδος should only be administered by experts. For ἰδιώταις 'laymen' cf. *Ion* 532d8.   **b7–9 Τοῖς ἄρχουσιν ... πόλεως:** S. switches from talking about what *poets* should and should not say to considering the possible benefits of falsehood for the *rulers* of the city. This is the first mention of rulers in the *Republic,* and foreshadows the division of the guardian class into ἄρχοντες (rulers) and ἐπίκουροι (auxiliaries) at 414a–b. Similarly the notion of the medicinal lie prepares the way for the 'myth' which the citizens must be told about their origins by the rulers at 414b8–415d5. See further Page (1991) 16–20.

c1–2 ἀλλὰ πρός ... φήσομεν 'but we shall say that it is the same mistake, but on a larger scale for a private person to deceive such rulers'.   **c5–6 ὅπως ... πράξεως ἔχει** 'about his own condition or that of his fellow sailors'. πράξεως is genitive of respect after ὅπως. S. stresses the importance of truthfulness amongst the population at large in order to differentiate between ordinary falsehood and the kind of falsehood his rulers may use for the benefit of the city. The comparisons to a doctor (carried on from b4–5), a trainer and a captain all emphasise the ruler's expertise in caring for others, but also reinforce the point that he will only be able to use the 'medicine' of falsehood for the good of the citizens in his care if they tell him the truth. These analogies remind us of the wider political context in which the education of the guardians is set, particularly the image of the captain and his ship (repeated at d4 below), which is applied to the city in the famous passage at 488a–489.

d1 λαμβάνηι: sc. ὁ ἄρχων.   **d2–3 τῶν ... δούρων:** Hom. *Od.* 17.383–4. In the Homeric context the people mentioned in this quotation are all experts, but for S. the only expert who will know how to use falsehood is the ruler. Hence if anyone other than the ruler is caught lying he must be punished.   **d6 Ἐάνπερ ... τελῆται** lit. 'if the deed is accomplished in accordance with the word' i.e. if we are as good as our word.   **d7 σωφροσύνης:** moderation or self-control, another of the four cardinal virtues discussed in book 4, will also be needed by the guardians of the state if they are to fulfil their function properly. Moderation consists not simply in controlling one's desires, but also in obedience to rulers (see further 430d–432a). Once again Homer's Achilles features prominently as an example not to be emulated. What is needed is a poetry which will encourage moderation in the young guardians so that the courage which they possess by nature (375a) can be disciplined into the service of the state. For the link between ἀνδρεία and σωφροσύνη see 399a–c.   **d9 Σωφροσύνης ... μέγιστα** 'for the mass of men aren't these the main points of self-control?'

e5 Ὁμήρωι 'in Homer'.   **e6 τέττα ... μύθωι:** *Il.* 4.412.   **e7 καὶ τὰ τούτων ἐχόμενα** 'and the words which are connected with these'.   **e8–9 ἴσαν ... σημάντορας:** these lines do not follow on from the previous one, nor do they occur together in our text of

Homer, but are a conflation of *Il.* 3.8 and 4.431. In choosing examples from Homer to illustrate his theme P. has combined lines which
occur in different books, but in similar contexts. In both cases the
self-restraint of the Achaeans is being contrasted with the clamour
and disorder of the Trojans. The fact that the verb ἴσαν occurs at
both 3.8 and 4.429 may also have facilitated the conflation of the
two passages. The resulting quotation provides an illustration of
σωφροσύνη of precisely the kind that P. wants to encourage in his
guardians: although fierce and courageous in battle, the Achaeans
are nevertheless obedient to their masters. P. is less interested in
quoting Homer's poetry verbatim than in using it to support the
particular points he wants to make. Cf. 379d2–8 and see further
Lohse (1965) 286.   **e13 οἰνοβαρές . . . ἐλάφοιο:** *Il.* 1.225, spoken by
Achilles to Agamemnon. Lines such as these must be censored because they are not conducive to σωφροσύνη, and encourage political
insubordination.

390a1 καλῶς sc. λέγεται.   **a2 νεανιεύματα** 'hot headed', 'insolent behaviour'. Achilles' words are particularly to be censured
because they are spoken to a superior.   **a5 εἰ δέ τινα . . . θαυμαστὸν οὐδέν:** cf. 387c3.   **a8 ἄνδρα τὸν σοφώτατον:** Odysseus' reputation as a σοφός is particularly associated with his self-control. See
further W. B. Stanford, *The Ulysses theme* (2nd edn Oxford 1968) 104–
8, 121–2, and below on d4–5. S.'s admiration for him is evident in
the myth of Er, when the soul of Odysseus is the only one to think
carefully and wisely about his choice of life: 'cured of ambition
through the memory of his former sufferings, he went about for a
long time seeking the quiet life of an ordinary man, and when he
found it at last lying neglected by the others, he chose it gladly'
(620c–d). For parallels between Odysseus and the philosopher see
further the suggestive remarks of Segal (1978) 321–3, 333–
5.   **a10–b2 παρὰ πλεῖαι . . . δεπάεσσι:** *Od.* 9.8–10 but with παρὰ
πλεῖαι ὦσι instead of the παρὰ δὲ πλήθωσι of the received text of
Homer.   **b5 λιμῶι . . . ἐπισπεῖν:** *Od.* 12.342.

b6–c1 ἢ Δία . . . ἐπιλανθανόμενον sc. ποιεῖν. ὡς should be taken
with ἐπιλανθανόμενον so that the construction is ἢ ποιεῖν Δία ὡς
ἐπιλανθανόμενον ἃ μόνος ἐγρηγορὼς ἐβουλεύσατο. The postpone-
ment of the relative emphasises the words μόνος ἐγρηγορὼς in con-

trast with καθευδόντων ... ἀνθρώπων. See Adam *ad loc*. Zeus stays awake thinking when all other gods and men are asleep at *Il.* 2.1–4. The story of Hera's seduction of Zeus is told at *Il.* 14.294–351.

c6–7 οὐδὲ Ἄρεώς ... τοιαῦτα: sc. ἐπιτήδειόν ἐστι λέγειν. δι' ἕτερα τοιαῦτα 'for similar reasons'. The story is told at *Od.* 8.266–332.

d1–3 Ἀλλ' εἴ πού ... ἀκουστέον 'But if there are any speeches and deeds of endurance against all odds by famous men, they must be seen and heard.' θεατέον refers to πράττονται, ἀκουστέον to λέγονται, suggesting dramatic representations as well as epic recitals. **d4–5 στῆθος ... ἔτλης:** Odysseus speaking at *Od.* 20.17–18. The particular quality of endurance associated with Odysseus makes him a more suitable role model than Achilles. See further Bloom (1991) 436; Hobbs (1990) 204–5, and above on a8. The same passage is quoted at *Phaed.* 94d8.   **d7–8 δωροδόκους ... φιλοχρημάτους:** the idea that love of money is incompatible with σωφροσύνη is further developed in book 8 (545b8ff) in relation to the moral degeneration of societies. See especially 555c7–d1: 'Isn't it clear that it is impossible for a society to honour wealth and to maintain adequate self-control (σωφροσύνη) among its citizens? One or other must be neglected.'

e3 δῶρα ... βασιλῆας: a traditional saying, attributed by some to Hesiod. See Suda s.v. δῶρα, and cf. *Alc.* 149e; Eur. *Med.* 964; Hor. *C.* 3.16; Ovid, *A.A.* 3.653–4.   **e4–7 τὸν τοῦ Ἀχιλλέως ... μήνιος** 'nor must we praise Achilles' tutor Phoenix on the grounds that he spoke reasonably'. These words refer to Phoenix' speech at *Il.* 9.515–605.   **e7–391a τὸν Ἀχιλλέα ... μὴ 'θέλειν:** Achilles receives Agamemnon's gifts at *Il.* 19.278–81, although earlier in the book at 146–53 he makes it clear that he will return to battle regardless of whether Agamemnon gives them or not. Priam offers Achilles ransom in return for Hector's body at *Il.* 24.501–2 and 555–6, but at 560–70 Achilles says that he will give back the body anyway in accordance with Zeus' wishes. P.'s characterisation of Achilles as φιλοχρήματος is therefore not strictly accurate. Hobbs (1990) 124–5 suggests that P. misrepresents Achilles, portraying him as materialistic rather than obsessed with honour, in a way that foreshadows one of the chief characteristics of the timocratic man in book 8

(549b1–2). Achilles, like the timocratic man, is dominated by thumoeidic values (see on 595a7–b1, 604e1–2) that are uncontrolled by reason, and therefore represents a political and ethical threat to the stability of the state. See further Hobbs (1990) 135–73.

391a3–5 Ὀκνῶ ... πείθεσθαι 'I hesitate to say it out of regard for Homer, but it is impious to say these things of Achilles or to believe them when others say them'. Cf. 383a7, 387b1–2.   **a6–7 ἔβλαψάς ... παρείη:** *Il.* 22.15 and 20. P. omits the intervening lines because the ones he quotes are enough to illustrate Achilles' insolent behaviour towards Apollo. See Lohse (1965) 286–7.

b1–2 πρὸς τὸν ποταμόν ... ἕτοιμος ἦν: Achilles' insolence and subsequent fight with the river god Scamander are described at *Il.* 21.130–2, 212–26, 233–382.   **b2–4 καὶ αὖ ... νεκρῶι ὄντι:** ἱεράς 'dedicated to', followed by the genitive. Understand ὡς with ἔφη. Achilles places the lock of his hair dedicated to the river Spercheus on the funeral pyre of Patroclus at *Il.* 23.138–51. P. quotes line 151 here.   **b5–6 Ἕκτορος ἕλξεις ... τὴν πυράν:** *Il.* 24.14–16, 23.175–6.

c2 Πηλέως ... ἀπὸ Διός: Peleus' father Aeacus was a son of Zeus.   **c3 Χείρωνι τεθραμμένος:** *Il.* 11.831–2 refers to skills which Achilles had been taught by Cheiron. Cf. Pi. *Nem.* 3.43–52.   **c4–6 νοσήματε ... ἀνθρώπων** 'two contradictory maladies, mean covetousness and arrogant contempt of gods and men' (Cornford). νοσήματε continues the body/soul analogy. Presumably these maladies of the soul are contradictory because the one involves meanness, the other excess. On both counts Achilles is a dangerous role model for the young, since the state needs 'obedient soldiers, not arrogant warriors' (Hobbs (1990) 121).   **c9–d1 Θησεύς ... ἁρπαγάς:** Theseus, aided by Peirithous, carried off Helen (see e.g. Plut. *Thes.* 31), who was rescued by the Dioscuri. Theseus and Peirithous also went down to the underworld together in an attempt to abduct Persephone (see e.g. Sen. *Phdr.* 93–5; Hyg. *Fab.* 79.2).

d5–6 μηδὲ ἡμῖν ... τοὺς νέους 'nor must they try to persuade our young men'.   **d7 ἐν τοῖς πρόσθεν:** 377e–380c.

e4 Καὶ μήν introduces the further point that these stories are not only untrue, but are also morally harmful, as discussed in the pas-

sage beginning at 386a. See especially 388d3–7.   **e5 ἄρα** dis-
sociates the speaker from the view he is expressing. Cf. 381e3.
e7–11 οἱ θεῶν ... δαιμόνων 'close kin of the gods, near to Zeus, to
whom belongs the altar of ancestral Zeus on Mount Ida in the sky,
in whom the blood of divinities is not yet extinct'. The quotation is
from Aesch. *Niobe* fr. 162 Radt, a play also quoted at 380a3–4. Cf.
Strab. 12.8.21.   **e12–392a1 μὴ ἡμῖν ... πονηρίας** 'lest they breed
in our young men a complete indifference to wickedness'.

392a3–c5

So far the discussion has covered what should be said about gods, daimons, he-
roes and the world of Hades. It remains to consider what should be said about
human beings, but this cannot be done until the nature of justice has been defined.

392a3–4 Τί οὖν ... καὶ μή; lit. 'What kind still remains to us defining about stories, what sort are to be told and what are not?' **λόγων**
πέρι: the accent of περί is thrown back because it follows the noun.
The word order perhaps suggests that there will be other things to
consider as well as the sort of stories that should be told, anticipating
the discussion of λέξις at 392c6–8. At 376e11 the distinction was
made between two types of discourse, τὸ μὲν ἀληθές, ψεῦδος δ'
ἕτερον. The stories considered so far necessarily belong to the latter
category, since human beings cannot have certain knowledge about
the divine (cf. 382c9–d3); but literature concerning human behaviour must be of the other type, i.e. must tell the truth.   **a10–11**
Ἀδύνατον δή ... τάξαι: it is not yet possible to prescribe guidelines
on stories about human beings because they have not yet decided on
the question of how human beings should live. Cf. c1–4 below.
a13 ἐρεῖν ὡς ἄρα: for this use of ἄρα to denote an idea whose truth
has not before been realised see Denniston (1954) 39.

b1 τὰ μέγιστα: poets and story-tellers are just as wrong about the
most important things in human life as they are about the gods. Cf.
377e6–7.   **b1–2 εἰσὶν ἄδικοι ... ἄθλιοι** 'many unjust men are
happy, whilst just men are miserable'. ἄδικοι and δίκαιοι are subjects, εὐδαίμονες and ἄθλιοι predicates. The proposition that the
unjust are happy and the just unhappy is put forward and discussed
in book 1; indeed the refutation of this popularly held view is one of

the central themes of the *Republic*. See e.g. 352d2–6 where S. insists that the question of whether the just live better and happier lives than the unjust is of the utmost importance since it affects our whole way of life. Hence the necessity of controlling what poets and story-tellers say on the subject. The idea that injustice pays provided that it is undetected is forcibly stated by Thrasymachus (344b–d), and reiterated in the tale of Gyges' ring (359c6).   **b3–4 ἡ δὲ δικαιο-σύνη ἀλλότριον μὲν ἀγαθόν, οἰκεία δὲ ζημία:** these words epitomise Thrasymachus' view that justice is the interest of the stronger. Cf. 343c3–5 ἡ μὲν δικαιοσύνη καὶ τὸ δίκαιον ἀλλότριον ἀγαθὸν τῶι ὄντι, τοῦ κρείττονός τε καὶ ἄρχοντος συμφέρον, οἰκεία δὲ τοῦ πειθομένου τε καὶ ὑπηρετοῦντος βλάβη. Cf. *Gorg.* 470c9–471d2 with Dodds (1959) *ad loc.*   **b4 ἀπερεῖν** is dependent on οἶμαι at a13 above.   **b8–9 Οὐκοῦν ἐὰν ... ἐζητοῦμεν** 'If you admit I am right, I shall say that you have now admitted the point we were trying to establish all along.' For this interpretation, and for a defence of the imperfect, ἐζητοῦμεν, the reading of all the MSS, see Slings (1990) 347–8.   **c1–4 Οὐκοῦν περί γε ἀνθρώπων ... τοιοῦτος εἶναι:** the investigation into the nature of justice is concluded at 588b–592b. P. does not explicitly return to the question of what sort of things should be said by poets and story-tellers about human life. But some have seen the myth of Er with which the *Republic* closes (614b2–621d3) as an example of the kind of story that should be told. S. prefaces the myth there with words which imply a contrast between the false tales of the poets and the truth contained in the story he is about to tell. See further Halliwell (1988) on 614b2 and b2–3.   **c3 λυσιτελοῦν** sc. ἐστι, for λυσιτελεῖ.

392c6–398b8

The discussion now moves from the content of literature to its form. S. dis-tinguishes between two different forms of narration which he calls διήγησις (narrative), when the author speaks in his own voice, and μίμησις (imitation), when he speaks in the voice of his characters. All literature uses one or other of these modes, or a mixture of both. Since μίμησις involves emotional identi-fication on the part of the speaker with the words he is reciting S. insists that it is to be used sparingly: the good man will only be willing to imitate the speech or action of a good character. All other types of imitation will have to be banned from the ideal state.

c6 λόγων πέρι: for the accentuation see on 392a3.   **c6–8 τὸ δὲ λέξεως … ἐσκέψεται:** lit. 'after this, I think, we must consider the question of form, and then we shall have thoroughly considered both *what* should be said and *how* it should be said'. For λέξις in a similar sense cf. *Ap.* 17d3, where S. claims to be unfamiliar with the style of speech used in a law-court. But Adeimantus' reply suggests that the meaning of the term here is by no means clear.

d2–3 ἆρ' οὐ πάντα … μελλόντων 'isn't everything related by story-tellers and poets a narration of things past, present or future?' The term διήγησις is used here of narration as a whole, but in the subsequent discussion beginning at d5 it denotes a species of narration, as noted by Else (1986) 29. The reference to things past, present and future recalls Hesiod's Muses who sing of τά τ' ἐόντα τά τ' ἐσσόμενα πρό τ' ἐόντα (*Th.* 38, cf. 32 with M. L. West (1966) *ad loc.*, Hom. *Il.* 1.70), but the words μυθολόγων ἢ ποιητῶν remind us that the discussion embraces literature as a whole, not just poetry. Cf. 376e9, 394b9–c1.   **d5–6 ἤτοι ἁπλῆι διηγήσει ἢ διὰ μιμήσεως γιγνομένηι** sc. διηγήσει 'either by pure narrative or by narrative conveyed through imitation'. Μίμησις here refers to a particular form of narrative style, which is further defined at 393c5–9. P.'s distinction between these two forms of narration, which we also find in Arist. *Po.* 1448a20–4, anticipates the telling/showing distinction which began to emerge in Anglo-American criticism at the end of the last century, and remains the starting-point for many twentieth-century narratologists. See further e.g. G. Genette, *Narrative discourse*, trans. J. Lewin (Oxford 1980) 162–70; S. Rimmon-Kenan, *Narrative fiction* (London 1983) 106–8. Nehamas (1982) 71 n.10 points out that P.'s distinction is repeated 'without significant alteration' by R. Wellek and A. Warren, *Theory of literature* (3rd edn London 1963) 215–16. For the ethical implications of μίμησις see below on 393c5–6.   **d7–8 Καὶ τοῦτο … ἀσαφής:** the elaboration stresses the importance, as well as the unfamiliarity, of the idea which S. is attempting to explain.   **d9–e1 οὐ κατὰ ὅλον … βούλομαι** 'I will try to show you what I mean by taking an example, not the subject as a whole.' For the significance of the example that S. chooses see Introduction p. 19.

393a4–5 καὶ ἐλίσσετο ... λαῶν: *Il.* 1.15–16.   **a6–7 οὐδὲ ἐπι-χειρεῖ ... ἢ αὐτός** 'and does not try to make us think (lit. 'turn our thoughts elsewhere') that the speaker is anyone other than himself'. Cf. 394c2–3n.

b1 ποιῆσαι ... δοκεῖν 'to make us think'.   **b3 οὕτω πεποίηται** 'in this way he has composed almost all the rest of his narrative', i.e. in a mixture of direct speech with narrative in between.   **b4–5 περὶ τῶν ... παθημάτων:** Adam notes the slight oddity of juxtaposing Ἰθάκηι, the place, and Ὀδυσσείαι, the poem, and suggests that the last twelve books of the poem, which take place on Ithaca, may have been known collectively as Ἰθάκη.

c1–3 ἆρ' οὐ ... ὡς ἐροῦντα lit. 'shall we not say that he then assimilates his style of speech as much as possible to that of each person whom he has announced as about to speak'. ἑκάστωι is for τῆι λέξει ἑκάστου.   **c5–6 ὁμοιοῦν ... μιμεῖσθαι:** to imitate someone is to make oneself like them in voice or bearing (σχῆμα). Imitation is not therefore a superficial activity, but involves a deep emotional identification on the part of the imitator with the speaker whose words he is impersonating. Μίμησις thus has ethical implications right from the start of the discussion, even though it is introduced at 392d5 in the context of narrative style. Speaking in the voice of another is in some sense to become that person, and therefore to acquire that person's habits; imitation affects the behaviour of the imitator (395c–e), so that style can never be simply an aesthetic phenomenon. Indeed at 400d6–7 P. explicitly states that style is an expression of character: Τί δ' ὁ τρόπος τῆς λέξεως ... καὶ ὁ λόγος; οὐ τῶι τῆς ψυχῆς ἤθει ἕπεται; On the ethical dimensions of μίμησις see further Ferrari (1989) 114–18. The point has to be understood in the light of the oral nature of Greek culture, in which the recitation of poetry involved the kind of performance which we would associate with acting. The reciter, whether schoolboy, rhapsode, poet or actor was expected to throw himself into his part in the manner described at *Ion* 535c4–8, on which see above. Havelock (1963) 21–2 further observes that P. here assumes that the poet's mental state when composing is analogous to that of a performer: he makes himself like the character whose words he portrays as if he were an actor. As in the *Ion*, where it is assumed that the experience of ἐνθουσιασμός is shared by poet, rhapsode and audience, no distinction is made between poet and performer. See further on *Ion* 532c8–9.   **c11**

ἀποκρύπτοιτο: Else (1986) 25 points out that this notion of μίμησις, whereby the poet hides himself and takes on the characteristics of someone else, involves a deception which P. finds deeply disturbing.

d5–6 ὡς Χρύσης γενόμενος lit. 'as if having become Chryses', emphasising the process of transformation that takes place when an author 'imitates' his character: he actually becomes that character. **d7** εἶχε ... πως 'it would have been something like this'.   **d8** φράσω ... ποιητικός implies that an important defining characteristic of poetry is metre. That poetry is defined by its form is also implied at 378e7–379a4, 601a4–b4, and cf. *Phdr.* 258d10–11: ἐν μέτρωι ὡς ποιητής ἢ ἄνευ μέτρου ὡς ἰδιώτης. One would expect, therefore, that to be skilled in poetry would involve a knowledge of metre, rhythm, diction and so on, but P. is reluctant to allow either poets or their interpreters that kind of technical expertise. Cf. *Ion* 540b3 and see further on 601a4–b4, cf. Introduction p. 9. Ferrari (1989) 115–16 points out a further implication of S.'s warning us that he is no poet: in the paraphrase which follows, S. in effect imitates or impersonates Homer, but in a way that deliberately contrasts with Homer's own impersonation of Chryses. S.'s use of imitation is severely limited and used strictly for educational purposes. Not being a poet himself, he makes no attempt to become Homer, but continues to speak in his own style, thus demonstrating the truly poetic nature of Homer's own imitations.   **d8–e3** Ἐλθών ... αἰδεσθέντας puts into reported speech the direct speech of Calchas at *Il.* 1.17–21.

e3–394a1 ταῦτα δὲ ... οἴκαδε ἔλθοι summarises *Il.* 1.22–32 which in Homer includes a mixture of narrative spoken by the poet in his own person, and the direct speech of Chryses.   **e8** γηράσειν μετὰ οὗ 'she would grow old with him', i.e. Agamemnon.

394a1–7 ὁ δὲ πρεσβύτης ... βέλεσιν summarises *Il.* 1.33–42, which is also a mixture of the two styles in the original.   **a6–7** ὧν δὴ χάριν ... βέλεσιν 'in return for which he prayed that the Achaeans should be made to pay for his tears by the arrows of the god'. ἃ here is, according to Adam *ad loc.*, the only instance of the possessive ὅς (= Latin *suus*) being used as a reflexive pronoun in Attic prose. Presumably this is due to the Homeric context, i.e. τὰ ἃ δάκρυα is what Homer would have put for Chryses' ἐμὰ δάκρυα if he had told the story as pure narrative.

b5 τὰ ἀμοιβαῖα 'the exchanges of conversation' i.e. dialogue. **b6** τὰς τραγωιδίας: the example of tragedy clarifies the meaning of μίμησις in relation to λέξις, but we should not therefore assume that tragedy is P.'s prime target. As Havelock (1963) 21 points out, P. is not concerned with the distinction between epic and tragedy as genres, but with different types of verbal communication. Both tragedy and epic, in so far as it uses the mimetic mode, are therefore open to the same kind of analysis and criticism, regardless of any generic differences that may exist between the two.

c2–3 ἡ δὲ δι' ἀπαγγελίας ... ποιητοῦ 'another consists of the poet's own report'. Cf. Arist. *Po.* 1449b26 where tragedy is defined as being performed by men acting οὐ δι' ἀπαγγελίας. **c3** ἐν διθυράμβοις: see on *Ion* 534c3–4. Although P. singles out the dithyramb here as being mainly narrative in character, the genre was becoming increasingly mimetic in his own day. See on 397a4–7. **c4–5** πολλαχοῦ δὲ καὶ ἄλλοθι 'and in many other places'. **c5** εἴ μοι μανθάνεις 'if you understand my meaning'. Cf. 392c9, 394b2, 3 and 6. S.'s emphasis on making his meaning clear suggests that what he is saying is unfamiliar to his interlocutors, and by implication to his readers. **c7–8** τὸ πρὸ τούτου ... σκεπτέον εἶναι: cf. 392c6–8.

d2–4 πότερον ἐάσομεν ... μιμεῖσθαι 'whether we shall allow our poets to use imitation in the composition of their narratives, or whether they should use it in parts, and if so what parts (lit. 'of what sort each is to be'), or whether they should not imitate at all'. The question relates to the form of λέξις which poets may be allowed to employ in the ideal state. **d5** Μαντεύομαι suggests that Adeimantus remains uncertain about his grasp of the argument, but he does try. And S. himself goes on to admit that he does not yet know how the argument will develop. **d5–6** εἴτε παραδεξόμεθα ...

εἴτε καὶ οὔ: at 373b5–8 S. says that their city will need πάντες οἵ τε μιμηταί, πολλοὶ μὲν οἱ περὶ τὰ σχήματά τε καὶ χρώματα, πολλοὶ δὲ οἱ περὶ μουσικήν, ποιηταί τε καὶ τούτων ὑπηρέται, ῥαψῳδοί, ὑποκριταί, χορευταί, ἐργολάβοι, which clearly implies that there will be performances of tragedy and comedy. But it is important to remember that S. is there building up a picture of a luxurious society (τρυφῶσαν πόλιν 372e3), of which he himself professes to disapprove. See e.g. 372e–373b where the true and healthy society, content with the bare necessities of life, is contrasted with the fevered society, replete with the luxuries of civilisation, which include poetry. The process of constructing an ideal state involves purging it of luxury (399e5–8), and the question of whether tragedy and comedy should be allowed is germane to this theme.   **d7–9 Ἴσως . . . ἰτέον:** this remark indicates that much more is at stake than the place of tragedy and comedy in the ideal state, and the status of particular genres of poetry. P. is concerned with the more fundamental question of the nature of poetry itself, as we see when he returns to the subject of μίμησις in book 10. But the image ὥσπερ πνεῦμα suggests that the course of the argument is not yet decided.

e1–2 πότερον μιμητικοὺς . . . ἢ οὔ: the argument now switches from poets to guardians, and we move from an artistic to an educational context. Should the guardians be imitative? This is not just a question of whether they should be allowed to perform or recite poetry which is imitative in the formal sense (i.e. consisting of direct rather than indirect speech), but also a question of whether they should acquire the imitative habits which such poetry fosters. When a Greek school boy recited Homer he imitated e.g. Achilles by throwing himself into the part like an actor; and in P.'s view this process of μίμησις demands an emotional identification on the part of the imitator which has permanent effects on the character, as the subsequent discussion makes clear. See further Havelock (1963) 23–4; Ferrari (1989) 115–16.   **e2–4 τοῖς ἔμπροσθεν . . . πολλὰ δ' οὔ:** at 370b S. argues that since nature equips us with different aptitudes, we should all exercise the particular skill to which we are suited rather than trying to practise several. This fundamental principle of one man one job is reiterated at 374a5–375.   **e4–6 εἰ τοῦτο . . . ἐλλόγιμος** 'if he tries his hand at many things, he will fail to be distinguished in any of them'. A double construction is involved here since both πάντων and the clause ὥστ᾽ εἶναί που ἐλλόγιμος depend on ἀποτυγχάνοι. See further Slings (1990) 348.   **e7 Τί δ᾽ οὐ μέλλει** sc. ἀποτυγχάνειν, lit. 'how is he not about to fail in everything?', i.e. 'certainly he will'. For the expression cf. 605c9.   **e8 περὶ μιμήσεως:** The term μίμησις covers both imitative poetry and imitative behaviour.

395a1–2 Σχολῇι ... μιμητικός sc. ὁ αὐτός. 'Scarcely, then, will the same man practise any worthwhile occupation and at the same time imitate many things and be imitative'. ἅμα should be taken with the second clause. It will be difficult for anyone to pursue a worthwhile occupation at the same time as being an imitator, because being an imitator involves imitating many things. S. here stresses that the principle of one man one job is incompatible with the imitative behaviour encouraged by poetry, since poetry by its very nature concerns itself with a plurality of subjects.   **a3–5 ἐπεί που οὐδὲ ...** **ποιοῦντες** 'since the same people cannot at the same time successfully accomplish even two forms of imitation which seem to be closely related to each other, composing tragedies and comedies, for example'. If poets, whose business is imitation, can only succeed in one form of imitation, still less will anyone else be able to combine being an imitator with any other kind of worthwhile pursuit. Despite the fact that he has just said that being an imitator involves imitating many things, S. now applies the principle of specialisation to the field of imitation as a whole. But the principle is only applicable at the formal level. Whilst it is true that poets and performers tend to specialise in particular types of imitation, or as we might say in particular genres of poetry, the subject-matter of these imitations is not correspondingly restricted to one area of activity. Both tragedy and comedy in their different ways depict the multiplicity and variety of human life. So, although the tragedian, for example, specialises in one form of imitation, his speciality consists in the depiction of various types of human behaviour. The argument that the same poet cannot compose in more than one genre is also used at *Ion* 534c3–4, though for different purposes, and without reference to tragedy and comedy. At *Symp.* 223d3 S. states that the same man ought to be able to write both tragedy and comedy, but his views there are hypothetical. See further on *Ion* 531e10. In fact we know of no Greek playwright who wrote both tragedy and comedy: as Dryden remarked: 'tragedies and comedies were not writ then as they are now, promiscuously by the same person; but he who found his genius bending to the one never attempted the other way ... the sock and buskin were not worn by the same poet' (*An essay of dramatic poesy*, 1688).　**a8 ῥαψωιδοί ... ὑποκριταί** sc. οἱ αὐτοὶ δύνανται εἶναι. At *Ion* 536a1 Ion is described as ῥαψωιδὸς καὶ ὑποκριτής. Elsewhere rhapsodes and actors are closely related, though different from each other. See further on *Ion* 532d6–7.　**a10–b1 Ἀλλ' οὐδέ ... οἱ αὐτοί:** the fact that separate contests were held for tragic and comic actors both at the City Dionysia and at the Lenaea confirms Plato's observation that actors specialised in one or the other genre. At the Dionysia such contests were introduced for tragic actors in 449, and for comic actors between 329 and 312; at the Lenaea between 440 and 430 for tragic actors, and about 442 for comic actors. See further R. C. Flickinger, *The Greek theater and its drama* (4th edn Chicago 1936) 202–3; Pickard-Cambridge (1988) 93–4, 124–5.

b3–6 Καὶ ἔτι γε τούτων ... ἀφομοιώματα lit. 'human nature seems to me to be cut up into pieces even smaller than these (i.e. it is even more specialised than these examples suggest) so that it is incapable of imitating many things well, or of doing well those things themselves of which the imitations are likenesses'. In other words, people are incapable of playing many different roles, whether in life or in art.　**b8–c2 τοὺς φύλακας ... τοῦτο φέρει:** cf. 374a4–e1. The guardians will be δημιουργοὶ ἐλευθερίας τῆς πόλεως because it will be their job to protect the city against enemies. But at a deeper level they will be responsible for the city's ἐλευθερία by ensuring that the lower levels of society are kept in check by the higher. The true meaning of freedom for both the individual and the state lies in freedom from the tyranny of bodily desires, a constant theme of the *Republic* from Cephalus' story about S. at 329b8–d6, to the discussion of tyranny at 577c5–e3, to the final moment of choice in the myth of Er at 617e1–5.

c4 μιμεῖσθαι ... ἐκ παίδων: they must imitate what is appropriate to them (i.e. to 'craftsmen of freedom') from childhood onwards. Cf. the importance of the early education of children at 377a4–c4.　**c7–d1 ἵνα μὴ ... ἀπολαύσωσιν** 'lest as a result of the imitation they are infected with the reality'. Cf. *Phdr.* 255d5 where ἀπολαύω is used of catching an eye disease. P.'s concern with the effects of imitation on character is at the heart of his critique of mimetic literature, for the reasons given in the following sentence. Cf. 605c6–606d7.

d1–3 ἢ οὐκ ᾔσθησαι ... τὴν διάνοιαν: 'Haven't you noticed that imitations, if continued from childhood onwards, become established into habits of body, voice and mind, which are second nature?' Any form of imitation, whether it involves imitating another person in life, or exposure to mimetic literature i.e. literature in which the poet or performer speaks in the person of his characters, leaves its mark on the imitator. Μιμήσεις κατὰ τὴν διάνοιαν are exemplified in the following sentence, κατὰ σῶμα at 396a8–b1 and κατὰ φωνάς at 396b5–7. Literature has this effect not only on the performer, but also on the listener, as P. makes clear at 605c10–d5. Cf. *Ion* 535d8–e3 for the effect which the rhapsode's recital produces on his audience.   **d5–6 ὧν φαμὲν ... αὐτούς:** instead of writing ὧν φαμὲν κήδεσθαι καὶ οὓς φαμὲν δεῖν ἄνδρας etc. P. shortens the construction and substitutes αὐτούς for οὕς. For the tendency to avoid the repetition of the relative in a different case in parallel clauses see Goodwin (1894) 222 and cf. e.g. *Rep.* 505d11, *Gorg.* 452d3–4. **d6–e2 γυναῖκα μιμεῖσθαι ... ὠδίνουσαν:** μιμεῖσθαι here refers not just to acting, but also to participation in epic and dramatic performances as listeners. Cf. 605c10 and *Ion* 535e2–3. The words πρὸς θεοὺς ἐρίζουσαν perhaps refer back to the complaints of Aeschylus' Niobe, quoted at 380a3–4. But the particular examples of unsuitable female behaviour in this passage point to the tragedies of Euripides. Cf. Ar. *Frogs* 1043–4 (with Stanford (1958) *ad loc.*) where Aeschylus contrasts himself with Euripides: ἀλλ' οὐ μὰ Δί' οὐ Φαίδρας ἐποίουν πόρνας οὐδὲ Σθενεβοίας, | οὐδ' οἶδ' οὐδεὶς ἥντιν' ἐρῶσαν πώποτ' ἐποίησα γυναῖκα. In his lost play *Auge*, Euripides apparently portrayed the heroine giving birth in a temple. See *Frogs* 1080 with Dover (1993) *ad loc.* However, the general description of women in 'misfortunes, griefs and lamentations' at e1 could apply equally to women in Homer as in tragedy, and it would be a mistake to assume that the discussion here is exclusively confined to drama. See further Stan-

ford (1973) 189–90.   **e2–3 πολλοῦ καὶ δεήσομεν** sc. ἐπιτρέπειν
μιμεῖσθαι: 'far less shall we allow them to imitate'.

396a3 οὐδὲ μαινομένοις ... **αὐτούς** 'nor must they form the habit of
likening themselves to madmen'.   **a4–6 γνωστέον ... οὐδὲ μιμητέον:** the guardians must recognise mad and bad men and women,
but they must not have direct experience of this type of behaviour
by indulging in it themselves or by imitating it. Cf. 409a–e where P.
says that a good judge will be an old man who has acquired a knowledge of wickedness, not through his own personal experience, but
by discerning it in other people.   **a8–b1 χαλκεύοντας ... κελεύοντας τούτοις:** these are examples of banausic activities which
involve bodily gestures (μιμήσεις ... κατὰ σῶμα at 395d1–3 above)
unsuitable for potential guardians.

b3–4 Καὶ πῶς ... ἐξέσται; 'how can they, since they won't be
allowed even to think of these things?' Cf. 395b8–c3.   **b5–7 ἵππους ... μιμήσονται:** Adam suggests that P. is referring to the
sounds produced by musical effects and stage machinery, such as
the βροντεῖον, and that he is thinking primarily of dramatic and
dithyrambic performances. In the *Laws* 669c–670a he laments the
modern habit of reproducing the noises of wild animals on musical
instruments, a kind of showmanship (θαυματουργία 670a2) which he
deplores. And the contemporary dithyramb evidently contained musical depictions of this type. See on 397a4–7. But is P. thinking primarily of the *musical* reproduction of the various sounds he lists, as is
generally assumed? Stanford (1973) objects that the discussion of
music does not begin until 398c, and suggests that P. is thinking primarily of vocal rather than instrumental μίμησις here. What P. has
in mind is the onomatopoeic use of language, particularly in
Homer, as was recognised by some of the ancient critics. Dio
Chrysostom, for example, praises Homer's diction, saying that he
'held himself back from no sound, but, in short, imitated the voices
(μιμούμενος φωνάς) of rivers and forests, of winds and fire and sea,
and also of bronze and stone, and of all animals and instruments'.
Or. 12.68. Cf. 71 and *Or.* 53.5; Dion. Hal. *De comp.* 15–16. For
detailed discussion of these passages see Stanford's article. That
Homer is still at the centre of the argument is strongly suggested by

the words ἵππους χρεμετίζοντας, which recall the description of Hector's horses at *Il.* 12.51, the only occurrence of χρεμετίζω in Greek poetry before P. If this general interpretation is correct then what we have here are examples of the imitations κατὰ φωνάς referred to at 395d3. See also on 397a4–7.   **b8–9 Ἀλλ' ἀπείρηται ... ἀφομοιοῦσθαι** 'But they have been prohibited from being mad or from making themselves like madmen.' Cf. 396a3–4. The implication is that imitating the sounds just described is the mark of a madman.   **b10 Εἰ ἄρα ... λέγεις:** S. tactfully suggests that Adeimantus is really contributing to the discussion, though we might detect a certain irony in this suggestion.   **b10–c3 ἔστιν τι εἶδος ... τραφείς:** the preceding discussion from 392c6 onwards leads us to expect that the form of speech which the good man will employ will be ἁπλῆ διήγησις without μίμησις, whereas the bad man will choose the opposite of this, i.e. imitation with no narrative interludes. But P. is not as concerned with the formal distinction made at 392d5–6 as with its ethical implications.

c2–3 οὗ ἂν ἔχοιτο ... τραφείς 'which a man of the opposite nature and education would always use for his narratives'.   **c5–d1 Ὁ μέν ... μέτριος ἀνήρ ... πράττοντα:** the good man will willingly imitate a good man acting sensibly, as if he were himself that man (ὡς αὐτὸς ὢν ἐκεῖνος), because imitating such a character will produce the requisite qualities in himself. Cf. 395c3–5. The emphasis here is on the ethical effects of imitation.

d1–3 ἐλάττω δὲ καὶ ἧττον 'in fewer respects and to a lesser degree' (Adam). Presumably the good man when he is ill, in love or drunk acts differently from a bad man, and to that extent is worth imitating.   **d3–e2 ὅταν δὲ γίγνηται ... παιδιᾶς χάριν:** the infinitives ἐθελήσειν and αἰσχυνεῖσθαι depend on δοκεῖ at c5 above. What is said here is hard to reconcile with the statement at 395c1–7 that the guardians, if they imitate at all, should only imitate men who are brave, self-controlled, righteous and free. The application of this principle turns out to be less rigid than we were led to expect, and the decent man will now be allowed to imitate someone worse than himself when he is doing something good, provided that the imitation is not serious. When he recites the words of a good man he will want to *be* that man (ἐθελήσειν ὡς αὐτὸς ὢν ἐκεῖνος ἀπαγγέλλειν, 396c7), but in the case of a worse man οὐκ ἐθελήσειν σπουδῆι ἀπεικάζειν ἑαυτὸν τῶι χείρονι. The crucial word here is σπουδῆι (cf. 397a3 and παιδιᾶς χάριν at e2). Earlier on, at 388d2, S. says that if the young were to listen seriously (σπουδῆι ἀκούοιεν) to Homer's tales of the gods lamenting and not laugh at them, they would find it hard to resist the temptation to behave in this way themselves. Similarly the guardian here must not seriously identify himself with the bad characters whose words he recites; he will be ashamed to do so (contrast his attitude to the imitation of the good man at 396c7–8: οὐκ αἰσχυνεῖσθαι ἐπὶ τῆι τοιαύτηι μιμήσει), feeling disgust at modelling himself (αὐτὸν ἐκμάττειν) on their patterns of behaviour. But he may recite their words for fun (παιδιᾶς χάριν). See further Ferrari (1989) 118–19. The contrast between doing things seriously and doing them for fun anticipates the condemnation of μίμησις itself as παιδιάν τινα καὶ οὐ σπουδήν at 602b8.

e4–7 Οὐκοῦν διηγήσει ... τῆς μιμήσεως: the relative οἷαι is attracted into the case of its antecedent, διηγήσει. τῆς ἄλλης διηγήσεως 'the other form of narration', i.e. the ἁπλῆ διήγησις illustrated at 393c11–394b1. The guardian will favour the form of narration used by Homer which includes both imitation and pure narrative, but with only a small element of imitation. Though he will be allowed to imitate certain types of character on the lines suggested above, the guardian should in any case imitate as little as possible, because the process of imitation itself encourages a multiplicity and variety which is inappropriate to his function. Cf. 394e1–6 and see Else (1986) 32. For Homer as a suitable stylistic model for the decent man cf. *Laws* 658d where it is said that the old men would prefer to listen to a recital of Homer or Hesiod, whereas educated women, young men and almost the entire population would choose tragedy. **e9–10 τοῦ τοιούτου ῥήτορος** suggests that P. is thinking not just of poetic recitals, but also of speech making. Cf. 397c8.

397a1 ὁ μὴ τοιοῦτος sc. ὤν, standing for the protasis of a conditional sentence. Hence the negative μή. **a1–2 ὅσωι ἂν ...** **διηγήσεται** 'the worse he is, the more he will narrate everything'. τοσούτωι should be supplied with μᾶλλον. Many editors adopt Schneider's emendation, μιμήσεται for the διηγήσεται of the main MSS. But there is no compelling reason to do so, since P. uses the term διήγησις of narration as a whole, as well as of a particular form of narration which does not use direct speech. See on 392d2–3, and for a cogent defence of the MS reading see Slings (1990) 352. In this passage S.'s point is that the worse the man, the less discriminating will he be about the subjects which he treats. He will therefore imitate everything (ὥστε πάντα ἐπιχειρήσει μιμεῖσθαι), treating imitation 'as an activity good in itself rather than dependent for its value on the goodness of what is imitated' (Ferrari (1989) 117). **a3–4 σπουδῆι τε καὶ ἐναντίον πολλῶν** 'seriously and in front of a lot of people'. The inferior man will identify himself whole-heartedly with everything he imitates in contrast with the good man described above at 396d4. And he will do this before large audiences. Presumably S. is thinking of epic recitals and dramatic performances. **a4–7 βροντάς ... φθόγγους:** S. extends the scope of vocal μίμησις referred to at 396b5–7 to include imitating the sounds of axles and pulleys, trumpets, oboes, pipes and all kinds of instruments, as well as the mimicry of animals and birds. Direct mimicry of this type is known to have been a feature of the contemporary dithyramb. The *Nauplios* of Timotheus, for example, which depicted a storm at sea, was ridiculed by the pipe-player Dorion, who said that he had seen a bigger storm in a boiling saucepan (Athen. 338a). See further Pickard-Cambridge (1962) 51; Zimmermann (1992) 127–8. And many examples of the imitation of animal sounds can be found in comedy. See e.g. Ar. *Plut.* 290–5 where Carion, imitating (μιμούμενος) the Cyclops, urges the chorus to follow him, crying and bleating like sheep and goats (ἐπαναβοῶντες | βληχώμενοί τε προβατίων | αἰγῶν τε κιναβρώντων μέλη). Cf. Ar. *Birds.* 227–62 for the imitation of bird sounds with Zimmermann (1992) 123–4. Having begun with Homer at 396b5–7, S. broadens the discussion of μιμήσεις κατὰ φωνάς with examples alluding to contemporary literature. See further Stanford (1973) 189.

b1–2 καὶ ἔσται ... διηγήσεως ἔχουσα 'his expression will be entirely through imitation, in voice and in gesture, or with a small narrative element'. Cf. 393c5–6 and 395d1–3. **b4 Ταῦτα ... τῆς λέξεως:** the two types of λέξις relate both to stylistic expression and to ethical content. One consists mainly of διήγησις with a small element of μίμησις, and the μίμησις will be primarily of the words and

deeds of the good man (396c5–e8). The other consists mainly of μίμησις of all kinds of things, with a small element of διήγησις (397a–b2). See further on 397c8–10. **b6–c1 Οὐκοῦν αὐτοῖν ...**
παραπλησίωι τινί; 'And so one of them involves small variations, and if the appropriate musical mode and rhythm is added to the expression, the correct speaker will speak in more or less the same mode (πρὸς τὴν αὐτήν sc. ἁρμονίαν) and in one mode – for the variations are small – and similarly in more or less the same rhythm.' For ὀλίγου meaning 'almost', 'more or less', see e.g. *Ap.* 17a3, 22b7, *Prot.* 361b8. On ἁρμονία see Barker (1984) 163–5. The assumption is that different forms of musical expression are needed for the representation of different characters. But since the good man will confine his imitations for the most part to good men performing good actions (cf. 396c5–d1), his style will be correspondingly uniform.

c5–6 διὰ τὸ παντοδαπὰς μορφὰς τῶν μεταβολῶν ἔχειν 'because of the manifold forms of its variations'. Since the λέξις of the inferior man involves imitation of all manner of things (397a–b), he will need all kinds of ἁρμονίαι (as opposed to the good man's single ἁρμονία at b7–9) and rhythms in order to express himself appropriately (οἰκείως). For παντοδαπός see 398a1. **c8–10 Ἆρ' οὖν πάντες ...**
συγκεραννύντες 'So all poets and speakers hit upon one or other of these patterns of expression, or on one that results from a combination of the two.' οἵ τι λέγοντες suggests P. is thinking of public speakers as well as of poets. Cf. 396e9–10. The triad here is not quite the same as that established at 392d5–6, where a distinction was made between ἁπλῆ διήγησις, μίμησις and a style that resulted from a mixture of both. Now all three forms of expression consist of both narrative and imitation, though the proportions in each case will be different. Cf. 397b4.

d1–3 πότερον εἰς τὴν πόλιν ... τὸν κεκραμένον; 'shall we admit all these patterns of expression into the city, or one or other of the unmixed, or the mixed?' Again this is not quite the same question as was posed at 394d5–6, and we were warned at that stage by S.'s reply (d7–9) that the issue was not as simple as it appeared to be. On formal grounds all three patterns of expression which have just been outlined are mixed. The discussion at this stage is certainly confusing, if not confused (see Annas (1982) 27 n. 37), but it is not incomprehensible. What emerges is that P. is not interested in purely stylistic matters, but in the ethical implications of literature. See on 393c1–3; Else (1986) 34–7; Ferrari (1989) 114–19.   **d4 Ἐὰν ἡ ἐμή** sc. γνώμη ... νικᾶι 'if my vote prevails'. Adeimantus no doubt thinks that some firm conclusion is in sight.   **d4–5 τὸν τοῦ ἐπιεικοῦς μιμητὴν ἄκρατον** 'the unmixed imitator of the good man' must refer to the kind of imitation outlined at 396c5–e8, whose stylistic features are further defined at 397b6–c1. In terms of the syntactical distinction made at 392d5–6, Adeimantus' choice of λέξις is not unmixed, since it contains both imitative and non-imitative discourse. But in terms of ethical content it will be, because it will consist of the imitation of the words and actions of a good man, whose expression will be correspondingly uniform and unvaried.   **d6–8 ἡδύς γε ... ὄχλωι:** οὗ is for ἐκείνου ὄν. The relative is attracted into the case of an antecedent which is omitted. The mixed form of expression refers to that which imitates many kinds of things, using a variety of ἁρμονίαι and rhythms (397a1–b2, c3–6). P. does not deny the pleasure afforded by the kind of λέξις of which he disapproves, pointing out that it will give the greatest pleasure to those who are least able to judge its worth. Cf. *Gorg.* 459a4 for the view that a popular audience means an ignorant one. At *Laws* 658d3–4 tragedy is said to give the greatest pleasure to women, young men and σχεδὸν ἴσως τὸ πλῆθος πάντων, but we should not therefore assume that the present discussion is confined to tragedy. The phrase παισὶ δὲ καὶ παιδαγωγοῖς καὶ τῶι πλείστωι ὄχλωι occurs at *Laws* 700c6–7, where P. laments the fact that these people are no longer controlled in the way that they used to be. Hence the degeneracy of modern performances, in which the various musical forms are all mixed up (700d6–8), and the only criterion of judgement is the pleasure of ignorant spectators (700e–701a). Cf. *Gorg.* 501d1–502d8 with Dodds (1959) *ad loc.*, and for the dangers of poetry which is pleasurable see *Rep.* 387b2–5, 601b1–4, 606b4, 607a5–8.

e1–2 οὐκ ἔστιν ... ἓν πράττει 'no man in our city plays two parts or many parts, since each person does one job'.   **e4–8 Οὐκοῦν διὰ ταῦτα ... πάντας οὕτω:** the implied contrast is with democratic Athens, where such multiple roles were the norm. Cf. *Prot.* 319d where S. points out that in matters of government anyone may give advice, whether he be a builder, a blacksmith or a cobbler, a merchant or a shipowner. χρηματιστὴν πρὸς τῆι πολεμικῆι: for the juxtaposition of money-making with warfare cf. 373d–e, where it is taken for granted that the motive for war is greed, and *Phaed.* 66c7–8 διὰ γὰρ τὴν τῶν χρημάτων κτῆσιν πάντες οἱ πόλεμοι γίγνονται.

398a1–2 Ἄνδρα δή ... χρήματα: ἄνδρα is governed by προσκυνοῖμεν at a4 below. σοφίας suggests the skill traditionally accorded to the poet. See on *Ion* 532d5 and d7–8. For παντοδαπόν see 397c5. The man able to imitate everything is the inferior type described at 397a–b and c3–6. **a3–4 αὐτός ... ἐπιδείξασθαι** 'wanting to show off himself and his poems'. ἐπιδείξασθαι implies a superficial display. See on *Ion* 530d4. The verb is intransitive with αὐτός, but transitive with ποιήματα (Adam *ad loc.*). **a4–6 προσκυνοῖμεν ... ἐγγενέσθαι:** προσκυνοῖμεν and ἱερόν suggest worshipping this poet as a sacred being, ironically alluding to the traditional idea of the divine poet. See on *Ion* 534b3–4 κοῦφον γὰρ χρῆμα ποιητής ἐστιν καὶ πτηνὸν καὶ ἱερόν. Gould (1992) 18 draws attention to the 'sneering tone' of προσκυνοῖμεν, the word regularly used of extravagant obeisance in the Oriental manner, on which see further E. Hall, *Inventing the barbarian* (Oxford 1989) 96–7, 206–7. θαυμαστόν also contains more than a hint of irony. At *Laws* 658a–c when the Athenian considers what would happen if they introduced a competition for pleasure, he says it would not be surprising if someone thought he could win by 'putting on a conjuring show' (θαύματα ἐπιδεικνύς); indeed if children were the judges they would choose τὸν τὰ θαύματα ἐπιδεικνύντα (658c11). Cf. Xen. *Symp.* 2.1 where the Syracusan brings in a flute girl and a dancing girl of the sort skilled in performing wonderful tricks (τῶν τὰ θαύματα δυναμένων ποιεῖν); he earns money from exhibiting them as a spectacle (ἐπιδεικνὺς ὡς ἐν θαύματι). These passages with their emphasis on tricks and displays suggest that P.'s use of the word θαυμαστόν here should not be taken at its face value. And we know already that pleasure is not an appropriate criterion by which to judge the value of poetry. See 397d6–8 and 387b2–5. The man described here cannot be admitted into the ideal state because he is the antithesis of the single-minded type on which the success of the state depends. Cf. 397d10–e2 and 394e1–6. **a6–8 ἀποπέμποιμέν ... στέψαντες:** continuing the irony, S. says that they would send the poet away, but anoint him and garland him with wool as if he were divine. Proclus commenting on this passage (*In remp.* 42 ed. Kroll) refers to the ancient custom of anointing and garlanding the images of the gods. cf. Paus. 10.24.6. **a8–b4 αὐτοὶ δ' ἂν ... παιδεύειν:** the more austere and less pleasing poet who would imitate the speech of a good man is the one described at 396c5–e10 and 397b6–c1. The mention of the story-teller as well (μυθολόγωι) takes us back to the beginning of the discussion at 377a, as does the word ὠφελίας, which reminds us that the point at issue is the question of how poetry and story telling can be useful in the moral education of the guardians. P. does not name specific poets in this final section, but we cannot help but think of Homer. On the purely formal level the decent man will use Homer as a stylistic model at 396e4–8, and Homeric epic could perhaps be seen as an example of the relatively uniform style described at 397b6–c1. But much of the content of Homer's poetry has been criticised as being unsuitable for the ears of young guardians. See 377d4, 378d5, 379c9, 383a7, 387b1, 388a5, 389a3, 391a3. Furthermore, the choice of Homer to illustrate what is meant by μίμησις at 392e2–394b1 is no accident: P. sees Homer as the originator of the dramatic method whereby the poet impersonates the characters whose words he is speaking, in a way that makes poetry so dangerous for all who come into contact with it. Cf. 607a2–3 and see further Else (1986) 24–37. τύποις at b3 recalls 379a2, στρατιώτας at b4 reminds us that the purpose of this programme is to educate the guardians of the state (see above p. 133), and παιδεύειν takes us back to the original question at 376e2: τίς οὖν ἡ παιδεία; The relative οἷς at b3 is attracted into the case of its antecedent.

b6–8 Νῦν δή ... εἴρηται summarises the subject of the preceding discussion. τῆς μουσικῆς is partitive genitive: 'the branch of music which is concerned with stories'. Cf. 376e9.

Republic 595–608b10

Book 10 opens with a return to the subject of poetry, last discussed in book 3. In the intervening section of the dialogue we have been introduced to the central doctrines of P.'s metaphysics and psychology: the theory of Forms (596a5–6), and the tripartite theory of the soul (595a7–b1). Both of these theories are now invoked in order to explain further the reasons for P.'s hostility to poetry, an issue which is here treated in a far more trenchant manner than in the earlier books. There P. was concerned to reform existing poetry through censorship, and was primarily interested in the effects of poetry on the young, whereas now his aim is to remove poetry from Greek culture altogether (607a3–5). A striking feature of P.'s description of the ideal state after book 3 is the absence from it of any mention of poetry in a public context, an absence which is all the more remarkable in view of the central role of poetry in Greek life (Introduction p. 15). P.'s ideal state is a *polis* without poetry, in marked contrast to his Cretan city in the *Laws*. Nehamas (1982) points out that P.'s return to the subject of poetry in book 10 is not as arbitrary as has often been supposed: 'the discussion of poetry in books 2 and 3 lays the foundations for the omission of any reference to poetry as a component in the city's life in the bulk of the *Republic*, and book 10 explains why that omission has been made' (53).

P.'s need to justify the exclusion of poetry from his ideal state in the final book of the *Republic* is an indication of the importance he attaches to this theme, as emphasised by e.g. Havelock (1963) 3–4; Nehamas (1982) 51–4; Lear (1992) 208–14. Book 10 has often been regarded as little more than an afterthought to the work as a whole, in which various loose ends are gathered together (see e.g. Nettleship (1901) 340; Crombie (1962) 1 143; Annas (1981) 335). And the two themes which dominate this final book, the nature of poetry (595a–608b) and the immortality of the human soul (608c–621d), have often been thought to have no intrinsic connexion with each other. But, on the contrary, there is a close link between the discussion of poetry and the myth of Er which follows it, and together they provide a fitting conclusion to a work whose fundamental theme is the salvation of the human soul. The myth of Er is an example of the kind of myth that should be told in order for people to understand the truth about the crucial issue which lies at the heart of the *Republic*: the way in which life should be lived. But there is no place for truth in a society nurtured on the false myths of the poets, and dominated by the criterion of pleasure. The particular danger of poetry, as P. sees it, lies not only in its falsehood, but rather in its irresistible power to corrupt (595b5, 605c10–606d7). By its very nature it appeals to the lowest part of the human soul, endangering the psychological health not only of the individual, but also of the community of which he is a part (605b7–8, 607e6–608a1). Society and its members can only be reformed by removing the source of corruption: hence the false myths of the poets must be replaced by the 'noble lies' of philosophy.

595a–595c6

S. says that they were right to have excluded mimetic poetry from the ideal state, especially now that the soul has been divided into parts, since poetry corrupts the minds of its listeners.

595a1 περὶ αὐτῆς: i.e. the city.   **a2 παντὸς ... μᾶλλον** 'more than anything' i.e. beyond all doubt.   **ᾠκίζομεν:** the imperfect suggests the process of trying to found the city.   **a3 οὐχ ἥκιστα ... λέγω** 'I say this thinking particularly about poetry'.   **a4 Τὸ ποῖον** sc. ἐνθυμηθείς, which also governs the infinitive in the next line.   **a5 Τὸ μηδαμῆι ... μιμητική:** lit. 'thinking of our in no way admitting as much of it as is mimetic'. αὐτῆς ὅση is for ὅσον αὐτῆς. This statement appears to conflict with the earlier discussion in book 3 (παραδέχεσθαι here picks up παραδεξόμεθα at 397d2), where mimetic poetry was not in fact completely banned from the ideal state, and it may also conflict with 607a3–4 (see below). At 395c3–5 it was suggested that the guardians may imitate appropriate models, and at 396c5–d1 we were told that the sensible man will willingly imitate a good man acting reasonably, since imitating such a character will produce the requisite qualities in himself. See also on 396e4–7, and cf. 398a8–b4. There is therefore a discrepancy between the total prohibition on mimetic poetry here and the earlier willingness to allow future guardians to perform mimetic poetry to a limited extent. Some have tried to eradicate this conflict by claiming that imitative poetry is of two kinds, one good, the other bad, and that it is only the latter which is to be banished, both here and at 398a–b. For this view see especially Tate (1928) and (1932); Belfiore (1984). But the discussion at 394d–398b does not provide a sufficient basis on which to differentiate between types of imitative poetry: the fact that

S. allows the young guardians to recite or listen to narratives which include imitations of good men, but forbids them to indulge in other kinds of imitation merely implies that the activity of μίμησις can have different objects, a point cogently argued by Nehamas (1982) 48–50. And there is nothing to indicate that the phrase ὅση μιμητική here should be restricted to poetry which imitates the wrong kind of objects. Furthermore, as Else (1986) 45 observes, if the phrase is meant as a limitation it does not amount to much, since all existing poetry seems to be included in the attack that follows. Homer and the tragedians are the prime targets, but comedy also features (606c2–9), and at 600e4–6 it is explicitly stated that *all* poets from Homer onwards are 'imitators of images'. It is only at 607a3–4 that the possibility of admitting any poetry at all into the city is considered, and it is not at all clear in what sense, if any, that poetry will be imitative. The matter is further complicated by the fact that, as will emerge, μίμησις now means something different from what it meant in book 3. See on 597e3–4. **a5–7 παντὸς γὰρ ... φαίνεται:** lit. 'beyond a doubt it is even more clearly evident, as it seems to me, that it [i.e. mimetic poetry] should not be admitted'. παραδεκτέα is the predicate, ἐναργέστερον a comparative adverb. **a7–b1 ἐπειδὴ χωρὶς ... εἴδη:** in book 4, 435c–441c S. distinguished between three parts or elements in the soul: τὸ λογιστικόν (the reasoning part), τὸ θυμοειδές (the spirited part) and τὸ ἐπιθυμητικόν (the desiring part). This psychology underpins the analysis of the decline of cities and the degeneration of the human soul in books 8 and 9, and is given vivid expression towards the end of book 9 in the image of the soul as a Chimaera-like hybrid, part human, part lion and part many-headed beast, but with the outward appearance of a human being (588b–589b). For discussion of this tripartite theory see I. M. Crombie, *An examination of Plato's doctrines* (London 1962) 1 341–59; Annas (1981) 123–46. Here it is signalled that the division of the soul into parts has a direct bearing on the banishment of mimetic poetry, though the connexion between the two is by no means clear, as the puzzlement of the interlocutor indicates. The argument will be further developed at 602cff.

b3 Ὡς ... εἰρῆσθαι 'to say it just to you', i.e. 'between ourselves'. For ὡς εἰρῆσθαι cf. 414a6–7, *Gorg.* 462b8–9. ὑμᾶς refers to the group of people gathered together at Polemarchus' house (327a–328c) in which the present conversation between S. and Glaucon is taking place. S.'s words draw attention, albeit in a somewhat playful way, to the shocking nature of what he is about to say. **b5–6 λώβη ... διανοίας:** πάντα τὰ τοιαῦτα is the subject, λώβη the predicate. λώβη, as Else (1972) 22 observes, is a strong word, implying radical damage. Cf. λωβᾶσθαι at 605c7; *Cri.* 47d4, e7; *Men.* 91c3–4, 92a3; *Laws* 890b1. The way in which poetry corrupts the minds of its audience will be further discussed at 605c10–606d7. For διάνοια of the mind as a whole cf. 603b10. The emphasis on listeners here suggests that this argument applies specifically to poetry, which is by implication differentiated from painting, the paradigm of μίμησις in book 10. The reason for the exclusion of poetry is not simply that it is mimetic, for in that case painting too should be banished, but rather that it corrupts the soul in a way that painting apparently does not. See further Nehamas (1982) 48 and 70 n. 2. **b6–7 ὅσοι μὴ ... ὄντα** 'all those who do not have knowledge of what these things actually are as an antidote'. The image implies that poetry is a poison requiring the 'medicine' of truth as an antidote (cf. 389b2–5, 382c8), but also hints at its magical powers. Cf. 598d3, 601b1, 602d2, 607c7, 608a3–5. **b9 Ῥητέον:** cf. 595c3. **b9–10 καίτοι φιλία ... λέγειν:** for the deference shown to Homer cf. 383a7, 387b1–2, 391a3–5, and see further on 607e7.

c1 καλῶν is ironical in tone, suggesting the specious appeal of poetry, which is repeatedly emphasised in this section. See e.g. 598d–e, 602a–b, and for the implications of καλός in this context see further on *Ion* 533e7. **c1–2 πρῶτος ... ἡγεμών:** the affinity between Homer and the tragic poets, which had already been implied in book 3, is now made explicit in this description of Homer as their master and leader. Cf. 598d8, 605c11, 607a2–3, *Theaet.* 152e4–5 (οἱ ἄκροι τῆς ποιήσεως ἑκατέρας, κωμωιδίας μὲν Ἐπίχαρμος, τραγ- ωιδίας δὲ Ὅμηρος) and 153a2. This is not just a reference to the fact that tragic plots tend to be taken from epic, but rather that Plato sees Homer as the originator of the dramatic method. See further on 398a8–b4. Arist. *Po.* 1448b35 agrees that Homer's imitations are essentially dramatic (Ὅμηρος ... μιμήσεις δραματικὰς ἐποίησεν), and discusses the similarities between epic and tragedy at 1449b9–

20. According to Athenaeus, *Deipn.* 8.347e Aeschylus himself is said to have remarked that his tragedies were 'slices from the great banquets of Homer' (τεμάχη τῶν Ὁμήρου μεγάλων δείπνων), a phrase whose meaning is interestingly discussed by J. Gould, 'Homeric epic and the tragic moment', in T. Winnifrith, P. Murray and K. Gransden (edd.), *Aspects of the epic* (London 1983) 32–45. Goldhill (1991) 171–4 draws attention to the social and cultural implications of the link between Homer and the tragic poets in that both were performed at civic festivals. The Panathenaea and the City Dionysia, the two public institutions for the performance of poetry in democratic Athens, provided the context in which these texts were communicated to the *polis* as a whole, thus endowing them with considerable normative force and ensuring the public role of the poet's voice within the city.   **c2–3 ἀλλ' οὐ γὰρ ... ἀνήρ:** on the paramount importance of truth cf. 607c7–8 and *Phaed.* 91c where S. urges his companions to think not of himself, but of the truth (σμικρὸν φροντίσαντες Σωκράτους, τῆς δὲ ἀληθείας πολὺ μᾶλλον). Aristotle seems to echo these words as a prelude to his criticism of P.'s theory of forms at *Eth. Nic.* 1.6, 1096a14–17: δόξειε δ' ἂν ἴσως βέλτιον εἶναι καὶ δεῖν ἐπὶ σωτηρίαι γε τῆς ἀληθείας καὶ τὰ οἰκεῖα ἀναιρεῖν, ἄλλως τε καὶ φιλοσόφους ὄντας. ἀμφοῖν γὰρ ὄντοιν φίλοιν ὅσιον προτιμᾶν τὴν ἀλήθειαν. Thereafter the thought became something of a *topos*. See Ferguson *ad loc.* for references to later literature. For the view that S.'s attitude here is 'authentically Socratic' see Halliwell *ad loc.*   **c3 ὃ λέγω** refers back to Ῥητέον at b9 above, the necessity of what must be said being emphasised by the repetition of ῥητέον at the beginning and end of this passage. For the use of the verbal adjective see on 377a1.   **c5–6 ἀποκρίνου.** Ἔρωτα makes explicit S.'s method of eliciting the truth by a process of question and answer, signalling that what follows will be a more strictly philosophical exchange conducted between S. and his interlocutor (contrast the singular here with the plural at 595b3).

595c7–597e9

S. now seeks a general definition of μίμησις, *invoking the theory of Forms. Taking the example of a couch, he argues that there are three categories of couch, the Form of Couch, a particular couch, and an image of a couch. Corresponding to these three couches are three makers: God, who makes the Form of Couch, the craftsman, who makes a particular couch, and the painter, who produces an image of what the craftsman makes. The painter is thus an imitator whose product is at third remove from reality. Similarly, the tragic poet, like all other imitators, is 'third from the truth'.*

c7 Μίμησιν ... ποτ' ἐστίν: prolepsis, cf. *Ion* 531c6–7n. The term μίμησις was first introduced at 392d5 where it was used primarily to denote a particular form of narrative style, but with the implication that wider issues were at stake. See on 393c5–6, 394d7–9, 395d1–3 and in general Else (1986) 24–46. S.'s request for a general definition (ὅλως) and his admission (in the usual ironic manner, cf. *Ion* 532d8–9) that he does not altogether understand what μίμησις means, suggest that the earlier discussion did not get very far in determining its nature.   **c9 Ἦ που ... συννοήσω:** που here is ironical in tone, the point being that if S. does not fully understand, *I* don't have much prospect.   **c10–596a1 Οὐδέν γε ... εἶδον** 'It wouldn't be surprising if you did, since people with duller eyes often see before those whose sight is sharper.' The gnomic aorist, used in generalised reflections (Goodwin (1929) 53–4, cf. 606c8), and τοι, indicating the application of a general truth to a particular situation (Denniston (1954) 542–3), give this sentence a proverbial ring. Halliwell *ad loc.* notes that the analogy between physical sight and intellectual perception plays a significant part in the dialogue. See e.g. 427d2, 432c7–8, 484c–d, 507b–509c (the simile which compares the Form of the Good to the sun), and particularly 514a–520d (the allegory of the cave).

596a4 ὅρα continues the sight motif.   **a5–6 ἐκ ... μεθόδου:** mention of 'the customary method' (cf. 533b–d for a description of ἡ διαλεκτικὴ μέθοδος) brings in the theory of Forms, which here, as elsewhere is introduced as being familiar to, and accepted by, S.'s interlocutors (cf 476a4, 505a2–3, 507a8–9). No systematic account of the theory is given, and there is no attempt to convince the sceptical reader that the Forms do in fact exist. For a helpful discussion of the Forms in this dialogue see Annas (1981) 195–41 with bibliography there given.   **a6–7 εἶδος γάρ πού ... ἐπιφέρομεν** 'for, as you know, we are in the habit of assuming a Form – one in each case – in relation to each group of particulars to which we apply the same name'. The distinction between Forms and particulars had been made at 476a–d and 507b–c, but this passage, which appears to suggest that there is a Form for *every* general term which can be applied to a set of particulars, is unique in Plato, and its interpretation has therefore been disputed. Although the natural way to take the Greek is as given above, an alternative and not impossible translation might be: 'we are in the habit of assuming a Form ... in relation to each group of particulars to which we apply the same name [as that which the Form has]'. Cf. *Phaed.* 78e2, 102b2, and for further discussion see J. A. Smith, 'General relative clauses in Greek', *C.R.* 31 (1917) 69–71; Nehamas (1982) 72f, and see on b3–4 below.   **a10**

Θῶμεν ... τῶν πολλῶν 'So now let's take any set of particulars you like.' But see the alternative translation proposed by Nehamas (1982) 73: 'let's now set whatever you want as among the manys (that is, among those groups to which Forms correspond)'.

b1 κλῖναι καὶ τράπεζαι: the choice of manufactured as opposed to natural objects is vital for S.'s purpose, since it allows him to denigrate the imitative artist by ranking him below the craftsman in the list ζωγράφος, κλινοποιός, θεός at 597b13. If he had chosen e.g. mountains for the painter to paint rather than couches, there would be no middle term in this list, as Adam notes *ad loc.* Else (1972) 36–7 makes the amusing suggestion that the examples of κλίνη and table may have come to P. whilst attending one of the symposia, which were apparently a regular feature of life in the Academy. The κλίνη was, of course, the couch on which the symposiast reclined. 'What more natural', asks Else, 'than that Plato should look round to the assembled company and say ... "Why yes, if you like, let's take these couches and tables" – not beds and tables, then (a pair whose inward connection has always seemed elusive), but banqueting couches and dining tables.' Whatever the origin of these particular examples, Else is surely right to associate them with the symposium. κλῖναι and τράπεζαι were absent from S.'s earliest society and were introduced at 373a2 together with the accoutrements of the symposium and other luxuries (including imitative artists, 373b5) which characterise the diseased community. Griswold (1981) 143 points out that couches and tables symbolise the desires for sex and food (and drink, one might add) which are associated with the lowest part of the soul, and would therefore be particularly suitable objects for the imitative artist to portray. And in fact representations of symposia and associated furniture are common on Greek pots.   **b3–4 Ἀλλὰ ἰδέαι ... τραπέζης:** the notion that there is a Form of Couch and a Form of Table, though consistent with the claim that there is a Form corresponding to each group of things with a common name, comes as something of a shock after the earlier discussion in which Forms are introduced as suitable objects of knowledge for true philosophers (475e–480, 521c–525e), and relate mainly to moral qualities (e.g. Beauty at 476c–d, 479e; the Form of the Good at 505a) and mathematical concepts (e.g. 'Oneness' at 524e6). The question of how far the theory of Forms should be extended is notoriously problematical, as P. himself was well aware. When the question is considered in the *Parmenides* (130b–d) S. is portrayed as being happy to maintain that there are Forms of Likeness and Unlikeness, Justice, Beauty and Goodness, less happy about Forms of Man, Fire and Water, and extremely doubtful about the existence of Forms of Hair, Mud and Dirt, although he does not altogether reject the possibility of their existence. According to Aristotle (*Met.* 1070a18), P. said that there were as many Forms as there are kinds of natural objects (οὐ κακῶς ὁ Πλάτων ἔφη ὅτι εἴδη ἐστὶν ὁπόσα φύσει), a statement which implies that P.'s theory did not extend to artefacts (cf. *Met.* 991b6 and b11). But, quite apart from the Forms of Couch and Table introduced here, *Crat.* 389b–c (on which see b6–8 below) refers to the Form of Shuttle and other kinds of tools. An anecdote in Diogenes Laertius (6.53) relates how Diogenes the Cynic, hearing P. talking about 'tableness' and 'cupness' (τραπεζότητα καὶ κυαθότητα) remarked that he could see a table and a cup, but not 'tableness' and 'cupness'. To which P. replied, 'Of course, since you have eyes with which to see a table and a cup, but no intelligence with which to see "tableness" and "cupness".' The peculiarity of the role of the Forms in *Rep.* 10 (on which see e.g. Annas (1981) 227–32; Nehamas (1982) 54–5, 72–4) was already noted in antiquity. Proclus (*In Tim.* 104f) remarked that the Form of Couch was introduced for the sake of the argument rather than as a serious proposition: οὐ γὰρ κατά τινας ἰδέας ὁ τεχνίτης ποιεῖ ἃ ποιεῖ, εἰ καὶ δοκεῖ τοῦτο λέγειν ὁ ἐν Πολιτείαι Σωκράτης, ἀλλ' ἐκεῖ μὲν τὰ εἰρήμενα παραδείγματος εἴρηται χάριν καὶ οὐ περὶ αὐτῶν τῶν ἰδέων, and it is difficult not to agree with this view. The Form of a manufactured as opposed to a natural object is necessary for Plato's argument for the reasons given at b1 above.   **b6–8 δημιουργὸς ... τραπέζας:** the notion that the craftsman looks at the Form as he makes his table or couch is curiously at odds with the emphasis in book 7 on the difficulties of perceiving the Forms, which can only be grasped by a select few after lengthy and arduous study. Clearly it does not require the same kind of rigorous training in mathematics and dialectic to see the Form of Table as it does to perceive the Form of the Good and the other moral and mathematical Forms discussed earlier. Some help in interpreting this passage is provided by *Crat.* 389a–d where S. explains that the carpenter making a shuttle looks towards the form (τὸ εἶδος) which we would call the absolute or real shuttle (αὐτὸ ὃ ἔστιν κερκίς, b5) in order to embody in the one he is making the elements which are essential for performing its proper function. Similarly it could be said (at any rate by a philosopher) that when the craftsman makes a table, rather than looking at a particular table, he considers what a table is for and then organises his material (pieces of wood, nails etc.) accordingly. Understood in this way the εἶδος of an object is a 'principle of organisation determined by its function' (Crombie (1962) I 144 and see Annas (1981) 230). Similar language is used of the craftsman's procedure at *Gorg.* 503e (on which see Dodds (1959) *ad loc.*), though without any suggestion that the εἶδος there has any existence outside the craftsman's own mind.   **b9–10 οὐ γάρ που ... δημιουργῶν:** these words reinforce the point that the Form of Couch or any other object (καὶ τἆλλα κατὰ ταὐτά) is not invented by the craftsman, but has an independent existence.   **b12 καὶ τόνδε ... δημιουργόν:** although the imitative artist about to be described is called a craftsman, whether χειροτέχνης or δημιουργός, the terms being used interchangeably, (cf. c5, d2, d8–9, e6) S. will argue that he does not deserve this title.

c2 Ὅς πάντα ... χειροτεχνῶν: the implied contrast between the craftsman who makes everything and the one who specialises in a particular craft picks up the theme of one man one job and recalls S.'s words at 397e4–398a2.   **c3 Δεινόν ... ἄνδρα:** for the ironic implications of these words, and particularly θαυμαστόν see on 398a4–6 above. For δεινόν, which implies wonder and awe, cf.

605c8 and see Nussbaum (1986) 52–3.   **c4 Οὔπω ... φήσεις** 'Not
yet, but soon you'll say so all the more.'   **c4–9 ὁ αὐτὸς γὰρ ...
ἐργάζεται: οἷός τε** sc. ἐστι. The repetition of πάντα ... ἅπαντα ...
πάντα ... πάντα ... ἅπαντα, ἐργάζεται ... ἐργάζεται and γῆν ...
οὐρανὸν ... οὐρανῶι ... γῆς (in chiastic order) ironically emphasises
this supposed craftsman's ability to make everything. This list can be
compared with the range of subject-matter attributed to the poet at
Ion 531c. For the phrase τὰ ἐν Ἅιδου cf. *Ion* 531c8. Adam *ad loc.*
draws attention to Polygnotus' painting of τὰ ἐν Ἅιδου at Delphi,
described by Paus. 10.28–31, as an illustration.

d1 Πάνυ ... σοφιστήν: the repetition of θαυμαστόν from c3 above
and the emphasis placed on σοφιστήν continues the irony. The term
σοφιστής, 'expert', was not in origin derogatory, and was used in
particular of people who were traditionally regarded as having privi-
leged access to knowledge, e.g. poets, seers and sages including the
Seven Wise Men (see e.g. *Prot.* 316c5–e5, and for further references
see G. Kerferd, 'The first Greek sophists', *C.R.* 64 (1950) 8–10). From
the latter part of the fifth century onwards it came to denote that
class of itinerant professional teachers, such as Protagoras, Hippias,
Gorgias and Prodicus, who are so vividly portrayed in P.'s dialogues.
See further Guthrie (1962–81) III 27–34; Kerferd (1981(b)). Here the
word suggests a slick superficiality shared by sophist and imitative
artist alike. Cf. *Soph.* 233e–235a with Else (1972) 26–8 for the comparison of the sophist to the painter.   **d2–4 τὸ παράπαν ... τινὶ
δὲ οὐκ ἄν** 'do you think that no such craftsman could possibly exist,
or that there might be a maker of all these things in one sense, but
not in another?' The word ποιητής here hints at a possible answer
to this question.

e4 φαινόμενα ... τῆι ἀληθείαι 'but only in appearance, not, I think,
as they are in reality'.   **e5 εἰς δέον ... λόγωι:** lit. 'you come in
opportunely for the argument', or, more elegantly, 'Bravo, you are
giving my argument the help it needs' (Else (1972) 25).   **e5–6 τῶν
τοιούτων ... ἐστίν** 'the painter too, I suppose, is one of such
craftsmen'. τῶν τοιούτων ... δημιουργῶν is partitive genitive. This is
the first mention of the painter, who is to become the prime example
of a μιμητής in the ensuing argument. See on 597e3–4. References

to painting in P.'s work are conveniently collected together and discussed by Demand (1975). See also Keuls (1978).

597a1–2 οὐκ ἄρτι ... ὃ ἔστι κλίνη: lit. 'didn't you just now say that
he doesn't make the Form, which we say is "what is" a couch', i.e.
the real couch. This refers to 596b9–10. The phrase ὃ ἔστιν (cf.
507b7, 532a7–b1, 533b2; *Phaed.* 75d2 with Rowe (1993) *ad loc.*) is a
technical term used in Platonic circles to characterise the Forms,
hence the significance of φαμέν. See Vlastos (1981) 261 n. 102. **a4–
5 Οὐκοῦν ... ὂν δὲ οὔ** 'So if he doesn't make "what is" a couch, he
makes something like what's real, but isn't real.' **a5 τελέως δὲ εἶναι ὄν** 'to be completely existent'. **a8–9 Οὔκουν ... διατρίβουσιν** 'not, at any rate, in the opinion of those who are familiar
with such arguments'. Those unfamiliar with the Platonic theory of
Forms might well be surprised at the proposition that a couch made
by a craftsman is not a real couch. **a10 καὶ τοῦτο:** i.e. τὸ τοῦ
κλινουργοῦ ἔργον. **ἀμυδρόν τι** 'somewhat dim'. For the
implications of the visual metaphor see on 595c10–596a1.

b2 ἐπ' αὐτῶν τούτων 'taking these very examples'. **b2–3 τὸν
μιμητὴν ... ἐστίν:** prolepsis, cf. *Ion* 531c6–7n. **b5–7 μία μὲν ...
ἐργάσασθαι:** for the phrase ἐν τῆι φύσει used of the Forms cf.
501b2, 597d3 and 7, *Phaed.* 103b5, *Parm.* 132d1 τὰ μὲν εἴδη ταῦτα
ὥσπερ παραδείγματα ἑστάναι ἐν τῆι φύσει, τὰ δὲ ἄλλα τούτοις
ἐοικέναι. P.'s language is consistent with Greek philosophical usage
in which φύσις commonly denotes 'the real constitution or character
of things' (Guthrie (1962–81) I 82). Hence the Forms, which are for
P. the ultimate reality, exist ἐν τῆ φύσει. This is the only passage in
P. where god (for the singular see on 379a7–8) is said to create the
Forms, which are elsewhere eternal and uncreated. Indeed at *Tim.*
28a–29a god looks to the Forms as patterns when he creates the
world. This contradiction can best be explained in terms of P.'s purpose in introducing it, which is to denigrate the mimetic artist: the
argument requires three types of maker to correspond to the three
classes of object, the Form of Couch, a particular couch, and a
painting of a couch, and god is introduced simply to provide a parallel with the craftsman and the painter. See further H. Cherniss,
'On Plato's *Republic* X 597B', *A.J.P.* 53 (1932) 233–42. Nehamas

(1982) 73–4 notes that the oddity of the idea of god creating the Forms is somewhat lessened if we remember that these are Forms of artefacts rather than of natural objects (though problems still remain, on which see Annas (1981) 229–30), and further that the potential optative ἦν φαῖμεν ἄν, ὡς ἐγῷμαι perhaps adds an ironical qualification to the statement, which might be translated: 'We could say, I suppose, that god makes it'. The following words ἢ τίν' ἄλλον; οὐδένα also contribute to this effect. Murdoch (1993) 12 remarks that 'Plato's use of "God", *theos*, here is picturesque'. **b13–14 Ζωγρά-φος ... κλινῶν:** this sentence, with no articles, no connectives and no verbs elegantly summarises the equation.

c3 μίαν ... κλίνη lit. 'only that very one "which is" a couch'. i.e. only that one real couch'. See on 597a2. μίαν, αὐτήν and ἐκείνην are attracted into the gender of κλίνη, as with ἐκείνη at c9 below. **c4–5 οὔτε ἐφυτεύθησαν ... φυῶσιν** 'have not been produced by god, and never will be'. οὐ μή with the subjunctive expresses strong denial. **c7–9 εἰ δύο μόνας ... οὐχ αἱ δύο** 'if god were to make no more than two, again a single one would appear whose Form the other two would possess, and that one, not the two, would be the real Couch'. The creation of two real Couches would necessitate the existence of another one in order to explain the characteristics shared by the two. On the problem raised here of an infinite regress see *Parm.* 132a–133a; Arist. *Met.* 990b17, and for further discussion see Annas (1981) 230–2, 241; Vlastos (1981) 342–65.

d2 ποιητής implicitly contrasts god as the true maker with the poet, who, like the painter, will be revealed as nothing more than a μιμητής. Cf. d11 where the designation ποιητής is specifically denied to the painter, and see on e6 below. **d3 μίαν ... ἔφυσεν** 'created one in its essential nature', i.e. one real Couch. Cf. 597b6 above. **d5–6 φυτουργὸν ... τοιοῦτον** 'shall we call him the nature-maker of this couch, or something of the sort?' That S. is using the term φυτουργός in the special sense of ὁ φύσει τι ποιῶν is made clear by Glaucon's reply. See further Adam *ad loc.* and, for the connotations of φυτουργός, which does not occur elsewhere in P., see Halliwell *ad loc.* **d7–8 Δίκαιον ... πεποίηκεν** 'justifiably so, since he has made this and everything else that exists in nature', i.e. that truly exists. See on 597b5–7. **d13 Ἀλλὰ τί ... εἶναι** 'Then what will you say he is in relation to the couch?' For this use of the genitive cf. 582c2, 585d5 and e3–4 below.

e2 μιμητής … δημιουργοί 'the imitator of what these make'. Although god as the φυτουργός of the real Couch (d5) has been distinguished from the carpenter, who is the maker (δημιουργός) of a particular couch (d9), both god and the carpenter are now called δημιουργοί (cf. *Tim.* 28a where the divine maker of the world is termed a δημιουργός), and contrasted with the painter, who is classed as a μιμητής rather than a maker. Contrast 400d–401a where ἡ γραφικὴ τέχνη is listed as a δημιουργία, cf. *Gorg.* 503e, and for painting as a τέχνη see on *Ion* 532e–533a.   **e3–4 τὸν τοῦ τρίτου … καλεῖς;** lit. 'do you, then, call the one concerned with that which is bred third [i.e at the third remove, because the Greeks counted inclusively] from reality an imitator?' γεννήματος continues the language of breeding and generation associated with nature (cf. φυτουργός at d5 above). The use of the genitive is parallel to that at d13. The definition of the μιμητής which they have been seeking (597b3, cf. 595c7) has now been supplied, and is markedly different from that put forward in book 3, see especially 393c5–6, 394b3–397b4. There μίμησις was defined in terms of the performing arts, the imitator being one who makes himself like someone else, and the emphasis was on the depth of emotional identification which such μίμησις requires. But now, somewhat surprisingly in view of 595a–b, which led us to expect a discussion which centred on poetry, painting is taken as the paradigm of μίμησις, and μίμησις is defined as the superficial activity of copying appearances. Elsewhere in the dialogue painting is presented in far less derogatory terms: at 400d–401a S. says that good painting can encourage good character, and on several occasions the philosopher's task is compared to that of a painter in terms which suggest much more than simple copying (see 420c, 472d, 484c–d, 500e–501c). But here S. deliberately restricts the painter's activity to that of mindless copying in order to produce an analogy which will denigrate poetry. See further Else (1972) 33–4; Annas (1981) 336–8 and (1982) 3–7; Nehamas (1982) 55–8.   **e6–8 Τοῦτ' ἄρα ἔσται … μιμηταί** 'Consequently then the tragic poet, too, since he is an imitator, will be, as it were, third from the king and from truth, as will all other imitators'. τοῦτο, 'therefore', is adverbial and stands in apposition to the sentence, as at *Laws* 686c4–5. τραγωιδοποιός is the subject, τρίτος τις the predicate. Although we were reminded that the tragic poet is an imitator at 595b3–4, and the use of the word ποιητής at d2 and d11 above perhaps keeps the poet in mind, the sudden intrusion of the tragic poet into this discussion about painting is very abrupt. The notion of μίμησις which was developed in relation to tragic poetry in book 3 is different from the one now proposed (see above on e3–4), and there is no attempt to prove that what is said about painting can be straightforwardly applied to poetry. The most plausible interpretation of the phrase τρίτος τις ἀπὸ βασιλέως καὶ τῆς ἀληθείας is that given by Adam *ad loc.* with appendix 1 (464–5). The metaphor is genealogical (cf. 391c2 Πηλέως, σωφρονεστάτου τε καὶ τρίτου ἀπὸ Διός; Aesch. *Pers.* 768), with the king corresponding to the φυτουργός (for God as βασιλεύς cf. *Laws.* 904a6). Thus the imitator is third in the line of descent from the king, just as his imitation is at third remove from reality (e3–4). Dante uses a similar metaphor (though with very different implications) at *Inferno* xi.105 where Virgil says, 'We may call this art of yours God's grandchild, as it were' (*Si che vostr' arte a Dio quasi e nipote*) because art is nature's daughter, just as nature is God's daughter. We should also recall that the Form of the Good is described as king (βασιλεύειν) of the intelligible realm at 509d2, and cf. *Phileb.* 28c7 νοῦς ἐστι βασιλεύς ἡμῖν οὐρανοῦ τε καὶ γῆς.

597e10–598d6

The painter can make anything because all he does is to imitate superficial appearances. For example, he can paint a portrait of a carpenter without understanding the carpenter's craft. Yet he deceives children and stupid people into thinking that his painting is real. We should beware, therefore, of being taken in by people who claim to be omniscient.

e10–598a1 Τὸν μὲν δὴ μιμητὴν ... τόδε: having established a link between poet and painter (however spuriously) S. now reverts to the painter as the prime example of a μιμητής.

598a1–2 πότερα ἐκεῖνο ... μιμεῖσθαι: the possibility that the painter might imitate the Forms, raised here only to be dismissed, was developed by later thinkers as a way of countering P.'s attack on the arts. Plotinus, in particular, declared: 'The arts do not simply imitate what they see ... they run back up to the forming principles from which nature derives ... and, since they possess beauty, they make up what is defective in things. For Pheidias too did not make his Zeus from any model perceived by the senses, but understood what Zeus would look like if he wanted to make him visible' (*Enneads* 5.8.1, trans. A. H. Armstrong (London and Cambridge, Mass. 1966–88) and see further Russell (1981) 104–6). This Neoplatonic view of the transcendental nature of art, sometimes wrongly attributed to P. himself (see Nehamas (1982) 58–60 with bibliography on p. 76 n. 60), was enormously influential in the subsequent history of Western aesthetics. See Abrams (1953) 42–6.   **a2–3 τὰ ... ἔργα:** see on 596b1.   **a8–9 μὴ τι διαφέρει ... ἀλλοία:** lit. 'it doesn't differ from itself, does it, or does it differ in no way, but appear different?' i.e. though the bed remains the same, it will look different according to the perspective of the viewer. Cf. 602c7–603b2.   **a10 Οὕτως ... οὐδέν** 'That's it, he said. It appears to be different, but isn't'.

b1–4 πρὸς πότερον ... οὖσα μίμησις: lit. 'towards which of these alternatives is painting directed in each case? Is it directed towards imitating the real as it is, or towards appearance, as it appears, being an imitation of appearance or of truth?' μιμήσασθαι is an explanatory infinitive which further specifies the purpose towards which painting is directed. For the construction cf. *Gorg.* 513e5–6 with Dodds (1959) *ad loc.* A painting of a bed is not only at third remove from reality in the metaphysical sense described at 597e3–8; it is also less real than a particular, material bed, because it is merely an appearance of a bed, which will vary according to the angle from which the painter has painted it, even though the bed itself has remained the same. Necessarily, then, the painter's representation of a bed can only be a partial one. As Adam points out *ad loc.* the painter can never capture the look of a bed in its completeness because painting is a two-dimensional medium.   **b6–8 Πόρρω ... εἴδωλον:** διὰ τοῦτο anticipates ὅτι. σμικρόν τι is an adverbial accusative qualifying ἐφάπτεται: 'the reason why it produces everything is that it has little grasp of anything, and that little is only an image'. πάντα ἀπεργάζεται recalls 596c1–e3, and also anticipates 598c7–d5 below. The term εἴδωλον is used of the images which cast shadows in the allegory of the cave at 532b–c, cf. 534c5, and of the illusory pleasures of the common man at 586b7–c5. For further references see Halliwell *ad loc*. The generalisation from painting to mimetic art as a whole (ἡ μιμητική sc. τέχνη) is slipped in unobtrusively; but the argument just used in relation to painting cannot be straightforwardly applied to a three-dimensional medium like sculpture, let alone poetry.

c1 περὶ οὐδενὸς ... τεχνῶν 'though in the case of none of them understanding their crafts'. The painter produces a superficial appearance of a carpenter without conveying the knowledge of carpentry which makes him a carpenter. Cornford 321 n. 1 points out that, though this argument is unconvincing in relation to painters, P. is more interested in its application to poets, who are said to have knowledge of everything which they depict in their poetry. See on c8 below.   **c1–4 ἀλλ' ὅμως ... τέκτονα εἶναι** 'but nevertheless, if he were a good painter, he might paint a carpenter and show it from a distance, and deceive children and stupid men into thinking it was a real carpenter'. Cf. *Soph*. 234b for the same idea. For ἐξαπατῶι cf. d3 and e6 below. The reference to παῖδας and ἄφρονας ἀνθρώπους perhaps anticipates 602b8, where μίμησις is defined as παιδιάν τινα. Demand (1975) 10 notes that, whereas in book 2 the poet was likened to an incompetent painter whose painting bears no resemblance to its original (377e1–3), in book 10 he is compared to the painter *per se*, and it is the painter's very success which condemns him (εἰ ἀγαθὸς εἴη ζωγράφος at c2). The popular belief that the best painters are those whose work is most realistic is reflected in the well-known anecdote about a painting contest between Zeuxis and Parrhasius recorded by Pliny (*NH* 35.65). Zeuxis painted a bunch of grapes which the birds came and pecked, whereupon Parrhasius secretly painted a curtain over the grapes. Zeuxis asked for the curtain to be drawn, but declared Parrhasius the winner of the contest when he discovered that the curtain was painted and not real. See further J. J. Pollitt, *The ancient view of Greek art* (New Haven and London 1974) 63.   **c6–7 τῶν τοιούτων** deftly generalises the discussion. **c8–d1 πάσας ... ἐπισταμένωι** lit. 'who knows all crafts and everything that each individual knows, and understands everything more exactly than anyone else'. οὐδὲν ὅτι οὐχί, i.e. ἅπαντα. Cf. 596c2–e4.

d3–4 γόητί ... πάσσοφος: the language refers us back to the example of the painter at c2–4, but also strongly suggests that this impostor will turn out to be a poet. The tragic poet was specifically described as a μιμητής at 597e6, and the connexion between magic, poetry and deception has already been well established. See on 380d1, 382c10 and 601b1. The heavily ironical πάσσοφος (cf. *Prot.* 315e7) also points to the reputation for wisdom traditionally accorded to the poet (cf. 398a1–2). The same tactics are employed at *Soph.* 233b2 where the Stranger says that only the young can be persuaded to believe that sophists are πάντα πάντων αὐτοὶ σοφώτατοι (cf. *Soph.* 234c7). **d4 αὐτός** is nominative because the subject of the infinitive is the same as the subject of the main verb ἐξηπατήθη: 'he has been deceived ... because he was unable to distinguish knowledge and lack of knowledge and imitation'.

598d7–601b8

It is often claimed that Homer is a master of all skills and understands everything, both human and divine. But if he had really known about the activities described in his poetry, he would have practised them rather than composing poetry about them. In fact all poets from Homer onwards have produced nothing but superficial appearances of the subjects which they treat. But they deceive ignorant people into thinking that they have knowledge by clothing their material in the magic of poetry.

d8 τραγωιδίαν ... Ὅμηρον: see on 595c2. **d8–e1 ἐπειδή τινων ἀκούομεν ὅτι οὗτοι** 'since we hear from some that these', i.e. Homer and the tragedians.

e2 καὶ τά γε θεῖα 'and even things divine'. The γε suggests ironic disbelief. S. had already exposed the dangers of treating poets as moralists and theologians in the earlier discussion at 364a–365d and at 377d5–392c5. For the range of subjects covered by Homer's poetry cf. *Ion* 531c4–d2, and 599c7–9 below. **e3–5 ἀνάγκη γὰρ ... ποιεῖν:** περὶ ὧν (for περὶ τούτων ἃ) ἂν ποιῆι is indefinite. The contention that the good poet must understand the subjects on which he composes his poems is at the heart of P.'s critique of poetry. The crucial point for P. is that composing fine poetry (καλῶς ποιήσειν) depends on knowledge of the truth, which poets do not have, how-

ever 'fine' their poetry may appear to be. Hence his exposure of the
falsity of the traditional tales of the poets in books 2 and 3, and his
insistence in the present section on the superficiality and worthlessness of the poets' so-called knowledge. Exactly the same argument is
used against rhapsodes in the *Ion* (530c1–5, cf. 531b6, 537c–541b5),
where the ambiguity of the term καλός is similarly exploited. See on
Ion 533e7 and cf. *Rep.* 377c1, 377d9.   **e5–6 πότερον ... ἐξηπάτηνται** 'whether these, meeting men who are imitators, have
been deceived'. οὗτοι refers back to τινων at d8, τούτοις to οὗτοι
(Homer and the tragedians) at e1. μιμηταῖς is predicative, as Adam
rightly notes.

599a1 τριττὰ ἀπέχοντα τοῦ ὄντος: cf. 597e7.   **a1–2 ῥάιδια [sc.
ὄντα] ... ἀλήθειαν** 'and are easy to produce for a man who does not
know the truth'. Cf. 596d8 where it is 'not difficult' to make anything
you like by picking up a mirror.   **a2–3 φαντάσματα ... ποιοῦσιν:** cf. 596e4, e11, 598b3–5, b8.   **a3 ἤ τι καὶ λέγουσιν** 'or
whether there is something in what they say'. καὶ emphasises λέγουσιν. See Denniston (1954) 306.   **a4 περὶ ὧν** is for ταῦτα περὶ ὧν
as at 598e3. δοκοῦσιν continues the language of illusion, leaving us
in no doubt as to the answer to the question posed here.   **a6–b1
Οἴει οὖν ... βέλτιστον ἔχοντα** 'Do you think that if a man were able
to make both the object of imitation and the image he would seriously give himself up to the manufacture of images, and put this in
the forefront of his life as his best possession?' μιμηθησόμενον is the
future passive participle, lit. 'the thing to be imitated'. Some take
προστήσασθαι (aorist middle infin. of προΐστημι) to mean 'set before as an aim', but 'put in the forefront' seems to make better sense.
See further Adam *ad loc.* For εἴδωλον cf. 598b8. The emphasis on
σπουδάζειν (cf. σπουδάσειεν at b5) recalls the discussion at 396d3–
e2, and prepares us for the condemnation of μίμησις at 602b8.

b3–5 Ἀλλ' εἴπερ ... τοῖς μιμήμασι: τῆι ἀληθείαι 'in reality'. The
argument is that if the poet really understood his subject-matter he
would put that knowledge into practice rather than producing poetry about it assumes that there is nothing to the composition of
poetry other than its subject matter. Cf. *Ion* 536d8–541e1 where S.'s
demonstration of the spuriousness of Ion's claim to knowledge depends on a view of poetry which equates it with its factual content

(see on *Ion* 531d6, 540b3). **b5–7 καὶ πειρῷτο . . . ἐγκωμιάζων:**
ἔργα picks up ἔργοις at b4 emphasising the importance of deeds
rather than their pale imitation in poetry. Exactly the opposite view
is expressed by Pindar at *Nem.* 4.6: ῥῆμα δ' ἐργμάτων χρονιώτερον
βιοτεύει. μνημεῖα reminds us of the traditional claim to fame and
immortality conferred by poetry, which P. is here attempting to sub-
vert. See e.g. Hom. *Il.* 6.357–8; *Od.* 8.580, 24.196–8; Theogn. 19–23,
245–52; Bacch. 3.90–8, 9.81–7; Pi. *Ol.* 10.91–6, *Pyth.* 5.45–9, *Nem.*
5.1–5, 6.29–30, 7.11–16, *Isthm.* 7.16–19, 8.56–62, and in general
Goldhill (1991) 69–166. P. himself puts this traditional view into the
mouth of Diotima at *Symp.* 209d where Homer and Hesiod are cited
as examples of mortals who have won immortal glory and fame
(ἀθάνατον κλέος καὶ μνήμην) through their poetry. On this passage
as a refutation of the positive view of poetry put forward by Diotima see Asmis (1992) 354. On ἐγκώμια see *Ion* 534c3. **b8 ὠφελία**
brings in the notion of usefulness which will be further discussed in
the following section. Cf. 599e2, 607d8. It is better to be the ἐγκωμιαζόμενος rather than the ἐγκωμιάζων because the former benefits
others as well as himself. Nevertheless at 607a4 (on which see below)
S. is prepared to allow ἐγκώμια to good men a place in his city,
which suggests that writers of such poems have their uses. **b9–
c1 Τῶν μὲν . . . Ὅμηρον** 'As far as other things are concerned, then,
let's not ask Homer for an account'. For the accentuation of πέρι see
on 392a3. The word order suggests that there will be more important things on which to interrogate Homer. ἀπαιτῶμεν takes a
double accusative. **c4–5 ὥσπερ Ἀσκληπιός . . . τοὺς ἐκγόνους:**
in Homer Asclepius has two sons, Machaon and Podalirius, to whom
he has passed on the skills of healing (*Il.* 2.731–2, 4.204, 11.517–18
and see on *Ion* 538b8–c5). But the term Ἀσκληπιάδαι (lit. 'sons
of Asclepius') came to be used of physicians in general. See e.g.
Theogn. 432, Pl. *Rep.* 405d–e with Adam *ad loc.* S.'s point here is not
that poets have no descendants or pupils (the mention of the Homeridae at 599e6 would refute that argument), but rather that they
leave no ἔκγονοι who can practise useful skills such as medicine.
Contrast *Symp.* 209d2–3, where Homer and Hesiod are praised for
their spiritual offspring (ἔκγονα), their poetry, which is valued more
highly than human offspring. **c6 περὶ δὲ ὧν** is for περὶ δὲ τῶν
μεγίστων τε καὶ καλλίστων ἅ. Cf. *Gorg.* 451d7–8 where Gorgias

claims that the art of rhetoric deals with τὰ μέγιστα τῶν ἀνθρω-
πείων πραγμάτων ... καὶ ἄριστα, and for the phrase τὰ μέγιστα
καὶ τὰ κάλλιστα cf. *Crat.* 421a2, *Pol.* 286a5–6; Arist. *Eth. Nic.*
1099b24.   **c7–9 πολέμων ... ἀνθρώπου:** for the range of subjects cf. 598e2, *Ion* 531c4–d2, and on generalship, *Ion* 540d1–5. The
significance of διοικήσεων πόλεων will not become clear until
600d1. παιδείας πέρι ἀνθρώπου reminds us of the centrality of
Homer in Greek culture, and refers back to the whole subject of
poetry and education which was discussed at 376e–398b8.

d2–4 εἴπερ μὴ τρίτος ... ὡρισάμεθα: cf. 597e1–8. εἰδώλου, echoing
εἴδωλον at 598b8, reinforces the paralleism between poet and
painter.   **d4–5 δεύτερος ... ποιεῖ:** the implication is that one
who understands the practicalities of training men in virtue (ἀρετῆς
πέρι at d3) would be second from the throne of truth, just like the
craftsman, who understands the function of the particular bed or
table he makes in a practical way (see on 596b6–9 and cf. 597b13–
14). For the view that the poet's job is to 'make men better' cf. Ar.
Frogs 1009 and cf. 600c3. The same claim is made for sophists at
Prot. 316c9.   **d5–6 ἰδίαι καὶ δημοσίαι:** cf. 600a9 and see on
600d1.   **d7 Λυκοῦργον:** the legendary law-giver, referred to by
Hdt. 1.65–6 as the originator of Spartan εὐνομία (good order). He
was traditionally regarded as the founder of the Spartan constitution and military system. See further O. Murray, *Early Greece*,
2nd edn (London 1993) 159–80. Although P. here contrasts Homer
unfavourably with law-givers, at *Symp.* 209d–e Homer and Hesiod
are linked with Lycurgus and Solon as examples of men who have
produced spiritual offspring.

e2 ὠφεληκέναι: cf. ὠφελία at 599b8.   **e2–3 Χαρώνδαν ...
Σόλωνα:** Charondas was a law-giver from Catana in Sicily, thought to
have lived in the sixth century B.C. He is mentioned several times by
Aristotle: see e.g. *Pol.* 1252b14, 1274a–b. Solon, the Athenian states-
man who was chief archon in 594/3, was renowned for his social,
economic and constitutional reforms. He was one of the Seven Wise
Men (cf. 600a6–7) and was also a poet, a fact which S. conveniently
ignores. See further O. Murray, *Early Greece*, 2nd edn (London 1993)
181–200.   **e5–6 οὔκουν ... Ὁμηριδῶν** 'it's not said even by the
Homeridae themselves'. οὔκουν ... γε introduces an emphatic neg-

ative answer. See Denniston (1954) 423. For the Homeridae see on *Ion* 530d7.

600a1 Ἀλλά δη is commonly used after a rejected suggestion. Cf. 600a4, a9, *Ion* 540b2 and Denniston (1954) 241–2.   **ἐπὶ Ὁμήρου** 'in the time of Homer'.   **a4–5 Ἀλλ' οἷα δὴ ... λέγονται:** lit. 'Well then, are many ingenious ideas and inventions in relation to crafts and other activities mentioned, such as are characteristic of a man who is clever in practical matters?' For this use of the genitive cf. 605e1. εἰς τὰ ἔργα depends on σοφοῦ.   **a6–7 Θάλεώ ... Σκύθου:** Θάλεω is the Ionic form of the genitive. Thales, like Solon, one of the Seven Wise Men, was well known for his practical wisdom. He was said, e.g., to have predicted the eclipse of the sun in 585 B.C. (Hdt. 1.74.2 cf. 1.75.4–5, 1.170.3). Aristotle refers to him as the founder of natural philosophy (*Met.* 983b), but also records that he was able to put his philosophical knowledge to practical use (*Pol.* 1259a). At *Theaet.* 174a, however, he appears as the archetypal absent-minded professor, so intent upon looking up at the sky in connexion with his astronomical researches that he falls into the well before his feet. Cf. Ar. *Clouds* 180, *Birds* 1009. Anacharsis the Scythian was a man of great knowledge who travelled extensively in Greece during the sixth century B.C. (Hdt. 4.76). Later writers list him among the Seven Wise Men, and he is credited by some with the invention of the anchor and the potter's wheel (Diog. Laert. 1.105).   **a9–b2 ἡγεμών ... Ὁμηρικήν:** Glaucon might have pointed out that although there is no private 'school of Homer' or Homeric way of life, Homer's poetry is at the centre of Athenian education and culture, as the discussion of παιδεία at 376e–398b has shown. And for Homer as ἡγεμών of tragedy cf. 598d8. ἐπὶ συνουσίαι 'for his company'.

b2–5 ὥσπερ Πυθαγόρας ... τοῖς ἄλλοις: Pythagoras, sixth-century philosopher and guru, left his native Samos for southern Italy where he founded a quasi-religious community. Despite the legendary nature of much of the evidence concerning his life and teaching, it is clear that he believed in metempsychosis, or the transmigration of the soul (Xenoph. fr. B 7 D–K; Hdt. 4.95–6, 2.123; Porph. *Vit. Pythag.* 19), that he was greatly revered, and that he bequeathed an esoteric way of life to his followers which involved the observance of various practices (e.g. abstinence from meat, ritual cleanliness, silence, self-examination) which set them apart from normal society. See e.g. Hdt. 2.81; Athen. *Deipn.* 161b–c, 238c–d; Diog. Laert. 8.22 and for other evidence Kirk, Raven and Schofield (1983) 214–38, 322–50. Hence the significance of ἰδίαι at a9 above: Pythagoras may not have performed any public services, but he was enormously influential through the way of life he initiated for his followers. ἐπὶ τούτωι 'on this account'.   **b6 αὖ** refers back to a8.   **b6–9 ὁ γὰρ Κρεώφυλος ... ἀληθῆ:** Creophylus of Samos was said to have composed a poem on Heracles' capture of Oechalia (Callim. *Ep.* 6 Pf.), or alternatively been given the poem as a gift from Homer himself (Strab. 14.1.8). Although described here as a companion of Homer's, according to another tradition he was Homer's son-in-law (*Suda*, s.v.). The name 'meat-stock' (derived from κρέας and φῦλον) suggests boorishness rather than culture, a tradition to which Sir Andrew Aguecheek alludes in *Twelfth Night* (Act 1, scene 3): 'I am a great eater of beef and I believe that does harm to my wit'.   **b9– c1 λέγεται γὰρ ... ὅτε ἔζη** 'for it is said that there was much ne- glect surrounding him (i.e. Homer) in his own lifetime, when he was alive'. The point is that if Homer had been a good teacher his dis- ciples would have put his παιδεία into practice and treated him with respect. The fact that he was neglected even in his own lifetime (the strong rhetorical emphasis of ὅτε ἔζη is correctly noted by Adam *ad loc.*) proves what an ineffective teacher he was. Contrast Protagoras and Prodicus at c6–7 below.

c2–6 ἀλλ' οἴει ... ἠγαπᾶτο ὑπ' αὐτῶν 'do you think that if Homer ... he would not have made many friends etc.' ἆρ' at c5 resumes the main argument after the ἄτε clause. Although the whole passage from c2–e2 is effectively one sentence, it has to be broken up into its separate parts when translating. For the claim that Homer educated people and made them better cf. 599d5 and d5–6 below.   **c6–d4 ἀλλὰ Πρωταγόρας ... οἱ ἑταῖροι** 'but Protagoras of Abdera and Prodicus of Ceos and many others are able to persuade their con- temporaries in private conversation that they won't be able to run either their households or their city unless *they* (i.e. Protagoras, Pro- dicus *et al.*) are in charge of their education, and they are so loved for this wisdom that their followers almost (μόνον οὐκ, lit. 'all but') carry them about shoulder-high'. The whole of this μέν clause, which is itself divided into a series of dependent clauses, is subordinate to the main statement, which begins at d5. Protagoras, one of the earliest and most distinguished of the sophists (*fl.* 450 B.C.), claimed to teach ἀρετή, or how to live. The tremendous enthusiasm of his followers is vividly depicted in the opening scene of the Platonic dialogue named after him (see esp. *Prot.* 315a–b). Prodicus, a contemporary of Protagoras, also appears in the same dialogue, where we are given a demonstration of his expertise in the right use of words (*Prot.* 337a–c, cf. 341a–e). As in the *Protagoras*, S.'s description of the excessive zeal of the disciples of these sophists is more than a little ironic. πόλιν ... διοικεῖν (d1) and παιδείας (d2) echo διοικήσεων πόλεων and παιδείας at 599c8–d1, underlining the parallel between poet and sophist: both claimed to be educators, both claimed to teach ἀρετή. Indeed at *Prot.* 316d7 Protagoras claimed that Homer was a sophist. Else (1972) 41 observes that, though S. makes no such direct comparison in this passage, the implication is that Homer has not even done as well as 'his fellow-sophists'.

d5–6 Ὅμηρον δ' ἄρα ... εἴων: ἄρα resumes the main argument as at c5 above. The word order lays emphasis on Homer. Hesiod is introduced almost as an after-thought, but prepares us for the extension of the argument to include all poets at e4–5 below. For the view put forward here cf. *Ion* 541b6–c2. ῥαψῳδεῖν is equivalent to ἀείδειν, on which see further above p. 96. **d7–e2 καὶ οὐχὶ μᾶλλον ... μεταλάβοιεν** 'wouldn't they have held on to them as more precious than gold, and forced them to stay at home with them [as opposed to περιιόντας at d6], or if they couldn't persuade them, wouldn't they have danced attendance on them until they had acquired enough education?' The duty of the παιδαγωγός was to supervise children, e.g. by accompanying them to and from school. Here P. playfully reverses the situation, using παιδαγωγεῖν of pupils 'dancing attendance' (Cornford's translation) on their masters. Cf. *Alc.* 1 135d where Alcibiades points out to S. that their roles are about to be reversed: οὐ γὰρ ἔστιν ὅπως οὐ παιδαγωγήσω σε ἀπὸ τῆσδε τῆς ἡμέρας, σὺ δ' ὑπ' ἐμοῦ παιδαγωγήσει.

e4–6 ἀπὸ Ὁμήρου ... ἅπτεσθαι: these words make it clear that the definition of the μιμητής at 597e3–4 extends to all poets from Homer onwards. **e6–7 ἀλλ' ὥσπερ ... ἐλέγομεν:** cf. 598b8–

c4.   **e7–601a2 ὁ ζωγράφος … θεωροῦσιν** 'the painter will produce what seems to be a cobbler, although he himself knows nothing
about cobbling, and [he produces it] for those who know nothing
about cobbling, but who judge from colours and shapes'. The dative
τοῖς μὴ ἐπαΐουσιν is best construed with ποιήσει, although some
take it with δοκοῦντα, i.e. 'what seems to be a cobbler to those who
know nothing about cobbling'. μή is generic, θεωροῦσιν is dative,
parallel with ἐπαΐουσιν. After devoting the whole section from
598d7–600e6 to Homer, P. slides back into using the painter as the
prime example of the μιμητής.

601a4–6 χρώματα ἄττα … μιμεῖσθαι 'applies the colours of every
art with words and phrases, though he understands nothing other
than how to imitate'. ἄττα is neuter plural of the indefinite
τις.   **a6–9 ὥστε ἑτέροις … λέγεσθαι:** ἑτέροις τοιούτοις, sc. τοῖς
μὴ ἐπαΐουσι περὶ σκυτοτομίας. The repetition of δοκεῖν emphasises
the unreality of what is depicted, cf. δοκοῦντα at 600e7. Metre,
rhythm and mode (for the meaning of ἁρμονία see on 397b7) in
poetry are the equivalent of colour and shape in painting.

b1–2 οὕτω φύσει … ἔχειν 'these things by their very nature possess
such great magical power'. αὐτὰ ταῦτα refers to μέτρωι καὶ ῥυθμῶι
καὶ ἁρμονίαι. S. here invokes the age-old view of poetry as a kind of
enchantment, embodied in the myth of Orpheus, the supreme example of the inspired musician exercising magical powers over nature itself. This idea is reflected in the use of the term θέλγειν and its
cognates to describe the magical, and potentially dangerous, effects
of song. See e.g. Hom. *Od.* 1.337, 12.40 and 44, 17.521; *h. Ap.* 161;
Hes. fr. 28; Pi. *Nem.* 4.3; Aesch. *Prom.* 173, and for further references
see Goldhill (1991) 60–6. The early connexion between poetry and
magic is usefully discussed by J. De Romilly, 'Gorgias et le pouvoir
de la poésie', *J.H.S.* 93 (1973) 155–62. See also on 382c8–10, 595b6,
598d3 and *Ion* 535e2–3.   **b2–4 ἐπεὶ γυμνωθέντα … τεθέασαι
γάρ που** 'for when the works of the poets are stripped of the colours
of music and spoken alone by themselves, I think you know how they
appear. For you must have seen.' τὰ τῶν ποιητῶν … οἷα φαίνεται:
prolepsis, cf. *Ion* 531c6–7n. Halliwell *ad loc.* compares γυμνωθέντα
with the use of the term ψιλός ('bare') to refer to prose (Arist. *Rhet.*
1404b14, *Po.* 1447a29) or to verses or speeches without musical

accompaniment (*Phdr.* 278c2, *Laws* 669d7). But S. is more concerned with the distinction between form and content in poetry itself than with different types of discourse. It is only when you strip poetry of its form that you realise how superficial its content is. For this distinction between form and content cf. 393d8 and *Ion* 540b3. This passage makes clear that it is the 'musical' elements which give poetry its magic powers, since if you remove these you are left with empty words. Cf. *Gorg.* 501d1–502d8 with Dodds (1959) *ad loc.*, where it is argued that poetry is simply a form of rhetoric, and cf. especially 502c5–7: εἴ τις περιέλοι [from περιαιρέω, 'to strip off'] τῆς ποιήσεως πάσης τό τε μέλος καὶ τὸν ῥυθμὸν καὶ τὸ μέτρον, ἄλλο τι ἢ λόγοι γίγνονται τὸ λειπόμενον; Cf. Isoc. *Evag.* 10–11. Gorgias himself had earlier described poetry as speech in metrical form: τὴν ποίησιν ἅπασαν καὶ νομίζω καὶ ὀνομάζω λόγον ἔχοντα μέτρον (*Hel.* 9). Aristotle, in contrast, argued that it is impossible to define poetry simply in terms of its form (*Po.* 1447a28–47b24b). It has been argued (notably by Annas (1981) 341–3 and (1982) 1–28) that S.'s insistence here on the triviality of poetry (cf. 602b8) conflicts with his insistence on its corrupting power (605c6–606d7). How can poetry be both trivial and dangerous? The implication of S.'s words here is that poetry is trivial in terms of its content, but dangerous because of the magic power of its 'musical' form. The danger of poetry lies in the pleasure it gives (387b2–4, 606b4), and that pleasure is particularly associated with its ability to arouse our emotions (605c10–d5, cf. *Ion* 535e2–3). Poetry, with its throbbing rhythms and seductive melodies, affects even the best of us so that, despite the triviality of its subject-matter ('What's Hecuba to him, or he to Hecuba ...?', quoted on *Ion* 535c7–8), we are nevertheless carried away and feel the emotions played out before us as if they were our own. Herein lies the crucial difference for P. between painting and poetry. A portrait of a bad man might be worthless, but it would not be dangerous because there would be nothing about it which would make us want to be like its subject. But poetry, by means of the natural magic inherent in μέτρωι καὶ ῥυθμῶι καὶ ἁρμονίαι (a8) seduces us into an emotional identification with the characters it portrays in a way which threatens the health of the psyche. **b6–7 ἔοικεν ... προλίπηι** 'they [sc. τὰ λεγόμενα] are like the faces of those who are in the bloom of youth, but who are not beautiful, as one can see when the bloom deserts them'. μή is generic, ἰδεῖν an explanatory infinitive after οἷα, lit. 'such as they are to see'. The true nature of the face, which has been disguised by the bloom of youth, only shows once that bloom has faded. Arist. *Rhet.* 1406b refers to this passage as an example of an εἰκών (simile).

601b9–602b11

S. makes the further point that there are three arts relating to any given subject: those of the user, the maker and the imitator. The user knows most about the merits and defects of any object; the maker, who incorporates the knowledge of the user into what he makes, has correct opinion; the imitator, however, knows nothing about the subjects which he imitates, but merely imitates what appeals to the ignorant masses. Therefore imitation in general, and poetry in particular, has no serious value.

b9–10 ὁ τοῦ εἰδώλου ... φαινομένου: it has now been established on the basis of the theory of Forms (cf. 596a6) that from a metaphysical point of view, the imitator produces an image of appearances rather than of reality, and is thus at the third remove from the truth. S. now proceeds to attack imitators, and especially poets, from another standpoint, namely their lack of practical knowledge. See on 601d1.

c11–13 ἢ οὐδ' ὁ ποιήσας ... ὁ ἱππικός 'or is it that not even the maker, the smith and the saddler [know what the reins and the bit ought to be like], but only the horseman, the one who knows how to use them'. The claim that it is not the maker, but the user, who has knowledge conflicts with 596b6–8, but see on e7 below. The words ἡμίσεως ... ῥηθέν at c3 above perhaps help to prepare for this shift.

d1–2 Περὶ ἕκαστον ... μιμησομένην: despite this passing reference to the τέχνη of the imitator, the nature of that τέχνη is never explored. P. sometimes pays lip-service to the notion of poetic τέχνη in his work (see on *Ion* 531e10, 532c6 and c8–9, *Rep.* 393d8), but it is never more than that; and poets are always unfavourably compared with craftsmen (see e.g. *Ap.* 22a–d). Painting is sometimes treated as a craft (see on 597e2, *Ion* 532e4–5), but when the painter is categorised as an imitator (see on 597d2, d11–12, e2 and *Soph.* 234b–c) his τέχνη amounts to very little. This triad of user, maker, imitator differs from the earlier one of god, craftsman, imitator (597b5–598c4) in that, whereas the earlier triad relates to different levels of reality (Form, particular, image), the present one concerns different ways of relating to objects at the same level of reality. See Annas (1981) 337; Else (1972) 37–40, who notes that in this new scheme 'god has been replaced by the customer'. **d4–6 Οὐκοῦν ἀρετὴ ... πεφυκός** 'are the excellence, beauty and rightness ... related to anything other than the use to which each thing has been made by man or nature?' For this relationship between ἀρετή and function cf. *Rep.* 352e–353e, *Men.* 72a; *Gorg.* 506d5 with Dodds (1959) *ad loc.*; Xen. *Symp.* 5.4; Arist. *Eth. Nic.* 1.7. **d8 ἐμπειρότατον:** for the same argument that the user's knowledge is superior to that of the maker cf. *Crat.* 390b–c. Halliwell *ad loc.* notes the oddity of this equation between experience and knowledge, since P. elsewhere distinguishes between the two. See especially *Gorg.* 463b, 465a. **d9–10 οἷα ἀγαθὰ ... ὧι χρῆται:** lit. 'what good or bad things the thing which he uses [i.e. the instrument] does when he uses it'. The subject of ποιεῖ is the antecedent to ὧι χρῆται, as explained by Adam *ad loc.* **d10–e2 αὐλητής ... ὑπηρετήσει** 'the pipe-player informs the pipe-maker about the pipes which would serve him in his playing, and will instruct him about what sort he ought to make, and he [the pipe-maker] will serve him'. The repetition of ὑπηρετῶσιν and ὑπηρετήσει with different subjects perhaps underlines the expertise of the user: both the instrument and the instrument-maker serve him.

e7–602a1 πίστιν ... ἐπιστήμην: the language recalls the simile of the Line at 509d–511e, where a distinction is made between four types of apprehension: νόησις or ἐπιστήμη, διάνοια, πίστις and εἰκασία. Of these categories the first two relate to the intelligible world, whereas the latter two operate within the world of appearances. In contrasting the ἐπιστήμη of the user with the πίστις of the maker P. maintains a similar distinction between levels of knowledge, but without implying that the user has knowledge in a metaphysical sense. According to the present argument, the user knows about his instrument because he understands its function; the maker has 'correct belief', which is inferior to the user's knowledge, because, although he makes the instrument correctly, he does so on the basis of what the user tells him, without understanding why. Cf. a4–5 below. This analysis of the activity of the maker conflicts somewhat with the description of the craftsman at 596b6, which suggests that he keeps his eye on the form of each object as he makes it. But in both cases the activity of the maker is favourably contrasted with that of the imitator. P.'s ultimate concern here is not with the craftsman, but with the imitator, and it is the imitator's lack of knowledge which both arguments are designed to show.

602a4 εἴτε καλὰ ... εἴτε μή: cf. *Ion* 531e10–11, 537c1–2, 538b1–2. **a4–6 δόξαν ὀρθὴν ... γράφειν:** one who has δόξα ὀρθή (cf. πίστιν ὀρθήν at e7 above) is dependent on an authority which has superior knowledge, a point which is underlined here by the emphasis on ἐξ ἀνάγκης (cf. ἀναγκαζόμενος at e8–9 above) and ἐπιτάττεσθαι (cf. ἐπιτάξει at e2 above). Cf. 430a–b with Adam *ad loc.* A distinction between δόξα, whose object is the world of appearances, and ἐπιστήμη, which concerns what truly exists, is developed at 477b–478d, but there is no such metaphysical framework here.   **a9 πρὸς ... πονηρίαν** 'with regard to goodness or badness'.   **a11–12 Χαρίεις ... ποιῆι** 'the poetic imitator would be an accomplished chap as regards wisdom on the subjects of his poetry'. Χαρίεις is clearly ironic, a nuance which Glaucon fails to grasp, as his reply indicates. The phrase ὁ ἐν τῆι ποιήσει μιμητικός could be taken to refer to mimetic activity in general, but the mention of σοφίαν suggests that it is poetic mimesis in particular that S. has in mind.

b1 Ἀλλ' οὖν δὴ ... μιμήσεται 'Well anyway, he will still go on imitating'. Ἀλλ' οὖν δή resumes the argument from a 8–9 after the passing comment at 11–12.   **b2–3 οἷον φαίνεται ... μηδὲν εἰδόσιν** 'the sort of thing that appears to be beautiful to the ignorant masses'. For the ignorance of the masses cf. 598c2–4, d3–5, 599a1–2, 601a1–2, a6–9. But there is the additional implication here, that the imitator's choice of subject-matter is dictated by his public.   **b8–10 ἀλλ' εἶναι παιδιάν ... ὡς οἷόν τε μάλιστα** 'but imitation is a form of play and not serious, and all those who compose tragedies in iambic and epic verse are imitators in the highest degree possible'. For the view of art as play cf. 396d3–e2, 598c1–4, 608a6–7 and Introduction p. 29. The description of tragedy as οὐ σπουδή ironically reminds us of the genre's claim to moral seriousness: cf. *Gorg.* 502b1–3, *Laws* 817a2, 838c4 and Arist. *Po.* 1449b24 ἔστιν οὖν τραγῳδία μίμησις πράξεως σπουδαίας. The reference to tragedies in epic verse is clearly to Homer, who was described at 595c1–2 (cf. 598d8) as πρῶτος διδάσκαλός τε καὶ ἡγεμών of all tragic poets. Homer thus frames the discussion of μίμησις from 595a–602c, which is devoted to the argument that all artists lack knowledge. Cornford 325 makes the pertinent point that throughout this section P. is concerned not with aesthetic matters, but with 'extravagant claims for the poets as moral teachers'. Homer, as the educator of the Greeks, is thus his prime target.

602c1–603b5

To what part of the soul does μίμησις *appeal? Painting, in that it relies for its effects on optical illusions, appeals to a part of the soul which is opposed to reason.*

c1–2 Πρὸς Διός ... τῆς ἀληθείας 'By Zeus, I said, this imitating, isn't it concerned with something third from the truth?' πρὸς Διός helps to mark a new stage in the argument. μέν is balanced by δέ at c4. τί is indefinite, the accent being thrown back from ἐστιν. The statement refers back to 597e3–8.   **c4–5 Πρὸς δὲ δὴ ... ἔχει:** lit. 'in relation to what sort of a thing of those in a human being does it have the power it has?' i.e. 'on what element in a human being does it exercise its power?'   **c6 Τοῦ ποίου ... λέγεις:** the word order perhaps emphasises Glaucon's perplexity.   **c10–11 Καὶ ταὐτά ... ἔξω:** refraction became a stock example to illustrate the unreliability of sense perception. See Cic. *Acad.* 2.19.   **c11–12 καὶ κοῖλά ... ὄψεως** 'concave and convex because sight is misled by colours'.   **c12–d1 καὶ πᾶσά τις ... ψυχῇ** 'and clearly there exists in our souls every kind of confusion (πᾶσά τις ταραχή) of this sort (αὕτη)'. Cf. *Prot.* 356d4–7 for the confusion caused by sense perceptions. For the language used here cf. 444b6–7 where injustice and other forms of wickedness are described as ταραχὴ καὶ πλάνη in the soul.

d1–4 ὧι δὴ ἡμῶν ... μηχαναί 'it's by exploiting this weakness in our nature that shadow-painting and conjuring and many other such tricks work their magic'. γοητείας οὐδὲν ἀπολείπει, lit. 'falls nothing short of wizardry'. Cf. 598d3. σκιαγραφία, developed by the Athenian painter Apollodorus in the late fifth century B.C., seems to have been a technique of using colours to render light and shade, possibly with perspective. The most important point for P.'s purposes here is that skiagraphic paintings were incomprehensible from close range, their subjects only becoming clear from a distance. Thus σκιαγραφία can be said to depend for its effect on optical illusion, providing P. with an appropriate illustration of the fallibility of human eyesight. See further Demand (1975) 5–20; Keuls (1978) 72–87. For θαυματοποιία see on 398a4–6. The word is used in connexion with the allegory of the Cave at 514b5, and of sophists at *Soph.* 235b5 and 268d2.   **d6 ἱστάναι** 'weighing'.   **d7–9 ὥστε μὴ ἄρχειν ... στῆσαν** 'so that what is apparently larger or smaller or more or heavier doesn't take control of our minds, but what has counted and measured or, if you like (ἢ καί) weighed'. i.e. counting, measuring and weighing enable us not to be taken in by appearances. The present infinitives μετρεῖν, ἀριθμεῖν and ἱστάναι at d6 refer to the activity or process of measuring, counting and weighing, whereas the aorist participles at d9 suggest an agent which performs these activities. On the importance of calculation as a check on the senses cf. *Euthyphr.* 7b–c, *Prot.* 356b–357b, *Phlb.* 55e; Xen. *Mem.* 1.1.9. For ἄρχειν see on 606d5.

e1–2 Ἀλλὰ μὴν ... ἔργον 'and this [i.e. τὸ λογισάμενον etc.] would be the task of the reasoning element in the soul'. ἀλλὰ μήν is progressive rather than adversative, as at 603a4 and cf. 388e5, 389b1. See Denniston (1954) 21–2. τὸ λογιστικόν, derived from λογίζεσθαι, as we are reminded here (cf. 525b with Adam *ad loc.*), was regularly used by P. of the reasoning element in the soul. In book 4 P. had distinguished between three parts of the soul, as we were reminded at 595a7–b1. But here the soul is divided simply between rational and irrational parts in a way which is not wholly consistent with the earlier tripartite division (see Else (1972) 46–9; Annas (1981) 338–40 and below on 603a7–8, 604d8–9, 605a8, 606d1–4). Nevertheless in both cases τὸ λογιστικόν is regarded as the superior element, whose task is to control the other parts.   **e4–6 Τούτωι δὲ πολλάκις ... περὶ ταὐτά:** lit. 'to this, when it has measured and shows that some things [ἄττα for τινά] are bigger or smaller than others, or the same, the contrary appearances are often presented about the same things at the same time', i.e. even when the rational element has performed its calculations, appearances may still contradict it: though we may know the correct size of an object because we have measured it, it still looks the same as it did before we measured it. Hence we can hold contrary opinions about the same object at the same time. For this interpretation see Penner (1971) 100, but for alternative possibilities see Adam *ad loc.* and 466–7. τούτωι strictly speaking implies that contradictory impressions appear to τὸ λογιστικόν, but since we are told in the next sentence that this is impossible, we must assume, with Halliwell, that τούτωι refers to the soul as a whole. Cf. 606a7–b2 and 440b–c.   **e8–9 Οὐκοῦν ἔφαμεν ...** **εἶναι** 'now we said that the same thing cannot have different opinions at the same time about the same object'. This principle was used at 436a–437d in connexion with the tripartite division of the soul, where it was argued that if the soul has opposing impulses or tendencies simultaneously, it must be because the soul itself is divided into parts. The principle is restated at 604b3–4.

603a1–2 Τὸ παρὰ τὰ μέτρα ... ταὐτόν 'so the part of the soul which contradicts the measurements would not be the same as the part which agrees with them'.   **a4–5 Ἀλλὰ μὴν ... τῆς ψυχῆς:** for ἀλλὰ μήν see on 602e1. For the association of λογισμός with the best part of the soul see 604d5 and cf. d6–9 above.   **a7–8 Τὸ ἄρα τούτωι ... ἡμῖν** 'so that which opposes it [the rational part] will be one of the inferior elements in us'. P. is vague about the nature of these inferior elements, and some have found it difficult to reconcile what is said here with the model of the soul proposed in book 4. Instead of the earlier tripartite division we now have a more straightforward distinction between a rational and a lower, irrational (ἀλόγιστον 604d9) element, which, unlike τὸ ἐπιθυμητικόν, is no longer specifically associated with desire. But we should not therefore assume that P. has abandoned the tripartite theory: for the purposes of his present argument he does not need to distinguish between the various aspects of the non-rational part of the soul. Nor should we assume that P. here attributes to the inferior part of the soul the power of forming opinions. As Penner (1971) 103 points out, δοξάζειν at 602e8 does not necessarily imply that the irrational part has done any thinking, but simply that it is taken in by appearances. The suggestion that the phrase τῶν φαύλων ... τι refers to an inferior aspect of the soul's *rational* part (see Murphy (1951) 239–43; Nehamas (1982) 64–6) seems unlikely in view of the derogatory terms in which it is described at a12–b1 and b4 below, and is incompatible with 605a9–b6.   **a10–b2 ἡ γραφικὴ ... ἀληθεῖ** 'painting and imitative art in general produces work which is far removed from the truth, and associates with that element in us which is far removed from wisdom, and is its companion and friend for no healthy or true purpose'. The personification contained in ἑταίρα and φίλη prepares us for the image of sexual union at b4. See also on 607e4–6. ὑγιεῖ hints at the body/soul analogy, implying that μίμησις is dangerous for the health of the soul. Cf. 595b, 605c7.

b4 Φαύλη ... μιμητική: the enclosing word order, the repetition of φαύλη ... φαύλωι ... φαῦλα and the sexual metaphor itself emphasise the tawdriness of all aspects of mimetic art. The same image is used of the bastard offspring spawned by spurious philosophers at 496a. For the image of breeding cf. 597e3–4. Asmis (1992) 356 notes that the language S. uses here is a negative version of Diotima's at *Symp.* 208e5–209e4, where the image of pregnancy and birth is used to describe the spiritual offspring of souls who love beauty.

603b6–605c5

We must not rely on the analogy with painting, but consider poetry independently to see which part of the soul it acts upon. Poetry encourages us to indulge in excessive displays of emotion which are contrary to the dictates of reason. Poetry therefore appeals to the non-rational part of the soul.

b7 τὴν ἀκοήν ... ὀνομάζομεν: for the emphasis on poetry as an oral activity cf. 387b2–4, 595b6, 605c10–11, 608a3, b1, and see Gentili (1988) 4–5.   **b9–c1 Μὴ τοίνυν ... μιμητική** 'let us not simply rely on the analogy from painting, but let us approach directly that part of the mind with which poetic imitation consorts'. For διάνοια used of the soul as a whole cf. 595b6. These words indicate that P. is aware that the analogy with painting has not yet proved anything about poetry.

c2 φαῦλον ἢ σπουδαῖον: πότερον should be supplied before φαῦ-λον. Since μίμησις, and particularly poetic μίμησις, has already been described as οὐ σπουδή at 602b8, the answer to this question would seem to be a foregone conclusion.   **c4–5 πράττοντας ... πράξ-εις:** βιαίους, 'forced', is a two-termination adjective here, agreeing with πράξεις. The emphasis on 'people doing things' suggests narra-tive and dramatic poetry (cf. 396c6, although in that section S. was more concerned with λέξις than with πρᾶξις). There are clearly par-allels between this passage and Arist. *Po.* 1448a1, but Else's sug-gestion (1972) 44–5 that the *Poetics* passage came first is refuted by Halliwell *ad loc.* and 195. Voluntary and involuntary actions (e.g. facing up to disasters such as injury or death) were discussed at 399a–c in connexion with the musical modes appropriate to each category. One difference between the treatment of poetry and that of painting, noted by Nehamas (1982) 66–7, is that whereas the dis-cussion of painting is concerned only with the *effects* of painting on the spectator (602d1–4 cf. 598c1–4), the discussion of poetry from 603c4–604e6 centres primarily on its content: conflicts of the soul provide poetry with its subject-matter (603c10–d3, 604e1–6).   **c7–8 μή τι ἄλλο ἦι παρὰ ταῦτα;** 'Can there be any other besides these?' Goodwin (1929) 93 cites this as an example of μή with the subjunctive 'in a cautious question with a negative answer implied', referring to *Phaed.* 64c and *Parm.* 163d as parallels. Others regard it as a regular use of μή with the subjunctive expressing a cautious as-sertion, and translate 'I suspect that there is something else besides these points', but this does not give good sense. Both Adam's edition and Burnet's Oxford Classical Text adopt Ast's emendation of ἦι to ἦν, which must be translated 'it was nothing beyond this, was it?', but the imperfect is difficult to explain. On the whole, therefore, it seems better to retain the best attested reading and accept Good-win's explanation.   **c10–d1 ὁμονοητικῶς ... διάκειται:** on the significance of this notion see on 380d5–6.

d1–3 ἢ ὥσπερ κατὰ τὴν ὄψιν ... αὐτὸς αὑτῶι: cf. 602c7–d1. For the metaphor of στάσις cf. 440b3 and e5, 442d1, 444b1, 560a1 where the strife in the soul is described in similar language. See further on 605b5. Despite this assertion it is difficult to see how the conflict engendered in the soul by the warring emotions of grief and joy is

parallel to that produced by the contradictory opinions which arise
in the case of optical illusions. See Annas (1981) 338–9.   **d5 τοῖς
ἄνω λόγοις:** the existence of conflicting motives in the individual
was analysed at 435e–441c, and provided the main argument for the
division of the soul into three parts.

e3–5 Ἀνήρ ... τῶν ἄλλων: cf. 387d5–e8. ῥᾷστα ... τῶν ἄλλων
'much more easily than the rest'.   **e8 μετριάσει** 'observe due
measure' (Cornford's translation). Cf. a4 above where measurement
is a function of the best part of the soul, and see further on 605a9–
b2.

604a1 τόδε νῦν is somewhat abrupt, but is preferable to τὸ δὲ νῦν,
the reading of most MSS, which involves taking τό as a demonstra-
tive.   **a10–b1 Οὐκοῦν ... τὸ πάθος** 'Now that which urges him
to resist is reason and custom, but that which pulls him towards his
sorrows is the experience itself'. Halliwell *ad loc.* suggests that,
though νόμος should not be interpreted in a strictly legal sense here,
P.'s use of the term in this context may well have been influenced by
the existence of funerary legislation at Athens, allegedly going back
to Solon, which attempted to control public displays of mourning
(see e.g. Cic. *De leg.* 2.64–6; Plut. *Sol.* 12.5; R. Garland, 'The well-
ordered corpse: an investigation into the motives behind Greek
funerary legislation', *B.I.C.S.* 36 (1989) 1–15; S. C. Humphreys, *The
family, women and death*, 2nd edn (Michigan 1993) 85–6).

b3–4 Ἐναντίας ... εἶναι 'Since there are contrary impulses in the
man concerning the same thing at the same time, we say that there
must be two elements in him.' Most MSS omit ἐν, which makes the
point more precise ('the two principles do not merely belong to the
man, but are *in* him' – Adam, *ad loc.*), but it could easily have fallen
out after φαμέν. For the same argument cf. 602e8–9.   **b6–7 ἧι
... ἐξηγεῖται** 'wherever custom leads'.   **b10–c3 ὡς οὔτε δῆλου
... τὸ λυπεῖσθαι** 'since the good and bad in such matters are not
clear, and taking it badly does not help anyone in the future; nothing
in human affairs is worth taking very seriously, and grieving prevents
us from attaining the very thing that we need as quickly as possible
in these circumstances'. For the mixture of genitive and accusative
absolutes cf. Thuc. 7.25.9. The use of οὐ rather than μή in the
clauses after ὡς shows that these are not suppositions but facts. ἐν

αὐτοῖς at c1 refers back to ταῖς συμφοραῖς at b10. For the view that nothing in human affairs is worth taking very seriously cf. 387d6, 486a8–10, and see the remarks of Murdoch (1977) 13.

c4 Τίνι is dative, like τούτωι, after ἐμποδών.   **c5–7** ὥσπερ ἐν πτώσει ... ἔχειν 'as with the fall of the dice, to regulate his affairs in relation to what has befallen in the way that reason decides is best'. P. alludes, in what is evidently a proverbial expression, to the game of κυβεία, in which the player had to place as skilfully as possible the pieces which fell to him by the luck of the dice. See LSJ s.v. τίθημι A. vii. 2, and for further discussion see Fraenkel (1962) on Aesch. *Ag.* 32 and 33. The image plays on the idea of life as a game (cf. 604c1), with τὰ πεπτωκότα suggesting that the misfortunes that befall us are no more significant than the fall of the dice. For the phrase ὁ λόγος αἱρεῖ cf. 440b5, 607b3, and e.g. Hdt. 2.33, 3.45.   **c8** παῖδας ... πληγέντος: cf. Demosth. *Phil.* 1.40 where Demosthenes compares the war with Philip to barbarians fighting: when one of them is struck he always covers the blow (ἀεὶ τῆς πληγῆς ἔχεται), and if someone hits him in another place, his hands are there.

d1 γίγνεσθαι πρός 'to attend to'.   **d2** ἰατρικῆι ... ἀφανίζοντα 'banishing lamentation with healing'. For the importance of medical imagery in relation to the soul see on 389b2–4 and cf. 595b6.   **d5–6** τὸ μὲν βέλτιστον ... ἕπεσθαι: the λογισμός is that suggested by νόμος at b9–c3, cf. a10 and c5–d2. The language echoes 603a4–5, linking what is said here with the earlier discussion of painting.   **d8–9** Τὸ δὲ πρός ... ἔχον αὐτῶν 'But the element which drives us towards the recollection of suffering and towards lamentation, and which can never have enough of these things ...'. This element does not correspond precisely with either of the two lower elements of the soul according to the tripartite model, but seems to be a mixture of both. Grief would be an emotion particularly associated with τὸ θυμοειδές (see on e1–2 below), whereas insatiability, laziness and cowardice would be characteristic of τὸ ἐπιθυμητικόν. But the crucial point (emphasised by the word order) is that this element is irrational.

e1–2 Οὐκοῦν ... τὸ ἀγανακτητικόν 'Now the one, the irascible element, lends itself to much and varied imitation'. The prominence of Achilles in the discussion of poetry in books 2 and 3 (see on 379d2–8,

386a6–7, c5–7) illustrates the point: volatile characters like him are much more exciting poetic subjects than the calm, wise man. Adam *ad loc.* notes that τὸ ἀγανακτητικόν can be seen as a 'degenerate variety' of τὸ θυμοειδές. At 411a–c, when discussing the nature of the musical education that the young guardians should receive, S. argued that the spirited element, if properly trained, makes men courageous. But if men indulge excessively in 'sweet and soft and mournful (θρηνώδεις cf. θρηνωιδίαν at d2 above) harmonies', they weaken their spirit, and become 'quarrelsome and irritable and full of bad temper' (ἀκράχολοι οὖν καὶ ὀργίλοι ἀντὶ θυμοειδοῦς γεγένηνται, δυσκολίας ἔμπλεωι). Cf. 440a–d for the connexion between anger (ὀργή) and the spirited part of the soul. For further discussion of τὸ θυμοειδές see J. Gosling, *Plato* (London 1973) 41–51.   **e2–3 παραπλήσιον … αὑτῶι** 'always at one with itself'. For the importance of this principle see on 380d5–6 and cf. 603c10. This wise, calm character is the one S. has in mind at 401b1–3, where he says that poets must either portray the image of good character in their poems or not write at all. But the question of what such poetry would be like in practice is not one that S. addresses.   **e3–6 οὔτε μιμουμένου … αὐτοῖς γίγνεται** 'nor, when it is imitated, is it easy to understand … for the imitation is of an experience which is foreign to them'. μιμουμένου is genitive absolute. The contrast between the consistency of the wise man and the variety and multiplicity of the inferior type is brought out at 397a–c. There too (397d6–8) S. recognises that the latter is far more attractive to the motley crowd than the former. Cf. 492b–c for the evil influence of crowds.

605a2–6 Ὁ δὴ μιμητικὸς … εὐμίμητον εἶναι 'So clearly the imitative poet is not by nature inclined towards this element in the soul, and his wisdom is not set on pleasing it if he wants to win popularity among the crowd, but towards the irascible and varied character, because it is easy to imitate.' For πέφυκε πρός cf. πεποίηται πρός at 598b1. οὐ has to be taken with πέπηγεν as well as with πέφυκε. For the view that poetry which appeals to the masses is bound to be worthless cf. 602b2–4, 493a–d and see further on 397d6–8. The part of the soul to which poetry appeals combines the characteristics of both spirit and appetite, since τὸ ἀγανακτητικόν is associated primarily with the former (see on e1–2 above), τὸ ποικίλον with the latter (cf. 580d11 which refers to the πολυειδία (diversity) of the lowest element in the soul, and cf. ποικίλου at 588c7). The phrase ὁ μιμητικὸς ποιητής (cf. 605b7) suggests that S. is focusing attention on the poet who imitates versatile characters such as the one described in book 3 (398a1–3, cf. 397a–b) whom S. has in mind at e1–2 above. It would be possible, therefore, to infer that there is another kind of non-imitative poet to whom these criticisms would not apply (see on 607a3–7). But if there is S. remains notably silent on the type of poetry that such a poet would compose.

a8–9 Οὐκοῦν δικαίως ... τῶι ζωγράφωι: τιθεῖμεν ἀντίστροφον lit. 'set him as corresponding to'. Cf. 603b9–10. The intervening discussion, P. claims, has proved that the analogy between poetry and painting is justified.   **a9–b2 καὶ γὰρ ... ὡμοίωται: καὶ ταύτηι** (b1–2) 'in this respect too'. The poet is the counterpart of the painter because (a) his products are inferior in relation to the truth (597e3–8, 598b1–d5, 600e4–601a2, 602b6–10) and (b) because he 'associates with the same part of the soul, which is not the best, but something else (ἕτερον)'. The nature of the part of the soul with which painting and poetry associate is left somewhat vague. At 602c4–603a8 it was established that painting acts on some inferior part of the soul which is taken in by appearances (602c10–d4) and which opposes the calculations of the best element (603a4–8). It seems to have little in common with τὸ ἐπιθυμητικόν, the lowest element of the soul according to the tripartite model. When it comes to poetry P. states that conflicts in the soul are its main subject-matter, and he specifically alludes to the previous discussion of such conflicts, on the basis of which the tripartite division of the soul was postulated (603d3–7). In the case of a good man who struggles to overcome the grief he feels for a son who has died, such a man will 'observe due measure in his grief' (μετριάσει at 603e8), and will follow the calculation which the best part of his soul makes (604d5–6). A parallel is thus set up between the calculation which a good man will make when he is grieving, i.e. a calculation in relation to emotions, and a calculation which involves the literal measuring and weighing of objects. But, we might object, the measurement of emotions and the measurement of objects are not parallel. P.'s notion of the inferior element of the soul in this section is imprecise, and it is not at all clear how we are to relate what is said here to the psychology of book 4. But the important point is that the inferior element, however it is defined, is opposed to reason. Whether we are talking about optical illusions exploited by painting, or the emotional conflict depicted and aroused by poetry, both painting and poetry appeal to the irrational element in the soul, and this is the point which P. wishes to emphasise.

b2–3 καὶ οὕτως … πόλιν: παραδεχοίμεθα sc. τὸν μιμητικὸν ποιητήν. These words refer back to 595a1–6, ἐν δίκηι (cf. δικαίως at a8 above) emphasising that the original decision to exclude poetry has now been justified. Despite the extended analogy between poet and painter, it is nowhere explicitly stated that painting too should be banished; but painting did not attack the emotions of 'the many' as poetry did in classical Athens.   **b3–5 τοῦτο … τῆς ψυχῆς** 'this part of the soul', referring back to ἕτερον τοιοῦτον … τῆς ψυχῆς. But poetry, unlike painting, does more than simply associate with this part of the soul (ὁμιλεῖν at 605b1, cf. 603b1): it arouses it and nurtures it, and by strengthening it it destroys the rational part of the soul. It is this emotive power of poetry which makes it so much more dangerous than painting, and which is ultimately responsible for its banishment. See on 601b4.   **b5–6 ὥσπερ ἐν πόλει … φθείρηι:** this parallelism between individual and state is central to the argument of the *Republic*; indeed the ideal state itself is constructed in order to find justice on a large scale before looking for its counterpart in the soul of the individual (368c–369b, 434d–435c2, 545b, 577c–578b). The analogy assumes that the structure of the psyche is parallel to the structure of the *polis*, and vice versa. Cf. 435e–436a, 544d–e, and see next note. So here, just as society degenerates when power is given to bad men, while the better ones are ruined (a process described at 555b2–562a where oligarchy declines into democracy; see also the description of the tyrant at 568a), so the soul is corrupted when the base element is strengthened at the expense of the best. The parallel is reinforced by the use of the term χαριεστέρους to describe the better men in the state, a verbal echo of 602d7 where measuring, counting and weighing are described as χαριέσταται βοήθειαι in relation to the soul.   **b7–8 ταὐτὸν …**

ἐμποιεῖν: ταὐτόν 'in the same way' is adverbial. For the phrase πολιτείαν ... ψυχῆι cf. 590e where P. underlines the importance of
education in establishing a 'constitution' in children just as in the
state (ὥσπερ ἐν πόλει πολιτείαν), 608b1, and for political language
used of the soul cf. 603d3. For P. psyche and *polis* are inter-
dependent, each being a product of the other. Here it is claimed
that the imitative poet sets up a bad constitution in the soul of each
individual; but at 568a–d tragic poets, and particularly Euripides,
are castigated for seducing great crowds with their beautiful, persuasive voices and literally drawing constitutions towards tyrannies
and democracies (εἰς τυραννίδας τε καὶ δημοκρατίας ἕλκουσι τὰς
πολιτείας). The more corrupt individuals become, the more corrupt
will be society, and vice versa; and the more corrupt the society, the
better will poets thrive: soul and state are bound up together in a
dynamic interrelationship in which the poet plays a vital part. For
this view see further Lear (1992), but for a different interpretation of
the state/soul parallel see B. Williams, 'The analogy of city and soul
in Plato's *Republic* ' in E. N. Lee, A. P. D. Mourelatos, R. M. Rorty,
(edd.), *Exegesis and argument: studies in Greek philosophy presented to Gregory
Vlastos*, *Phronesis* supplementary volume 1 (1973) 196–206, and Annas
(1981) 301–5. For τὸν μιμητικὸν ποιητήν see on 605a2.   **b8–c3**
τῶι ἀνοήτωι ... σμικρά: by claiming that the poet panders to the
senseless part (τῶι ἀνοήτωι) of the soul, which cannot distinguish
between greater and less, P. reminds us again of the analogy with
painting (cf. 602c1–603b5). But it is difficult to see how the part of
the soul which perceives objects and their representations in painting
can be nurtured and strengthened by poetry. See on a9–b2 above.

c3–4 εἴδωλα ... ἀφεστῶτα qualifies τὸν μιμητικὸν ποιητήν at b7
and restates the point made at a9–10, (cf. 598b6–8, 599a7), the repetition of εἴδωλα εἰδωλοποιοῦντα and the alliteration of πόρρω
πάνυ giving the whole phrase an emphatic ring.

605c6–607a9

*The gravest charge against poetry is that it corrupts even the best of us. By fos-
tering and encouraging feelings which ought to be suppressed poetry weakens the*

control of reason and makes us slaves to our desires. Despite their appeal, Homer and the other poets must be banished from the ideal state because of the drastic effects they have on the constitution of the human soul.

605c6 Οὐ μέντοι ... αὐτῆς 'But we haven't yet laid the greatest charge against it', sc. ποιήσεως, with the emphasis on μέγιστον. What follows concerns poetry alone, the legal language (cf. 607b1) suggesting that poetry itself is on trial.　**c6–8 τὸ γὰρ καὶ ... πάνδεινόν που:** cf. 595b5–7, and for the implications of πάνδεινον see on 596c3. For other examples of που at the end of a sentence see Denniston (1954) 493. The 'very few' good men who will be able to resist the corrupting power of poetry are those who are true philosophers. Cf. 498a7, 499b4, 606b6.　**c9 Τί δ' οὐ μέλλει,** sc. πάνδεινον ἔσεσθαι. Cf. 394e7. εἴπερ γε δρᾶι αὐτό suggests that Glaucon feels some doubt as to whether poetry does in fact have such power.　**c10–11 ἀκροώμενοι ... τραγωιδοποιῶν:** for the emphasis on listening see on 603b7, and for Homer and the tragic poets see on 595c1–2.

d1–2 τινὰ τῶν ἡρώων ... κοπτομένους: cf. 387d1–2. Adam sees here a contrast between a ῥῆσις or set speech, and κομμοί, the lyric laments between chorus and one or more actors in tragedy, which were sung; but the emphasis seems rather to be on excessive lamentation of any kind. μακρὰν ῥῆσιν ἀποτείνοντα suggests a speech drawn out to unnecessary lengths (for parallels see Fraenkel (1962) on Aesch. *Ag.* 916, where Agamemnon caustically remarks that Clytaemnestra's speech of welcome was long drawn out to suit his absence). Or it might refer to the 'big speech' for the lead role(s) which all tragedies exemplify. ἄιδοντας does not necessarily imply singing (see on *Ion* 532d7–8 and cf. 388d7 θρήνους ἂν ἄιδοι καὶ ὀδυρμούς). Taken together the words ἄιδοντάς τε καὶ κοπτομένους suggest a wallowing in misery of the kind that was discussed at 387d–388e, where all the examples were taken from the *Iliad*. For the transition from the singular to the generalising plural (τινὰ ... ἄιδοντας), see Adam on 347a.　**d3–5 χαίρομέν ... οὕτω διαθῆι:** the pleasure we experience in listening to poetry (cf. 387b2–3, 601b1) is here specifically associated with its power to make us feel the painful emotions of the characters which it portrays, for which see *Ion* 535e2–3. For συμπάσχοντες cf. Arist. *Pol.* 1340a12 ἔτι δὲ ἀκροώ-

μενοι τῶν μιμήσεων γίνονται πάντες συμπαθεῖς. For the view that
we positively enjoy the weeping induced by tragedy cf. *Phil.* 48a5–6
τάς γε τραγικὰς θεωρήσεις, ὅταν ἅμα χαίροντες κλάωσι, and *Laws*
800d where P. says that we judge the excellence of a poet in relation
to his ability to affect us in this way. The paradox that the depiction
of pain can be a source of pleasure, was already recognised by
Homer (see e.g. *Od.* 15.399–400, 23.301–8). Macleod (1982) 4–8 discusses this phenomenon, observing that the poet's ability to make us
empathise with the feelings of another corresponds to the Greek notion of pity as an emotion aroused by the realisation that the sufferings of another are such as we might suffer, or indeed have suffered,
ourselves (Arist. *Rhet.* 1385b and cf. Soph. *Aj.* 121–6, *O.C.* 560–68;
Hdt. 1.86.6).   **d8 ἡσυχίαν ἄγειν:** cf. 604b9–10.

e1–2 ὡς τοῦτο μὲν ... ἐπηινοῦμεν 'because this is characteristic of a
man, whereas that which we were just now praising, is characteristic
of a woman'. For the association of women with lamentation see on
387e10–11.   **e4–6 Ἦ καλῶς ... ἐπαινεῖν:** 'Is this praise right? Is it
right not to feel disgusted, but to feel pleasure and give praise when
you see the sort of man you would despise and be ashamed to be
yourself?' τὸ ὁρῶντα ... ἐπαινεῖν is in apposition to Ἦ καλῶς ...
ἔχει. Cf. 604a7–8.

606a1 Ναί ... σκοποίης 'That's right, especially if you look at it in
this way'.   **a3–7 τὸ βίαι κατεχόμενον ... χαῖρον:** lit. 'the part
which is forcibly kept in check then [i.e. ὅταν δὲ οἰκεῖόν τινι ἡμῶν
κῆδος γένηται] in our own misfortunes, which hungers after tears
and having its fill of lamentation, since it is the sort of thing which
naturally desires these things, this is the part which the poets then
[i.e. on those occasions] satisfy and please'. ἐπιθυμεῖν and the meta-
phorical use of πεπεινηκός clearly link this part of the soul with τὸ
ἐπιθυμητικόν. See e.g. 439d6–8. The difficulty of controlling this
part is brought out by βίαι.   **a7–b1 τὸ δὲ φύσει ... θρηνώδους
τούτου:** cf. 604c9–d2 where lamentation was described as a disease
which the best part (the rational part cf. 603a4–5, 604d5–6) must
accustom (ἐθίζειν 604c9) the soul to cure, ἰατρικῆι θρηνωιδίαν ἀφανίζοντα (604d2). The training of the soul was, of course, the function of the entire system of παιδεία discussed in the earlier books.
See further Gill (1985) and above p. 133. The image of the best

part relaxing its guard against this desire for lamentation picks up ἐνδόντες ἡμᾶς αὐτούς at 605d3 and underlines the difficulty of the task, cf. βίαι at a3 above.

b1–3 ἅτε ἀλλότρια … ἐλεεῖν 'because it [τὸ βέλτιστον] is looking at sufferings which are not its own, and if a man claiming to be good laments out of season, there is no disgrace to oneself in praising and pitying him'. θεωροῦν (which suggests a spectator) is nominative, αἰσχρὸν ὄν is the accusative absolute. With ἑαυτῶι there is a shift from the best part of the soul to the person as a whole, as explained by Adam *ad loc.* For ἐπαινεῖν and ἐλεεῖν cf. d3–5, e6.   **b3–5 ἀλλ’ ἐκεῖνο … ποιήματος:** lit. 'but he thinks that thing a gain, pleasure, and wouldn't consent to being deprived of it by despising the whole poem'. The word order emphasises ἡδονήν. The only way to guard against the corrupting effects of poetry (cf. the φάρμακον required at 595b6) is to despise it altogether, but this people will not do because poetry gives them pleasure. P.'s puritanism (on which see Murdoch (1977) 12–14) is epitomised in this statement.   **b5–8 λογίζεσθαι γὰρ … τὰ οἰκεῖα** 'For I think few people are capable [lit. 'there is a share to few'] of reasoning that the enjoyment we derive from other people's experiences inevitably affects our own.' For ἀπολαύειν cf. 395d1. The point is that the process of emotional identification involved in performing or listening to poetry has serious psychological consequences. Cf. 393c5–6, 395d1–3. The ὀλίγοι are those referred to at 605c7–8.   **b7–8 θρέψαντα γὰρ … κατέχειν** 'for it is not easy to restrain pity in one's own sufferings when a person has nurtured it and made it strong on those of others'. This view contrasts markedly with that of Aristotle, who, in answer to Plato, maintains that tragedy, by arousing the emotions of pity and fear in its audience, brings about a beneficial κάθαρσις of those emotions. (*Po.* 1449b and for discussion of the concept of κάθαρσις see Halliwell (1986) 184–201, 350–6).

c2–5 Ἆρ’ οὖν οὐχ … ἐν τοῖς ἐλεόις 'Well, doesn't the same argument apply to the ridiculous too? In relation to jokes which you would be ashamed to make yourself, but which you very much enjoy hearing in comedy or in private and don't despise as being morally bad, aren't you doing the same thing as in the pitiable cases?' ἄν, which might equally well have been written ἃ ἄν, is Schneider's correction of the ἄν of the MSS. ἅ has no antecedent in the main clause and is best regarded as an adverbial accusative. ἄν has to be taken both with the potential optative αἰσχύνοιο, and with the indefinite subjunctives χαρῇς and μισῇς. For discussion of the text see Adam *ad loc.* and 467–8. αἰσχύνοιο picks up αἰσχύνοιτ' ἄν at 604a7, reinforcing the parallelism between excessive grief and excessive laughter. The section as a whole expands on 388e5–389a7, where indulgence in laughter had already been designated as unsuitable behaviour for the good man.   **c5–9 ὃ γὰρ τῶι λόγωι ... κωμωιδοποιὸς γενέσθαι** 'For that which you used to hold in check in yourself through reason when you wanted to play the fool, being afraid of a reputation for buffoonery, you then release; having made it vigorous there [i.e. at the theatre], you don't notice that you have often been carried away in your private life so that you have become a comedian.' The first αὖ at c5 connects the argument about laughter with the argument about tears, the second, τότ' αὖ at c7, contrasts ἀνίης with κατεῖχες, as explained by Adam *ad loc.* ἔλαθες is gnomic aorist, denoting a general truth or habitual action. Cf. 596a1. The sentence reiterates the argument at a3–b8 above, the language carefully mirroring that of the earlier passage. For τῶι λόγωι at c5 cf. λόγωι at a8; for κατεῖχες at c6 cf. κατεχόμενον at a3 and κατέχειν at b8; for ἀνίης at c7 cf. ἀνίησιν at a8; for νεανικὸν ποιήσας at c7 cf. θρέψαντα ... ἰσχυρόν at b7; for ἐν τοῖς οἰκείοις at c8 cf. τὰ οἰκεῖα at b7. The βωμολόχος, according to Arist. *Eth. Nic.* 1128a–b, cf. 1108a24, is the man who cannot resist a joke, however inappropriate it may be, and whose humour is of the coarse and offensive type particularly associated with Old Comedy.

d1–4 Καὶ περὶ ἀφροδισίων ... ἐργάζεται 'And concerning sex and anger and all the desires and pains and pleasures in the soul, which, we say, accompany all our actions, the same argument applies in that poetic imitation produces similar effects on us.' ὅτι, like ὅτι at c2 depends on ὁ αὐτὸς λόγος which must be supplied from c2. ἐργάζομαι takes a double accusative. Anger, according to the tripartite theory, was characteristic of the spirited part of the soul, τὸ θυμοειδές, but here all emotions are treated together as being simply opposed to the rational part.   **d4–5 τρέφει γὰρ ... αὐτά:** δέον is accusative absolute, ἄρχοντα is neuter plural, agreeing with ταῦτα.

For τρέφει cf. θρέψαντα at 606b7, and for ἄρδουσα cf. 550b2. For the metaphor of ruling cf. 602d7, and see especially 444d8–11 where it is said that justice is produced in the soul when its various parts are put in their natural relations of authority and subordination: οὐκοῦν … τὸ δικαιοσύνην ἐμποιεῖν τὰ ἐν τῆι ψυχῆι κατὰ φύσιν καθιστάναι κρατεῖν τε καὶ κρατεῖσθαι ὑπ' ἀλλήλων, τὸ δὲ ἀδικίαν παρὰ φύσιν ἄρχειν τε καὶ ἄρχεσθαι ἄλλο ὑπ' ἄλλου; Poetry is so dangerous precisely because it subverts this order.   **d6–7 ἵνα βελτίους … γιγνώμεθα:** this reminds us that one of the primary purposes of the *Republic* is to demonstrate that living the right kind of life makes people happy. See further on 392b1–4.

e1–5 Ὁμήρου … ζῆν: Ὁμήρου ἐπαινέταις are here simply 'admirers of Homer', but see *Ion* 536d3 where the phrase may have a more specific meaning. For Homer as the educator of Greece see Introduction p. 19, 600a9 and, for the implied comparison between Homer and the sophists as educators, see 600c2–d4.

607a2–3 Ὅμηρον … τραγωιδοποιῶν: ποιητικός and ποιητικώτερος were used of Homer's poetry at 387b3–4, but this is the only instance of the superlative in P., perhaps with a hint of ironic exaggeration. Cf. *Soph.* 234c7 quoted at 598d3–4 above, and see further Goldhill (1991) 170. For Homer as the first of the tragedians cf. 595c1–2, 598d8, and see on 398b1–2.   **a3–5 εἰδέναι … εἰς πόλιν:** lit. [you must] 'know that only as much of poetry as consists of hymns to the gods and encomia to good men is to be admitted into the city'. For encomia see on *Ion* 534c3 and cf. 599b7 above. Despite the fact that, according to the arguments of book 10 *all* poetry is by definition μίμησις, and all poets from Homer onwards are condemned as worthless imitators of images (see especially 600e4–601c), S. is now prepared to accept some kinds of poetry into the state after all. How can we justify this discrepancy? Some claim that there is no discrepancy. For example, Adam *ad loc.*, maintains that the quarrel is 'not with Imitation as such, but only with Imitation of the false and immoral', and connects this passage with 398b1–3, where S. says that they will be content with the more austere and less pleasing poet who would imitate the λέξις of the good man in accordance with guidelines laid down by the rulers. For arguments against this interpretation see on 595a5. The problem arises partly from the fact that the term μίμησις is used in two different senses. On the metaphysical level, as argued in book 10, all poetry is μίμησις and therefore worthless, because poets have no knowledge of their subject-matter and produce only a pale imitation of what is truly real. But on the stylistic level, in the sense in which the term μίμησις was used in book 3, although μίμησις is generally thought to be a bad thing, there are certain limited circumstances in which it would be acceptable. Perhaps it is the kind of poetry outlined at 398b1–3, referred to above, that S. is thinking of here. If so he is contradicting his own statement at 595a5 that they were right to have excluded mimetic poetry from the state. It is not entirely clear that hymns to the gods and encomia to good men need to be mimetic in the stylistic sense defined in book 3. So it might be that S. here envisages the possibility of non-imitative poetry (i.e. narrative), which does not yet exist, but which could be composed for strictly defined purposes. Hymns to the gods were included in S.'s earliest society (372b7–8); 459e5–460a2 refers to hymns which will be needed for the religious ceremonies when brides and grooms are brought together; at 468d9 virtuous men and women will be rewarded with hymns composed in their honour. These scattered references give some idea of the kind of role which poetry might be allowed to play in the ideal state. Cf. *Laws* 801e1–4 where hymns to the gods and encomia to heroes will similarly be permitted. What is clear, however, is that no existing poetry is acceptable (600e4–601c): all the great works of Greek literature are to be excluded. As Gould (1992) 17 puts it, P.'s 'aim is directed not at the marginal, the allegedly outrageous fringe art-works that offend his moral sensibility, but at the entire literary heritage, including all its master-works, from the *Iliad* onwards to the greatest masterpieces of fifth-century tragedy'. Such poetry as is allowed will be 'tailor-made for special occasions' (Nehamas (1982) 69) and will be strictly subordinate to the purposes of the rulers.   **a5–6 εἰ δὲ τὴν ἡδυσμένην ... ἔπεσιν:** τὴν ἡδυσμένην Μοῦσαν, 'the sweetened Muse' is poetry which is pleasurable (for the dangers of which cf. 387b2–4, 397d6–8, 606b4), but with the implication that the 'seasoning' or 'sweetening', i.e. metre, rhythm and melody, disguises what is really there. Cf. 601b1–4; *Gorg* 463–5 for the analogy between rhetoric and cookery, and 502c3 where tragedy too is described as κολακεία; Arist. *Po.* 1460b2 where it is said that Homer disguises the absurdities of his plot by flavouring it with other good features, τοῖς ἄλλοις ἀγαθοῖς ὁ ποιητὴς ἀφανίζει ἡδύνων τὸ ἄτοπον. μέλεσιν, 'lyrics' must refer primarily to the lyric metres of tragedy, since there has been no mention of other kinds of lyric poetry in the preceding discussion.   **a6–8 ἡδονή ... λόγου** 'pleasure and pain will rule in the city instead of custom and the rational principle which in every instance seems in general best'. For λόγος and νόμος as guiding principles see 604a10–c7, and for the political threat posed by poetry cf. 605b2–c4. In the *Laws* (801c8–d4) P. states categorically that a poet should compose nothing that is contrary to the laws and customs of society (τὸν ποιητὴν παρὰ τὰ τῆς πόλεως νόμιμα καὶ δίκαια ἢ καλὰ ἢ ἀγαθὰ μηδὲν ποεῖν ἄλλο), and advocates strict censorship to achieve this aim. Goldhill (1991) 175 points out that the adverb κοινῆι ('in general' or 'in common') in the present passage is a reminder of the background of democratic Athens against which the *Republic* is set, and suggests that the customary formula for recording state decisions, ἔδοξε τῆι βουλῆι καὶ τῶι δημῶι, may add a further layer of meaning to κοινῆι δόξαντος.

607b–608b10

If anyone were able to prove that poetry is not only pleasurable, but also beneficial, we would be happy to welcome it back into the city. But as it is, we must renounce our passion for poetry because it has no serious claim to truth and has a destructive effect on the human soul.

b1–3 Ταῦτα δή ... τοιαύτην οὖσαν: lit. 'Let this defence have been made by us recalling about poetry, that we banished it then from our city with good reason, such being its nature'. The perfect imperative suggests a note of finality summing up P.'s ἀπολογία or defence of his banishment of poetry. Cf. e.g. Hdt. 1.92. For the legal metaphor cf. 605c6, 607d3. τότε refers to 398a–b.   **b3 ὁ γὰρ ... ἤιρει:** cf. 604c7.   **b5 καταγνῶι** 'accuse', followed by the genitive of the person with accusative of the grounds of accusation, continues the legal language.   **b5–6 παλαιὰ μέν ... ποιητικῆι:** examples of philosophers criticising poets are not difficult to find. See e.g. Xenophanes' criticisms of Homer, discussed in the notes to 377d4, 378d6–7 and 380d5–6, and cf. Heraclit. B 42 and 57 D–K. But there is less evidence for poets attacking philosophers. Aristophanes' portrayal of Socrates in the *Clouds* is, of course, an example, but Adam is right to point out that we should not take παλαιά too literally: P. is anxious to establish the antiquity of the quarrel between philosophy and poetry, but one suspects that it was largely of his own making. See Nussbaum (1986) 123–4 on the lack of distinction between the two before P.'s time.　**b6–c3 καὶ γὰρ ἡ ... ἐναντιώσεως τούτων** 'for example, that "yapping bitch barking at her master", and "great in the empty talk of fools", and "the crowd of know-alls holding sway", and "the subtle thinkers" that they after all "starve", and there are countless other signs of the old opposition between these [i.e. philosophy and poetry]'. We do not know the source of any of these quotations, but presumably they are all attacks by poets on philosophy. *Laws* 967c–d refers to attacks on philosophers for their atheistic views about the heavenly bodies (Anaxagoras must have been a prime target, cf. *Phaed.* 97b–c), and says that poets in particular joined in the abuse, comparing philosophers to 'bitches howling in vain' (καὶ δὴ καὶ λοιδορήσεις γε ἐπῆλθον ποιηταῖς, τοὺς φιλοσοφοῦντας κυσὶ ματαίαις ἀπεικάζοντας χρωμέναισιν ὑλακαῖς). There is some uncertainty about the text of the third quotation. διάσοφος is otherwise unknown, though διασοφίζεσθαι occurs at Ar. *Birds* 1619. Adam suggests κράτων ('the crowd of know-all heads') for the κρατῶν of the MSS, which gives good sense, but the absence of any context for the quotation makes emendation difficult. See further Adam *ad loc.* and 468–9. The fourth quotation alludes to the stock figure of the penniless intellectual, on which see Dover (1968) xxxii–xl. For the connotations of λεπτός see Ar. *Clouds* 153 with Dover (1968) *ad loc*, and for μεριμνάω, *ibid*. 101.　**c4–5 ἡ πρὸς ... μίμησις** 'poetry for pleasure and imitation'. Here S. seems to allude to μίμησις in general (cf. 595c7), which would presumably include painting as well. But Halliwell takes the phrase as an example of hendiadys, and translates, 'poetic mimesis designed for pleasure'. This may well be right, since it is poetry in particular rather than μίμησις in general which has been banished.　**c6 καταδεχοίμεθα** 'we would receive back from exile', cf. κατιέναι at d3.　**c6–8 ὡς σύνισμεν ... κηλῆι:** for the magical effect of poetry, emphasised by the repetition of κηλουμένοις and κηλῆι, cf. 595b6, 601b1, 608a3, and for the paramount importance of truth cf. 595c2–3.

d1 ὅταν δι' Ὁμήρου … αὐτήν 'when you see her through the medium of Homer'. For the quasi-personification of poetry see on e4–6 below.   **d3–4 κατιέναι … μέτρωι: κατιέναι** 'to return from exile', cf. c6. For ἀπολογησαμένη see on 607b1. The suggestion that poetry might successfully plead for her return in lyric or some other metre is surely playful, in view of the terms in which she is described in the following section.   **d6 τοις προστάταις αὐτῆς:** Halliwell notes that the legal sense of the term προστάτης ('patron' of a resident alien) may well be relevant here, with the implication that poetry has no natural right to belong to the city.   **d8 ἡδεῖα … ὠφελίμη:** cf. 599b8 and e2 which implied that poets have brought no benefit to society. At 398b1 S. concedes that the austere and less pleasing poet can be of some use, but what he consistently denies is that poetry can be both pleasing and useful. P. here sets the terms of a debate which was to continue for centuries to come. See the classic formulation in Horace's *Ars Poetica, aut prodesse uolunt aut delectare poetae* (333) and *omne tulit punctum qui miscuit utile dulci* (343).

e4–6 ὥσπερ οἱ ποτέ … ἀπέχονται 'like those who have once fallen in love with someone, and if they think the love is not beneficial, though they must force themselves, they nevertheless refrain from it'. For βίαι cf. 606a3. Poetry is, as it were, a woman, who can 'charm and coax and wheedle and enthral' (Havelock (1963) 5), but who must be resisted at all costs. Cf. 603a10–b1 for the image of ἡ γραφική καὶ ὅλως ἡ μιμητική as a ἑταίρα.   **e6–608a1 διὰ τὸν ἐγγεγονότα … τροφῆς:** this is presented almost as an excuse for P.'s love of poetry. Cf. 595b9–10 where S. refers to his love of Homer ἐκ παιδός, which, in the light of what is said here becomes more than simply a childhood love: it is a love which has been engendered through education, παιδεία. Else (1972) 22 makes the further point that what was earlier described in respectful terms as φιλία and αἰδώς has now become an ἔρως (cf. a5), a passion whose analogue is the master-passion which takes control of the tyrant's soul at 572e–575a8 (see especially 573b6–7 τύραννος ὁ Ἔρως λέγεται). τροφῆς recalls the imagery which had been used at 606b7 and d4 of poetry which nurtures the lowest part of the soul. And the sarcastic use of καλῶν (see on 595c1 and cf. 562a4 where tyranny is described as ἡ καλλίστη … πολιτεία) underlines the link between the superficial appeal of worthless poetry and the flawed nature of contemporary constitutions. Once again the political dimension of the argument about poetry is highlighted: culture and politics go hand in hand; the right sort of education produces the right sort of society and vice versa, and the welfare of the individual human soul is intimately linked with the cultural and political climate in which it is nurtured. Hence the justification for P.'s entire educational programme. See further Introduction p. 23.

608a1–2 εὔνοι ... ἀληθεστάτην: lit. 'we shall be glad for her to be shown to be best and truest'. εὔνοι is followed by the accusative and infinitive.   **a2 ἕως δ' ἂν ... ἀπολογήσασθαι** 'as long as she is unable to defend herself'.   **a3–4 ἐπᾴδοντες ... τὴν ἐπῳδήν:** the arguments that have been adduced in the discussion above will work as a charm against the magic of poetry, providing the φάρμακον referred to at 595b6–7. Philosophy is thus the only effective antidote to the dangerous influence of poetry.   **a6–b2 ᾀσόμεθα ... ποιήσεως:** lit. 'we shall chant, therefore, that such poetry must not be taken seriously, as though it were serious and grasped the truth, but that the man who hears it must be careful, fearing for his own constitution, and what we have said about poetry must be believed'. ᾀσόμεθα, continuing the image implied by ἐπᾴδοντες, is Madvig's emendation of the αἰσθόμεθα of the MSS, a form of αἰσθάνομαι which is not used in classical Greek. ὡς οὐ σπουδαστέον ... δεδιότι depends directly on ᾀσόμεθα and thus constitutes the ἐπῳδή referred to at a4. This sentence, which brings the discussion of poetry towards its end, encapsulates P.'s criticisms of it: it is (a) trivial (595c7–602c2) and (b) dangerous (602c4–606d7). The phrase ἐν αὑτῶι πολιτείας brings out the interdependence of state and individual, reminding us of the political dimensions of the arguments against poetry.

b4–8 Μέγας γάρ ... ἀρετῆς: the repetition of μέγας, and the direct address to Glaucon, heightens the emotion at this point, and underlines the significance of S.'s words. For the metaphor of life as a contest, and particularly an athletic contest, cf. c2, 613b–c, 621c–d (the closing sentence of the *Republic*), and see further Halliwell *ad loc.* ὅσος 'as small as', cf. *Phaed.* 83b9. τὸ χρηστὸν ἢ κακὸν γενέσθαι is in loose apposition to ὁ ἀγών. οὐδέ γε 'nor even', after the series οὔτε

... οὔτε ... οὔτε marks poetry as the crucial case. Cf. 499b2 οὔτε πόλις οὔτε πολιτεία οὐδέ γ᾽ ἀνήρ and see Denniston (1954) 156. The corrupting effects of honour, wealth and power are discussed in the account of the moral degeneration of society and the individual in books 8 and 9. But the implication here is that poetry is even more dangerous than these because it is more insidious. Havelock (1963) 4 rightly emphasises the evangelical tone of this peroration, in which P. 'exhorts us to fight the good fight against poetry, like a Greek Saint Paul warring against the powers of darkness'.

APPENDIX

POETIC INSPIRATION IN PLATO

The theme of poetic inspiration in P.'s work is discussed in the Introduction pp. 6–12 and 25–8. The principal passages on which that discussion is based are collected together here for the convenience of the reader.

1. In the *Apology* S. describes how he investigated the meaning of the Delphic oracle's pronouncement that there was no one wiser than himself by questioning people with a reputation for wisdom. First he went to the politicians, then he went to the poets. But when he questioned them about the meaning of their poems they were unable to explain their compositions:

ἔγνων οὖν αὖ καὶ
περὶ τῶν ποιητῶν ἐν ὀλίγωι τοῦτο, ὅτι οὐ σοφίαι ποιοῖεν
ἃ ποιοῖεν, ἀλλὰ φύσει τινὶ καὶ ἐνθουσιάζοντες ὥσπερ οἱ   c
θεομάντεις καὶ οἱ χρησμωιδοί· καὶ γὰρ οὗτοι λέγουσι μὲν
πολλὰ καὶ καλά, ἴσασιν δὲ οὐδὲν ὧν λέγουσι. τοιοῦτόν
τί μοι ἐφάνησαν πάθος καὶ οἱ ποιηταὶ πεπονθότες, καὶ
ἅμα ἠισθόμην αὐτῶν διὰ τὴν ποίησιν οἰομένων καὶ τἆλλα   5
σοφωτάτων εἶναι ἀνθρώπων ἃ οὐκ ἦσαν.

And I soon realised that the poets did not compose their poems through wisdom, but by nature, and that they were inspired like seers and soothsayers. For these say many fine things, but know nothing of what they say. It seemed to me that poets experienced something similar; at the same time I noticed that because of their poetry, they regarded themselves as the wisest of men in other respects also, which they were not. (*Ap.* 22b8–c6)

For discussion of these lines see Introduction p. 10.

2. At the end of the *Meno* S. claims that it is not through knowledge that politicians succeed in public life:

Σω. Οὐκοῦν εἰ μὴ ἐπιστήμηι, εὐδοξίαι δὴ τὸ λοιπὸν
γίγνεται· ἧι οἱ πολιτικοὶ ἄνδρες χρώμενοι τὰς πόλεις ὀρ-   c

θοῦσιν, οὐδὲν διαφερόντως ἔχοντες πρὸς τὸ φρονεῖν ἢ οἱ χρησμῳδοί τε καὶ οἱ θεομάντεις· καὶ γὰρ οὗτοι ἐνθου-
σιῶντες λέγουσιν μὲν ἀληθῆ καὶ πολλά, ἴσασι δὲ οὐδὲν ὧν
5 λέγουσιν.

ΜΕΝ. Κινδυνεύει οὕτως ἔχειν.

ΣΩ. Οὐκοῦν, ὦ Μένων, ἄξιον τούτους θείους καλεῖν τοὺς ἄνδρας, οἵτινες νοῦν μὴ ἔχοντες πολλὰ καὶ μεγάλα κατορθοῦσιν ὧν πράττουσι καὶ λέγουσι;

10 ΜΕΝ. Πάνυ γε.

ΣΩ. Ὀρθῶς ἄρ' ἂν καλοῖμεν θείους τε οὓς νυνδὴ ἐλέγομεν
d χρησμῳδοὺς καὶ μάντεις καὶ τοὺς ποιητικοὺς ἅπαντας· καὶ τοὺς πολιτικοὺς οὐχ ἥκιστα τούτων φαῖμεν ἂν θείους τε εἶναι καὶ ἐνθουσιάζειν, ἐπίπνους ὄντας καὶ κατεχομένους ἐκ τοῦ θεοῦ, ὅταν κατορθῶσι λέγοντες πολλὰ καὶ μεγάλα πράγματα,
5 μηδὲν εἰδότες ὧν λέγουσιν.

If it is not through knowledge, it must be by using good opinion that men who take part in public affairs guide cities. So far as knowledge is concerned, they do not differ from seers and soothsayers who, when inspired, say many true things, but they know nothing of what they say.

So it seems.

Isn't it right, Meno, to call men divine who, without thinking, are often highly successful in what they do and say?

Indeed.

We would be right then to call divine those seers and sooth-sayers whom I just mentioned, and poets of every description. And we would say that men who take part in public affairs no less than these are divine and inspired, being possessed and held by god, when they are successful in speaking on many important subjects, although they know nothing about what they are say-ing. (*Men.* 99b11–d5)

The application of the language of inspiration to politicians in this example ironically plays on the familiar opposition between inspira-tion and knowledge, suggesting that S. is more interested in the ig-norance of inspired people than in their divine status. On the irony of the passage see Bluck (1961) *ad loc.* and Tigerstedt (1969) 41–5.

3. In the *Phaedrus* S. suggests that our greatest blessings come to us through god-sent madness, of which there are four types: prophetic madness, which comes from Apollo; telestic or ritual madness, whose patron is Dionysus; poetic madness, inspired by the Muses; erotic madness caused by Aphrodite and Eros. Of poetic madness he says:

τρίτη δὲ ἀπὸ Μουσῶν   245
κατοκωχή τε καὶ μανία, λαβοῦσα ἀπαλὴν καὶ ἄβατον ψυχήν,
ἐγείρουσα καὶ ἐκβακχεύουσα κατά τε ὠιδὰς καὶ κατὰ τὴν
ἄλλην ποίησιν, μυρία τῶν παλαιῶν ἔργα κοσμοῦσα τοὺς
ἐπιγιγνομένους παιδεύει· ὃς δ' ἂν ἄνευ μανίας Μουσῶν ἐπὶ   5
ποιητικὰς θύρας ἀφίκηται, πεισθεὶς ὡς ἄρα ἐκ τέχνης ἱκανὸς
ποιητὴς ἐσόμενος, ἀτελὴς αὐτός τε καὶ ἡ ποίησις ὑπὸ τῆς
τῶν μαινομένων ἡ τοῦ σωφρονοῦντος ἠφανίσθη.

The third type of possession and madness comes from the Muses: taking a tender and virgin soul it rouses and excites it to Bacchic frenzy in lyric and other sorts of poetry, and by glorifying the countless deeds of the past it educates the coming generations. Whoever comes to the doors of poetry without the madness of the Muses, persuaded that he will be a good enough poet through skill, is himself unfulfilled, and the sane man's poetry is eclipsed by that of the insane. (*Phdr.* 245a)

For discussion of this passage see Introduction pp. 10–12.

4. In the *Laws* the Athenian Stranger suggests that poets might welcome the regulations imposed by a law-giver, saying:

Παλαιὸς μῦθος, ὦ νομοθέτα, ὑπό τε αὐτῶν   c
ἡμῶν ἀεὶ λεγόμενός ἐστιν καὶ τοῖς ἄλλοις πᾶσιν συνδε-
δόγμενος, ὅτι ποιητής, ὁπόταν ἐν τῶι τρίποδι τῆς Μούσης
καθίζηται, τότε οὐκ ἔμφρων ἐστίν, οἷον δὲ κρήνη τις τὸ
ἐπιὸν ῥεῖν ἑτοίμως ἐᾶι, καὶ τῆς τέχνης οὔσης μιμήσεως   5
ἀναγκάζεται, ἐναντίως ἀλλήλοις ἀνθρώπους ποιῶν διατιθε-
μένους, ἐναντία λέγειν αὑτῶι πολλάκις, οἶδεν δὲ οὔτ' εἰ ταῦτα
οὔτ' εἰ θάτερα ἀληθῆ τῶν λεγομένων. (*Laws* 719c)

For translation of these lines see Introduction p. 12. Here *mimesis* is used in the same sense as in *Rep.* 3 (see on 393c5–6), and the notions of inspiration and *mimesis* are merged into one. (See Velardi (1989) 115–21.) The image of the Muses' tripod exploits the ancient analogy between poetry and prophecy (see on *Ion* 534b7), and the simile of the spring plays on the traditional association between poetry and flowing liquids (*Ion* 534b1–2), suggesting the effortless and unstoppable flow of the poet's words. The poet is pictured as divinely inspired, but also as a mindless imitator of the characters whom he portrays: either way, the poet is unaware of what he does, and though P. refers to the poet's *techne*, that *techne* is something over which he has no control.

BIBLIOGRAPHY

Editions, commentaries and translations of the *Ion* and *Republic* are usually cited in the Introduction and Commentary by author alone. All other works are cited by author and date, e.g. Flashar (1958).

Abrams, M. H. *The mirror and the lamp: Romantic theory and the critical tradition* (New York 1953)

Adam, J. *The Republic of Plato*, 2nd edn (Cambridge 1963)

Annas, J. *An introduction to Plato's Republic* (Oxford 1981)

'Plato on the triviality of literature', in Moravcsik and Temko (1982) 1–28

Asmis, E. 'Plato on poetic creativity', in R. Kraut (ed.) *The Cambridge companion to Plato* (Cambridge 1992) 338–64

Baldwin, A. and Hutton, S. (edd.) *Platonism and the English imagination* (Cambridge 1994)

Barker, A. *Greek musical writings. Vol. 1: The musician and his art* (Cambridge 1984)

Barker, A. and Warner, M. (edd.) *The language of the cave* (Alberta 1992)

Belfiore, E. 'A theory of imitation in Plato's *Republic*', *T.A.P.A.* 114 (1984) 121–46

'"Lies unlike the truth": Plato on Hesiod *Theogony* 27', *T.A.P.A.* 115 (1985) 47–57

Bloom, A. *The Republic of Plato*, 2nd edn (New York 1991)

Bluck, R. S. *Plato's Meno* (Cambridge 1961)

Boter, G. *The textual tradition of Plato's Republic* (Leiden 1989)

Bowie, E. L. 'Lies, fiction and slander in early Greek poetry' in Gill and Wiseman (1993) 1–37

Brandwood, L. *A word index to Plato* (Manchester 1976)

Brisson, L. *Platon: les mots et les mythes* (Paris 1982)

Brommer, F. *Vasenlisten zur griechischen Heldensage*, 3rd edn (Marburg 1973)

Buffière, F. *Les mythes d'Homère et la pensée grecque* (Paris 1956)

Burkert W. *Greek religion*, trans. J. Raffan (Oxford 1985)

Burnet, J. *Plato's Euthyphro, Apology of Socrates and Crito* (Oxford 1924)

Buxton, R. *Imaginary Greece: the contexts of mythology* (Cambridge 1994)

239

Chantraine, P. *Dictionnaire étymologique de la langue grecque. Histoire des mots* (Paris 1968–80)

Cornford, F. *The Republic of Plato translated with introduction and notes* (London 1941)

Crombie, I. M. *An examination of Plato's doctrines*, 2 vols. (London 1962)

Curtius, E. R. *European literature and the Latin Middle ages*, trans. W. R. Trask (London 1953)

Delatte, A. *Les conceptions de l'enthousiasme chez les philosophes présocratiques* (Paris 1934)

Delcourt, M. 'Socrate, Ion et la poésie: la structure dialectique de l'Ion de Platon', *Bulletin de l'Association Guillaume Budé* 55 (April 1937) 4–14

Demand, N. 'Plato and the painters', *Phoenix* 29 (1975) 1–20.

Denniston, J. *The Greek particles*, 2nd edn (Oxford 1954)

De Romilly, J. 'Gorgias et le pouvoir de la poésie', *J.H.S.* 93 (1973) 155–62

  Magic and rhetoric in ancient Greece (Cambridge, Mass. and London 1975)

Dodds, E. R. *The Greeks and the irrational* (Berkeley and Los Angeles 1951)

  Plato: Gorgias (Oxford 1959)

  Euripides: Bacchae, 2nd edn (Oxford 1960)

Dorter, K. 'The *Ion*: Plato's characterisation of art', *Journal of Aesthetics and Art Criticism* 32 (1973) 65–78

Dover, K. *Aristophanes: Clouds* (Oxford 1968)

  Aristophanes: Frogs (Oxford 1993)

Edelstein, L. 'The function of the myth in Plato's philosophy', *J.H.I.* 10 (1949) 463–81

Edwards, M. (ed.) *The Iliad: a commentary. Vol.* v: *books 17–20* (Cambridge 1991)

Else, G. F. '"Imitation" in the fifth century', *C.P.* 53 (1958) 73–90

  The structure and date of book 10 of Plato's Republic (Heidelberg 1972)

  Plato and Aristotle on poetry (Chapel Hill and London 1986)

Ferguson, J. *Plato: Republic book X* (London 1957)

Ferrari, G. 'Plato and poetry', in Kennedy (1989) 92–148

Flashar, H. *Der Dialog Ion als Zeugnis platonischer Philosophie* (Berlin 1958)

Fraenkel, E. *Aeschylus: Agamemnon*, 2nd edn (Oxford 1962)

Friedländer, P. *Plato: an introduction*, trans. H. Mayerhoff (New York 1958)

Gadamer, H. 'Plato and the poets', in *Dialogue and dialectic*, trans. P. C. Smith (New Haven 1980) 39–72

Gentili, B. *Poetry and its public in ancient Greece from Homer to the fifth century*, trans. A. T. Cole (Baltimore 1988)

Gill, C. 'Plato and the education of character', *Archiv für Geschichte der Philosophie* 67 (1985) 1–26

  'Plato on falsehood – not fiction', in Gill and Wiseman (1993) 38–87

Gill, C. and Wiseman, P. (edd.) *Lies and fiction in the ancient world* (Exeter 1993)

Goldhill, S. *Reading Greek tragedy* (Cambridge 1986)

  The poet's voice. Essays on poetics and Greek literature (Cambridge 1991)

Goodwin, W. *Greek grammar*, 2nd edn (London 1894)

  Syntax of Greek moods and tenses (London 1929)

Gould, J. 'Plato and performance', in Barker and Warner (1992) 13–25

Griswold, C. 'The Ideas and the criticism of poetry in Plato's *Republic*, book 10', *Journal of the History of Philosophy* 19 (1981) 135–50

Guthrie, W. K. C. *A history of Greek philosophy*, 6 vols. (Cambridge 1962–81)

Halliwell, S. 'Plato and Aristotle on the denial of tragedy', *P.C.P.S.* 30 (1984) 49–71

  Aristotle's Poetics (London 1986)

  Plato: Republic 10 (Warminster 1988)

  Plato: Republic 5 (Warminster 1993)

Hankins, J. *Plato in the Italian Renaissance*, 2 vols. (Leiden 1990)

Harriott, R. *Poetry and criticism before Plato* (London 1969)

Havelock, E. A. *Preface to Plato* (Oxford 1963)

Herington, J. *Poetry into drama: early tragedy and the Greek poetic tradition* (Berkeley and Los Angeles 1985)

Heubeck, A. and Hoekstra, A. *A commentary on Homer's Odyssey, Vol. II, books ix–xvi* (Oxford 1989)

Heubeck, A., West, S. and Hainsworth, J. B. (edd.) *A commentary on Homer's Odyssey, vol. I, books i–viii* (Oxford 1988)

Hobbs, A. *Homeric role models and the Platonic psychology*, unpublished Ph. D. thesis (Cambridge 1990)

Janaway, C. 'Craft and fineness in Plato's *Ion*', *Oxford Studies in Ancient Philosophy* 10 (1992) 1–23

Kambylis, A. *Die Dichterweihe und ihre Symbolik* (Heidelberg 1965)

Kennedy, G. (ed.) *The Cambridge history of literary criticism* Vol. I (Cambridge 1989)

Kerferd, G. (a) *The sophists and their legacy* (Wiesbaden 1981)
(b) *The sophistic movement* (Cambridge 1981)

Keuls, E. *Plato and Greek painting* (Leiden 1978)

Kirk, G., Raven, J. and Schofield, M. *The Presocratic philosophers*, 2nd edn (Cambridge 1983)

Klagge, J. C. and Smith, N. D. (edd.) *Methods of interpreting Plato and his dialogues* (Oxford 1992)

Labarbe, J. *L'Homère de Platon* (Paris 1949)

Ladrière, C. 'The problem of Plato's *Ion*', *Journal of Aesthetics and Art Criticism* 10 (1951) 26–34

Lear, J. 'Inside and outside the *Republic*', *Phronesis* 37 (1992) 184–215

Linforth, I. M. 'The Corybantic rites in Plato', *University of California Publications in Classical Philology* 13 (1946) 121–62

Lohse, G. 'Untersuchungen über Homerzitate bei Platon I', *Helikon* 4 (1964) 3–28
'Untersuchungen über Homerzitate bei Platon II', *Helikon* 5 (1965) 248–95
'Untersuchungen über Homerzitate bei Platon III', *Helikon* 7 (1967) 223–31

Lucas, D. W. *Aristotle: Poetics* (Oxford 1968)

Macgregor, J. *Plato: Ion* (Cambridge 1912)

Mackenzie, M. M. *Plato on punishment* (Berkeley and Los Angeles 1981)

McKeon, R. 'Literary criticism and the concept of imitation in antiquity', in R. S. Crane, *Critics and criticism: ancient and modern* (Chicago 1952) 147–75

Macleod, C. *Homer: Iliad book XXIV* (Cambridge 1982)

Marrou, H. *Histoire de l'éducation dans l'antiquité*, 6th edn (Paris 1965)

Méridier, L. *Platon, œuvres complètes*, v: *Ion, Ménexène, Euthydème* (Paris 1931)

Miller, A. *Plato's Ion* (Bryn Mawr 1981)

Moore, J. 'The dating of Plato's *Ion*', *G.R.B.S.* 15 (1974) 421–40

Moravcsik, J. and Temko, P. (edd.) *Plato on beauty, wisdom and the arts* (Totowa, New Jersey 1982)

Murdoch, I. *The fire and the sun: why Plato banished the artists* (Oxford 1977)

Metaphysics as a guide to morals (Harmondsworth 1993)

Murphy, N. *The interpretation of Plato's Republic* (Oxford 1951)

Murray, P. 'Poetic inspiration in early Greece', *J.H.S.* 101 (1981) 87–100

'Inspiration and *mimesis* in Plato', in Barker and Warner (1992) 27–46

Nagy, G. 'Early Greek views of poets and poetry', in Kennedy (1989) 1–77

Nehamas, A. 'Plato on imitation and poetry in *Republic* 10', in Moravcsik and Temko (1982) 47–78

Nettleship, R. *Lectures on the Republic of Plato*, 2nd edn (London 1901)

Nussbaum, M. *The fragility of goodness* (Cambridge 1986)

Page, C. 'The truth about lying in Plato's *Republic*', *Ancient Philosophy* 11 (1991) 1–33

Penner, T. 'Thought and desire in Plato', in G. Vlastos (ed.) *Plato II: Ethics, politics, and philosophy of art and religion* (New York 1971) 96–118

Pfeiffer, R. *History of classical scholarship from the beginnings to the end of the Hellenistic age* (Oxford 1968)

Pickard-Cambridge, A. *Dithyramb, tragedy and comedy*, 2nd edn rev. T. B. L. Webster (Oxford 1962)

The dramatic festivals of the Athenians, 2nd edn rev. J. Gould and D. Lewis (Oxford 1988)

Pratt, L. *Lying and poetry from Homer to Pindar* (Michigan 1993)

Reeve, C. D. *Philosopher-kings: the argument of Plato's Republic* (Princeton 1988)

Richardson, N. J. 'Homeric professors in the age of the sophists', *P.C.P.S.* 21 (1975) 65–81

Riginos, A. *Platonica. The anecdotes concerning the life and writing of Plato* (Leiden 1976)

Robinson, R. *Plato's earlier dialectic*, 2nd edn (Oxford 1953)

Rösler, W. 'Die Entdeckung der Fiktionalität in der Antike', *Poetica* 12 (1980) 283–319

Rowe, C. *Plato: Phaedrus* (Warminster 1986)

Plato: Phaedo (Cambridge 1993)

Russell, D. *Criticism in antiquity* (London 1981)

Russo, J., Fernandez-Galiano, M. and Heubeck, A. (edd.) *A commentary on Homer's Odyssey, Vol. III, books xvii xxiv* (Oxford 1992)

Saunders, T. J. *Plato: early Socratic dialogues* (Harmondsworth 1987)

Plato's penal code (Oxford 1991)

Schaper, E. *Prelude to aesthetics* (London 1968)

Scheinberg, S. 'The bee maidens of the Homeric *Hymn to Hermes*', *H.S.C.P.* 83 (1979) 1–28

Sealey, R. 'From Phemius to Ion' *R.E.G.* 70 (1957) 312–55

Segal, C. 'Gorgias and the psychology of *logos*', *H.S.C.P.* 66 (1962) 99–155

'"The myth was saved": reflections on Homer and the mythology of Plato's *Republic*', *Hermes* 106 (1978) 315–36

Shorey, P. *Platonism ancient and modern* (Berkeley 1938)

Slings, S. 'Critical notes on Plato's *Politeia*, I', *Mnemosyne* 41 (1988) 276–98

'Critical notes on Plato's *Politeia*, II', *Mnemosyne* 42 (1989) 380–97

'Critical notes on Plato's *Politeia*, III', *Mnemosyne* 43 (1990) 341–63

Smith, J. S. 'Plato's use of myth in the education of philosophic man', *Phoenix* 40 (1986) 20–34

Sperduti, A. 'The divine nature of poetry in antiquity', *T.A.P.A.* 81 (1950) 209–40

Sprague, R. *Plato's philosopher-king: a study of the theoretical background* (Columbia, S.C., 1976)

Stanford, W. B. *Homer: Odyssey*, 2 vols. (London 1947)

Aristophanes: the Frogs (London 1958)

'Onomatopoeic *mimesis* in Plato, *Republic* 369b–397c', *J.H.S.* (1973) 185–91

Stewart, J. *The myths of Plato*, 2nd edn (London 1960)

Stock, St. G. *The Ion of Plato* (Oxford 1909)

Tate, J. '"Imitation" in Plato's *Republic*', *C.Q.* 22 (1928) 16–23

'Plato and "imitation"', *C.Q.* (1932) 161–9

Taylor, A. E. *A commentary on Plato's Timaeus* (Oxford 1928)

Thomas, R. *Literacy and orality in ancient Greece* (Cambridge 1992)

Tigerstedt, E. N. *Plato's idea of poetical inspiration* (Helsinki 1969)

'*Furor poeticus*: poetic inspiration in Greek literature before Democritus and Plato', *J.H.I.* 31 (1970) 163–78

Turner, B. *The Republic of Plato. Book X* (London 1889)

Van der Valk, M. *Researches on the text and scholia of the Iliad*, 2 vols. (Leiden 1963–4)

Velardi, R. *Enthousiasmos: possessione rituale e teoria della communicazione poetica in Platone* (Rome 1989)

Verdenius, W. J. 'L'Ion de Platon', *Mnemosyne* 11 (1943) 233–62

'Plato's doctrine of artistic imitation', in G.Vlastos, (ed.) *Plato: a collection of critical essays* 11 (New York 1971) 259–72

'The principles of Greek literary criticism', *Mnemosyne* 36 (1983) 14–59

Vicaire, P. *Platon: critique littéraire* (Paris 1960)

Vlastos, G. *Platonic studies*, 2nd edn (Princeton 1981)

Walsh, G. *The varieties of enchantment: early Greek views of the nature and function of poetry* (Chapel Hill and London 1984)

Waszink, J. H. *Biene und Honig als Symbol des Dichters und der Dichtung in der griechisch-römischen Antike* (Opladen 1974)

Weinberg, B. *A history of literary criticism in the Renaissance*, 2 vols. (Chicago 1961)

West, M. L. *Hesiod: Theogony* (Oxford 1966)

'The singing of Homer and the early modes of Greek music', *J.H.S.* 101 (1981) 113–29

The Orphic poems (Oxford 1983)

West, S., Heubeck, A. and Hainsworth, J. (edd.) *A commentary on Homer's Odyssey: vol. 1, introduction and books i–viii* (Oxford 1988)

White, N. *A companion to Plato's Republic* (Indianapolis 1979)

Woodruff, P. 'What could go wrong with inspiration? Why Plato's poets fail', in Moravcsik and Temko (1982) 137–50

Plato, two comic dialogues: Ion, Hippias Major (Indianapolis 1983)

Zimmermann, B. *Dithyrambos: Geschichte einer Gattung* (Gottingen 1992)

INDEXES

1. General

actors 17, 110, 121, 123, 170–1, 173, 175
aesthetics, 1–2, 28
allegory 103, 140–1
anacoluthon 115
arithmetic 107, 127

Bacchic ecstasy 115–16, 237
body/soul analogy 151, 162, 166, 216

carpenter 127, 197, 200
censorship 2, 21, 145, 158, 164, 185
chorus 16–17, 155
comedy 107–8, 173–5, 226–7
Corybantic ritual 115, 125
courage (see also ἀνδρεία) 156–7, 163
craftsmen (see also δημιουργός) 10, 127, 193–5, 210–12

dancing 16, 115, 124–5
death 21, 156–61
democracy 23, 182, 223, 230
dithyramb 16–17, 119, 172, 177, 180

education 15–19, 30, 102, 133–4, 141, 163, 175, 184, 223, 233
encomia 15, 119, 203, 228–9
epic 17, 114, 119, 142, 152, 172, 188, 212–13
ethic dative 100, 128, 139, 160

falsehood, see lies
fear 21, 122, 157–9, 226
festivals 17, 20, 30, 155, 189
fiction (see also lies) 135–6, 153
funeral legislation 161, 218

gnomic aorist 190, 227
god, as maker of the Forms 195–8

gods 21, 134, 137–49, 155
guardians 133, 157, 160, 162–3, 175, 178–9, 184, 186–7

honey 25, 116–17
hymns 15, 119, 228–9

iambics 119–20, 212–13
imitation, see mimesis
inspiration 6–12, 25–8, 98, 113–25, 235–8
irony, 96, 99–101, 103–9, 112, 119, 129–30, 132, 142, 178, 183–4, 190, 194, 207, 212, 236

justice (see also δικαιοσύνη) 133, 137, 153, 168, 228

lamentation 21, 121, 159–61, 176, 224–6
laughter 21, 162, 227
lies (see also ψεῦδος) 135–6, 140, 150–3, 162–3, 185–6, 201–2
lyric 17, 115–19, 142, 230

magic 23, 145–6, 149, 151, 188, 201, 208–9, 231, 233
magnet 10, 27, 112–13, 124
medicine 107, 127–8, 151, 162–3, 188, 203, 219, 225
memory 97, 126, 129
mimesis 3–6, 12–14, 16, 19, 22, 28–30, 122, 138, 160–1, 168–82, 186–90, 197–200, 212–16, 228–9, 237–8
mirror 29, 202
myth 29, 135–41, 152, 162, 168, 185–6

orality 18, 24, 108, 158, 170, 216, 224

246

2. Proper names

3. Greek words